MEDIEVAL AND RENAISSANCE DRAMA IN ENGLAND

Editorial Board

Leeds Barroll
University of Maryland (Baltimore)

Catherine Belsey
*University of Wales
College of Cardiff*

David M. Bevington
University of Chicago

Barry Gaines
University of New Mexico

Jean E. Howard
Columbia University

Arthur F. Kinney
University of Massachusetts

Anne C. Lancashire
University of Toronto

William B. Long
Independent Scholar

Barbara Mowat
Folger Shakespeare Library

Lee Patterson
Yale University

John Pitcher
St. John's College, Oxford

E. Paul Werstine
*University of Western
Ontario*

MEDIEVAL AND RENAISSANCE DRAMA IN ENGLAND

Volume 21

Edited by
S. P. Cerasano

Book Review Editor
Heather Anne Hirschfeld

Madison • Teaneck
Fairleigh Dickinson University Press

© 2008 by Rosemont Publishing & Printing Corp.

All rights reserved. Authorization to photocopy items for internal or personal use, or the internal or personal use of specific clients, is granted by the copyright owner, provided that a base fee of $10.00, plus eight cents per page, per copy is paid directly to the Copyright Clearance Center, 222 Rosewood Drive, Danvers, Massachusetts 01923. [978-0-8386-4180-4/08 $10.00 + 8¢ pp, pc.]

Associated University Presses
2010 Eastpark Boulevard
Cranbury, NJ 08512

The paper used in this publication meets the requirements of the American National Standard for Permanence of Paper for Printed Library Materials Z39.48-1984.

International Standard Book Number 978-0-8386-4180-4 (vol. 21)
International Standard Serial Number 0731-3403

All editorial correspondence concerning *Medieval and Renaissance Drama in England* should be addressed to Prof. S. P. Cerasano, Department of English, Colgate University, Hamilton, N.Y., 13346. Orders and subscriptions should be directed to Associated University Presses, 2010 Eastpark Boulevard, Cranbury, New Jersey 08512.

Medieval and Renaissance Drama in England disclaims responsibility for statements, either of fact or opinion, made by contributors.

PRINTED IN THE UNITED STATES OF AMERICA

Contents

Foreword	9
Contributors	11

Articles

The Presence of Africans in Elizabethan England and the Performance of *Titus Andronicus* at Burley-on-the-Hill, 1595/96 GUSTAV UNGERER	19
"The Sanctuarie is become a plaiers stage": Chapel Stagings and Tudor "Secular" Drama JEANNE H. MCCARTHY	56
Begging at the Gate: *Jack Straw* and the Acting Out of Popular Rebellion STEPHEN SCHILLINGER	87
Foul Papers, Promptbooks, and Thomas Heywood's *The Captives* JAMES PURKIS	128
Women and Crowds at the Theater ANDREW GURR AND KAROLINE SZATEK	157
"Follow the Money": Sex, Murder, Print, and Domestic Tragedy PETER BEREK	170

Notes and Documents

An Illustration of Traveling Players in Franz Hartmann's Early Modern *Album amicorum* JUNE SCHLUETER	191

Review Essay

Perspectives on Shakespeare and 1599 WILLIAM B. LONG	203

Reviews

Robert A. Logan, *Shakespeare's Marlowe: The Influence of Christopher Marlowe on Shakespeare's Artistry* CHARLES R. FORKER	225

Andrew Hadfield, *Shakespeare and Republicanism* GRAHAM HAMMILL	232
Julie Crawford, *Marvelous Protestantism: Monstrous Births in Post-Reformation England* GRACE TIFFANY	236
Donna B. Hamilton, *Anthony Munday and the Catholics, 1560–1633* JOHN D. COX	242
Ton Hoenselaars, *Shakespeare's History Plays: Performance, Translation and Adaptation in Britain and Abroad* BRIAN WALSH	245
Zachary Lesser, *Renaissance Drama and the Politics of Publication* RICHARD PREISS	248
Garrett A. Sullivan, Jr., *Memory and Forgetting in English Renaissance Drama* ANTHONY B. DAWSON	255
Peter Holland, ed., *Shakespeare, Memory and Performance* R. A. FOAKES	258
Deborah G. Burks, *Horrid Spectacle: Violation in the Theater of Early Modern England* EMILY DETMER-GOEBEL	266
Alexander Leggatt, *Shakespeare's Tragedies: Violation and Identity* RAPHAEL FALCO	271
Philip Butterworth, *Magic on the Early English Stage* MARINA FAVILA	274
Lukas Erne and Margaret Jane Kidnie, eds., *Textual Performances: The Modern Reproduction of Shakespeare's Drama* BRIAN WALSH	278
Henry S. Turner, *The English Renaissance Stage: Geometry, Poetics, and the Practical Spatial Arts, 1580–1630* DAVID GLIMP	281
Edward L. Rocklin, *Performance Approaches to Teaching Shakespeare* SHARON A. BEEHLER	285
Sarah Hatchuel, *Shakespeare, from Stage to Screen* DOUGLAS M. LANIER	288
Katharine Goodland, *Female Mourning and Tragedy in Medieval and Renaissance Drama: From the Raising of Lazarus to King Lear* KATIE NORMINGTON	292

Pamela Allen Brown and Peter Parolin, eds., *Women Players in England, 1500–1660: Beyond the All-Male Stage* 294
  SHEILA T. CAVANAUGH

Melissa D. Aaron, *Global Economics: A History of the Theater Business, the Chamberlain's/King's Men, and Their Plays, 1599–1642* 296
  NORA JOHNSON

Edward Gieskes, *Representing the Professions: Administration, Law, and Theater in Early Modern England* 299
  REBECCA LEMON

Ivan Cañadas, *Public Theatre in Golden Age Madrid and Tudor-Stuart London: Class, Gender, and Festive Community* 301
  OLGA VALBUENA

Index 304

Foreword

The publication of volume 21 of *Medieval and Renaissance Drama in England* features essays on issues ranging from chapel stagings (Jeanne McCarthy) to textual issues (Stephen Schillinger, James Purkis) to the presence of Africans in Elizabethan England (Gus Ungerer). Additional essays take up historical and theoretical issues relating to women at the early modern theater (Andrew Gurr and Karoline Szatek) and domestic tragedy (Peter Berek). We are also pleased to print June Schleuter's essay concerning an illustration of traveling players in Germany, and William Long presents a detailed commentary on James Shapiro's *A Year in the Life of William Shakespeare.* Other reviews—long and short—complete the volume.

S. P. CERASANO
Editor

Contributors

SHARON A. BEEHLER is Professor of English at Montana State University, Bozeman, where she teaches Shakespeare and English pedagogy. Recently she published *Women, Violence, and English Renaissance Literature: Essays Honoring Paul Jorgensen* (coedited with Linda Woodbridge) and *Shakespeare Yearbook: Shakespeare and Higher Education—A Global Perspective* (coedited with Holger Klein).

PETER BEREK, Professor of English at Mount Holyoke College, has published recently on Renaissance Jews, cross-dressing in the Beaumont and Fletcher plays, and generic terms on early modern titled pages and the authority of print.

SHEILA T. CAVANAUGH is Masse-Martin/NEH Distinguished Teaching Professor at Emory University and editor of the *Spenser Review*. She is the author of *Cherished Torment: The Emotional Geography of Lady Mary Wroth's "Urania"* (2001), *Wanton Eyes and Chaste Desires: Female Sexuality in "The Faerie Queene"* (1994), and numerous articles on Renaissance literature and pedagogy. She is the Director of the Emory Women Writers Resource Project, which received a major grant from the NEH. Cavanaugh received her PhD from Brown University in New Hampshire, where she focused on cognition and learning.

JOHN D. COX is DuMez Professor of English at Hope College. He is the author of *Shakespeare and the Dramatugry of Power* and *The Devil and the Sacred in English Drama, 1350–1642*. He coedited *A New History of Early English Drama* with David Scott Kastan and the Third Arden edition of Shakespeare's *3 Henry VI* with Eric Rasmussen.

ANTHONY B. DAWSON is Professor Emeritus at the University of British Columbia. His recent publications include *The Culture of Playgoing in Shakespeare's England* (with Paul Yachnin) and the New Cambridge Edition of Shakespeare's *Troilus and Cressida*.

EMILY DETMER-GOEBEL is Assistant Professor of English at Northern Kentucky University where she teaches courses on Shakespeare, Renaissance drama, and composition. Her work appears in various journals including *Shakespeare Quarterly* and *Shakespeare Studies.* She received her doctorate from Miami University.

RAPHAEL FALCO is Professor of English at the University of Maryland, Baltimore County. His publications include *Charismatic Authority in Early Modern English Tragedy* (2000) and, most recently, articles in *Diacritics, MLN,* and the *Shakespearean International Yearbook.*

MARINA FAVILA is Associate Professor at James Madison University. She has published on film and Shakespeare.

R. A. FOAKES is Professor Emeritus at UCLA. He is the editor of the Arden edition of *King Lear,* and of many works pertaining to performance studies.

CHARLES R. FORKER is Professor of English Emeritus at Indiana University, Bloomington. His recent publications include the Third Arden edition of Shakespeare's *Richard II* and the Revels edition of Marlowe's *Edward II.*

DAVID GLIMP is Associate Professor in the English Department at the University of Colorado, Boulder. He is the author is *Increase and Multiply: Governing Cultural Reproduction in Early Modern England* (2003) and coeditor of *The Arts of Calculation: Quantifying Thought in Early Modern Europe* (2004). His current research centers on the literature of emergency in Renaissance England.

ANDREW GURR is Professor Emeritus at Reading University. His most recent books are *The First Quarto of King Henry V* (2006), the third edition of *Playgoing in Shakespeare's London* (2004), and *The Shakespeare Company* (2004).

GRAHAM HAMMILL is Assistant professor of English at the University of Notre Dame. He is the author of *Sexuality and Form: Caravaggio, Marlowe, and Bacon,* as well as a variety of essays on early modern literature and literary theory.

NORA JOHNSON is Associate professor in the Department of English at Swarthmore College. She is the author of *The Actor as Playwright in Early Modern Drama* (2003). Her essays and reviews have centered on Shakespearean romance, the history of authorship, and the history of sexuality.

DOUGLAS M. LANIER is Associate Professor of English at the University of New Hampshire. His publications include *Shakespeare and Modern Popular*

Culture (2002), as well as numerous articles on Shakespeare and contemporary media. He is also a contributor to the Sourcebooks edition of Shakespeare. His most recent article is "Shakespeare on the Record" in *A Companion to Shakespeare and Performance,* ed. Barbara Hodgdon and William Worthen (2006).

REBECCA LEMON is Associate Professor in the Department of English at the University of Southern California. She is the author of *Treason by Words: Literature, Law, and Rebellion in Shakespeare's England* (2006), and coeditor of the forthcoming volume, *The Blackwell Companion to the Bible and Literature.* Her essays have appeared in *SEL, Theatre Journal,* and *Women and Culture at the Court of the Stuart Queens* (ed. Clare McManus).

WILLIAM B. LONG is an independent scholar who has published numerous essays in the areas of textual studies and theater history.

JEANNE H. MCCARTHY is a Visiting Associate Professor of Core Programs at Oglethorpe University. With articles forthcoming or published in *ELR, JEMCS,* and *Studies in Philology,* she is currently completing a book on the early modern children's theatrical companies, which originated in an award-winning dissertation completed at the University of Texas at Austin and for which she received an NEH Folger Shakespeare Library Fellowship in 2004.

KATIE NORMINGTON is Professor of Drama at Royal Holloway, University of London. She has published on medieval and modern drama: *Gender and Medieval Drama* (2004), *Modern Mysteries: Contemporary Productions of Medieval English Cycle Dramas* (2007), and coauthored *Making a Performance: Devising Histories and Contemporary Practices* (2007).

RICHARD PREISS is Assistant Professor of English at the University of Utah. His most recent publications are "Natural Authorship," in *Renaissance Drama* 34 (2006), and "Robert Armin Do the Police in Different Voices," in *From Performance to Print in Shakespeare's England,* ed. Peter Holland and Stephen Orgel (2006).

JAMES PURKIS is an Assistant Professor at the University of Western Ontario, Canada. He has published on Shakespeare's comedies for *The Year's Work in English Studies* and is currently completing a book on mauscript drama.

STEPHEN SCHILLINGER is a Lecturer at The University of Vermont. He has published on Christopher Marlowe's *The Massacre at Paris.* He is currently writing on the theoretical implications of how drama is used in the scholarship of cultural historians.

JUNE SCHLUETER, Charles A. Dana Professor of English at Lafayette College, is coauthor of *Reading Shakespeare in Performance: "King Lear"* and coeditor of *Acts of Criticism: Performance Matters in Shakespeare and His Contemporaries.*

KAROLINE SZATEK, a Shakespeare and early modern drama scholar, is an Associate Professor at Curry College. Szatek is a contributing editor of the *The Shakespeare Newsletter* and has recently coedited *From Around the Globe: Secular Authors and Biblical Perspectives,* which includes her article, "The Measure of Un-marked Vows in Two Early Modern Dramas." As well, Szatek has published "*The Merchant of Venice* and the Politics of Commerce" in *The Merchant of Venice: New Critical Essays.*

GRACE TIFFANY is a Professor of Shakespeare and Renaissance Literature at Western Michigan University. She is the author of *Erotic Beasts and Social Monsters: Shakespeare, Jonson, and Comic Androgyny* (UDP, 1995) and *Love's Pilgrimage: The Holy Journey in English Renaissance Literature* (UDP, 2006).

GUSTAV UNGERER, retired Professor of English literature at the University of Berne, is currently working on the English forerunners of black slavery who resided in early modern Andalusia (1480–1531). His findings are due to be published by Verbum (Madrid).

OLGA VALBUENA teaches Shakespeare and early modern literature at Wake Forest University. Since her last book was published in 2003 she has been focusing on conquest-era Spanish literature and Anglo-Hispanic relations.

BRIAN WALSH teaches in the English Department at Yale. He has published essays in *Shakespeare Quarterly, Studies in English Literature,* and *Theatre Journal,* and reviews in *Renaissance Quarterly, Shakespeare Bulletin, Sixteenth Century Journal,* and *PAJ.*

MEDIEVAL AND RENAISSANCE DRAMA IN ENGLAND

Articles

The Presence of Africans in Elizabethan England and the Performance of *Titus Andronicus* at Burley-on-the-Hill, 1595/96

Gustav Ungerer

IN 1594 Shakespeare confronted the Elizabethans with the dramatic figure of Aaron, a literate African trained in the classics. Shakespeare's characterization of Aaron presented a striking departure from the established discourse of black inferiority. The novelty was calculated, in the first place, to unsettle the average Elizabethan theatergoer. It could not, however, have been a surprise to those playgoers who had a university education or to those courtiers and noblemen, like the Haringtons and Sidneys, who had been cultivating cultural relations with the Continent and had learned how to shape their beliefs and views in the light of the Spanish and Portuguese experience. There was, moreover, another category of spectators, the descendants of those English merchants who had pioneered slaveholding and dealing in early modern Andalusia from 1480 to 1532. The Mediterranean apprenticeship of slavery has been left unrecorded owing to the one-sided attention of Africanists and historians to the development of English slavery in the seventeenth century. I am going to make some use of the material I have uncovered from Spanish archives at the end of the present paper.

We must, moreover, bear in mind that the Elizabethans had witnessed the haphazard attempts made by the authorities to accommodate the presence of black Africans and Moors to the structure of Elizabethan society. The black presence, particularly in the last decade of the sixteenth century, had raised anxieties about interbreeding that asked to be addressed. This was the case particularly between 1592 and 1594, when the government was embroiled in the hitherto little noticed scandal caused by the legal and illegal importation of slaves from Guinea. I have, therefore, felt obliged to unfold the still poorly documented history of the black presence in Elizabethan England before turning my attention to Shakespeare's *Titus Andronicus* as performed at Burley-on-the-Hill by the Chamberlain's Men on January 1, 1596. The performance had been designed by Sir John Harington to be the political and cultural climax of his lavish Christmas festivities.

The Presence of Africans in Elizabethan England

The presence of Africans in early modern England has remained a subject in its infant stage of studies. As late as the 1980s, historians clung to the view that there is no way of establishing how many colored persons had been taken to or had settled in early modern England. However, Rosalyn L. Knutson has opened up new research strategies. She is the first to have undertaken systematic investigation and has succeeded in gathering fresh material from the entries of baptisms and burials kept in the London parish records.[1]

The major difficulty in gathering reliable information has proved the absence of a regulated slave trade in early modern England. Whereas in Portugal and Spain the import of slaves was a government monopoly, England disposed of no legal code for operating a slave system under the Tudor monarchs. Hence there were no customs duties levied on imported slaves. There was, however, an annual per capita tax. This was, in effect, a poll tax of 8d levied by the municipal authorities.[2] The English authorities came close to conceding a royal monopoly on the import of slaves in the Guinea charter of 1588, a memorable event of its own that took place in the year of the Armada and that, surprisingly, Africanist historians have not taken any notice of (see below).

The majority of the Africans were black domestic slaves, a few were freedmen, and some of them were Moors, mostly Berbers from North Africa. The contemporary blanket term for them all was blackamoor. The seeming absence of records documenting their presence would argue the case for the existence of a negligible number of colored servants.[3] On second thoughts, however, the marginalized African population must have assumed a sizable volume, conspicuous and large enough to be of concern to the government, which thought it opportune to take countermeasures. The "discontented" queen, in view of the "great numbers of Negars and Blackamoors which . . . are crept into this realm," issued two expulsion edicts in July 1596 and a third in 1601. The royal orders, however, were of no consequence, for as long as the Africans were granted no legal status and the owners enjoyed the freedom of an unregulated market, the queen's policy of containment was simply ignored. The 1590s were a decade of poor harvests, food shortages, and poverty, but the queen's anxiety that, I dare say, approximately half a percent of London's population were taking jobs away from the English seems to be unwarranted. Similar concerns had been raised in Portugal in the 1560s when the African population of the Portuguese capital had risen to 10 percent.[4]

English Female Slaveholders

A good many misconceptions about the black and colored population in early modern England are due to the fact that the issue of the black presence has not yet overcome the difficulties and misconceptions of a nascent discipline. Thus the majority of the African servants were not curiosities, neither were they oddities nor status symbols, as some scholars would make us believe. On the contrary, they were like their cousins in Spain and Portugal hardworking domestic servants whom, to put it in Shylock's terms, the Venetian (English) owners would "use in abject and in slavish parts." Moreover, a serious oversimplification perpetrated by current historical work has been to neglect the problem of gender difference as regards both the slaves and the slave owners. I have, therefore, thought it opportune to discuss some records that shed new light on the ignored gender issue. It is a most striking feature that Englishwomen of all social classes, from low to high class, and even to royalty, should emerge as slave owners as if they had been emulating their Spanish and Portuguese counterparts, who did not hesitate to attend public auctions, selling and buying slaves in great numbers.[5] Thus the queen kept black artists, Lady Ralegh called a black servant her own, Lady Anne Clifford numbered Grace Robinson, a black laundress, and John Morocco, a black servant, among her household staff at Knole some time after 1609, and the seamstress Millicent Porter was present at the christening of her black slave Mary Phillis in 1597.[6]

Grace Robinson has been singled out by Kim F. Hall, in her insightful article "Reading What Isn't There" (see note 4), as an instance demonstrating that the personal histories of black women are bound to remain irretrievable and that the black female domestic servants, unnamed and stripped of a history of their own, are doomed to remain invisible. Grace Robinson's alleged invisibility, I dare say, was a matter of social status rather than of color or ethnicity; for it is a commonplace that the personal histories of white female servants are equally difficult to recover. The black laundress Grace Robinson shared the fate of being elided from the narrative of Lady Anne Clifford's *Diary* together with her white fellow laundresses. She stands nonetheless the chance of coming into her own if we attempt to pry into the position held by the laundry maids and into their daily work in the large household of Lady Anne Clifford, countess of Dorset after 1609 and countess of Montgomery and of Pembroke after 1630.[7]

From the inventory or "Catalogue of the Household and Family of the Right Honourable Richard, Earl of Dorset," which was begun in 1613 and completed on the earl's death in 1624, it emerges that Grace Robinson was one of several dozen servants who are all mentioned by name and listed according to their seating order at various tables, from the lord's table, the parlor table, the clerks' table, the long table, the laundry maids' table, the nursery, the kitchen and scullery.[8] The comprehensive inventory, which still hangs framed under glass at Knole House, Kent, is obviously conceived to convey to the reader the socializing policy of the earl of Dorset and his wife Lady Anne Clifford, who saw to it that all the members of their household, from the gentlemen ushers, grooms of the great horse, to the brewers, gardeners, and huntsmen met in the dining hall on festive occasions. The members seated at the "Laundry Maids' Table" were, besides Grace Robinson, Mrs Judith and Mrs Grace Simpton, obviously two gentlewomen overseeing the laundry; Penelope Tutty, the maid of Margaret Sackville, Lady Anne's eldest daughter; Anne Mills, the dairymaid; the two goodwives Burton and Small; William Lewis, porter; and what must have been the four fellow laundresses of Grace Robinson: Prudence Butcher, Anne Howse, Faith Husband, and Elinor Thompson. The catalogue reveals no trace of social or racial marginalization, getting the message across to the reader that the "Blackamoor" laundress was well integrated in the Knole household.

Grace Robinson was indeed working in a team of five laundresses whose duties must have entailed washing, repairing, and possibly sewing the linen and clothes of the household. This was no doubt a burdensome task which demanded great skill and endurance. There is some evidence proving that Lady Anne developed a personal relationship with her personnel and maid-servants. Thus in April 1617, she was lying ill in Judith Simpton's chamber and in her old age, when she was too weak to attend divine service on Sundays, she used to send her four laundry maids and her washerwoman Isabel Jordan to attend the sermon preached by parson Samuel Grasty at Ninekirks Church, Wetsmoreland. A fortnight before she died at Brougham Castle on March 23, 1676, she took the seamstress Margaret Montgomery, who had come from Penrith to make up twenty pairs of sheets and pillows, to her chamber, and kissed her and talked to her.[9]

Whether Lady Anne Clifford's personal relations with Grace Robinson were as intimate as with the seamstress Margaret Montgomery remains unproven. But in view of the fact that she felt bound to take special care for the spiritual welfare of her laundresses, it is not unreasonable to assume that she must have developed a particular interest in an African maid who had become a Christian convert. There is historical precedent for the privileged treatment of black female converts by aristocratic women in Europe. Catherine of Austria, wife of the Portuguese king Joao III, who on average numbered some twenty-five black African and Amerindian slaves among her royal household, gave evidence of her particular concern for the welfare of her female maid-servants in manumitting her three black laundresses Margarida da Silva, Clemencia da Santa Maria, and Catarina da Cruz, in 1554.[10]

A female slaveholder of much lower social profile was Widow Stokes. She dwelt in the parish of All Hallows Barking, Tower Ward, London, where she paid an annual per capita tax of 8d for her servant "Clare, a Negra," in October 1598 and 1599.¹¹ Widow Stokes may have exploited Clare as a single maid-of-all-work for the full range of household tasks and may thus have offered Clare immunity from sexual abuse at the hand of fellow servants. Sleeping arrangements still used to be mainly communal. Servants of either sex slept in the same room, and servants of the same sex often shared the bed, a fact that was well known to raise the female servants' vulnerability to rape, seduction, and, worst of all, the specter of miscegenation.¹² The possibility that the bedrooms of early English households were immune to color discrimination cannot be ruled out. In Spain miscegenation was endemic among the servant class; in Elizabethan England it was certainly on the rise. The bold interracial bedroom scene in *Othello* (act 5) may have been inspired by the reality experienced in middle-class English households.

A well documented case of a female slaveholder in early modern England is that of Millicent Porter, seamstress. It shows that also women at the lower scale of the social order knew how to take advantage of slaveholding. In January 1584, she was found guilty of "ffornication and adulterye" and was, against her will, "enioyned to make her canonycall purgation" in the "consistorye place" in St Paul's, London. After having done public penance, she returned to her parish of St Botolph Aldgate. When exactly the black slave Mary Phillis joined her household is not known, but we do know that on June 3, 1597, Millicent Porter attended the christening of the twenty-year-old Mary together with the curate's wife, the sexton's wife, and three other women who stood as godparents to Mary Phillis. We have it on the authority of Thomas Harridaunce, the clerk of St Botolph Aldagte, that Mary Phillis answered the curate's questions about her faith "verie Christenlyke,"and recited the Lord's Prayer and the "articles of her beliefe." Thereupon the curate took Mary to the font and baptized her. These two women, a black slave and what looks like a repentant prostitute, transcended the habitual relegation of the black African females and of the female delinquents to the margins of society.¹³

The parishioners of St Botolph were certainly unaware of the fact that the christening of Mary was an infringement upon her African past. They looked upon the baptismal rite as conferring a new lease of life on an English-speaking Christian convert, who despite her new cultural and religious identity remained a slave. The presence of a curate officiating the ceremony in a London parish church is proof of the Anglican Church's toleration of slavery as a necessary evil. The Anglican authorities considered slavery as reprehensible only when English merchants were sold to the Muslims and enticed to convert.

The case of Mary Phillis does not correspond to the culturally defamed representations of the black female domestic figure in Elizabethan and Jacobean drama, nor does the hitherto unrecovered case of twelve-year-old Polonia. On May 5, 1597, Mrs Piers ("Peires"), the mistress of "Polonia, the blackmor maid," consulted Simon Forman about her servant's illness. Forman, in the absence of the patient, cast an astrological figure and below it set down a humoral diagnosis, according to which the poor girl was suffering from "Moch pane syd[e] stom[ach]" and was "Lyk to vomit." Moreover, he found "a feuer in her bones" and diagnosed a "fa[i]nt harte, full of melancoly & cold humors mixed with collor," i.e., choler. The remedy he prescribed for her cure was to "purg her of Neptune" and of her vapors.[14]

The absence of the patient during the medical consultation was nothing extraordinary. Of the 132 consultations for children in 1597, forty-five were visits of a parent on behalf of a sick child, and only in thirty-two cases was the child present for the consultation.[15] With the benefit of hindsight we may venture to put down the illness of the twelve-year-old Polonia to menstrual disorders rather than to the social stress of deculturation.

Polonia's case marks a watershed event in the annals of cross-cultural encounters insofar as it records the first rapprochement between a black African and a self-made London medical practitioner. Simon Forman, though much maligned and denounced by the College of Physicians as a quack, must be given his due for having treated Polonia as a patient irrespective of race, ignoring the ethnic boundaries erected by the cultural discourse of white supremacy. An unconventional man operating on the outer fringes of academic life, he seems to have been aware of the historic moment in his medical career, for he was meticulous about the patient's identity, adding a definite article that seems to be charged emotionally: "Polonia, the blackmor maid at Mr Peires." Forman's professionally impeccable behavior is out of line with the depiction of non-European women in literary and other writings of the period as being "either dangerous . . . and needing to be . . . annihilated, or alienated from their own society and made tractable, and therefore ready to be converted and assimiliated into European family and society."[16]

Mrs Piers was aged twenty-one and had previously consulted Forman on May 3, 1597, regarding an illness of her own. She might also be the mother of "John Peire," aged three, who had consulted Forman on April 14, 1597.[17] This young woman felt morally obliged to look after the well-being of her juvenile black maidservant although she must have known that black servants enjoyed no legal status in early modern England and therefore was under no legal obligation whatsoever to offer her servant medical treatment.

Polonia's age profile is worth comment. In Europe the age of twelve was generally considered to mark a girl's transition from childhood to adult life. Thus in early modern England, the age of consent for marriage was set at twelve for girls. The age of twelve years was also taken to be the ideal age for slave girls to be introduced to the household domestic chores as maids-of-all-work or as companions or nursemaids for young children.[18] This might have been Polonia's lot if "John Peire," aged three, was indeed the son of Mrs Peirs. But it was also an age fraught with the danger of a young girl being raped and becoming pregnant. The bawd in Shakespeare's *Pericles* has brought up her daughters to the age of eleven and then has reduced them to serve in the brothel.[19] Juliet's nurse swears by her own "maidenhead at twelve year old," implying that she was deflowered as soon as she reached the age of twelve.[20] Launcelot, the primary go-between in the play, who shuttles between religious communities and ethnic minorities, commits an act of interracial sex in Portia's domain at Belmont, impregnating the offstage Mooress, whose age must be put to twelve or thereabouts. His impregnation of the Mooress may have been meant to evoke a real-life incident in London.[21]

English Merchant Slaveholders

Slaveholding in early modern England was not gender bound; but whereas in the case of female slaveholders all the social classes seem to have participated in the business, in the case of men, slaveholding was mainly concentrated in the hands of the upper echelons of the merchant class. The English merchants stationed in Spain at the turn of the fifteenth/sixteenth century and John Hawkins's ventures in the Guinea-Caribbean slave trade of 1562/63 and 1564/65 had prepared the ground for holding colored slaves in England, and the English merchants doing business in the Mediterranean and in West Africa in the closing decades of the sixteenth century took their cue from them. Among the foreign merchants residing in England, the Portuguese New Christians or *conversos,* who had been accustomed to keeping and handling slaves before they took refuge in England in the 1540s, enjoyed the privilege of keeping up their old lifestyle, practicing their Jewish rites on the sly, and developing their commercial networks with their old *converso* partners in Amsterdam, Antwerp, and Constantinople. (See below.)

The double-career men like the Gonsons, the Hawkinses, and the Winters, who had a lifelong experience as members of the inner circle of the naval administration in charge of the royal fleet, had no scruples to take advantage of their public offices to promote their private enterprises. They became involved in slaving voyages as investors, ship owners and seafaring businessmen and did not hesitate to staff their households with colored servants. Evidence, however, is scarce to come by, but as regards Sir William Winter (ca. 1525–89) it is conclusive.

William Winter, keeper of the naval records (1546), master of the naval ordnance (1557), invested in and sailed on Thomas Wyndham's 1553 voyage to Guinea. He then joined the syndicate of Guinea merchants which in 1561 advanced the project of building a fort in Guinea. He was also one of the investors of John Hawkins's second slaving voyage of 1564/65, and in 1565 he financed, in partnership with his brother George, the voyage of their ship the *Mary Fortune,* which the Portuguese sank off the Guinea coast, taking the crew prisoner. It is also on record that in 1570 one ship of a fleet of three, owned by William Winter and bound for Guinea to participate in the transatlantic slave trade, sailed back home without reaching the Caribbean. For his services rendered to the navy and for his private ventures he was knighted in 1573.[22]

Had Thomas Harridaunce, the parish clerk of St Botolph Aldgate, not been keeping separate memoranda besides the ordinary parish registers, we might never have known that Sir William Winter even in his old age could not do without a Guinea slave or two working in his household. On August 17, 1587, Harridaunce recorded in his daybook the death of "Domingo Beinge a ginnye Negar" who was "servaunt to the Right worshipfull Sr William Winter" and had died in his London manor house at East Smithfield.[23] We do not know when Domingo entered Winter's service, it may have been before or after 1570. He may have been part of Winter's personal booty taken in Guinea from a former Portuguese owner, in which case Domingo would have been an institution among possible black fellow servants, or Winter may have bought him in London from a business partner any time after 1570.

The Guinea Charter of 1588–98

The diplomatic interventions of the Portuguese and the subsequent treaty signed by the English and the Portuguese governments in 1576 brought about a slump in the English Guinea trade. However, the exile of Dom Antonio, the claimant to the Portuguese throne, gave an unexpected impetus to the resumption of the Guinea or rather the Senegambian slave trade. Dom Antonio sought refuge in England in the aftermath of the Portuguese dynastic crisis of 1578/80, accompanied by a retinue of some forty-eight attendants, among them the mulatto Pedro Fernandes. The renewal of the slave trade under the auspices of the English government and Dom Antonio has passed unnoticed by English historians. A comprehensive study of the historical, cultural, and ethnic dimensions of the first Guinea charter (1588–98) remains a desideratum. The following comments lay claim to being nothing more than a first step on the road to recovering a fascinating story of cross-cultural encounters, political machinations, and African dominance in imposing the terms of the slave export and foreign trade with the Portuguese, Spaniards, French, and English.[24]

On his arrival in England in July 1581, Dom Antonio was penniless, but he had taken the precaution to seize the Portuguese crown jewels, the precious spoils of the Portuguese East and West Indies. Queen Elizabeth welcomed Dom Antonio not as a claimant, but as a sovereign brother, and set her mind on making use of him as a trump card in the political trials of strength waged between the English, French, Spanish, and Moroccan courts. When Dom Antonio ran out of his financial resources, he resorted, with the approval of the English government, to unorthodox methods of financing his campaign to recover the Portuguese throne from Philip II.[25]

The Guinea charter, signed on May 3/13, 1588, by the English government and on May 20/30, 1588 by Dom Antonio, was a contract concluded, in the first place, for the benefit of both sides and, in the second, as a warrant for Dom Antonio's financial survival. It granted some English merchants of Exeter, Colyton, Barnstaple, and London, for the space of ten years, license to trade with Senegambia, that is, a stretch of the mainland littoral lying between the rivers Senegal and Gambia in Upper Guinea and some 240 miles long. The first 140 miles, reaching from the estuary of the Senagal to the peninsula of Cape Verde and known as the Great Coast, were inhospitable terrain without any ports and therefore irrelevant to the transatlantic trade. The international traffic was concentrated on the Small Coast, reaching from Cape Verde to the estuary of the Gambia. This part of the coast was dotted with a number of busy ports and slave emporia, the most important being Bezeguiche, Rufisque, Portudal, and Joal. [26]

Dom Antonio, though ousted from the Portuguese throne by Philip II, kept claiming the Senegambian littoral as his overseas possession. Thus he enjoined the English patentees to fit out three vessels bound for Guinea every year; to accept two Portuguese agents on board the English vessels to register the goods on the outward and homeward voyages; to pay duties of 5 percent on all the goods sold from ivory, hides, amber, wax, gold, and silver to slaves, and to hand the taxes over to Dr Rodrigo (Ruy) López, the queen's physician, whom the Privy Council had appointed collector of the duties and had charged to use the incoming money to indemnify Dom Antonio's English creditors. The debts Dom Antonio had incurred between 1581 and 1588 amounted to £4000, and he was about to accrue further debts with the disastrous Portugal expedition of 1589 under the command of Sir Francis Drake and Sir John Norris.[27]

The most prominent patentee to sign the Guinea charter was the Barbary merchant Anthony Dassell. He staked his money on the vessels which sailed under the command of his brother Thomas. The two brothers looked upon the resumption of the Guinea trade as a fat chance of lining their own pockets. They committed a number of violations, which were endemic among international slaving merchants, such as flouting the legal machinery set up to recover the import duties levied on the goods. Dom Antonio, therefore, brought a lawsuit against them for refusing to allow his agents to board their vessels in order to inspect the commodities and to remit the duties to Dr López's account. What is of utmost relevance to the present investigation is the attempt of the Dassell brothers to bypass the rules of the Guinea charter in surreptitiously importing black Africans and evading the import taxes to the detriment of Dom Antonio and the English authorities. Thus it transpires from the interrogatory drawn up by the High Court of Admiralty and put to four English sailors, who had obviously sailed to Guinea in 1592, that the Dassell brothers were suspected of smuggling a considerable number of Guinea slaves into England. The four sailors summoned to appear before the judges of the High Court of Admiralty were to be questioned about the number of Africans transported on the two ships of the Dassells. The judges also wanted to know "what are their names and in whose custodye and keeping are they at this tyme, and whether were they transported with the good will and leave of their parents and frends and the leave of the kinge of the said cuntrye, yea or no, and of what account are such as are so transported in the saide cuntrye to your knowledge, or as you have hearde by credible reporte."[28]

It emerges from the wording of the interrogatory (items 11 and 20) that Dom Antonio, in cooperation with the English government, was the instigator of the resumption of the English Guinea slave trade in 1588. The English government tacitly approved of the view held by an exiled potentate, who had had a lasting experience in slaveholding, that exporting slaves from Guinea was a legal enterprise provided the European exporter secured a license from the native kings or chieftains. This is borne out by the accusation laid by Dom Antonio before the High Court of Admiralty against Anthony Dassell and his brother Thomas in 1592. Dom Antonio accused the Dassell brothers of having "cast in prison the king of Portingall his agent," that is, his own Guinea agent, and of having "transported" to England two Africans "against the king[e] of that realme and his officers comma[u]ndements".[29]

The two Africans were said to be "cheife yonge negroes, . . . sonnes to the cheife justice of that contrey." Dom Antonio and the English authorities, therefore, feared that the Dassells' fraudulent practices would bring about "the utter overthrow[e] and disturba[u]nce of that trade in those partes," and awaken "the prejudice of other marchants of that societie, by reason wherof" the queen and Dom Antonio were bound to lose "tenn thowsand[e] crownes yearlye" (Nunes Costa, Document 40). Richard Kelley was one of the Guinea merchants who disapproved of Anthony Dassell's behavior. He was afraid to return to Guinea because he believed that the two "Neygrose of some accompt" had been taken to England "against their wills." He argued that "by suche indiscreete dealinge it is greatlye to be feared that the trade into those partes wilbe very muche hindred." He was, therefore, not ready to return to Guinea unless "some order be taken for the saffe bringinge backe of the sayde ij Negrose into the sayde countrye" (National Archives, Kew, HCA 24/59/49–51).

In his defense, Anthony Dassell countered that the "two yonge negroes they of themselfes made sute to come, and voluntarie came to see England without any compulsion," adding that their "good entertaynment heere wil be more benefficiall and comodius" to the queen "in regarde of the trade then all the serva[u]nts" of Dom Antonio "canne doe good in goinge thither."

And to justify his blatant breach of the Guinea charter he went to the length of invoking the example set by the French, who had been trading in Guinea "above thirtie yeares" without paying "duties" to their king. No "nation" was "better beloved nor so well wellcome to the negroes" as the French, who "cheifflie proceded by bringinge negroes nowe and then into France and usinge them well" (Nunes Costa, Document 41).

Anthony Dassell's violation of the Guinea charter and his brother's resort to violence lends little credence to Anthony's argument that the measures he had taken were inspired by altruistic motives in the interest of England's economic development. He revealed his true turn of mind when he complained to the judges that he was now constrained to keep the two noble Africans in his own house at his great cost for the benefit of the queen and his country (Nunes Costa, Documents 44 and 45).

The documents uncovered so far in the English and Portuguese national archives yield only a fraction of the economic enterprises undertaken by the eight patentees of the Guinea charter, that is, by William Brayley, Gilbert Smith, Nicholas Spicer, John Derricott, all four of Exeter, John Young of Colyton (Devon), Richard Dodridge of Barnstaple (Devon), and Anthony Dassell and Nicholas Turner, both of London. Further investigations are likely to bring to light the actual number of the black Africans whom the Dassells illicitly imported into London and whom the other merchants may have legally freighted to England, paying the export licenses issued by the African chiefs and the import duties exacted by Dom Antonio and the English government.

Two contemporary witnesses and chroniclers of the arrival of the English merchants in Senegambia in the early 1590s, one a Portuguese and the other an Englishman, throw some additional light on the memorable encounters between the English and some African kings as well as on the nature and conditions of the trade. It emerges from the chronicle of André Alvares d' Almada, citizen of Sao Tiago, the principal among the Cape Verde Islands, and from the report of Richard Rainolds, one of the factors on Anthony Dassell's ship the Nightingale, that Dom Antonio was woefully out of touch with the realities in Senegambia. The Portuguese and the Spaniards had lost the favor of the native kings, who since the 1570s had been encouraging the French and, in the 1590s, the English, among them Thomas Dassell, to trade with them directly irrespective of the regulations of the 1588 Guinea charter, which obliged the English merchants to sail under the supervision of Dom Antonio's agents.[30]

Alvares d'Almada provides invaluable information on the profitable and successful relations between the Creolized Luso-Africans or Afro-Portuguese and the English merchants who had chosen Bezeguiche (Beseguiache in Rainolds) on the Cape Verde Peninsula, its large bay sheltered by the islet of Palma, as their favorite port of call. The Luso-Africans, disdainfully dismissed by the Portuguese authorities as "lançados," were the middlemen who specialized in bartering goods between the Africans and the foreign merchants, the Spaniards, French, and English. They became the main purveyors of slaves when the monopoly of the Portuguese began to decline after 1570. The business partners were in a festive mood when the deals were concluded and the goods handed over to the foreign traders. The English used to banquet the Luso-Africans, entertaining them with music played on viols and other instruments.[31]

Alvares d' Almada also raises the issue of sending Senegambians to England. He records that owing to the amicable relations established between the Bawal kingdom and the English merchants some Africans went to England to learn English and to visit the country. It was the governor of Portudal (Porto d'Ally in Rainolds), also acting as overseer of king Amar Malik's exchequer, who had given the order. This statement seems to contradict the accusation, brought against the Dassell brothers by Dom Antonio, of having conveyed to London two noble Africans, the sons of the chief justice, against the orders of king Amar Malik (or Mamalik) and his officials.[32] The case of the Dassells looks very much like being a precedent of the business venture to be arranged between some London Guinea merchants and the king of the river of Cess in Upper Guinea. The king sent his son Derij Iaquoah to London, where he was baptized in the church of St Mildred Poultry on January 1, 1611, some of the English merchants attending the ceremony of the baptism as godparents and sureties. John Iaquoah, the new convert, was obviously trimmed as a black Christian factor in the hope of boosting the shipment of goods, presumably slaves, between England, Guinea, and the Caribbean.[33]

The Senegambians participated in the Atlantic trade as equal partners. Rainolds in his travel account does not tire of foregrounding the understanding and amity between the African rulers, the state officials, and the English merchants. One of the first professional obligations Rainolds fulfilled in November 1591 after landing at the islet of Palma, which he calls the "litle Iland . . . of liberty," was to receive the governor of Beseguiache. The governor came "with a great traine . . . aboord in their canoas" to collect king Melek Zamba's "dueties for ankerage." Rainolds rose to the occasion, giving the governor "and all his company courteous entertainment" so as "to purchase the more love." The governor then conducted Rainolds and his company to his "house" on the mainland at Beseguiache, where the English merchants "were gently and friendly feasted after their maner, and with some presents returned safe aboord againe." These ceremonies, observed on the occasion of what was the official opening of trade relations, were concluded the following day when the governor came aboard the English ship "to wil" Rainolds "to send some yron and other commodities . . . to traffike with the Negros." The same procedure was repeated at Rufisque (Refisca) and at Portudal. Portudal was ruled by king Amar Malik, son of Melek Zamba, whose subjects "befriended and favoured" the English and were "ready to ayde, succor and defend" them against the hostile followers of Dom Antonio. "In" these Africans, Rainolds commented, "appeared more confident love and goodwill towards us, then ever we shall finde either of Spaniards or Portugals."[34]

The alleged influx of Guinea slaves in the early 1590s, whether legal or illegal in terms of the Guinea charter of 1588, generated a sense of anxiety about the black presence in late Elizabethan London. The government, therefore, took measures to defuse the situation. In the wake of the investigations conducted by the High Court of Admiralty in 1592–94, the queen under the pretext of a threat to economic stability, was induced to issue the ineffective deportation acts of 1596, 1599, and 1601. It is one of history's ironies that the English government, put under pressure by Dom Antonio's impecunious circumstances, should have condoned the import of Guinea slaves. Government measures alone were not sufficient to allay the fear of the citizens. By 1594 the Londoners had come to perceive the presence of Africans as an anomaly within the social body of their city and country which asked to be confronted on a public platform. This was the moment for Shakespeare to step in to make an attempt to defuse the situation by confronting his contemporary audiences with the extraordinary figure of Aaron, a literate African, in 1594.

The Mediterranean Traders

Besides Guinea as an export region of black slaves, the countries bordering the Mediterranean were another frequent source of supply. Trade in the Mediterranean and later on in the West Indies afforded Paul Banning or Bayning (d. September 30, 1616), member of the Grocers' Company, alderman of Farringdon Without, called Fleet Street Ward (1593–1602), the opportunity to build up a vast business empire. Banning was one of the dominant figures of the Venice Company (1583–89) and the Levant Company, also known as the Turkey Company (1581–88), which was granted a new charter in 1592. As a merchant promoting privateering, he had a powerful galleon built, the Golden Phoenix, designed with an eye to war and trade. At the turn of the century, he pursued a policy of investing the capital, which he had accumulated while trading in Venice and Turkey in the 1580s, in the first expedition of the East India Company.[35] He was treasurer of the East India Company 1600–1602.

The head of a vast household made up of many retainers, clerks, and servants, Banning had by 1593 bought at least three "blakamores," all of them female domestic servants, who constituted a high-risk group in his crowded household. He is the only English merchant known so far to own more than one black servant except for the naturalized Portuguese *conversos* dwelling in England. A fourth black household servant was "Iulyane," twenty-two years old when she was christened in St Mary Bothaw on March 29, 1601, and "namyd" Mary by her godparents. These were obviously responsible for her integration into Banning's teeming household and for her assimilation of English cultural values.[36]

The Portuguese New Christians as Slaveholders in England

The most experienced slaveholders in early modern England were the Portuguese New Christians or *conversos* who sought refuge in English ports when in 1536 Portugal, under Spanish pressure, established an Inquisition of its own and instituted the purity of blood statutes. The community of the Portuguese *conversos* reached its peak in the last decades of queen Elizabeth's reign when it numbered between eighty and ninety members. Their presence was most welcome in England because of their widespread international commercial networks, their inveterate disapproval of Spain's annexation of Portugal in 1580, and their unanimous backing of Dom Antonio's cause. Their impressive performances won them much acclaim among the English circles of power and secured them long-lasting government backing and many a special privilege, the most important being the tacit acceptance by the English authorities of their commitment to rejudaization.[37]

The dominant *converso* families maintained their old elite lifestyle in their new English environment. The ingrained legacy of their self-image as prominent bankers, merchants, ship owners, physicians, diplomats, and court astronomers stood them in good stead when they struggled to pursue their old careers in England.[38] The way of life led by the wealthy Portuguese *conversos,* whether they settled in London, Amsterdam, or Antwerp, required running large households, staffed by native and foreign male and female servants. The foreign domestic personnel of the Portuguese merchants of Antwerp were mostly black African servants. Their presence in Jewish Antwerp households is rather well documented; as for London *converso* households it is, unfortunaley, poorly documented.[39]

Dr Hector Nunes [Núñez] (1520–91) scored an unparalleled success as one of the most prominent multi-career Portuguese *conversos* to opt for exile in England. He was a renowned court physician, an enterprising merchant, shipowner, marine insurance broker, intelligencer, and banker who supported the cause of Dom Antonio, the pretender to the Portuguese throne. He was monitoring anti-Spanish resistance from his exile in England, besides being secretary Walsingham's accredited negotiator in putting out secret peace feelers in 1585/86 in order to assess the mounting preparations made for the sailing of the Spanish Armada. As head of the Portuguese community in London, he was running a syndicate of *converso* merchants linked by close family ties. Their policy was to pioneer commercial relations with the Mediterranean countries, Morocco included. He and his partners were among the first to import Moroccan sugar, molasses, paneles (brown unpurified sugar), and rameals (inferior sugar), via Antwerp in ships flying the Moroccan flag in the late 1560s. In March 1571, he and his partner William Curtis invested money in a voyage to Guinea, obviously with an eye on seizing slaves, but the Portuguese ambassador put the Privy Council under pressure to stop the enterprise. There is also evidence that he suffered serious financial setbacks due to daring commercial ventures and to the dangers of Anglo/Spanish hostilities. [40]

In 1582, Dr Nunes's household consisted of his wife Leonor Freire of Antwerp, a butler, three clerks, all of them Portuguese New Christians (Fernando Alvarez, senior, Francisco Alvarez, and Francisco de Tapia), and two black female domestics, Gratia and Elizabeth Anegro. Elizabeth obviously bore the name of Dr Nunes's sister-in-law Elizabeth Freire, who in 1582 married Alvaro de Lima, and Gratia, the name of Grace Freire, another sister-in-law, who had died in 1578. Gratia died a young woman; she was buried in the parish of St Olave Hart Street on July 13, 1590.[41]

Elizabeth and Gratia Anegro, who were members of the Anglican Church, were to play a decisive role in confirming the accusation that the Nunes and Alvarez households were practicing Jewish observances in secret. While Dr Nunes saw to the worldly and economic affairs of his household, he left the daily observance of religious conduct to his wife and his brother-in-law Fernando Alvarez, the husband of Philippa Freire. Dr Nunes had been endenizened as an English subject in 1579 and then had publicly conformed to the Church of England while allowing the members of his family to practise Judaism in the privacy of his house. The evidence that his was a judaizing family is unmistakable. His wife had obviously assumed the role of judaizer since in rabbinic law it was held that Jewishness was transmitted through the mother.[42]

As a slaveholder the distinguished physician was surprisingly out of touch with the legal realities in Tudor England. After having spent some forty years in England, Dr Nunes assumed that there were laws regulating the slave traffic as there had been in his native Portugal. Thus, in 1587, he submitted a formal complaint to the Court of Requests, stating that he had bought an Ethiopian, meaning a black African, from an English mariner at a price of £4 10s. The slave, however, "vtterly" refused "to tarry and serve him." Dr Nunes apparently made the painful experience that he had "not any ordinarye remedie at and by the course of the comon Lawes" unless the queen through her secretaries in the Court of Requests would "compell the sayde Ethiopian to serve him during his liffe." Should the court refuse to oblige the African to serve him, he requested the court to "Recover this sayd ffowre poundes Tenne shillinges" from the English mariner who had sold him the slave.

This case confirms that owing to the absence of a black slave's legal status in early modern England the law courts and even the secretaries of state in the Court of Requests, some of whom were personally acquainted with Dr Nunes, had no authority to intervene. The conclusion of Rosalyn L. Knutson, who has unearthed the document, that the English slaveowner who bought a black slave at the market "did not have the help of the law of England to enforce the bond at the level of enslavement, though they may well have had other kinds of power," is quite relevant. It was precisely the absence of the legal status of a slave that offered the slave a loophole to refuse and at the same time gave the owner free hand to enslave his black African, exploiting him or her as an unpaid domestic servant.[43]

The complaint lodged by Dr Nunes casts a fresh perspective on the hazards of an unregulated black slave market in early modern England. The black slave took advantage of his legally undefined status in refusing to accept the sale and serve Dr Nunes for the rest of his life. He may have been a second-generation African, born in Europe, who had created an image of himself and did not hesitate to challenge European concepts of ownership. Dr Nunes's complaint, moreover, reveals for the first time in an English document what was the actual market value of a black male slave in 1587 London.

Dr Nunes's leadership went uncontested among the Portuguese New Christians in Elizabethan London. His merits, however, have remained undervalued by literary and cultural scholars, who have preferred to focus their attention on another Portuguese converso, on Dr Rodrigo (Ruy) López, physician and collector of the customs duties which the patentees of the Guinea charter owed Dom Antonio. His execution, on June 7, 1594, on a charge of being a secret judaizer plotting to poison the queen has been more newsworthy. C. J. Sisson holds the view that the judaizing New Christians of Portuguese descent Shakespeare is likely to have met in London were not Shylocks but men like Dr Nunes.[44]

The Performance of *Titus Andronicus:* Sir John Harington's Political and Cultural Credo

My first article on *Titus Andronicus* was, as it were, the by-product of my extensive researches into Antonio Pérez's exile in Essex House, London (1593–95). The historic defection of the astute secretary to Philip II and the secret royal audiences he was granted by queen Elizabeth aroused the indignation of the Spanish court. His defection, however, as seen through the prism of English history, was a marginal event worth comment but of little consequence for Elizabethan foreign policy. Even as a man of letters, as a leading aphorist and Tacitist in his day, Antonio Pérez has remained underrated in Spain. Surprisingly, though officially a persona non grata in the eyes of the Elizabethan authorities, he was championed as Spain's foremost Tacitean writer by the learned secretaries of the earl of Essex.[45]

Most of the earl of Essex's secretaries and advisers had taken to Tacitism as a mode of political inquiry and, while Pérez was dwelling in London, were pooling their resources to disseminate the Spaniard's writings among the members of the Essex faction and the Elizabethan court. They even went to the length of harnessing the skills of Richard Field, Shakespeare's first printer, to publish Pérez's famous *Pedaços de Historia o Relaçiones* (1594) in a cross-border campaign framed to exonerate the notorious exile at home. In the *Pedaços de Historia,* Pérez drew on Tacitus's histories in order to provide ideological justification for tyrannicide and for the Aragonese rebellion against Philip II, which had been unleashed by Pérez's imprisonment in Zaragoza. Pérez escaped from his Aragonese prison to the court of Navarre and, in 1593, to the French embassy in London until he eventually took refuge in Essex House. There a set of like-minded scholars came together in the earl's secretariat; one of them, Henry Wotton, produced an English synthesis of the book; another, Arthur Atey, turned out an English translation under the supervision of Anthony Bacon, the earl's foreign secretary.

While Pérez, as a politician, was ignored by the English court or rather, the English court pretended to ignore Pérez, he was held in high esteem by the Tacitean scholars in the service of the Essex faction. To them Pérez offered a model for studying the rule of a tyrant. In his *Pedaços de Historia,* Pérez posed as the favorite who had fallen victim to Philip II's tyranny. Thus what they read in Tacitus and in Pérez sustained their republican principles of imposing legal limits on royal power. In their opinion, to put it in terms of John Guy, the queen's capriciousness, especially in the matter of favorites, bore the "distinguishing mark of tyranny." [46]

Pérez also made a name for himself as an epistolomaniac. He used to shower the English courtiers and the followers of the Essex circle, male as well as female, with epistles, penned in Latin and Spanish, which he used to lard with political aphorisms. His favorite English muse was Penelope Devereux, Lady Rich, to whom he addressed at least five Spanish letters. The climax of Pérez's literary and social prestige was, no doubt, his three-day visit to Cambridge, which was stage-managed by the earl of Essex. On the occasion of the B.A. Commencement at the end of February 1595, which was celebrated with the performance of several plays at Trinity and Queens Colleges and a series of academic disputations, over a dozen guests of the earl of Essex, among them noblemen and courtiers, were awarded honorary M.A. degrees. Among the honorands were Antonio Pérez and Giovanni Battista Basadonna.[47]

Giovanni Battista Basadonna was a patrician merchant, whom the republic of Venice had despatched to England as agent to the Elizabethan court. A nobleman with some literary pretensions, who presided over a miniature court in the city of London, which used to be frequented by Anthony Bacon in his capacity as foreign secretray to Essex, he acted as a banker to Pérez and assisted him in erecting, on behalf of the earl of Essex, an intelligence service in Italy. The pregnant news that this "royal merchant," as he is called in contemporary documents, kept among the records of the Court of Admiralty, was building up an impressive merchant fleet of his own, has gone unnoticed by scholars. His vessels, manned with English and Italian sailors, were flying the Venetian flag while navigating the waters of the Thames in those years in which Shakespeare happened to be writing *The Merchant of Venice*.[48]

For Richard Field printing a book coming from the pen of the expatriate Spaniard, who was biding his time in Essex House, in a quarto edition of over 389 pages with a faked imprint, was quite an outstanding professional achievement. An address of the printer, "El Impressor à Todos" (sig. Ddd3r–Ddd4v), is appended at the end of the book, in which Field declares, "Yo he Impresso este libro con poca notiçia de la lengua Española" (I have printed the book with little knowledge of the Spanish language). This was not quite true.[49]

Bearing in mind that Richard Field had been commissioned by the Essex faction to print the *Pedaços de Historia* and that the earl of Essex had subsidized its printing, it is not rash to speculate that one of the earl's secretaries may have suggested to Shakespeare to pen a stage portrait of the notorious Spaniard for the entertainment of the Essex followers. In my study *A Spaniard in Elizabethan England* I have marshaled various arguments to bring home to the modern reader that Shakespeare conceived Don Adriano de Armado in *Love's Labour's Lost* as a downgraded stage portrait of Antonio Pérez. Shakespeare's parody of Pérez as an insider of Spanish history endowed with rare linguistic accomplishments is grafted on the dramatic stock figure of the Spanish braggart, who originally strutted on the stage of the commedia dell'arte. I have not changed my mind since the 1970s and still hold, to put it in terms of A. L. Rowse, that Shakespeare's stage portrait of Antonio Pérez is "very near the bone."[50] The original audience of the comedy was invited to take King Ferdinand of Navarre's description of Armado at face value:

> Our court, you know, is haunted
>   With a refinèd traveller of Spain,
> A man in all the world's new fashion planted,
>   That hath a mint of phrases in his brain,
> One who the music of his own vain tongue
>   Doth ravish like enchanting harmony,
> A man of compliments, whom right and wrong
>   Have chose as umpire of their mutiny.
> This child of fancy, that Armado hight,
>   For interim to our studies shall relate

> In high-born words the worth of many a knight
> From tawny Spain, lost in the world's debate.
> How you delight, my lords, I know not, I,
> But I protest I love to hear him lie,
> And I will use him for my minstrelsy.[51]

There are, admittedly, other candidates for Shakespeare's satirical portrait of Armado, the Spanish braggart. Thus Tom Cain has demonstrated that the play was written within the tradition of representing recognizable contemporaries in a satirical vein. His candidate for Armado is Gabriel Harvey, the Cambridge scholar. But unlike Pérez, Harvey simply does not fit in with King Ferdinand of Navarre's description of the "refinèd traveller of Spain."[52] It was none other than Pérez, hailed as the "refinèd" exile "of Spain," who was haunting the Elizabethan court. Pérez had taken refuge at the court of Navarre before haunting the court of Queen Elizabeth. Stage-cast in the shape of Armado, he finds access to the court of Navarre and its noblemen who have vowed to impose on themselves a three-year exile as students. Some commentators have noted that the king's promise of an excursion into Spanish history is not fulfilled in the play. It was probably never meant to be fulfilled, for Shakespeare apparently assumed that the play's original audience, that is, the members of the Essex faction and the Inns of Court students and lawyers, did know that "the worth of many a knight / From tawny Spain, lost in the world's debate" was inscribed in the London edition of the *Pedaços de Historia,* a handwritten English and even Latin translation of which were available to them.

What may clinch the controversy over the satire's target in favor of Antonio Pérez is the following argument I forgot to advance in my study of 1976: the closeness of *Love's Labour's Lost* to the Inns of Court culture of wit and satire which fostered the mock recitation of private correspondence. Given that Pérez was a frequent visitor to Gray's Inn, where he shared Francis Bacon's private rooms, as well as a guest of the Gray's Inn revels of 1594, which climaxed with the performance of Shakespeare's *The Comedy of Errors* on December 28, it is not far-fetched to assume that the inmates, the lawyers, and the law students of Gray's Inn had more than a passing knowledge of the Spaniard as an obtrusive epistolomaniac and Tacitean historian à la mode, whose advocacy of limited sovereignty was deemed subversive by the Elizabethan authorities. His epistles are likely to have been made the object of quipping comments circulating among the Inn's members, such as the poet Francis Davison, who were in close touch with the Bacons and the followers of the earl of Essex. Armado's pretentious letter, read out in act 1 before the court of Navarre by King Ferdinand, sounds like a concerted take-off of Pérez's overblown epistolary style.[53]

Antonio Pérez was an exacting exile. His political expectations, demands, and whims inevitably put an unbearable strain on Anthony Bacon's frail physical condition. Bacon therefore appointed, with the approval of the earl of Essex, a string of servants to attend upon the "refinèd" Spaniard, who in his heyday had commanded an army of officials to see to his business and body of curators to look after his famous collection of Titians, Correggios, and Parmigianino's *Cupid*.[54] One of them was the Gascon Jacques Petit, who prided himself on being blessed with an academic turn of mind that stood him in good stead while he was in attendance upon Pérez.

After the Spaniard's departure for France in July 1595, Anthony Bacon commissioned Petit to repair to Burley-on-the-Hill, Rutland, and there to further the French studies of Sir John Harington's son and heir John, a three-year-old child prodigy. While in Rutland, Petit maintained a steady correspondence with his master in London which discloses some nuggets of precious information on the Christmas festivities celebrated at Burley-on-the-Hill in December 1595/January 1596. Thus Sir John Harington, though beset with economic difficulties after marrying his adolescent daughter Lucy to Edward Russell, third earl of Bedford, in December 1594, lavishly and generously entertained some two hundred private guests, many of them his relatives, and up to nine hundred neighbors, copyholders, and tenants. Petit likened the vast concourse of aristocratic Christmas revelers to a "royal" court. It looks as if in 1595/96 Sir John inaugurated a series of Christmas festivities which John Chamberlain in 1602 was to qualify as "royal."

The memorable Christmas celebrations climaxed with a double bill on New Year's Day, first, with the amateur performance of a masque written by Sir Edward Wingfield, Sir John's brother-in-law, obviously with an eye to offering his young niece, the countess of Bedford, a stage début among her relatives, and second, with a professional performance of Shakespeare's *Titus Andronicus*, given by the Chamberlain's Men.[55] Petit, our informant, failed to live up to the importance of the event. An uninspired onlooker, he contented himself with the terse comment that "Les commediens de Londres son[t] venus icy po[u]r en auoir leur p[ar]t . . . on a aussi ioué la tragedie de Titus Andronicus mais la monstre a plus valeu q[ue] le suiect."[56] Petit did not even bother to find out what had induced Sir John to commission the Chamberlain's Men to stage *Titus Andronicus* for the entertainment of his guests. He haughtily assumed the pose of a would-be chronicler who looked down on dramatic entertainments as products of minor quality, missing the opportunity to record the emotional impact the play made on the select audience. On the other hand, he had felt it his bounden duty, on the occasion of Antonio Pérez's departure for France, to compose a doggerel farewell sonnet and two adulatory lamentations each couched in an execrable quatrain. In the first quatrain, he deplores Pérez's absence "Manquant le médecin qui chassoit mon esmoy"; in the second, he laments that he will no longer be able to converse with Pérez and his "dons célestes."[57]

The play Sir John Harington had commissioned for the entertainment of his Christmas guests at Burley-on-the-Hill was not brand-new considering that its first performance had already been given on January 24, 1594. But the play's political message, which argues the case for a more constitutional form of government capable of making up for individual failure as well as for the failure of political institutions in Rome and, by implication, in Elizabethan England, had not lost its immediacy in 1595/96.[58] In 1594, the earl of Essex had been positioning himself to weather the imminent issue of succession, aspiring to change England's destiny on the queen's death.[59] In 1594/95, the earl had also been championing the international campaign raised by the exiled Antonio Pérez, who as Spain's leading Tacitean historian and former secretary to Philip II had adopted a critical discourse to reveal the machinations of Philip II's government against him. Sir John Harington had always been gravitating toward the Leicester/Essex nexus. He had been a staunch supporter of the earl of Leicester, who as second husband of Lettice Knollys (1578–88) had been stepfather of the earl of Essex.[60] Sir John's scheme to stage *Titus Andronicus* as the climax of the Christmas festivities at Burley-on-the-Hill in 1595/96 was no doubt motivated by political considerations. It looks as if the Christmas festivities in Rutland served him as an instrument for letting his entourage know in public that he was positioning himself as a member of the Essex faction. His extravagant twenty-two-year-old son-in-law, Edward Russell, earl of Bedford (1572–1627), who on December 12, 1594, had married his daughter Lucy a month before her fourteenth birthday, followed suit. In February 1601, the earl was tried and heavily fined for being implicated in the rebellion of the earl of Essex.

Besides the contemporary relevance of the play's political message, *Titus Andronicus* broke new ground in its attempt to cast doubt on the conventional perception of the African other as an inferior being. The racial discourse had not lost its immediacy in 1595/96. The foundation of the Guinea Company in 1588 had led to an increased influx of black Africans and by 1593/94, when Shakespeare was writing the play in the form it has come down to us, the black presence in Elizabethan England had reached a peak. The illicit arrival of two young African notables, the sons of the chief justice of Senegambia, and of some black students to be indoctrinated in English culture, was a conspicuous event, which alarmed the English government (see above). Shakespeare responded to these social, legal, and ethnic tensions in staging forms of cross-cultural encounters that called in question the entrenched English position on racial hierarchies; and George Peele, considered by some scholars as coauthor of *Titus Andronicus,* seized the opportunity to publish his old play on *The Battle of Alcazar* with its Moroccan and European settings, which he had written in 1589 as a caveat against the imminent dangers of an English alliance with a Muslim country.[61]

Titus Andronicus, besides being Shakespeare's first revenge tragedy, can claim to be the first Elizabethan play to undercut the racial discourse of positioning white over black. It challenges the ideological assumptions about the black man's racial inferiority. Aaron, the black outsider, does not correspond to the black African slaves the Londoners had come to know in increasing numbers after 1588. His most salient deviation from the real-life enslaved blackamores kept in London households is his literacy. Aaron is a literate black African well versed in the classics. He knows Ovid and Horace better than the sons of Tamora, the white queen of the Goths. Moreover, Aaron's sexual behavior does not conform to the entrenched belief and stereotyped representation of a black man's uncontrollable sexuality. Whereas Tamora herself and her two sons are figures of unrestrained sexuality, Aaron is capable of practicing sexual restraint. He thereby contradicts the current notion of the black man's boundless sexual potency. He also outdoes the Romans in setting examples of moderation and self-discipline and in acting as a vehicle of moral commentary.[62] As a father he is pitted against Titus Andronicus, an embodiment of Roman values, who does not hesitate to resort to infanticide for political and moral considerations. Aaron, however, poses as a paragon of paternal love in his frantic attempt to save his son's life. The assumption that civilized Rome cannot be barbaric is shown to be incorrect.

The play's two miscegenated babies, I think, must be seen as projections of contemporary cultural anxieties about miscegenation: a black baby, the biological product of a black man (Aaron) and a white woman (Tamora), and an offstage "fair" baby, begotten by a black African (Muly) on the body of his white wife. However, the different skin color of the two babies goes against one of the basic tenets of the racial discourse that black men invariably produce black children. The play's daring instance of nature's waywardness was obviously orchestrated by Shakespeare to cast doubt on the popular view, spread by George Best in the *True Discourse of the Late Voyages of Discoverie* (1578), that he had seen a black baby born on English soil to an Englishwoman and an Ethiopian, "whereby it seemeth this blacknes proceedeth rather of some natural infection of that man, which was so strong, that neither the nature" of the salubrious English climate, nor the fair "complexion of the mother concurring, coulde any thing alter" (262). In passing off the anomaly of interbreeding as an "infection," Best, of course, touched a sensitive nerve: his country's fear of losing its identity.

In contrast to Best, Shakespeare's play suggests what Sir Thomas Browne was to formulate in his *Pseudodoxia Epidemica* (1646) that the Blacks descend from "the seed of Adam" just as the English and are endowed with the powers of body and mind to do good and bad things. Thus the play gives the liminal Aaron a public platform to voice his bottomless pride in blackness. "Coal-black," he speaks out undauntedly "is better than another hue / In that it scorns to bear another hue."[63] He does not hesitate to mount a counterattack to bring home to Tamora, to the nurse, and emphatically to Tamora's sons that far from being "as loathsome as a toad" (4.2.69) the black baby is their brother "sensibly fed / Of that self blood that first gave life" to them (4.2.124–25). This is not meant to be a humanitarian plea, but rather a challenge to drop their "exclusiveness and see in themselves" the consanguineous "evil they see in their black brother."[64]

Sir Thomas Browne's position was not a novelty in the context of European cultural history, nor was Shakespeare's. Thus Greek ceramicists and vase painters used to give voice to their belief in the equality of Blacks and Whites in creating janiform kantharoi, two-headed drinking-jugs, representing a white and a black head. The naked black Africans, romping around together with their white partners in Hieronymus Bosch's *The Garden of Earthly Delights* (painted about 1510), convey the painter's message to the world that humans born black are equal to those born white. His contemporary Albrecht Dürer was most impressed by his encounters with black Africans when he was in Flanders in 1521. He portrayed two black domestic slaves, bringing their personalities to life with his masterful pencil strokes. The black slave is unnamed, but the female slave is identified as Katherina, aged twenty, serving in the household of Joao Brandao, commercial representative of the king of Portugal in Antwerp.[65]

Shakespeare's approach to the imminent issues of cultural otherness must have struck a chord with Sir John Harington. The Haringtons had had close interconnections with the Spanish nobility since Margaret Harington, one of Sir John's many sisters, had left England for Spain in July 1559 in the suite of her twenty-year-old cousin Jane Dormer, lady-in-waiting to the late queen Mary. Jane had been married in London to Gómez Suárez de Figueroa, fifth count of Feria, on December 29, 1558. The Feria household in Madrid was to become the hub of the English recusants in Spain, the countess relentlessly supporting the activities of the English Catholics on the Continent besides keeping her Protestant cousins in England, the Haringtons and Sidneys, au courant with the latest flourishing of Spanish culture. Margaret Harington remained affiliated to her cousin's retinue until 1588 when she married don Benito de Cisneros, a member of a prominent Castilian family. As a present Jane gave her cousin Margaret a dowry.[66]

Bearing in mind that Sir John Harington was a patron of the arts who had a cousin, a sister, and a brother-in-law, the three of them members of the Spanish nobility, it is obvious that his family connections singled him out as one of the best informed English noblemen about Spanish matters. We can, therefore, be almost certain that he knew that Portugal had brought forth a mulatto dramatist, Afonso Alvares, and Spain a black neo-Latin poet, Juan Latino, who was the first Afroeuropean writer to construct a Latin discourse of black pride.[67] Given the absence of his sister Margaret and his Spanish brother-in-law, who had not been able to honor the invitation to join the Harington reunion at Burley-on-the-Hill in December 1595, Sir John was, no doubt, the best qualified playgoer, watching the performance of *Titus Andronicus* and ready to awaken the response of his numerous private guests, among them his relatives, friends, and neighbors, to the the play's ethnic position. He may indeed have succeeded in bringing home to his select audience the redeeming qualities of Aaron as a father as well as his outstanding literacy and grounding in classical authors, which entitle him to shed the image of a barbarian. Both the fictional Aaron and the real-life Juan Latino defined themselves by their classical literacy as a measure of human worth. The Latinity was for the two of them a means to fashion their own identities and in the case of Aaron even to claim cultural superiority.

It is not possible to do justice to the play's attempt to question the hostile response to the African in Elizabethan England without taking into account, besides the black presence, the early history of English slavery, the whole body of experience made by the English slaveholders and dealers dwelling in early modern Spain, which cultural historians, literary scholars, and Africanists have brushed aside as nonexistent. Ignorance of early English real-life encounters with Africans has spawned Winthrop Jordan's long-harbored and infectious myth that the encounter of the early modern English with Blacks was a traumatic experience—for the English.[68]

The historical records I have uncovered open up a new dimension in assessing the cross-cultural encounters between the Africans and the English merchants residing on the Christian/Muslim frontier, the European/African intersection in the Mediterranean ports of early modern Spain. It emerges from the documents retrieved from Spanish archives that all the English merchants residing in lower Andalusia after 1480 were potential owners of domestic slaves, black Africans and Moors, and that they were deeply immersed in the slave trade as dealers in human merchandise. The most prominent of them, Thomas Malliard and Robert Thorne, operated as capitalist leaseholders of soap factories in Seville and Malliard as an early colonist and joint tenant of one of the first sugar farms in the Canaries, the two of them exploiting unskilled and skilled labor force from Africa for the industrial production of white soap and sugar. [69]

Despite the institutionalization of the slave market, which affected all social classes in Spain, from top to bottom, in buying and selling slaves, the foreign merchants included, there were moments in which the white masters did look beyond the immediate exploitation of their slaves, whom they were legally entitled to own as their chattels. Thus Robert Thorne, facing his sudden return to England, sold seven Berbers and six Negroes to Bartholomäus Welser and Heinrich Gessler on May 2, 1531, and manumitted his two Berber master soap makers on May 10, 1531. He was somehow looking beyond harnessing their skills for the sole purpose of exploiting them as pieces of productive property. But it was still a "manumissio sub conditione."[70] There is also unmistakable evidence that the authorities in England were disposed to acknowledge the black man's human nature and personhood. The judges of the High Court of Admiralty in a London lawsuit of 1548 granted the Guinea diver Jacques Francis the status of a witness against the fierce opposition of some Italian merchants resident in Southampton. (See my paper on the Guinea diver Jacques Francis.)

Richard Hakluyt, the historian of England's maritime ventures and collector of travel narratives, unlike his Spanish and Portuguese colleagues, who were eloquent chroniclers of the incipient slave trade in their countries, failed to record the experiences made by the English merchants as slave dealers in early modern Spain. It looks as if the chaplain-turned-geographer pursued an editorial policy of withholding information in order to protect his compatriots against being lumped together with the ignominious record of the Spaniards and Portuguese. His nationalist discourse of discovery was primarily aimed at glorifying his country's naval achievements and praising its moral superiority. Thus in his *Divers Voyages* (1582), he edited Robert Thorne's text on the polar passage to Cathay and another on "A declaration of the Indies" without making a reference to Thorne as an experienced slaveholder.[71]

Despite Hakluyt's reticence about England's early Mediterranean experience with black slaves, the extensive involvement in the slave business of William de la Founte, Thomas Malliard, Robert Thorne, his brother Nicholas Thorne, Roger Barlow, Nicholas Arnold, Thomas Bridges, Francis Bawdwyn, Emmanuel Lucar (1494–1574), William Ostriche, Henry Patmer, Martin Pollard, Thomas Waters, (Guatres) and many other English merchants cannot have completely been lost on their English partners, colleagues, friends, and acquaintances in England.

When Robert Thorne was back in England in 1531, he took like most of his wealthy partners testamentary measures to preserve the survival of his memory in perpetuity. In his will he donated £300 toward the foundation of St Bartholomew Grammar School, Bristol. This foundation was an expression of the wish "he shared with his brother Nicholas from adolescence, as they both tried to establish navigational instruction and foreign language tuition in the city of Bristol." (See entry on Robert Thorne in *ODNB*.) What the two brothers in their capacity as mercantile and intellectual go-betweens envisaged was obviously a transfer of scientific knowledge of modern navigation and cartography from Spain to England, a transfer that was eventually to be brought about after 1547, when Sebastian Cabot, Robert Thorne's old partner, settled in England.[72] Thorne's endowment of the grammar school was apparently financed by money he had made by holding and selling slaves.

Emmanuel Lucar, Robert Thorne's onetime apprentice, later on partner and overseer of the Seville soap factory, turned out to be a competent go-between and transmitter of past events. He returned to England in 1531, though Thorne had commissioned him to look after the two manumitted Berber master soap makers, who had been sold to the German Welser Company and were bound to work on for another five years. Thorne, who died in 1532, and Lucar were members of the Merchant Taylors' Company. Lucar was elected master of the Company in 1560/61, the year in which the famous Merchant Taylors' School was founded. He was in an ideal position to keep alive the memory, legacy, and life story of his former master Robert Thorne. His son, Ciprian Lucar, is said to have transmitted the Thorne papers to John Dee and Richard Hakluyt.[73]

In my essay on "Portia and the Prince of Morocco," I argue that the Davenants, who were members of the Merchant Taylors' Company, called Shakespeare's attention to the story of the Gores, who have gone down in the annals of the Merchant Taylors as the first Anglo-Moroccan family. The involvement of the Gores in the bankruptcy of the prominent Moroccan Jew Isaac Cabeça and in the ensuing lawsuit, which dragged on in the High Court of Admiralty for over a decade, was common knowledge in London's mercantile community. The numerous bankruptcies of English Christians and Moroccan Jews, who happened to be interlocked in transnational business partnerships and cross-border money lending, was quite alarming. The Gore/Cabeça partnership and subsequent lawsuit is, to my mind, a real-life contemporary parallel to the Antonio/Shylock bond. The involvement of English merchants in the slave trade of early modern Spain may likewise have been brought home to Shakespeare through his contacts with the members of the Merchant Taylors' Company. It would help explain why about 1592–94 Shakespeare, at the height of the scandal caused by the illicit import of Guinea slaves, embarked on a policy of facing up to the new cultural realities and of provoking changes in the Elizabethan perception of cultural otherness. He was to pursue his policy in the Mediterranean plays, *The Merchant of Venice*,[74] *Othello, Anthony and Cleopatra,* and *The Tempest,* addressing in all of these plays the hotly debated issues of cross-cultural marriages, miscegenation, and manumission of slaves in *The Tempest.*

Notes

1. See Rosalyn L. Knutson, "A Caliban in St. Mildred Poultry," in *Shakespeare and Cultural Traditions. The Selected Proceedings of the International Shakespeare Association World Congress Tokyo 1991,* ed. Tetsuo Kishi et al. (Newark: University of Delaware Press, 1994), 110–26. Imtiaz Habib of the Department of English, Old Dominion University, Norfolk, Virginia, is pursuing his search for black Africans in London parish records (see n. 14). The family of a freedman is recorded by Knutson and another instance is erroneously given by Habib. Habib, an authority on the colonial discourse in Shakespeare's plays, has been misled by Folarin O. Shyllon's study, *Black People in Britain, 1556–1833* (London: Oxford University Press, 1972), into

identifying a Spanish or Italian mercenary serving in the army of king Henry VIII as an African. The identification of Sir Peter Negro as a black officer does not take into account that the Negros were of Genoese descent. Dozens of them settled in Spain and Portugal in the course of the fourteenth and fifteenth centuries, far too many to be listed here. The factor Paolo di Negro, for whom Columbus was working in Madeira in 1479, may stand for the others. I have consulted all the available contemporary records in Spanish and English; none mentions that Sir Peter was black. I therefore can't help concluding that the career of the mercenary Pedro Negro under king Henry VIII is quite irrelevant to the study of Othello. See Imtiaz Habib, *Shakespeare and Race: Postcolonial Praxis in the Early Modern Period* (Lanham: University Press of America, 2000), 128 ff.

2. For the confusion of the legal status of black Africans in England see Kenneth Little, *Negroes in Britain. A Study of Racial Relations in English Society* (London: Routledge and Kegan Paul, 1972), 192–93. For the poll tax levied in the parish of All Hallows, Barking, Toward Ward, see W. E. Miller, "Negroes in Elizabethan London," *Notes and Queries,* n.s. 8 (April 1961): 138.

3. The view still prevails that black Africans were rarities in England until slaving reached its full development in the late seventeenth century. See William D.Phillips, Jr., *Slavery from Roman Times to the Early Transatlantic Trade* (Manchester: Manchester University Press, 1985), 155.

4. For the expulsion edicts see James Walvin, *Black and White: The Negro and English Society 1555–1945* (London: Allen Lane, The Penguin Press, 1973), 8–9; Carole Levin, *The Reign of Elizabeth I* (Basingstoke: Palgrave, 2002), chap. 6, 120–1, For the Portuguese complaints about the superfluity of slaves and alleged disruption of economic stability see A. C. de C.M. Saunders, *A Social History of Black Slaves and Freedmen in Portugal 1441–1555 (*Cambridge: Cambridge University Press, 1982), 48; and Didier Lahon, "Black African Slaves and Freedmen in Portugal during the Renaissance: Creating a New Pattern of Reality," in *Black Africans in Renaissance Europe,* ed. T. F. Earle and K. J. P Lowe (Cambridge: Cambridge University Press, 2005), 261–79. For the issue of an immigrant coloured minority becoming the national scapegoat for an economic problem and Shakespeare's ironic response to this issue through the figures of Launcelot and the Mooress in *The Merchant of Venice* see Kim F. Hall, "Reading What Isn't There: 'Black' Studies in Early Modern England," *Stanford Humanities Review* 3 (1993), 23–33.

5. Doña Catalina de Ribera is an extreme instance. On her death in 1505, she owned seventy-one slaves. See Alfonso Franco Silva, *La esclavitud en Andalucía al término de la edad media* (Madrid: Pons, 1984), 145; Leonor de Guzmán, duchess of Medina Sidonia, claimed thirty-three slaves in 1511. See Miguel-Angel Ladero Quesada, *Los señores de Andalucía: Investigaciones sobre los nobles y señores en los siglos XIII a XV* (Cádiz: Universidad de Cádiz, 1998), 252–53; Leonor de Aznar bought thirteen slaves on January 17, 1511 (Archivo Histórico Provincial de Sevilla, legajo 3969).

6. For Lady Ralegh and Lady Clifford see Peter Fryer, *Staying Power: The History of Black People in Britain* (London: Pluto Press, 1984, rpt. 1992). Fryer makes the outdated statement that is was the privilege of titled and propertied families to secure blacks as an exotic status symbol (p. 8). For Grace Robinson and John Morocco

see Edward Scobie, *Black Britannia: A Study of Blacks in Britain* (Chicago: Johnson, 1972), 23. African musicians in the service of Tudor monarchs have been recorded by Africanist scholars. The "Blynd More," one of the musicians in Leicester's service in 1559, has not. See Simon Adams, ed., *Household Accounts and Disbursement Books of Robert Dudley, Earl of Leicester, 1558–61, 1584–86* (Cambridge: Cambridge University Press, 1995).

7. The paucity of biographical records shedding light on the lived experience of ordinary black people has aroused the comment of James Walvin. Very little is known about black women and black family life in Britain. See James Walvin, "From the Fringes: The Emergence of British Black Historical Studies," in *Essays on the History of Blacks in Britain,* ed. Jagdish S. Gundara and Ian Duffield (Aldershot: Avebury, 1992), 225–42.

8. See D. J. H. Clifford, ed., *The Diaries of Lady Anne Clifford* (Stroud: Alan Sutton , 1990), appendix 1. The Catalogue, I think, must have been drawn up by Edward Marsh, Lady Anne's secretary.

9. D. J. H. Clifford, *The Diaries,* 53, 231, 234, 238, 241, 242, 244, 251, 254, 258, 264, 265.

10. For more information on the three black laundresses see Annemarie Jordan, "Images of Empire: Slaves in the Lisbon Household and the Court of Catherine of Austria," in T. F. Earle, *Black Africans in Renaissance Europe,* chap. 7.

11. The other slaveowners listed as paying the same tax in the parish of All Hallows were Richard Woods, the owner of Mary; Oliver Skinner, the owner of Maria; and one Mr Mitons, obviously a Dutchman. See W.E. Miller, "Negroes in Elizabethan London," *Notes and Queries,* n.s. 8 (1961): 138, and R. E. G. Kirk and Ernest P. Kirk, *Returns of Aliens in the City and Suburbs of London,* Publications of the Huguenot Society of London 10 (1907), pt. iii, 28, 54.

12. See Sara Mendelson and Patricia Crawford, *Women in Early Modern England 1550–1720* (Oxford: Clarendon Press, 1998), 89, 106–7, who do not mention miscegenation.

13. For more detailed information on slave and slaveholder see Rosalyn L. Knutson, "A Caliban in St. Mildred Poultry," 113, 120, 124.

14. Bodleian Library, MS. Ashmole 226, fol. 84v. A. L. Rowse in his study of *The Case Books of Simon Forman: Sex and Society in Shakespeare's Age* (London: Picador, 1976) has ignored Polonia's case. I have managed to read Forman's hand but have failed to decipher his astrological shorthand. There is a cursory reference to this case in Imtiaz Habib's article "Elizabethan Racial-Medical Psychology, Popular Drama, and the Social Programming of the Late-Tudor Black: Sketching an Exploratory Postcolonial Hypothesis," in *Disease, Diagnosis, and Cure on the Early Modern Stage,* ed. Stephanie Moss and Kaara L. Peterson (Aldershot: Ashgate, 2004), 93–112.

15. See Barbara Howard Traister, *The Notorious Astrological Physician of London. Works and Days of Simon Forman* (Chicago: University of Chicago Press, 2001), 64, 70.

16. Quotation from Ania Loomba, *Shakespeare, Race and Colonization* (Oxford: Oxford University Press, 2002), 28.

17. I owe this information to Dr. Lauren Kassell who has been so kind as to consult

her microfilm of Forman's case books. Dr. Kassell does not discuss Polonia's case in her study *Medicine and Magic in Elizabethan London. Simon Forman: Astrologer, Alchemist, Physician* (Oxford: Clarendon Press, 2005).

18. See Iris Origo, "The Domestic Enemy: The Eastern Slaves in Tuscony in the 14th and 15th Centuries," *Speculum* 30 (1955), 321–66.

19. William Shakespeare, *Pericles,* The Arden Edition, ed. F. D. Hoeniger (London: Methuen, 1963), 4.2.13–16.

20. William Shakespeare, *Romeo and Juliet,* The Oxford Shakespeare, ed. Jill L. Levenson (Oxford: Oxford Univerity Press, 2000), 1.3.2–3. Juliet is fourteen years old.

21. William Shakespeare, *The Merchant of Venice,* The New Cambridge Shakespeare, ed. M. M. Mahood (Cambridge: Cambridge University Press, 1987), 3.5.30–35. For Launcelot's role as go-between and advocate of religious, racial and sexual exchange see Steven R. Menth, "The Fiend Gives Friendly Counsel: Launcelot Gobbo and Polyglot Economics in *The Merchant of Venice,*" in *Money and the Age of Shakespeare: Essays in New Economic Criticism,* ed. Linda Woodbridge (Houndmills: Palgrave Macmillan, 2003), 177–87. For Portia's anxieties about miscegenation see my article on "Portia and the Prince of Morocco," *Shakespeare Studies* 31 (2003): 89–126. Miscegenation was endemic among the servant class in Spain. See Ruth Pike, *Aristocrats and Traders: Sevillian Society in the 16th Century* (Ithaca: Cornell University Press, 1972)*,* 188. It was on the increase in late Elizabethan London and in the Netherlands. The rudimentary bilingual word list *Duyts-Guineets*, appended to Pieter de Marees' *Beschryvinge ende historische verhael van het Gout Koninckrijk van Gunea* (Amsterdam, 1602), was challenging and novel in the sense that its language lessons conceived for the professional guidance of Dutch merchants in Guinea did not shy away from raising the issue of sexual intercourse, thus encourging the Dutch merchants, in conversational scraps, to pull down the racial and sexual barriers: "Give me a fine woman" and "Woman, do you want to sleep with me?" See the modern English translation *Description and Historical Account of the Gold Kingdom of Guinea (1602),* ed. Albert van Dantzig and Adam Jones (Oxford: Oxford University Press, 1987), 246–59. The registers of St. Benet Fink, London, record, on June 2, 1606, the christening of a boy born to a black woman. The father was supposed to be John Edwardes, a border in the house of William Connrador. See Rosalyn L. Knutson, "A Caliban in St. Mildred Poultry," 113.

22. For William Winter's career as a naval administrator see entry in the *ODNB* (2005); as a mercantile venturer exploiting the commecial resources of Guinea see John W. Blake, *West Africa: Quest for God and Gold 1454–1578* (London: Curzon Press, 1977), 163–64, 172; Kenneth R. Andrews, *Trade, Plunder and Settlement. Maritime Enterprise and the Genesis of the British Empire, 1480–1630* (Cambridge: Cambridge University Press, 1984, rpt. 1991), 105. The *ODNB* does not record Winter's stake in the Guinea ventures.

23. Rosalyn L. Knutson, "A Caliban in St. Mildred Poultry," 114–15. Sir William's son, Edward, kept a black African working as his porter in Lydney, Gloucestershire, in the 1590s. Edward Winter dispossessed the African of his original identity, calling him his own under the name of Edward Swarthey. I owe this information to Miranda Kaufmann, Christ Church College, Oxford, who is working on "Africans in Britain 1500–1640."

24. Kenneth R. Andrews in *Trade, Plunder and Settlement,* has argued that the possibility of English trade to Guinea returned in 1585 with the open outbreak of the Anglo-Spanish hostilities. The English slave trade, he noted, was not resumed until after 1650 (pp. 111/12). For the Portuguese members of Dom Antonio's household in February 1585, see the inventory drawn up by one of Sir Francis Walsingham's clerks and edited by E. M. Tenison, *Elizabethan England,* vol. 7 (Leamington Spa: 1940), 202–4. As a person of high rank Dom Antonio used to keep colored slaves in his household. Thus he brought from Tangiers, where he had been governor, the Muslim slave Antonio Luis, whom he kept to look after his stables in Portugal. See Jorge Fonseca, "Black Africans in Portugal during Cleynaert's Visit 1533–1538," ed. T. F. Earle and K. J. P Lowe, *Black Africans in Europe,* 113–21.

25. Thus he issued privateering letters and letters of marque in 1582 and 1584. See Pauline Croft, "English Commerce with Spain and the Armada War, 1558–1603" and Simon Adams, "The Outbreak of the Elizabethan Naval War against the Spanish Empire: The Embargo of May 1585 and Sir Francis Drake's West Indian Voyage," both papers ed. M. J. Rodríguez-Salgado and Simon Adams, *England, Spain and the Gran Armada, 1585–1604,* 240 and 53, resp. For a financial memorandum Dom Antonio addressed to the English government in 1592 see E. M. Tenison, *Elizabethan England,* vol. 9, 165 ff, 269–75, 449ff.

26. For a short description of the two coasts see Jean Boulègue, *Les anciens royaumes Wolof (Sénégal), vol. I: Le Grand Jolof, XIIIe–XVIe siècle* (Paris: Karthala, 1987), 124–29.

27. The documents concerning the renewal of the English Guinea trade in 1588 have been published by Mario Alberto Nunes Costa, "D. Antonio e o trato Ingles da Guiné (1587–1593), *Boletim Cultural da Guiné Portuguesa* 8 (1953): 683–797. Nunes Costa has edited the material he found in the Portuguese National Archives, the Arquivo Nacional da Torre do Tombo, but has not made use of the documents kept at the National Archives, at Kew, High Court of Admiralty, 24/59/28–51. The date 1587 as given by the Portuguese editor is in Old Style. The regulations of the charter provided that the proceedings from the sales of slaves, "qualquer dinheiro . . . de qualquer venda de escravos," were to be inventoried. See the Portuguese text of the charter in Nunes Costa, document 4, pp. 711–17, resp.715–16. The English original text of the Guinea charter was published by Richard Hakluyt in *The Principal Navigations, Viages and Discoveries of the English Nation* (London, 1589), Hakluyt Society, Extra Series, no. 39, vol. 1 (Cambridge: Cambridge University Press, 1965), 240–42. Nunes Costa has edited the original French translation of the Guinea charter (see document 3). For a concise history of the Guinea charter see John Milner Gray, *A History of Gambia* (London: Frank Cass, 1966), chap. 3: "The arrival of the English in Gambia, 1588–1622;" William Robert Scott, *The Constitution and Finances of English, Scottish, and Irish Joint-Stock Companies to 1720,* 3 vols. (Cambridge, 1910–12), vol. 2, 10–14. The best informed English historian on the first Guinea Company is John William Blake. However, his study "English Trade with the Portuguese Empire in West Africa 1581–1629," published in *Quarto congreso do mundo portugues,* vol. 4, t. 1 (Lisbon, 1940), 314–35, though meticulously researched, remains incomplete. Blake overlooked the important body of material which Nunes Costa was to recover from Portuguese archives. Blake's article has been reedited by

Jeremy Black in *The Atlantic Slave Trade: Origins-1600* (Aldershot: Ashgate, 2006), vol. 1, item 15.

28. Nunes Costa, document 43, pp. 776–78. A copy of the same document is also kept at the National Archives, at Kew, HCA 24/59/45–46. Evasion of duties was rampant among merchants and slavers operating on the upper Guinea coast. Under the Hispano-Portuguese regime the colony went through the golden years of trade in slaves and ivory. See Walter Rodney, "Portuguese Attempts at Monopoly on the Upper Guinea Coast, 1580–1650," *Journal of African History* 6 (1965): 307–22.

29. Nunes Costa, documents 1, 37, 38.

30. André Alvares d'Almada, *Tratado breve dos rios de Guiné do Cabo Verde (1594)*, ed. Antonio Brasio, *Monumenta Misionaria, Africa Ocidental, 1570–1650*, 5 vols. (Lisbon: Agencia Geral do Ultramar, 2a serie, 1958–79), vol. 3 (1964), 230–376, chap. 2, pp. 247ff. Richard Rainolds, "The voyage of Richard Rainolds and Thomas Dassel to the rivers of Senega and Gambra [*sic*] adjoyning upon Guinea, 1591, with a discourse of the treasons of certain of Don [*sic*] Antonio his servants and followers," in Richard Hakluyt, *The Principal Navigations, Traffiques and Discoveries of the English Nation* (1598–1600), ed. with an Introduction by John Masefield, 8 vols. (London: J. M. Dent and Sons, 1927), vol. 5, 44–52.

31. To put it in terms of Alvares d' Almada: "E o dia de eles receberem as pagas e entregarem as suas mercadorias, lhes dao os Ingleses em terra banquetes, com muita música de violas de arco e outros instrumentos músicos. E por esta causa estao estes resgates de toda esta costa do Cabo Verde até Rio de Gâmbia perdidos" (p. 251). For more information on the Luso-Africans see Walter Rodney, *A History of the Upper Guinea Coast, 1545–1800* (Oxford: Oxford University Press, 1970), 74 ff; Jean Boulègue, *Les Luso-Africains de Sénégambie, xvi–xix siècles* (Lisbon: Instituto de Investigaçao Cientifica Tropical, 1989), 37–39; and the first chapters in Peter Mark, *"Portuguese" Style and Luso-African Identity: Precolonial Senegambia, Sixteenth–Nineteenth Centuries* (Bloomington: Indiana University Press, 2002).

32. The relevant passage in Alvares d' Almada reads: "e agora, depois de terem amizade com os Ingleses, foram já alguns a Inglaterra aprender a língua Inglesa e ver a terra, por mandado do alcaide de porto de Ale, que serve de veador da fazenda de el-Rei" (p. 250). The earliest instance of five West Africans taken to England in order to be broken in as interpreters, in emulation of Portuguese practice to boost commercial relations, dates from 1555. See Peter Fryer, *Staying Power*, 5. The difference between the two events is that in 1555 the initiative was taken by the English, in 1592 obviously by the Africans.

33. See Rosalyn L. Knutson, "A Caliban in St. Mildred Poultry."

34. See "The voyage of Richard Rainolds," 46, 50, 51. The central theme of John Thornton's incisive study *Africa and Africans in the Making of the Atlantic World, 1400–1680* (Cambridge: Cambridge University Press, 1998) is that "the Africans were active participants in the Atlantic world, both in African trade with Europe (including the slave trade) and as slaves in the New World" (p. 7). Slavery in Africa was endemic before the arrival of the Europeans; the Africans themselves were given to exporting slaves. As soon as the Portuguese abandoned their early strategy of raiding for commerce, exporting slaves took a dramatic turn upward (p. 95). It was African strength, not weakness, that became a key factor in shaping the transatlantic slave trade.

35. For Paul Banning's career as a merchant and privateering magnate see Kenneth R. Andrews, *Trade Plunder and Settlement,* 98, 245–47, 251–52, 257, 261, 263; and T. S. Willan, "Some Aspects of English Trade with the Levant in the 16th Century," *The English Historical Review* 70 (1955): 399–410.

36. The three black servants are listed in Irene Scouloudi, ed., *Returns of Strangers in the Metropolis, 1593, 1627, 1635, 1639. A Study of an Active Minority,* Proceedings of the Huguenot Society of London 16 (1937–41): 149. The christening of "Iulyane" has been retrieved by Rosalyn L. Knutson, "A Caliban in St. Mildred Poultry," 113. For John Abel, one of Banning's many retainers, who "purloined" £70 from his wealthy master to squander them on the maintenance of Mary Newborough see my article on "Prostitution in Late Elizabethan London: The Case of Mary Newborough," *Medieval and Renaissance Drama in England* 15 (2003): 89–126, n. 74.

37. The groundwork for studying the Portuguese *conversos* in early modern England has been laid by Lucien Wolf in the "Jews in Elizabethan England," *Transactions of the Jewish Historical Society of England* 11 (1926): 1–91. For an overview of the Jewish presence see James Shapiro, *Shakespeare and the Jews* (New York: Columbia University Press, 1996), 68ff.

38. For a modern approach to defining *converso* identity see Miriam Bodian, "'Man of the Nation': The Shaping of *Converso* Identity in Early Modern Europe," *Past and Present* 143 (1994): 48–76; and *Hebrews of the Portuguese Nation: Conversos and Community of Early Modern Amsterdam* (Bloomington: Indiana University Press, 1997).

39. For the Antwerp Jews see Hans Pohl, "Die Portugiesen in Antwerp (1567–1648): zur Geschichte einer Minderheit," *Vierteljahrschrift für Sozial- und Wirtschaftsgeschichte* 63 (1977): 1–439.

40. For Dr Nunes's biography see the entry in the *ODNB* (2004), vol. 41, 274; and Lucien Wolf, "Jews in Elizabethan England," 8–9, 23, 30, and appended documents. For the uncalendared Moroccan trade see my article on "Recovering a Black African's Voice, in an English Lawsuit," *Medieval and Renaissance Drama in England* 17 (2005): n. 38; and for the abortive Guinea voyage see John W. Blake, *West Africa: Quest for God and Gold ,* 188. For his financial reverses see Charles Meyers and Edgar Samuel, "Debt in Elizabethan England: the Adventures of Dr Hector Nunez, Physician and Merchant," *Jewish Historical Studies* 34 (1994–96): 125–40.

41. See Lucien Wolf, "Jews in Elizabethan England," 8–9, 13. Gratia's death is recorded by Rosalyn L. Knutson, "A Caliban in St. Mildred's Poultry." Knutson gives two burial dates, one is July 13, 1590 (p. 114), the other is September 13, 1591 (p. 115). For the role played by the Freire sisters within the international network of Jewish trade relations see Alan Stewart, "Portingale Women and Politics in Late Elizabethan London," in *Women and Politics in Early Modern England, 1450–1700,* ed. James Daybell (Aldershot: Ashgate, 2004), chap. 5.

42. For the Alvarez household, which is said to have contained several black servants, and for the part played by Elizabeth Anegro see C. J. Sisson, "A Colony of Jews in Shakespeare's London," *Essays and Studies* 23 (1938): 38–51. Fernando Alvarez was a member of the Spanish Church of London and when it was disbanded in 1563, he joined the Italian Church under Girolamo Ferlito. See William McFadden, "The Life and Works of Antonio del Corro (1527–1591)" (PhD thesis, Faculty of

Arts of Queen's University, Belfast, 1933), 2 vols, chap. 22; and Luigi Firpo, "La chiesa italiana di Londra nel cinquecento e i suoi rapporti con Ginevra," in *Ginevra e l'Italia*. Biblioteca Storica Sansoni, ed. Delio Cantimori et al. n.s., 34 (1959): 342.

43. The document has been unearthed and commented on by Rosalyn L. Knutson in "A Caliban in St. Mildred Poultry," 116. Knutson has not realized that the misspelt name of the physician "Hector Novimeis" stands for Dr Nunes. Penal slavery did exist in early modern England under the anti-vagrancy and poor relief acts.

44. C. J. Sisson, "A Colony of Jews in Shakespeare's London," 38–51. Gondomar, the Spanish ambassador to the Jacobean court, was to allege that Dr López had been innocent and unjustly executed. See the biographical entry of Dr López in *ODNB* (2004).

45. On the earl of Essex's secretaries and his patronage of Antonio Pérez see Paul E. J. Hammer, "The Uses of Scholarship: The Secretariat of Robert Devereux, second Earl of Essex, ca. 1585–1601," *English Historical Review* 109 (1994): 26–51, and *The Polarisation of Elizabethan Politics. The Political Career of Robert Devereux, Second Earl of Essex, 1585–1597* (Cambridge: Cambridge University Press, 1999). My article on the play is titled "An Unrecorded Elizabethan Performance of *Titus Andronicus*," *Shakespeare Survey* 14 (1961): 102–9.

46. John Guy, "The 1590s: The Second Reign of Elizabeth I?" ed. John Guy in *The Reign of Queen Elizabeth I. Court and Culture in the Last Decade* (Cambridge: Cambridge University Press, 1995), 1–19.

47. The letters have been edited in Gustav Ungerer, *A Spaniard in Elizabethan England: The Correspondence of Antonio Pérez's Exile* (London: Tamesis Books Limited, 1 (1974), 2 (1976); see vol. i, nos. 41, 42, 44, 45, 48, 50. The visit to Cambridge has been uncovered by Paul Hammer in *The Polarisation of Elizabethan Politics*, 304.

48. Basadonna's presence in London (1593–99) has been blotted out from Italian and English historiography. Some day I hope to write an essay on Basadonna's embassy, his commercial and social activities, and his purchases of expensive vessels from London brokers. Basadonna was undoubtedly the best qualified Venetian in London to give an English author, such as Shakespeare, an insider's account of Venice. He was in touch with John Byrd, brewer, of Southwark, and with Henry Stradling, draper, who in 1594 sold him three vessels, the Hopewell, the Elizabeth of London, alias the Golden Noble, of 240 tons, and the Bona Speranza, a "royally furnished ship," of 280–300 tons, at a price of £650. See my essay on "Prostitution in Late Elizabethan London: The Case of Mary Newborough," *Medieval and Renaissance Drama in England* 15 (2003): 138–223, n. 71.

49. Richard Field had already some experience in publishing a Spanish/English language manual. In 1591, he had printed William Stepney's *The Spanish Schoolemaster* and between 1596 and 1600 he was to print several books of the Spanish reformer Cipriano de Valera under the imprint "En casa de Ricardo del Campo." See Gustav Ungerer, "The Printing of Spanish Books in Elizabethan England, *The Library*, 5th ser. 20 (1965): 177–229.

The presence of Pérez in London and the publication of his book under the pseudonym of Raphael Peregrino were reason enough for the Essexians to learn Spanish. In his instructions to Robert Naunton, Essex wrote that "to have Signor Perez willingly helpe yow in the Spanishe yow must pretende to studye the tonge as well, because it is hys, as for the excellencye of itselfe . . . If you will use an amplificacion, yow maye saye yow learne Spanishe to understande Raphael Peregrino's booke as well as Bartas did Englishe to understande Sir Philip Sydney's Arcadia." See Hammer, *The Polarisation of Elizabethan Politics*, 310, n. 215.

50. A. L. Rowse, *Shakespeare's Globe. His Intellectual and Moral Outlook* (London, 1981), 117.

51. William Shakespeare, *Love's Labour's Lost*, ed. G. R. Hibbard in *The Oxford Shakespeare* (Oxford: Oxford University Press, 1990), 1.1.161–75.

52. Tom Cain, "'Comparisons and wounding flouts': *Love's Labour's Lost* and the Tradition of Personal Satire," ed. John Batcheler, Tom Cain, and Claire Lamont in *Shakespearean Continuities: Essays in Honour of E. A. J. Honigmann* (London: Macmillan, 1997), 193–205. Not Armado but the Spanish braggart Huanebango in George Peele's play *The Old Wives Tale* (1593–94) is in part a parody of Gabriel Harvey's style.

53. On the play's similarity to the Inns of Court culture see Lynne Magnusson, "Scoff Power in *Love's Labour's Lost* and the Inns of Court Language in Context," *Shakespeare Survey* 57 (2004): 196–208. On Francis Davison's acquaintance with Pérez, his obvious knowledge of Spanish and participation in the Gray's Inn Revels of December 1594 see Gustav Ungerer, *A Spaniard in Elizabethan England*, i, 256–57.

54. For Pérez's famous collection of paintings see Gustav Ungerer, *A Spaniard in Elizabethan England*, i, 193.

55. I have addressed the issues raised by the performance of the Chamberlain's Men in Rutland and those by the Christmas festivities sponsored by Sir John Harington in two separate papers. The first, dating from 1961, focuses on the identification of the London company of players (see note 45). The second deals with the social and economic dimensions of the Christmas festivities and with the great drain the financial resources of Sir John Harington which was caused by his ambitious life style. It was published by the Rutland Record Society under the title "Shakespeare In Rutland," *Rutland Record* 7 (1987): 242–48. The original French text of Jacques Petit has been dropped by the editor and replaced by my English translations.

56. Jacques Petit's letter containing the reference to *Titus Andronicus* can be read in the original French in the appendix to my 1961 essay and in a modern English version in Daphne du Maurier's *Golden Lads. A Study of Anthony Bacon, Francis and Their Friends* (London: Victor Gollancz, 1975), 146–47. A team of record agents under the supervision of Mrs St. George Saunders has transcribed over three hundred original letters. The quality of the transcriptions is very uneven and occasionally quite inaccurate. See, for instance, A. Bacon's letter in *Golden Lads*, p. 160, and my transcript in *A Spaniard in Elizabethan England*, i, 276–77.

57. Petit's sonnet and lamentations can be read in *A Spaniard in Elizabethan England*, i, 238–40. While Petit immersed himself in effusions of second-rate farewell verses, the earl of Essex was constrained to borrow £500 from the Dutch jeweler and stonecutter Peter van Lore in order to finance Pérez's return to Henry IV in Paris. (See my essay on "Prostitution in Late Elizabethan London," n. 33). Medical tropes were fashionable in the Elizabethan age. When Thomas Platter, the physician from Basel, visited White Hall Palace in September 1599, he was ushered into a hall which jutted out over the Thames and which was crammed with emblematic devices. One of them

in Latin hexameters praised the queen as the writer's "medicine," light, and fountain. See Emmanuel Le Roy Ladurie, ed., *L'Europe de Thomas Platter: France, Angleterre, Pays-Bas, 1500–1600. Le siècle des Platter III* (Paris: Fayard, 2006), 362, n. 579.

58. See Andrew Hadfield, *Shakespeare and Republicanism* (Cambridge: Cambridge University Press, 2005), 165–67. Quentin Taylor, "'To order well the state': The Politics of *Titus Andronicus*," *Interpretation: A Journal of Political Philosophy* 32 (2005): 125–50

59. Paul E. J. Hammer, *The Polarisation of Elizabethan Politics,* 168–69.

60. For Sir John's relations with Leicester see Jan Broadway's entry of Sir John in *ODNB,* vol. 25.

61. Accurate figures of black slaves in England are hard to come by. Further investigations into the mercantile and legal activities of the Guinea Company are bound to yield reliable figures. The year 1593 happens to be the year in which the mortality rate of black domestic servants in London was high. Four black servants are entered as having been buried in the parish of St Botolph Aldgate: Suzanna Pearis, servant to John Despinois, on August 8; Simon Valencia on August 20; Cassangoe, servant to Thomas Barbor, merchant, on October 8; and Robert, servant to William Matthew, gentleman, on November 29. See Rosalyn L. Knutson, "A Caliban in St. Mildred Poultry," 113–14.

62. Glenn Odom and Bryan Reynolds, "Becomings Roman/Comings-to-be Villain: Pressurized Belongings and the Coding of Ethnicity, Religion, and Nationality in Peele and Shakespeare's *Titus Andronicus,*" ed. Bryan Reynolds, *Transversal Enterprises in the Drama of Shakespeare and his Contemporaries. Fugitive Explorations* (Houndmills: Palgrave/Macmillan, 2006), chap. 8. Francesca T. Royster, "White-Limed Walls: Whiteness and Gothic Extremism in Shakespeare's *Titus Andronicus,*" *Shakespeare Quarterly* 51 (2000): 432–55.

63. William Shakespeare, *Titus AndronIcus,* The Arden Shakespeare, ed. Jonathan Bate (London: Routledge, 1995), 4.2.101–2. In his article on "Kind and Unkindness: Aaron in *Titus Andronicus,*" Brian Boyd holds the view that nowhere in the play does Shakespeare presume "that the blackness of race means vileness of character" (69). Boyd has edited his article in *Words that Count. Essays on Early Modern Authorship in Honor of MacDonald P. Jackson* (Newark: University of Delaware Press, 2004), 51–77. The governors of Bridewell have recorded a number of cases which disprove that the fear of "natural infection" was inhibitive. The taboo of sex between a white woman and a black man was repeatedly broken in the London brothels. Thus alone in 1577 Jane Thompson, obviously a prostitute, was detained in Bridewell for committing "whoredome" with "Anthonye, a blackamore;" and Rose Brown for admitting "dyvers & many blackamores" as customers to her establishment; and Margery Williams confessed to the governors that she had sexual intercourse with Peter Peringoe, a "blackamore." In 1604, the governors issued a warrant to arrest a London hatmaker "whoe had gott the blacke more with child." See Duncan Salkeld's review of Michael Neill's edition of Shakespeare' *Othello* in *The Times Literary Supplement,* August 18/25, 2006, p. 26. A thorough search for further evidence among the Bridewell Court Books is a desideratum. Were the black customers slaves or freedmen? Did these white prostitutes give rise to the fashion of deriding harlots as "dark ladies" which was in vogue among the Inns of Court students in the 1580s and 1590s?

64. Quotation taken from Alexander Leggatt, *Shakespeare's Tragedies: Violation and Identity* (Cambridge: Cambridge University Press, 2005), 15.

65. Ladislas Bugner, general ed., *L'image du noir dans l'art occidental,* vol. ii *Des premiers siècles chrétiens aux grandes découvertes,* ed. Jean Devisse and Michel Mollat, *Les Africains dans l'ordonnance chrétienne du monde, 14e—16e siècle* (Fribourg: Office du Livre, 1979).

66. See Albert J. Loomie, S.J., *The Spanish Elizabethans: The English Exiles at the Court of Philip II* (New York: Fordham University Press, 1963), 107; *ODNB,* vol. 53, under Suárez de Figueroa, Jane and Suárez de Figueroa, Gómez. Don Benito de Cisneros must have been a descendant of Don Benito Jiménez de Cisneros, nephew of Francisco Jiménez de Cisneros (1436–1517), primate and regent of Spain, grand inquisitor, initiator of the mass conversion of the Moors, the guiding spirit behind the Spanish campaign in North Africa (1505–10), and patron of the Complutensian Polyglot Bible. Bartholomew Yong (1560–1612), the son of a Roman Catholic family, known as translator of Jorge de Montemayor's pastoral novel *Diana,* had "conference with the duchess of Feria" while he was touring Spain (1578–80). The subject of the conference remains unknown. See Dale B. J. Randall, *The Golden Tapestry. A Critical Survey of Non-chivalric Spanish Fiction in English Translation, 1543–1657* (Durham: Duke University Press, 1963), 77ff. Yong may have been introduced to Sir Philip Sidney after he had completed his translation. See Judith M. Kennedy, *A Critical Edition of Yong's Translation of George of Montemayor's Diana and Gil Polo's Enamoured Diana* (Oxford: Clarendon Press, 1968), lix, n. 8. There is an entry on B. Yong in *ODNB.*

67. On Juan Latino's classical literacy see Baltasar Fra-Molinero, "Juan Latino and His Racial Difference," ed. T. F. Earle, *Black Africans,* chap. 15; on Diego Jiménez de Enciso's seventeenth-century play on Juan Latino's life and career see the same author, *La imagen de los negros en el teatro del Siglo de Oro* (Madrid: Siglo XXI, 1995), chap. 6; on Afonso Alvares see T. F. Earle, "Black Africans versus Jews: Religious and Racial Tension in a Portuguese Saint's Play," ed. T. F. Earle, *Black Africans,* chap. 16. Juan Latino's work that stood the greatest chance of being known in sixteenth-century England and Scotland was his poem *Austrias Carmen* (1573), a panegyric in hexameters praising don John of Austria as victor of the battle of Lepanto in 1571, putting an end to the myth of Turkish naval invincibility. King James composed a poem on Lepanto about 1584. The British Library copy of Juan Latino's panegyric, which has an accession stamp of 1872, has the following handwritten title page motto: "Satiabor cum apparuerit gloria tua 1573." I owe this information to Dr Barry Taylor, Curator of the Hispanic Collections 1501–1850.

68. Winthrop Jordan, *White Over Black: American Attitudes Towards the Negro, 1550–1812* (Chapel Hill: University of North Carolina Press, 1968, rept., New York, 1977), 6.

69. The findings of my investigations into the early history of English slavery will be published by Verbum, Madrid, in 2008.

70. Archivo Histórico Provincial de Sevilla, Protocoles Notariales, legajo 3289, fol. 23 r–24 v; fol. 125 r–v; fol. 126 r–v. These records together with some others will be published in the appendix of the above mentioned study.

71. For Hakluyt's "economic nationalism" shaping his editorial policy see Emily

C. Bartels, "Imperialist Beginnings: Richard Hakluyt and the Construction of Africa," *Criticism* 34 (1992): 517–38. For a discussion of Thorne's document see Roger Barlow, *A Brief Summe of Geographie,* ed. E. G. R. Taylor, The Hakluyt Society, 2d ser., no. 59 (1931; Nendeln: Kraus Reprint, 1967), xxv ff. Hakluyt had no scruples about eliminating narratives, abridging materials, and excising records for political reasons. See James P. Helfers, "The Explorer or the Pilgrim? Modern Critical Opinion and the Editorial Methods of Richard Hakluyt and Samuel Purchas," *Studies in Philology* 94 (1997): 160–86.

72. See David Loades's entry on Sebastian Cabot in *ODNB,* vol. 9. For Cabot's role as innovator and mediator in handing down to the English pilots his knowledge of mathematical navigation acquired as Spain's pilot major see Eric H. Ash, *Power, Knowledge and Expertise in Elizabethan England* (Baltimore: Johns Hopkins University Press, 2004).

73. For the transmission of the Thorne papers see R. C. D. Baldwin, "Robert Thorne, the younger," ODNB, vol. 54, p. 606; G. C. Moore Smith, *The Family of Withypoll,* Walthamstow Antiquarian Society 34 (1936): 38.

74. Venice is a transposed image of mercantile London, Shylock and Antonio operating as mirror images of Elizabethan society. Shylock, who is pressed by the court to forgive Antonio, claims the same rights to sell human flesh as the Venetian (English) merchants have and urges them to free their own slaves and grant them the rights of free subjects: "You have among you many a purchased slave, / Which, like your asses and your dogs and mules, / You use in abject and in slavish parts / Because you bought them. Shall I say to you, / 'Let them be free! Marry them to your heirs! / Why sweat they under burdens?" Quoted from M. M. Mahood's edn. of the play in The New Cambridge Shakespeare (Cambridge: Cambridge University Press, 1987), 4.1.90ff. There is evidence that some English contemporaries of Shakespeare, who were operating in the Mediterranean, were working hand in glove with the Venetian elite as purveyors of slaves. Thus, in 1594, the captain of the English vessell *Susanna* sold seven slaves to the "magnifico Giovanni Maria Canevali, cittadino e mercante," three men, three women, and a boy, all of them presumably Moors. See Alberto Tenenti, "Gli Sciavi di Venezia alla fine del Cinquecento," *Rivista Storica Italiana* 67 (1955): 52–69.

"The Sanctuarie is become a plaiers stage": Chapel Stagings and Tudor "Secular" Drama

Jeanne H. McCarthy

WHEN Anthony Munday issued his oft-cited rebuke of players and theater in *A Second and Third Blast of Retrait from Plaies and Theatres* (1580), the use of the church as a playing space received particular attention. While he railed against traveling household players who "are privileged to . . . publish their mametree in euerie Temple of God, and that through England, vnto the horrible contempt of praier [; s]o that now the Sanctuarie is become a plaiers stage,"[1] the sometime-playwright seemed to be implying that such a use of sacred space was "now" a new and troubling Elizabethan phenomenon. Despite Munday's relatively marginal status as a minor playwright and pageant-maker in the era, this pamphlet and another of his works have had an enormous influence on the narrative of theater history. As the principal author of *The Book of Sir Thomas More* (ca. 1590), his treatment of a play within a play given by "My Lord Cardinalls players" (ll. 918–37) is one of the primary sources informing David Bevington's analysis of the popular tradition. Munday is thus frequently cited as an authority for both emerging anti-theatrical sentiments and the argued link between professional players and the traveling interluders and halls.[2] And yet, at least in regards to the use of churches for playing, he is occasionally misleading. His implication that church playing was a novelty appears to be particularly inaccurate, for plays were certainly being performed in "sanctuaries" long before 1580.

Surviving records suggest, for instance, that between 1339 and 1642[3] for "some sixteen villages and towns, . . . the church seems to have been the normal playing space"[4] for performances by local and traveling players, and performances of religious plays like *The Assumption* or *The Coronation of the Blessed Virgin* occurred in major cathedrals both before and after the Reformation even in London, including at Lincoln Cathedral, Westminster Abbey, and some eleven other churches.[5] Paul Whitfield White has found that churches were such "a popular venue for Reformation dramatic performances"[6] that in many villages the *preferred* site for evangelical drama was the local church and that such uses continued throughout the Reformation.[7] Church performance for quasi-religious drama thus actually persisted long after a critically assumed evolution from sacred to secular popular drama—that is, the imagined linear journey from the church to the courtyard to the inn yards, halls, and theaters—supposedly occurred. Indeed, John M. Wasson's finding that "it is arguable that far more than half of all vernacular plays of the English Middle Ages and Renaissance were in fact performed" in such religious sites,[8] only buttresses White's assessment that there was no "steadily evolving progress from the sacred to the secular in sixteenth century English theatre."[9] And, in fact, a closer scrutiny of Munday's pamphlet confirms that the theater that most preoccupies him is not yet that of the London public stages. Rather, the would-be reformer's repeated references to boy actors ("yong boies . . . trained vp in filthie speeches, vnnatural and vnseemlie gestures, . . . brought up by these Schoole-maisters in bawderie, and in idlenes"),[10] to household servants and traveling players, to schools, and to chapels, as well as his likening of theater to "the Schoolehouse of Satan and chappel of il counsel,"[11] point to a much more complicated context, one for which the traditional description "popular" theater may be an anachronistic imposition.

Reviving an early critical tradition suggesting that the anonymous *Godly Queen Hester* (ca. 1525–29) and John Heywood's comedies *The Pardoner and the Frere* and *The Play of the Wether* (ca. 1519–33) were staged within a chapel, while drawing on recent research in theater history and approaches looking to the text as evidence of stage practice,[12] I want to question such assumptions. I will argue that not only these plays, but two other moral interludes from the early Henrician era, ca. 1513–14—the anonymous *Youth* and *Hick Scorner*—long considered "household plays" performed by small professional troupes in halls and deemed "unquestionably" part of the popular canon by Bevington,[13] bear signs of performance by household chapel personnel in a chapel setting. Notably, *Youth* and *Hick Scorner* reference chapel furnishings, decor, church rituals, and vestments, and, like the apparent household chapel plays of Heywood and *Godly Queen Hester,* they allude to child performers and chapel personnel. Though possibly within the "popular" tradition, these plays are not purely secular.

More importantly, that earlier performance context is one in which such distinctions as "sacred" and "secular" may not yet apply. Rather, given the significant overlap between touring players and the professional repertory, and the ongoing difficulties authorities in the provinces had determining which dramas were free of questionable religious doctrine, the idea that chapel or church stagings involved only *religious* drama is increasingly on unsafe ground.[14] Among Wasson's findings, for instance, is the discovery of the use of parish churches for performances by professional players whose repertories did not include overtly religious plays: "the Records of Early English Drama project has identified sixteen different professional companies who performed in churches," thus far. Notably, Queen Elizabeth's Players "appear seven times in four different churches" and Leicester's Men "were paid 20 shillings 'for playing in the Churche' at Doncaster."[15] In his discussion of traveling players, Peter H. Greenfield conjectures that their "[p]erformance in inns, churches, and private houses may have occurred just as often" as in town halls, "and perhaps even more frequently, but have gone unrecorded unless connected with legal action."[16] Moreover, the Elizabethan children's company, Children of Paul's, who in the early years of Elizabeth's reign appeared more frequently at court than any other company, appear to have rehearsed and performed "either in the Cathedral . . . or in the small church built next to it, St. Gregory's, where the singing school had been housed since the twelfth century."[17]

The chapel remained associated with student performances in the universities as well throughout the period. While interpretations of surviving records from the universities appear to suggest that the use of a hall was a more likely site for a performance than the chapel—e.g., "There can be little doubt that performances [at King's College] were in the college hall"—it is nonetheless true that clear evidence of such "is lacking."[18] Meanwhile, although references to performances at Jesus College in Cambridge are "extremely sparse," Alan H. Nelson finds that "[t]he college chapel is the only sixteenth-century Cambridge performance site still regularly used for plays."[19] Evidence of this tradition also appears in entries for 1568–69 in which "two fellows of the college received £4–6-0 'spent at the playes in the chappell,'" and a payment from 1567–68 for "'glasse for the chappell after the playe.'" The specificity of a related reference dated 1578, which indicates an alternate playing space when that year's play was instead "pleyed publiklie in the Hawlle,"[20] may suggest, ironically enough, that the hall staging was the exceptional use. A Marian entry for "Candelles waxe & linckes for the chappell and hall for the showes in chri*s*tom*a*s,"[21] from Trinity College in 1553–34 suggests, moreover, that both the chapel and the hall were used for its Christmas "showes."

Assimilating such a context into our understanding of playing in the period, however, has not proved easy. Although the use of churches for non-liturgical playing was acknowledged in seminal studies by E. K. Chambers and Bevington,[22] for most contemporary scholars, even those who long ago "abandoned the 'big bang' theory that secular drama was expelled from nave to market-place because of its comic coarseness,"[23] a church performance renders a play outside the bounds of discussions of the critically favored professional drama, so much so that if "those sites most neglected by twentieth century scholars for performance of early English religious drama have been the churches themselves,"[24] neglect is all the more pronounced for the performance of drama not identified as "religious." After all, Suzanne Westfall's observation that "Protestantism discouraged clerical dramatic performances and isolated the chapel as a space dedicated solely to worship"[25] only becomes true after English reformers had successfully employed the staging of plays, even iconoclastic ones, in churches and chapels. Nevertheless, even though concerted resistance to church playing such as that expressed in Munday's tract was, as White has shown, a late development, there is little willingness to consider the possibility that sacred spaces might have influenced the imaginations of Tudor playwrights and players.[26] Certainly, earlier, passing suggestions that a few extant Tudor plays may have been performed in churches or chapels have been allowed to dwindle away as they have been replaced by an emerging consensus, reflected recently in Greg Walker's anthology of *Medieval Drama* (2000), that *all* surviving influential "secular" interludes were designed for a vague, nonspecific playing space, such as a hall.[27] Indeed, even as most scholars of the period remain aware of church stagings, household productions, and even the use of chapel players—both children and gentlemen—in dramatic performance, any particular attribution of an interlude, at least some of which appear to have been written by household chaplains or chapel personnel,[28] to a chapel or church setting has been challenged or questioned. Westfall doubts, for example, whether sufficient evidence still exists to support Bevington's and Chambers's suggestion that the Henrician era biblical play *Godly Queen Hester* would have been staged in a chapel, and Ian Lancashire, curiously, finds the notion of staging of the moral interlude *Youth* in a church setting an uninformed anachronism.[29]

Wasson's assessment that only a "stubborn" critical reluctance prevents us from integrating evidence of church stagings into our current narrative of the drama may indeed be true. However, Westfall's unwillingness to read surviving secular interludes with a church or chapel setting in mind in her study of household performances—she denies the possibility of a chapel location to *any* extant secular plays[30]—may be due less to stubbornness than to her having restricted her claim that the early Tudor household chapel "could also be exploited for theatrical effect[,] the choirs and lofts provid[ing] playing space, and the aisles an ease of movement and scope for ceremonial processions" to liturgical drama so that the chapel itself became a stage only when "the Chapel could stage religious plays; vestments became costumes, chapel structures became sets, and hangings became backdrops."[31] Although she finds it more likely that sacred plays—Nativity plays, Shepherd plays, and Easter plays of the Resurrection—were performed in the chapel itself and non-sacred ones, such as the conventionally secular chapel-produced Shrove Tuesday plays, were staged in the hall, the basis for such a distinction reflects her tacit assumption of late Protestant, even post-puritan attitudes toward theater as profane. When she argues, for instance, that the early morality *Mankind* does "not suit Chapel performance" partly because "the irreverence of the vices and the lewdness of the music are inappropriate to Chapel style which, while it could be boisterous, was usually not bawdy,"[32] her analysis echoes not only those late Reformation ideas expressed in Munday's diatribe against abuses of the sanctuary, but those of an intriguing pamphlet issued in 1569 objecting that the "pretty vpstart youthes" of Elizabeth's Royal Chapel (later the first occupants of the Blackfriars) were frequently "profan[ing] the Lordes day" by "feigning bawdie fables gathered from the idolatrous heathen poets"—that is profane secular plays—". . . in her maiesties chappel."[33] Oddly enough, she accepts the late puritan valuation while overlooking the acknowledgment of church stagings of secular drama in their pamphlets.

The exclusion of chapel stagings from discussions of performance not only raises interesting epistemic questions regarding the use we make of certain types of historical evidence in the still fascinating narrative of dramatic professionalization, but invites a reexamination of the dominant narrative that still informs theater history. It is, seemingly, an emphasis on—or desire for—secularization that makes the argument that a transformation from medieval to early modern drama was enabled by movement outside the church to the hall and into the hands of the adult traveling players tradition appealing. The argument appears most vividly, to cite two influential examples, in Richard Southern's assertion that an entirely "separate [non-sacred] source informs the development of secular drama,"[34] and Hardin Craig's claim that "medieval drama existed for itself . . . and not as an early stage of the secular drama."[35] Such a narrative retains the terms of what O. Hardison, Jr., called the "Chambers-Young hypothesis," that began with Chambers's declaration that "With the advent of humanism . . . drama at last 'put off its exclusively religious character, and enter[ed] upon a new heritage,'" only to be refined by Karl Young so that humanism itself became identified with "secularization,"[36] and which now supports contemporary discussions of professionalism and the marketplace. It is a history of medieval and Renaissance drama that has its roots, as Hardison observes, in a nineteenth-century spirit of English "anticlericalism" and a suspicion of "theological dogma"[37] that, in application, identifies "amateur" with schools, and religious or sacred plays with pre-Reformation Catholicism, while linking "professional" with secularism, and Protestantism with humanism, as if to say that throughout the Reformation, the dramatic tradition somehow acquired a protective barrier from any primitively sacred influences.

I

The terms of a biased disciplinary denial of chapel or sacred influences on the popular drama can be found in an examination of the resistance that greeted the argument that the presumably Henrician era biblical interlude *Godly Queen Hester* was originally performed by a chapel company and therefore *in* a chapel, even as such a review reveals grounds for reassessing such a position. Frederick Gerard Fleay first advanced the possibility that chapel personnel rather than a troupe of traveling players performed *Godly Queen Hester* based, reasonably enough, on the stage direction, "than the chappell do sing," in response to Queen Hester's line, "Call in the chapell to the intent they maye / Syng some holy himpne to spede vs this day" (ll. 860–61).[38] The early Tudor chapel in noble and royal households, which consisted of twenty-eight to thirty-seven chapel personnel, and of which six to twelve were children, provided a ready group of trained performers for meeting elite household entertainment needs. The Tudor monarchs, for instance, maintained private chapels at Windsor "and another—the Chapel Royal—which moved with the court to the larger standing houses in and around London. . . . [T]he Windsor Chapel had ten choirboys and the Chapel Royal twelve" in addition to their resident gentlemen.[39] Chapel personnel were frequently called upon to perform in sacred and secular performances throughout the Tudor era, and so the assignment of any play with a large cast and musical requirements to the chapel repertory has conventionally been seen as plausible. After all, a large cast informs the similarly uncontested argument that Heywood's *Play of the Wether* was performed by the child choristers of one of the royal chapels. However, Fleay's related inference that such lines and related stage directions similarly imply a chapel *setting* has never been fully adopted, perhaps plagued with the same kind of disciplinary assumptions about sacred spaces that led the play's early editor W. W. Greg to dismiss the possibility as being entirely "without weight."[40]

However insubstantial the argument may have seemed to Greg, it was a metatheatrical reference to a prominent stage element in *Godly Queen Hester,* a traverse—a curtained or enclosed closet space or private balcony—that eventually led Chambers to declare it "not inconceivable that the play, which was very likely performed by the Chapel, was actually performed in the chapel,"[41] a point with which Bevington later concurred.[42] Indeed, Bevington concluded more confidently that "It seems likely that the play was actually produced in the chapel by the chapel choir, using for its stage the same structures employed in religious ceremony."[43] A traverse is explicitly used for the exits of Hester's husband, King Assuerus at lines 139 and 635, the latter of which includes the stage direction, "Here the kynge entreth the trauerse & Hardy Dardy entreth the place." Chambers's and Bevington's conclusion that the venue for the performance was actually a chapel was based on the fact that household chapels typically had closets and traverses that provided for a patron's privacy during services. Stage directions in Heywood's *Play of the Wether,* which seemingly also call for the use of a curtained traverse by Jupiter for his sudden revelations and "withdraw[als]" from the playing space similarly suggested its chapel setting as well.[44]

As Chambers observes, the traverse is a piece of church architecture most "familiar . . . from the records of the royal chapel."[45] In fact, Elizabeth is known to have made use of both a traverse and a closet in her palace at St.

James: "it is from the records of the royal chapel that [their] Elizabethan use can best be illustrated. Thus when Elizabeth took her Easter communion at St. James in 1593, she came down, doubtless from her 'closet' above, after the Gospel had been read, 'into her Majestes Travess,' whence she emerged to make her offering, and then 'retorned to her princely travess sumptuously sett forthe' until it was time to emerge again and receive the communion."[46] (The architectural plans for the sixteenth-century Percy seat at Wressle indicate that its chapel also contained a traverse, in this case a small private, curtained balcony, accessible from the lower Nether Chapel by a spiral stair, that served as "my lordes pew of stat" during services.)[47] Another significant use of a chapel traverse by a royal is suggested by the alterations to King College's Chapel undertaken to prepare the site for the performance of plays during Elizabeth's visit to Cambridge in 1564. In addition to setting up her throne "hanged with a clothe of state" along the south wall of the chapel's nave, the court's Office of Works constructed "a fayr closet glased towards the Queer . . . made in ye mydle of the Rode lofte" so that "ye queens maiestie" could "repose herself" out of view if she should tire during the performances.[48] The construction recalls a surviving drawing by Wenceslaus Hollar of Elizabeth I's remodeled chapel at Windsor that reveals two prominent glazed traverse-like "holy closets" set over the choir screen.[49] Royal chapel traverses tended to serve the same function as closets and were often used in tandem with them.[50]

Despite the association of the traverses with church architecture, other critics have nevertheless been less than convinced of the connection. Southern, seemingly unaware of the religious uses of the term, drew on alternate "grounds," including ancient Chinese and Indian theater practices, to argue for a hall setting for *Godly Queen Hester*. He referred to "the technical . . . requirements of the script, . . . contemporary meanings of [traverse], and . . . near contemporary paintings," to claim that the traverse was a "small two-part curtain" set on the floor before the hall screen.[51] Southern's argument for a hall setting seems to have held. Thus, while concurring with Bevington and Chambers regarding evidence of the play's "Chapel auspices," including its "[c]ast size, the number of costumes, the complexity of the staging, . . . the actual summoning of a Chapel, and the sophistication of the music," Westfall, like Greg, nonetheless felt compelled to challenge the conclusion of a chapel rather than hall setting for the performance. Noting that a non-sacred use of the traverse by a monarch (in a household site other than a chapel) is suggested by Edward Hall's observation that Henry VIII watched Anne Boleyn's coronation banquet from a traverse in a great hall,[52] she argues that Hester's late call for a banquet and the use of a traverse seems equally suggestive of a hall setting, and then abruptly deems that the more likely option.[53] Alistair Fox has also argued that a chapel setting for the play was "unlikely," although on differing, practical grounds regarding the availability of a chapel to the play's presumed female patron,[54] while Walker, based on an argument that the play's patron was likely an ecclesiastical group intimately affected by Wolsey's policies, found it most plausible that the play was performed by a chapel in "an abbot or prior's *hall,* perhaps even that at Westminster" (emphasis added).[55] Walker's position, then, not only assumes Southern's anachronistic argument that hall stagings were the norm in the era, but recalls Bevington's conjecture that "ecclesiastical auspices" for earlier religious moralities like the late fifteenth-century *Wisdom* play (*Wisdom Who Is Christ or Mind, Will, and Understanding*) do not necessarily imply the use of a monastic chapel; rather a chapel may well have been only one of the "different localities" that could have been used.[56]

Although a number of plausible reasons may yet inform critical skepticism of a chapel location for the performance of this and other plays, a certain bias toward the argument that hall stagings and traveling players gave rise to the professional theaters also informs such resistance.[57] And yet, by Greg's own criterion, the argument for hall stagings is seemingly even less weighty than that for chapels. After all, the primary texts informing Bevington's analysis of the link between professional players and the traveling interluders and halls is the late Elizabethan play *The Book of Sir Thomas More* (ca. 1590), among whose collaborators was the somewhat unreliable author of the antitheatrical pamphlet discussed above, Anthony Munday; a 1639 recollection of a performance of a lost play, *The Cradle of Security,* witnessed by the author of *Mount Tabor,* R. Willis, when he was a boy, ca. 1570–80;[58] the post-Reformation title pages of interludes offering prescriptions for doubling; and the assumption that most interludes were performed by some version of a "four men and a boy" troupe. For Southern, the primary source is, even more tenuously, the mummer's traditional entrance into a house and their "impromptu" creation of space.[59] And, of course, there is for both Bevington and Southern the clear use of a "hall" in Henry Medwall's formative interlude, *Fulgens and Lucrece* (ca. 1493–97), certainly the most definitive evidence that a hall was used for some interludes. Essential to Southern's inventive proposals for the staging of other interludes in halls, however, is the notion that a sense of place was achieved solely through "acting and not through elaborate setting."[60] Repeatedly, the obvious references to stage properties like a bed in *Magnyfycence* or the traverses in *Godly Queen Hester* and *Play of the Wether* are problems resolved by the introduction of stage properties into the otherwise amorphously imagined, unprepared hall.[61] Southern's argument for hall stagings relies, then, upon a "juxtaposition of evidence," that is, "the sum of all the fragments of information that helps to clarify each separately,"[62] as does, arguably, Bevington's, but there is no single compelling "fragment" that would disavow a chapel setting for a number of the interludes discussed, except for the implicit assumption that anything "profane" would have been deemed inappropriate for a sacred space.[63]

Yet a profane use of a sacred space may well be evidenced in John Heywood's less examined *The Pardoner and the Frere* (ca. 1530, printed 1533),[64] where the apparent appropriation of another type of chapel furniture for the delivery of dueling sermons by the Pardoner and the Frere, the epistle and gospel pulpits, seems to argue strongly for its chapel setting. Upon his entrance, the friar or Frere declares his purpose is "The gospell of Chryst / openly to preche" (A1r, l. 17), a line that may allow him to claim the gospel pulpit on the stage left side of the altar that was used solely by the clergy, while the Pardoner's desire to speak may lead him to claim the epistle lectern stage right of the altar, reserved for nonclerical personnel. Such a staging would make possible their simultaneous preaching, which begins with the stage direction, "Now shall the Frere begyn his sermon, and evyn at the same tyme the Pardoner begynneth also to shew and speke of his bullys, and auctorytes com from Rome" (Aiiir, s.d. ll. 194–96). Both the description of the friar's lines as a "sermon" and the religious content of the Pardoner's text suggest that a church setting was at least implied if not actualized. When the two are later interrupted by the Parson, who claims their mischief will "polute my churche" (Biiiv, l. 559), however, the implied church or chapel setting is more or less confirmed. At least imaginatively, in this play, the characters' comic "profanity," which is associated with their fallen, human condition, appears not to have been barred from "polluting" the sacred space, but rather to have been both tolerated and then exorcised in the play's staged expulsion of the two offenders. The possibility that the play may have been performed in a chapel is reinforced, moreover, by a detail suggesting the participation of chapel children. Chapel children were already licensed to play in churches during the seasonal Boy Bishop festival that commenced on St. Nicholas Day (December 6), in which one child would be chosen to take on the role of Bishop to appear richly dressed with a bishop's garb while presiding over the liturgy until Innocents Day (December 28).[65] It is worth noting, then, that during the brawl between the Parson and the Frere, the fourth character in the play, Neighbor Prat, who is himself battling with the Pardoner, calls the Frere an "elfe" (Bivv, l. 643), a term that is similarly used, interestingly enough, to describe Merry Report in Heywood's known children's play, *The Play of the Wether* (l. 120). The modern diminutive or childlike associations with the word "elf" were extant in the period, suggesting the participation of a child actor in both plays.[66] If a chapel boy played one of the major roles in *The Pardoner and the Frere,* Bevington's apt insight that there is "something akin to the saturnalian rule of the Boy-Bishop" in *The Play of the Wether* may apply as well to Heywood's earlier play.[67] Such a casting would also suggest that Heywood's later association with child actors may well have begun earlier in his career.

Indeed, Heywood's use of chapel personnel would align this interlude with his *Play of the Wether* as well as with the biblical interlude *Godly Queen*

Hester, all of which point to stagings in chapels rather than halls. Both casting and staging "problems" or opportunities posed by these interludes can, after all, be just as easily met by chapels as halls. Halls provided screens with openings for entrances and exits, a location for costume changes in the kitchen beyond it, a festive atmosphere, and a crowded space necessitating the call for "room" that appears in so many of the interludes. But then again, so did pre-Reformation chapels in which fixed pews were not yet common. Chapels also had other architectural features beyond traverses and pulpits that could have been exploited by players, including choir lofts or stalls and rood screens that closely resembled hall screens. A choir loft or stall may have been invoked in *Godly Queen Hester,* for instance, when Hester calls for a chapel to sing ("Call in the chapell to the intent they maye / Syng some holy himpne to spede vs this day" [ll. 860–61]), since a choir entering into an upper or lower choir loft could easily have satisfied the request. That a chapel organization may actually have performed a play *in a chapel* is thus more likely when there is a suggested use of such chapel furniture and architecture.

II

The pre-Reformation chapel was, in fact, much better suited to dramatic presentation than modern notions of a strictly sacred space allow. Chapels were vividly animated spaces; their walls were enlivened with paintings of such popular themes as the harrowing of hell, the Passion Cycle, including scenes of the flagellation and road to Cavalry, and Our Lady of Pity, as well as depictions of the lives of saints and martyrs, events from the Bible, church history, and catechetical teachings.[68] Embroidered tapestries also provided richly suggestive scenic backdrops, and in the royal chapels of Henry VIII, the story of Esther, the heroine of *Godly Queen Hester,* was a popular subject.[69] Similarly dramatic imagery was also the subject of windows and statuary. Roger Martin's "detailed account" of the "furnishings and iconography" of a parish church at Long Melford as it looked "before the iconoclastic storms of Edward's reign" thus includes a vivid description of a statue depicting Our Lady of Pity holding "the afflicted body of her dear Son, . . . lying along on her lap, the tears as it were running down pitifully upon her beautiful cheeks, as it seemed bedewing the sweet body of her Son."[70] As late as 1546–47, the Duke of Norfolk's chapel at Kenninghall contained not only an altar retable painted with "a gilded Passion of Christ sequence 'wrought upon wainscot,'" but six tapestries, "each of 9 square yards," also evocatively "depicting the story of the Passion."[71] An evocative sense of character apparent in statuary and windows was also echoed in wood carvings found on pews and baptismal fonts, a frequent subject of which was the Seven Deadly Sins. As Eamon Duffy records, such figures had colorful and archetypal features: "At Wigginhall St. German, Lust is represented by a man and woman embracing, Avarice clutches his money bags, while Gluttony pours wine from a bottle into a cup. At Thornham, Sloth dozes over his rosary. At Blythburgh, Gluttony hugs a distended paunch, while Pride is a hypocritical devotee."[72] Frequently bawdy secular and folk imagery, often emblematically depicting folk proverbs and lore incorporating animals like geese and lions as well as pagan classical figures, were found carved into the misericords. In short, the pre-Reformation church or household chapel would not have allowed the distinction between the sacred and the profane we seem now to require.

Indeed, the chapel's function was often secular. Particularly before Edwardian reforms diminished the opulent Royal Chapel's function as a site for ceremony, it could often display secular "magnificence" while buttressing majestic iconography.[73] Fiona Kisby has argued, for instance, that the "pre-Reformation Henrician chapel" played a "preeminent" role in the "display of royal power."[74] Royal chapels were thus typically adorned not only with religious iconography but with heraldic glass displaying shields of arms, badges, mottoes, and scrolls, incorporating images of worldly kings and queens along with the saints.[75] According to articles in the household ordinances reflecting the practices of Henry VII and Henry VIII, even "the holy days when both kings went to chapel services were the 'festa ferienda' of the household," accompanied by lavish banquets and the keeping of "open house" at court.[76] The king's journey to the chapel, moreover, "was a highly formal ceremonial procession. . . . [T]he route he processed went through the Privy Chamber, into the Presence Chamber, past the Great Chamber through a gallery and into the chapel."[77] Such an overlay of sacred and secular activity reflected a tendency that was true of household revelry generally, that is, to "blur the distinction between communal and personal space, public and private experiences, liturgical and secular activities."[78]

The chapel's suitability for household performance is further demonstrated by Elizabeth's court uses. For her 1564 Cambridge visit noted above, for instance, Elizabeth deemed the chapel more, not less, suited to performance than the originally intended hall.[79] Prior to the queen's arrival, university authorities begged for assistance meeting her expectations since they were "poor and unfamiliar" with court practices. In response, the court requested, and bore the cost for, dismantling a temporary stage that had been erected in the college hall for the occasion and rebuilding it in the King's College Chapel.[80] Deeming the original hall "to[o] lytle, and to[o] close for her Highnes . . . and also to[o] farre from her Lodgynge," the stage was erected instead "in ye Bodye of ye churche" with "ye chapels . . . serv[ing] for howses."[81] Significantly, the chapel was chosen because it was "most elegant on account of (its) design and quite extensive on account of its size," as well as nearer the queen's lodging—preferences recalling the virtues of household chapels generally. Likewise, efforts were undertaken to grant Elizabeth the distinctions her own chapel provided her through the construction of the aforementioned closeted traverse should she wish to retire during the play.[82] That Elizabeth's use of the chapel at Cambridge for the student performances in 1564 drew so little notice suggests that it was indeed consistent with her practices at court, especially since the heads of the university had requested help conforming to them.

Evidence that a link between chapels and performance did in fact exist at court in the period can be found elsewhere in the entertainment records of Elizabeth I, which suggest not only her frequent use of her Royal and Windsor chapel personnel to entertain her with secular plays during the winter season, but the little-noticed observation that she actually used her own royal chapel as a performance space at least through the early years of her reign. More promising even than Michael Shapiro's finding of thirty-three performances by the Royal and Windsor Chapels at Elizabeth's court between 1558 to 1603, with twenty-three to twenty-six play titles associated with the Royal Chapel and four with the Windsor Chapel in the same period,[83] is the record of puritan opposition to such a use of her Royal Chapel by the Children of the Chapel Royal who, as noted above, were frequently "profan[ing] the Lordes day" by "feigning bawdie fables gathered from the idolatrous heathen poets . . . in her maiesties chappel."[84]

Monarchs were hardly alone in recognizing the household chapel's utility as a stage for promoting and justifying their status and power. The chapel's prominence in sixteenth-century architecture is underscored by Andrew Boorde's recommendation "that as many of the rooms that looked into the court as possible should have a view of the chapel."[85] The size and grandeur of the Tudor era chapel at the Percy family's Wressle, whose chapel rooms included a Nether Chapel, a High Chapel, and a Rood Loft and whose dimensions, significantly for playing, "rivaled . . . the Great Hall," appears to have figured prominently in displays of the noble family's wealth and power.[86] Its "importance as a gathering and performing place" is further suggested by its location in the western wing of the building, adjacent to the Dyning Chamber which was in turn adjacent to the Lorde's Chamber.[87] Connected by entryways and passageways on all floors, the rooms in this wing enabled members of the household to move freely and easily between the Dyning Chamber and the Chapel, while a balcony in the Rood Loft of the Nether Chapel that overlooked the Dyning Chamber allowed the Chapel choir to do so as well. From the two balconies in this loft, the same choir that sang "the Gloria as the nativity play was enacted below" could then turn and "entertain from above while [Percy's] family and guests supped" in the adjoining hall.[88] It seems unlikely, however, that this religious play would have been the only instance of such a practice. Indeed, the chapel's centrality in the early Tudor household contrasts markedly with its later isolation from the rest of the rooms of the household, a late development encouraged by much later Protestant reformers; the seemingly anomalous lack of interior entrances to the chapel of Haddon House reflects alterations to the chapel completed prior to 1782, but certainly after the sixteenth century.[89] By contrast, another sixteenth-century manor house, Woodlands Manor, has a layout similar to that found at Wressle whereby "a lobby and stair connecting the chapel . . . to the hall . . . [offer] a clear indication that movement between these two locations was frequent and necessary" in the earlier period.[90]

The interconnectedness of pre-Reformation architecture, in which passageways linked the chapel to the other rooms of the house could be exploited in the household entertainments, and such fluidity is one key to reconceptualizing the chapel as a playing space for Tudor interludes. Festivities for special occasions and feast days were often extensive, involving a number of events and activities scheduled throughout the day and week, and events staged in the chapel and hall were often but one part of a more elaborate entertainment. Surviving accounts further indicate that not only the chapel's spectacular setting—its statuary, painted walls, plate, altar cloths, and lighting—but its rich chapel vestments appear to have been pointedly incorporated in sacred and secular productions, entertainments, and festivities with great ease.[91] And, the chapel's theatrical potential could also be enhanced, as is implied in notations indicating that Percy decorated his chapel with arras for his daughter's wedding, as well as the Duke of Norfolk's recorded expenditures for hooks, wires, canvas cloth, and workmen for alterations to his chapel, possibly for a Christmas nativity play in 1481.[92] By Westfall's own account, "at family occasions such as christenings and weddings, the entire property could be theatre space, as ceremonial processions progressed throughout the space from chapel, to antechamber, to great hall, to bedchamber, and outdoors for hunting and dancing."[93] Chapels could even be secularized or "transmogrif[ied]" on such occasions as weddings, and the altars hung with arras and used to display "silver and gilt church plate."[94] Their use on such occasions and for liturgical drama certainly suggests that they may well have been appropriated for other plays, particularly those performed by chapel personnel, as part of household entertainments.

Interestingly, a number of plays previously conjectured to have been performed in or by chapels provide evidence of the opportunity for the characteristic movement from or to the chapel into the plot. A seeming difficulty posed, for instance, at the end of *Godly Queen Hester* when Assuerus orders the preparation of a feast in response to Hester's request and the stage direction reads, "Here must bee prepared a banket in y[e] place" (s.d., l. 885), a requirement that might seem to make the play more suitable to a banqueting hall setting, can easily be resolved if this sense of contiguous space and movement is recalled. Soon after the request for a banquet appears, the intended meal is, pointedly, interrupted when Aman's treachery is uncovered, and the banquet itself never commences before, by the end of the play, Assuerus dismisses the players and audience: "Let us then cesse thy conuocatione, / And this tyme dyssolue this congregation" (ll. 1176–77). Although the possible allusion to a church gathering in the use of the term "congregation" has been disputed, the accompanying reference to "convocation," which also has both sacred and secular associations, certainly does not rule out a church setting.[95] And while banquets and ales were sometimes served in churches,[96] a just as likely setting for the post-play banquet would be a hall. If the concluding lines of the play are used as a prompt for the dishbearers to lead the audience into the adjacent banqueting hall for the meal, both implied settings could be accommodated. Like the similarly late allusion to a banquet in *The Play of the Wether,* when the Boy, the play's final suitor, says he has heard that his "godfather, god almighty" has come "This nyght" to "suppe here with my lorde" (ll. 1025, 1027), such lines may be read as anticipating an upcoming banquet, rather than alluding to an ongoing one, and as initiating the fluid extension of the entertainment from the play to the meal that sixteenth-century architecture invited.

Not only did household architecture allow ease of movement from chapel playing to dining in the banquet hall, but chapels generally posed fewer problems in performance than halls, for the staging possibilities and orientation of the audience to the actors in chapels were more numerous. (Here we must again recognize that fixed pews are a late innovation in English churches.) Wasson suggests that the "logical" playing space in a church would have been, as modern churchgoers or visitors might expect, "the east of the nave, before the choir screen."[97] Indeed, chapel choir or rood screens appear to have functioned, quite easily, very much like hall screens or the *frons scenae* of the indoor theaters, although playing could also occur behind and in front of such a choir screen. Thus, while "In 1483 *The Assumption* and *The Coronation of Mary* were both performed in the nave just west of the choir,"[98] John C. Coldewey finds that the Easter "*quem queritas*" trope was likely performed between the altar and the choir screen with the monastic audience seated in the choir stalls and the nave excluded from the playing space.[99] But the known seating arrangement for the staging of plays at King's College Chapel at Cambridge for Elizabeth's 1564 visit to the university suggests that even more options for staging were available.[100] At Cambridge, the playing space was located in the nave area reserved in contemporary churches for the pews, and the queen's throne faced not the altar area but the long north wall of the chapel nave, while the courtiers stood in the east end altar and choir areas. Such an arrangement allowed the actors a variety of entrances and exits and the ability to use the various side chapels as "houses" or setting locations. The few surviving records on the matter suggest that whether before or within the choir or rood screen, in the nave, or employing side chapels as houses, church and chapel architecture afforded many useful playing spaces.

Although Elizabethan records show that traveling household players and professional companies could perform in churches, household accounts indicate that a play set in a household chapel would most likely be performed by chapel personnel or schoolboys. By the Elizabethan era, companies formed from the chapel seem no longer to have included gentlemen, but to have drawn exclusively on the talents of boy actors. When that change formally occurred has not yet been determined, but that the chapel children became increasingly prominent in court records during the reign of Elizabeth is certainly clear. Several elements of *Youth* and *Hick Scorner* indicate that they may well have been early entries in such a tradition of chapel children plays.

III

That these morality interludes are early Henrician era plays is clear, although their precise date of composition and performance auspices are less so. Ian Lancashire's suggestions of a date of composition of ca. 1513–14 for *Youth* and ca. 1514 for *Hick Scorner* seem plausible.[101] Shrewdly contending that allusions to locations in London and Southwark point to a performance of *Hick Scorner* at the Duke of Suffolk, Charles Brandon's grand London house, Suffolk Place,[102] he similarly suggests, on the basis of in-text staging directions and hints of a northern dialect, that "the northern household that probably sponsored the interlude [*Youth*] . . . is that of Henry Algernon Percy, fifth earl of Northumberland," presumably at Percy's seat in York, Wressle.[103]

Lancashire's attribution of *Youth* to Percy's patronage is supported by records that Percy himself was keenly interested in performance. The surviving household account books of the Tudor Percys, a primary source for Westfall's discussion of the Tudor chapel, demonstrate a large and lavish household (retaining 166 domestic servants) for which elaborate Christmas and Twelfth Night festivities, including both secular and liturgical dramas, were sumptuously staged. The performers of such entertainments would have been drawn from minstrels, "a four-person troupe" of players, and a large Chapel, which consisted of an almoner, who was, significantly, a "maker of interludys,"[104] and "as many as eleven chapel gentlemen, one of whom was master of the chapel's six children."[105] Westfall observes that "We should expect great household Chapels to perform liturgical plays in Latin," including the "*Quem queritas*" performed at Easter, nativity plays at Christmas time, and a secular Shrovetide play perhaps "at or after a banquet"—or even before.[106] But the Percy revels during the Christmas season also included a procession through the household, "scriptural plays and concerts of religious music," impersonations of the Abbot of Misrule, a lavishly costumed Boy Bishop at St. Nicholas, secular carols, disguisings, musical accompaniment at banquets, and morris dances.[107] The boy choristers of his chapel annually participated in performances before "his lordship" in "my Lordes Chappell"—"the Play of the Nativitie uppon Christymas-Day in the mornynge," and the other on "Esturday in the Mornynge"[108]—as well as the Boy Bishop.[109] But the use of his chapel personnel in secular celebrations is suggested by the fact that the household accounts of Northumberland, Oxford, and Norfolk "frequently record [Chapel] expenses for articles of non-religious clothing" around the Christmas season.[110]

As Lancashire finds, the penitential theme of the interlude *Youth* and its prodigal youthful title character would have been well suited to a Shrovetide occasion and to a household that included Lord Percy's romantic son and heir, Henry, who had been recently called to court. Its didactic tenor would also comport well with the father's notable adornment of his family's rooms with moralizing verse dialogues, including one between youth, "sensatyue," and maturity, "intellectyue."[111] That Percy was the patron of the play, then, certainly seems more than plausible. Equally persuasive is Lancashire's argument that Percy's chapel performed the play, for the signs of the involvement of chapel personnel in *Youth* are numerous. Citing as chapel references an allusion to evensong (l. 570) and to a choir rector or leader (l. 473), a call for an extemporized harmony or "descant" on a song (l. 693), and the use of three-part song (ll. 472–75, 546), Lancashire quite reasonably suggests that it may well have been performed by "Chapel gentlemen."

Less persuasively, he speculates further that the group might have been organized in such a way as to resemble "an economical, mobile Tudor troupe . . . of familiar make-up, 'Foure men and a boye.'"[112] Such a grouping would require four adult choristers to take on the roles of Youth, Charity, Riot, and Pride and one "child or adolescent" chorister to play both "little" Lady Lechery and Humility.[113] This casting draws on several prevailing and influential assumptions about Tudor drama—that the parts in early interludes were regularly doubled, that the actors were already organized as small traveling companies of four men and, sometimes, a boy, that boys typically tended to play only the smaller female parts, and that performances were conventionally staged in halls—that were not as universally applicable to surviving plays as has been assumed. Indeed, it is a tribute to Bevington's compelling discussion of five-actor traveling troupes performing in halls within a secular interlude tradition that it has somehow become so entwined in the imaginations of most readers with interludes themselves that it is hard to find an editor who does not impose such expectations, even exploring presumed doubling assignments when none are explicitly given.[114] The prominence of the small professional troupe is, admittedly, supported, as Bevington demonstrates, by a number of printed plays that *do* offer doubling prescriptions on their title pages.[115] But can we really infer that such practice was the rule for all plays and performers even when no suggestions for doubling survive? Since the Henrician play *Youth* makes no such recommendations and little evidence beyond critical convention exists to support the imposition of such expectations on the play, I believe we should not, especially where other possibilities were certainly available.

While the title character Youth certainly could have been played by an adult, not to consider a boy actor having played the role would not only overlook an obvious casting choice, but anachronistically underestimate the significance of alternate "company" structures beyond the five-actor, four men and a boy, troupe that were in existence by the early 1500s. Revels Accounts under Henry VII, for instance, bear an entry showing that choirboys performed *Christi Descensus ad Infernos* at St. Swithun's and Hyde Abbey for the christening of Arthur in 1486,[116] while others indicate that William Cornish was using the Chapel Children in a knighting ceremony that occurred in 1493 at Westminster late in the reign of Henry VII.[117] In 1508, "iiij children *that* played afore *the* king" were paid 3s. 4d,[118] and in January, 1509, the last Christmas season of Henry VII, there is a reward given to "diu*er*se of the king*es* Chapell that playde afore the king vpon xij*th* nyght."[119] In both January and March of 1517, Cornish and the Chapel Children were rewarded £6.13s. 4d. for performing at court, the latter performance on Shrove Tuesday.[120] And, Cornish was later being rewarded for playing interludes with the Children of the Chapel before Henry VIII in 1519 and 1520.[121]

Not only were the chapel children frequently performing in the era, but schoolboys, White has argued, would perform "Protestant drama" during the Henrician Reformation.[122] Earlier still, the appointment of William Lily, who "had studied in Italy under Pomponio Leto (the first modern producer of Roman plays in Europe)," to be the first schoolmaster of the grammar school at Paul's for the poor founded by John Colet in 1512, led Shapiro to conjecture that he too promoted "the pedagogical value of dramatic performance."[123] Certainly, Lily's surmaster, John Rightwise brought his schoolboys of St. Paul's to court to perform a Latin play, *Phormio,* in 1528,[124] and an intensely political anti-Luther play also performed in Latin before visiting ambassadors in 1527, an indication that grammar school performance had by then gained status at court.[125] We must at least consider, then, the possibility that ca. 1514 *Youth* may have been performed by chapel children rather than "Gentlemen," especially given that didactic youth/prodigal plays are later known to be common in the children's repertory. Indeed, in such contexts it is worth noting that not only did "Percy's court ha[ve] a school, [and] a children's choir,"[126] but *Youth* offers a number of internal clues to suggest that the six parts in the play were most likely performed by the six child choristers of Northumberland's chapel rather than four chapel gentlemen and a boy, and likely in a chapel.

Beyond its focus on teaching a moral lesson about the dangers of dishonest recreation, *Youth* shares with known schoolboy plays like John Redford's *Wit and Science* some telltale signs of a boy company performance. Most suggestive is its prodigal son motif as it attempts to guide a youthful aristocrat back on the right path. More particularly, while adopting a didactic tone resembling that in *Wit and Science, Youth* also includes a number of references to lessons and schools, a trope widely used in the *Wit* plays, as when Youth refuses to follow Charity's "school" (l. 128) and has his decision reinforced by Riot who tells him he will "hold thee a fool, / And thou follow [Charity's] school" (ll. 616–17). Charity elsewhere takes on the trappings and rhetoric of a schoolmaster. He enters the play promising to interpret God's "laws to your behove" (l. 4) while citing a catechetical primer as a source ("In the A.B.C., . . . it is written" [ll. 25–26]), and Youth scornfully refuses to accept his authority by inverting the master-pupil relationship and putting foolish questions to him: "Soil me a question . . . Why do men eat mustard with salt fish?" (ll. 116, 120). Youth's fall is secured, moreover, when he agrees to "commit me even now / Under the teaching of Riot" and Pride (ll. 356–57). Youth, then, may well have been meant to be performed by a boy struggling to leave his school days behind him and to assert, unconvincingly, his maturity. If *Youth* were indeed performed for the Percy household with the young Henry Percy in mind, it is worth noting that the Percy's son was "about twelve years old in 1514;"[127] the prodigal Youth may, then, have been meaningfully assigned to a young chorister of like age.

But Youth is not the only youthful character in the cast. Tradition already assumes that the part of Lechery was played by a boy actor and certainly the use of childlike diminutives throughout *Youth* to describe "sister Lechery" (l. 405) as "a little pretty pie" who goes "full gingerly" (ll. 413–14) is suggestive of the boy company practice of using one or more younger and shorter actors to take on the part of smaller, but often comical and theatrically challenging, cross-gendered, roles. At least one character other than "pretty" Lady Lechery and Youth is also a youth, however: Pride is called a "noble swain" (l. 322), and he too is given the adjective conventionally used for a boy actor when he is described as "pretty" (l. 324). The possibility that several of the remaining characters in the cast may also be youths is suggested by their addressing one another as "brothers," as when Youth wishes "my brother Riot would help me / For to beat Charity / And his brother too" (ll. 207–9), since such familial references are more suggestive of a children's group than an adult's troupe in which age and status relationships tend to be more complex. If Humility is also played by a child actor, then it is possible that all of the characters—except, perhaps, Charity—would have been performed by chapel children, while a chapel gentleman could have taken on the role of the schoolmasterly Charity. In 1514–15, when mixed performances of chapel gentlemen and children like those in Cornish's court entertainments staged for Henry VIII were still familiar, it is certainly possible that some of the roles in Youth were performed by adults. However, that child actors played several, if not all, of the prominent roles in the play and that their presence dominated the play's rhetorical effect are suggested by its infusion with school references suggestive of a child's concerns.

Moreover, that one of the characters in *Youth,* the saturnalian Riot, was traditionally associated with a child actor and the boy companies' association with the parodic prodigal son genre of plays is evident in a late Elizabethan allusion to Riot's "huffing" entrance lines that appears in the later boy company playwright John Marston's *Histrio-Mastix* (1599) written for the Children of Paul's where, as Lancaster has found, "Post-Hast's script for 'the new plot of the prodigall childe' has two lines possibly based on *Youth:* 'Huffa, huffa, who callis for me? / I playe the Prodigall child in iollytie' (Sig. C1ʳ)."[128] Although in his discussion of the children's repertory, Shapiro considers seventeenth-century parodies of the earlier moralities with a prodigal son theme to be a late development in the children's drama, it is possible that Marston's allusion merely aligns his play with a long-standing children's tradition that included *Youth.*[129] After all, a 1557/58 entry in the Stationer's Register licensing John Walley as the printer of, presumably, the Q2 edition of *Youth* actually places the play in a list with a children's play, *Wealth and Health,* and several other child-centered texts. The reference to *Youth* (citing its three main characters) appears fourth in an entry that reads: "*Welth and helthe / the treatise of the ffrere and the boye / stans puer ad mensam* another of *youghte charyte and hymylyte* an *a b c for cheldren* in englesshe *with syllables . . .*"[130] While certainly not necessarily indicative that the play was recognized as part of a children's repertory, this entry as well as the interlude's compatibility with a later children's dramatic tradition are at least suggestive that its earliest auspices may have originally involved child choristers.

It is likely, as suggested above, that child choristers may well have performed a play like *Youth* not in a hall, but a chapel. Indeed, the play's extensive religious content and rhetoric comports well not just with the religious function of the chapel children choristers, but also with the iconographic features of their chapel rooms. The walls of the chapel of Wressle, which had once been praised by the chronicler Leland as "fair," would have been decorated with wall paintings, pew carvings, windows, and statuary, a practice that had not yet gone out of fashion in England in 1514 and was certainly fashionable in 1380 when Wressle was built. The allegory of *Youth* would have had a particular resonance in such a chapel setting which, beyond providing myriad theatrical opportunities for staging, offered a possibility of heightened meaning linking certain scenes to a broader catechism. In a number of scenes throughout *Youth,* for instance, such as that in which Charity sermonizes and prays (ll. 1–39, ll. 105–12, ll. 165–69), Youth receives prayer beads (s.d., l. 770), Latin biblical texts and Latin prayer forms are cited (ll. 25–26; l. 110), and in Youth's conversion itself, which involves a ritualistic kneeling in submission to a priestly and Christlike Charity (ll. 732–41), a chapel staging would have amplified the echoes of church teachings. In this context, the entrance of Charity from "above"—"I desire audience till I have made an end, / For I am come from God above" (ll. 4–5)—could easily have begun in the upper lofts of a chapel. It would then have had particular resonance in a church or chapel given Catholic teaching on the symbolic meaning of particular elements of church architecture, particularly the conventional association of the roof of the church with "charity, which covers a multitude of sins."[131] That the virtues of *Youth* are clerics and priests (and one of the vices represents a dissolute chapel gentleman) only enhances the numerous references to religious properties and rituals that clearly suit the play to a staging in a chapel.

If *Youth* seems suited to a chapel, the closely allied *Hick Scorner* seems even more so. The buried stage directions suggestive of actual decor in the opening speech of *Hick Scorner* likely function as a tour of a household chapel's trappings, here delivered by a character named Pity, and manage to situate the moral lesson of this play within a chapel's broader scriptural context. Among the Christian iconography described with surprising immediacy by Pity is the iconic scene of Our Lady of Pity in which he asks the audience to contemplate a virtual character onstage: "This delicate colour, that goodly lady, / Full pale and wan" who looks on "her son all dead, / Splayed on a cross with the five wells of pity, / Of purple velvet, powdered with roses red" (ll. 17–20). The lines, one editor rightly suggests, appear to indicate that "Mary's image is then visible."[132] The suspicion that Pity may actually be gesturing toward the chapel's furnishings instead of the velvet *costume* Lancashire believes he displays is prompted by Contemplation's first speech in which he too refers to such frequent subjects of statuary, windows, and wall paintings as "John Baptist, Antony, and Jerome" (l. 53), as well as to such iconic imagery associated with the Stations of the Cross as Christ "to a pillar bound / With scourges . . . lashed" (ll. 35–36) and to his "fall" under the "burden . . . so heavy" of the cross (ll. 38–39). Later, Perseverance refers to "the ladder of grace" (l. 83), a frequent image in church wall paintings, and, in the redemption scene, he asks the wayward Imagination to contemplate such vivid pictorial details of the crucifixion as God "hanged on a tree / And all his precious blood spent. / A spear did rive his heart asunder" while "the gates" of purgatory open to deliver "Adam and Eve" (ll. 943–47). So many are the religious allusions that they render the discordantly anachronistic description of *Hick Scorner* as a "secular play" unconvincing and enhance thereby the likelihood of a chapel staging.

As in *Youth,* a number of details in *Hick Scorner* are likewise suggestive of the involvement of Chapel personnel. The virtues of *Hick Scorner,* Contemplation and Perseverance, are apparently dressed, appropriately for a chapel space, in clerical robes, for when Free Will sees Perseverance, he wonders if he is "a priest, a doctor or else a frere" (l. 696), Imagination claims he is from a family of "clerks" (l. 266), and Contemplation announces that he is the patron of "prelates and priests" (l. 49). As Perseverance and Contemplation preside over Free Will's confession (ll. 850–68), moreover, "the two virtues act as priests."[133] Perseverance's final lines in which he prays that the audience too might be brought "unto Vertuous living" and the "bliss of heaven . . . Amen" (ll. 1025, 1028–29), are, fittingly, a benediction. Moreover, just prior to the closing prayer, Perseverance has provided Imagination and Free Will, newly adorned in "new coats," with an apparent cue to ascend into the choir loft: "Then to heaven ye shall go . . . / Where ye shall see in the heavenly quere / The blessed company of saints so holy" (ll. 1019–21). Their assimilation into the "quere" or choir suggests that the new coats that they have received are chapel robes.

The possible use of a choir loft here is but one of the staging requirements of *Hick Scorner* that could be well met by a chapel setting. Indeed, several scenes, such as Free Will's confession or Pity's sermon-like complaint (ll. 546–600), would be particularly effective in a chapel. The binding of Pity in "fetters and rope" (s.d. at l. 505), introduced by a discussion of having him falsely arrested for a theft of "forty pound" (l. 504) and "forty pence" (l. 516) that is rich in allusions to Judas's forty pieces of silver, suggests an episode suitable for a Passion play. More subtly, Free Will's metatheatrical summation of his fight with Hick Scorner, "Is not this a great farce?" (l. 446), sandwiched between such oaths as "God us save!" (l. 443) and "for the passion of my soul" (l. 449), recalls the liturgical meaning of "farsa" which, as Lancashire finds, the *O.E.D.* defines as "the various phrases interpolated in litanies . . . ," that served as an "expansion[n] of . . . liturgical formulae."[134] Here, the scene interpolates an ironic struggle for Free Will's soul. At the same time, elements arguably unsuitable for a chapel, like the "stews" and taverns to which Free Will resorts (ll. 184, 650) or the ship upon which Hick Scorner purportedly arrives (l. 301), are left offstage. Since ships were brought into the halls for the masks of Henry VIII, the coy evasion here, coupled with the attention to church properties, suggests an alternate playing space.

In this play, a mixed cast of choir members may well be implied. Contemplation and Perseverance address each other as "brother" (ll. 95, 125), as do Free Will and Imagination (l. 231), suggesting a parity in ages among the pairs. The virtues, however, are older and wiser than the wayward vice-like characters. Contemplation, adopting a paternal role, calls Free Will "good son" (l. 721), for instance, while Free Will refuses to follow Contemplation's "school" (l. 731), an assertion that seems to draw attention to Contemplation's schoolmaster's authority and Free Will's schoolboy status. Free Will's youth is further indicated when he later boasts that he could "play the man" and beat Contemplation in a fight if only he had help (l. 765). Imagination's youth is similarly suggested when Free Will insults his "father" and "mother" (ll. 421, 424), a point of attack that would cut more keenly were

Imagination still a school-age boy. While certainty about the identity of the original performers of *Hick Scorner* cannot be hoped for, such details in the dialogue and its staging requirements nonetheless warrant serious consideration of a chapel or song school production performed in a household chapel rather than a hall. With or without resorting to doubling, a chapel or singing school would have yielded enough actors for an all-children cast (or a mixed cast of gentlemen and children) and would have been especially suited to performing both the songs and the snatches of Latin—as when Contemplation invokes the Office of the Dead—*"qui est in inferno nulla est redemption"* (l. 787)—in the play.

A use of child choristers to impersonate clerics and priests in both *Youth* and *Hick Scorner* would, moreover, have mitigated any then-current hostility to priestly theatricality, such as had been incited by the Dean of St. Paul's, Colet, in his recent notorious sermon offered on February 6, 1511/12, exhorting "the clergy to reform themselves."[135] Among the priestly abuses Colet explicitly criticized was the willingness of priests to "take part in sports and playes" rather than devoting themselves to their studies.[136] Colet clearly endorsed children's acting, however, given his already noted hiring of Lily and Rightwise as masters at Paul's. If the parts of *Hick Scorner* were performed by child actors, playwright and patrons may well have avoided accusations of impropriety and, as later authors of children's plays found, the satiric jabs at the clergy and court would have been better tolerated in such a quasi-saturnalian context.

A child cast would certainly have enhanced some of the comedy of the plays, especially since child actors tend to accentuate the satiric effect of any scene in which the behavior of a gentleman or a braggart is imitated. In later plays by children's companies, for instance, jokes about the child actor's size had a metatheatrical effect, drawing attention to the boy actor's comic difference from the role he plays.[137] The convention also appeared in adult actor interactions with boys playing pages in adult company plays, perhaps most familiarly in Shakespeare's *Love's Labour's Lost* when the grammar school teacher Holofernes overrides Armado's objections to the page Moth's suitability to perform one of the Worthies because "he is not quantity enough for that Worthy's thumb" by declaring that the boy will play the part of Hercules "in minority."[138] Such metatheatrical attention to the actor's physical inadequacy for the part he plays may be detected in *Hick Scorner,* as when Free Will ostentatiously invites the audience's admiration—"am not I a goodly person" (l. 156)—his overbearing insistence on being ceded room—"Aware, fellows, and stand a-room!" (l. 155)—and his unproven sexual boasts of having spent on "a piece of flesh ten pence" (l. 174). All of these claims would have acquired a more comical air if spoken by a youth. Similarly, in *Youth,* the humor of the title character's threatening entrance—"Aback fellows, and give me room, / Or I shall make you to avoid soon!" (l. 40–41)—followed by his preening before the audience as he draws its attention to his "royal" and "thick" hair, his "big and strong" arms, and his chest as "big as a tun" (ll. 48–54), would have been more pronounced if the lines were uttered by a child actor, particularly a small one. After all, none of the other characters appear to be particularly threatened by Youth; Charity, for one, hardly seems to react to Youth's warning that "with my dagger I [will] thee slay!" (l. 161). A chapel setting would also amplify the comic effect of the saturnalian utterance of oaths and the sporting of clerical garb by one of the vices.

Though certainly not proof of the appropriateness of either of these plays to a church location, it is worth noting that two of the most successful stagings of the *Youth* play were done in churches, though purportedly under "the pall" of "medieval methods of staging."[139] Nugent Monck's 1924 revival of the play was in "an eighteenth-century Catholic church;"[140] it made use of a "'high altar under a canopy' at the hall's eastern end" and faithfully restored elements from a 1905 production, including an entrance being staged as "a procession of one priest, two monks and a three-boy choir, bearing a crucifix and chanting *Adeste Fideles*," and having Charity appear "with the wings of a 'pre-Raphaelite angel.'"[141] The play also became "a staple" of Barry Jackson's repertory whose 1907 production evoked an imaginative church setting when it included "the chanting of an *Ave Maria* by an unseen choir, and a procession (accompanied by a hymn) . . . [of] 'acolytes swinging censers and carrying tapers.'"[142] Although some have found the use of medieval or Catholic iconography in the productions anachronistically informed by recent productions of *Everyman,* there is actually much in the texts to invite a rethinking of such cursory dismissals.

Given the range of effects available in a chapel setting for the plays discussed above, especially within the context of recent analyses finding that churches were a popular venue for performance in the period, it is perhaps time to ask whether a banqueting hall was inevitably the site where other surviving plays—particularly those with large or clerical casts requiring chapel actors or choristers, extensive or elaborate song, chapel furniture, vestments, ritual actions, concluding prayers, or religious imagery otherwise assumed to be mere spoken décor—were first performed. In short, we should reconsider the prevailing orthodoxy, indeed, virtually the default assumption, that secular plays, particularly extant ones, were always performed in halls throughout the Tudor period, or, for that matter, question the presumed distinction between sacred and secular staging practices. Just as the boundary between household chapel and the rest of the house was far from distinct in Tudor England, so the perceived boundary between what has come to be called "professional secular drama" and "amateur," "sacred," or "household" drama was likewise porous. If actors in the religious dramas could be at least imaginatively included in secular plays, as when the Pardoner in Heywood's secular comedy *The Four P's* (ca. 1519–33) claims the devil guarding the gate to Hell is an "olde acquaintance / For oft in the playe of Corpus Christi / He hath played the devyll at Couentry" (Dii^{v,} l. 947–49),[143] so too might alternate notions of space. It is, then, at the very least, possible that we have too quickly dismissed the insight that early Tudor plays like *Godly Queen Hester, The Pardoner and the Frere,* and *Play of the Wether* were indeed staged in chapels and thus missed the fact that *Youth* and *Hick Scorner* contain more hints about earlier staging practices in churches and chapels than earlier readers allowed.

Notes

1. Cited in Paul Whitfield White, *Theatre and Reformation: Protestantism, Patronage and Playing in Tudor England* (Cambridge: Cambridge University Press, 1993), 135; and E. K. Chambers, *The Medieval Stage,* 2 vols. (London: Oxford University Press, 1903), 2:191.

2. David Bevington, *From Mankind to Marlow: Growth of Structure in the Popular Drama of Tudor England* (Cambridge: Harvard University Press, 1962), 18–19.

3. "The last professional performance in a church seems to have been in 1625–26, the earliest in 1339; the last nonprofessional church play . . . was in 1642, the earliest in 1348"; see John M. Wasson, "The English Church as Theatrical Space," *A New History of Early English Drama,* ed. John D. Cox and David Scott Kastan (New York: Columbia University Press, 1997), 25–38; here, citing 35.

4. John M. Wasson, "Professional Actors in the Middle Ages and Early Renaissance," 1984; cited in White, *Theatre and Reformation,* 134; also see Peter H. Greenfield, "Drama Outside London after 1540," *The Cambridge History of British Theatre: Volume 1, Origins to 1600,* ed. Jane Milling and Peter Thomson (Cambridge: Cambridge University Press, 2004), 178–99. Greenfield cites Rosalind Conklin Hays's discovery that both church houses and churches themselves were used as playing spaces at "Sherborne, Dorset, and . . . in Doncaster" (194); see her "Dorset Church Houses in the Drama," *Research Opportunities in Renaissance Drama* 31 (1992): 13–23.

5. "Between 1317–18 and 1543–44, records survive for no fewer than seventeen different plays performed" in Lincoln Cathedral; see Wasson, "The English Church as Theatrical Space," 27.

6. White, *Theatre and Reformation,* 131.

7. Paul Whitefield White, "The Bible as Play in Reformation England," in *The Cambridge History of British Theatre: Volume 1, Origins to 1600,* ed. Jane Milling and Peter Thomson (Cambridge: Cambridge University Press, 2004), 87–115; here, citing 88. White offers as evidence of the extent of such a movement John Bale's scriptural dramas typically written for three to four players, a professional troupe-performed *Mary Magdalene,* the learned school drama *Jacob and Esau,* and Nicholas Udall's university play based on a biblical episode popular with Protestant iconoclasts, *Ezechias.*

8. Wasson, "The English Church as Theatrical Space," 25.

9. White, "The Bible as Play in Reformation England," 88.

10. Cited in E. K. Chambers, *The Elizabethan Stage,* 4 vols. (Oxford: Clarendon Press, 1923), 4:212.

11. Cited in William Hazlitt, The *English Drama and Stage under the Tudor and Stuart Princes, 1543–1664* (London: Roxburghe Library, 1868), p.140.

12. See, for instance, the approach exhibited in Alan C. Dessen and Leslie Thompson, *A Dictionary of Stage Directions in English Drama, 1580–1642* (Cambridge: Cambridge University Press, 1999). A close reading of the plays for insights about past staging practices is demonstrated in Bevington's explication of the visiting players' scene in *Sir Thomas More* for the itinerant troupe tradition in *Mankind to Marlowe,* 18–19.

13. Bevington, *Mankind to Marlowe,* 50.

14. See Greenfield, "Drama Outside London after 1540," 182.

15. Wasson, "The English Church as Theatrical Space," 36.

16. Greenfield, "Drama Outside London after 1540," 194.

17. White, *Theatre and Reformation,* 138. See also Michael Shapiro, "Patronage and the Companies of Boy Actors," in Paul Whitfield White and Suzanne R. Westfall, ed., *Shakespeare and Theatrical Patronage in Early Modern England* (Cambridge: Cambridge University Press, 2002), 272–94; here, citing 281; and M. C. Bradbrook, *The Rise of the Common Player: A Study of Actor and Society in Shakespeare's England* (London: Chatto & Windus, 1962), 217, 227.

18. Alan H. Nelson, *Early Cambridge Theatres: College, University, and Town Stages, 1464–1720* (Cambridge: Cambridge University Press, 1994), 62.

19. Ibid., 71.

20. Ibid.

21. Alan H. Nelson, *Records of Early English Drama: Cambridge,* 2 vols. (Toronto: University of Toronto Press, 1989), 1:87.

22. Bevington, *Mankind to Marlowe,* 12; and Chambers, *The Medieval Stage,* 2:191.

23. Suzanne R. Westfall, "'An example of courtesy and liberality': Great Households and Performance," in *The Cambridge History of British Theatre: Volume 1, Origins to 1600,* ed. Jane Milling and Peter Thomson (Cambridge: Cambridge University Press, 2004), 200–224; here, citing 223.

24. Wasson, "The English Church as Theatrical Space," 25.

25. Suzanne R. Westfall, *Patrons and Performance: Early Tudor Household Revels* (Oxford: Clarendon Press, 1990), 23.

26. For a related claim of an "amateur" tradition's influence on Shakespeare, see Rowland Wymer, "Shakespeare and the Mystery Cycles," *English Literary Renaissance* 34.3 (2004): 265–85.

27. Walker's synthesis of the argument for a general audience in his anthology of *Medieval Drama* is instructive. While acknowledging in his general introduction that "Moral Plays and Interludes [were] performed in great halls and domestic and religious spaces throughout Britain in the late fifteenth and sixteenth centuries" (vii), he proposes a hall staging, in line with Medwall's *Fulgens and Lucrece,* for each of the interludes he presents (307, 351, 410, 434, and 457). The exceptions are Bale's plays; for one, he offers no conjecture as to staging (493) and another he suggests was staged

"indoors or outside" (481), while Lindsay's *Ane Satyre of the Thrie Estates,* he observes, was performed outdoors (537). Greg Walker, ed., *Medieval Drama: An Anthology* (Oxford: Blackwell Publishers, 2000).

28. Henry Medwall is identified as the "late chapelayne" to Cardinal Morton in the title page for *Fulgens and Lucres* (printed ca. 1512) and "Henry Medwall chapleyn" in that of *Nature* (printed ca. 1530). A chaplain would have been responsible for conducting religious services for a lord in his private chapel, which in a noble household such as Morton's would have included a large number of personnel, among which would have been gentlemen and child choristers. The staffing notices for the Chapel in the *NHB* includes a desire that the almoner be a "Maker of Interludes" and, if so, to be provided with a servant "to the intent for Writyne of the Parts"; *The Earl of Northumberland's Household Book: The Regulations and Establishment of the Household of Henry Algernon Percy, the Fifth Earl of Northumberland, at the Castles of Wressle and Leckonfield, in Yorkshire. Behun Anno Domini MDXII. A New Edition,* ed. Bishop Percy (London: A Brown and Sons, 1905), xx; hereafter, cited as *NHB.*

29. Westfall, *Patrons and Performance,* 55–56; Ian Lancashire, ed., *Two Tudor Interludes: The Interlude of "Youth," "Hick Scorner"* (Manchester: Manchester University Press, 1980), 268–71.

30. See "Table 1. Chapels and Interludes," Westfall, *Patrons and Performance,* 59–60.

31. Westfall, *Patrons and Performance,* 27.

32. Ibid., 54.

33. "The Children of the Chapel Stript and Whipt" (1569); cited in Chambers, *Elizabethan Stage,* 2:34–35. All that remains of the pamphlet is the following passage: "Plaies will never be supprest, while her maiesties unfledged minions flaunt it in silkes and sattens. They had as well be at their Popish service, in the deuil's garments. . . . Even in her maiesties chappel do these pretty vpstart youthes profane the Lordes day by the lascivious writhing of their tender limbs, and gorgeous decking of their apparell, in feigning bawdie fables gathered from the idolatrous heathen poets."

34. Richard Southern, *The Staging of Plays before Shakespeare* (London: Faber and Faber, 1973), 20.

35. Hardin Craig, *English Religious Drama of the Middle Age* (Oxford: Clarendon Press, 1955), 7.

36. O. B. Hardison, Jr., *Christian Rite and Christian Drama in the Middle Ages: Essays in the Origin and Early History of Modern Drama* (Baltimore: Johns Hopkins University Press, 1965), 16, 19. Hardison cites Chambers, *Medieval Stage,* 2:18.

37. Hardison, *Christian Rite and Christian Drama,* 16, 14.

38. W. W. Greg, ed., *A New Enterlude of Godly Queene Hester: Edited from the Quarto of 1561* (Louvain: A. Uystpruyst, 1904), xii.

39. Michael Shapiro, *Children of the Revels: The Boy Companies of Shakespeare's Time and their Plays* (New York: Columbia University Press, 1977), 6.

40. Greg, *Godly Queen Hester,* xii.

41. Chambers, *Elizabethan Stage,* 3:27.

42. Cited by Westfall, *Patrons and Performance,* 56n.14.

43. Bevington, *Mankind to Marlowe,* 31.

44. More specifically, the staging requires that Jupiter, at the opening of the play, be "revealed in his throne" (s.d. l. 1), and that "a song [be] played in his trone" (s.d. l. 178); several time he "withdraws" (s.d. l. 185, l. 284, l. 379), and at the end of the play, he apparently descends to award the suitors so that he may fulfill the final stage direction, "Song as Jupiter ascends and withdraws" to his "trone celestyall" (s.d. l. 1254, l. 1254); see John Heywood, *The Play of the Wether,* in *The Plays of John Heywood,* ed. Richard Axton and Peter Happé (Cambridge: D. S. Brewer, 1991), 184–215. Here, too, conventional resistance to a chapel auspice hovers. Walker, who even doubts the play was performed by children, believes, like Bevington, that it was "intended for an evening performance in a dining hall"; see Walker, *Plays of Persuasion,* 134; and David Bevington, *Tudor Drama and Politics: A Critical Approach to Topical Meaning* (Cambridge: Harvard University Press, 1968), 65. Walker argues that the play was performed during a banquet based on the Boy's statement that Jupiter has come "This nyght to suppe here with my lorde" (l. 1050).

45. Chambers, *Elizabethan Stage,* 3:26.

46. Ibid.

47. Westfall, *Patrons and Performance,* 22.

48. "Stokys' Book," *CUA: Misc. Collect. 4,* ff. 70v; transcribed in Nelson, *REED: Cambridge,* 1:234.

49. Reproduced in W. H. St. John Hope, *Windsor Castle: An Architectural History,* 2 vols. (London: Country Life, 1913), 1:267, 283.

50. According to Fiona Kisby, the royal chapel closets tended to be located above the ante-chapel, that is, the area of the chapel where "members of the household gathered to hear the services": "Above the ante-chapel were two enclosed spaces . . . known as great or holy day closets, one each for the sole use of the king and queen . . . [E]ach closet was richly furnished and lavishly decorated. Staircases, which led down into the main body of the chapel, were placed at the outer corners of each closet and . . . were used frequently by the monarch during the services." Fiona Kisby, "'When the King Goeth a Procession': Chapel Ceremonies and Services, the Ritual Year, and Religious Reforms at the Early Tudor Court, 1485–1547," *The Journal of British Studies* 40.1 (January, 2001): 44–75; here citing 49.

51. Southern, *Staging of Plays before Shakespeare,* 270.

52. Edward Hall, *Hall's Chronicle; containing the History of England, during the Reign of Henry the Fourth and the Succeeding Monarchs, to the End of the Reign of Henry the Eighth* (London, 1809), 304–5, cited in Westfall, *Patrons and Performance,* 56.

53. Westfall, *Patrons and Performance,* 55, 56. Westfall accepts Southern's "implicit" argument that "many early interludes were designed to be staged in the great halls of ecclesiastical or noble households"; Westfall, *Patrons and Performance,* 154.

54. Alistair Fox, *Politics and Literature in the Reigns of Henry VII and Henry VIII* (Oxford: Basil Blackwell, 1989), 244.

55. Walker, *Plays of Persuasion,* 131. Walker accepts Southern's observation that the "traverse was probably a small booth fronted by curtains and placed against the screens at the lower end of the hall."

56. Bevington, *Tudor Drama and Politics,* 34.

57. For a related claim addressing the critical tradition's exclusion of humanist,

educated drama from discussions of the development of the popular drama, see Kent Cartwright, *Theatre and Humanism: English Drama in the Sixteenth Century* (Cambridge: Cambridge University Press, 1999).

58. Bevington, *Mankind to Marlowe,* 13–15.
59. Southern, *Staging of Plays before Shakespeare,* 48, 63, 19–20, 165.
60. Ibid., 166.
61. See, for example, ibid., 198–99.
62. Ibid., 21–22.
63. Ibid., 19.
64. John Heywood, *The Pardoner and the Friar, 1533; The Four P's, 1544?* ed. G. R. Proudfoot (Oxford: Malone Society Reprints, 1984); also see Axton and Happe, *The Plays of John Heywood,* "Introduction," 16–18.
65. Percy, *NHB,* 423.
66. In the *Oxford English Dictionary,* "elfe" is defined as "The name of a class of supernatural beings" (*OED* 1) . . . believed to be of dwarfish form" (*OED* 1A); "A diminutive being" (*OED* 3); "A dwarf, mannikin" (*OED* 3A), "Applied to a child" (*OED* 3B). One roughly contemporary example is cited from a 1530 entry in Palsgrave in which the equation between "Elfe or dwarf" occurs.
67. Bevington, *Tudor Drama,* 65; for a discussion of the boy-bishop, see Chambers, *Medieval Stage,* 1:336–71. As the 1541 edict banning the boy-bishop from "sing[ing] mass and preach[ing] in the pulpit" revealed, the comic usurpation of the pulpit or a willingness to "put down the mighty from their seat" in such plays had a precedent, for comic elements in the medieval religious drama and the Boy Bishop tradition had already allowed for the introduction of comic ribaldry into the sacred space; see Harold N. Hillebrand, "The Child Actors," *University of Illinois Studies in Language and Literature* 11.1 (February 1926): 25–26.
68. See, for instance, the images of the church at Pickering, N. Yorks reproduced on the Web site, *Medieval Painting of the Passion Cycle,* at *http://www.painted church.org/pickerpc.htm* and the vivid illustrations of churches and church architectural features for sites used as playing spaces on the *Records of Early English Drama* Web site, such as those of St. Olaf's Church in Cornwall at http://link.library.utoron to.ca/reed/venue_ps.cfm?PSID=76&VenueListID=197.
69. David Starkey, ed. *Henry VIII: A European Court in England* (Greenwich: Collins and Brown, 1991), 102.
70. Cited in Eamon Duffy, *The Stripping of the Altars: Traditional Religion in England c. 1400–c. 1590* (New Haven: Yale University Press, 1992), 38.
71. Maurice Howard, *The Early Tudor Country House: Architecture and Politics, 1490–1550* (London: George Philip, 1987), 114.
72. Duffy, *Stripping of the Altars,* 64.
73. Diarmaid MacCulloch, *The Boy King: Edward VI and the Protestant Reformation* (Berkeley: University of California Press, 1999), 81. Cambridge and Oxford Universities were thus both encouraged to "follow Chapel Royal liturgical practice" in forbidding processions and ceremonial movements, the recitation of the rosary, and "the burning of candles in front of . . . the rood" which was "one of the few exceptions for devotional lights which Henry VIII had allowed"; MacCulloch, *Boy King,* 82, 70–71.

74. Kisby, "'When the King Goeth a Procession,'" 75.

75. Hilary Waymen, "Stained Glass in Henry VIII's Palaces," in *Henry VIII: A European Court in England,* ed. David Starkey (Greenwich: Collins and Brown, 1991), 28–31.

76. Kisby, "'When the King Goeth a Procession,'" 53, citing Eustace Chapuys, *LP VIII,* no. 826, 315.

77. Kisby, "'When the King Goeth a Procession,'" 53.

78. Westfall, "'An example of courtesy and liberality,'" 206.

79. Nelson, *REED: Cambridge,* 1:228.

80. "Stokys' Book," *CUA: Misc. Collect. 4,* ff. 70v; transcribed in Nelson, *REED: Cambridge,* 1:234.

81. "Stokys' Book," transcribed in Nelson, *REED: Cambridge,* 1:234; also quoted in Frederick S. Boas, *University Drama in the Tudor Age* (Oxford: Clarendon Press, 1914), 91. Other recorders refer to the stage as "a large scaffolde" (*Miscellany, CUL: Ff.5.14,* ff. 87v-8; cited in Nelson, *REED: Cambridge,* 1:230.

82. "[Nicholas] Robinson's Book," ff. 33–3v, (Folger: V.a.176); translated in Nelson, *REED: Cambridge,* 2:1136. Hollar's drawing of the Windsor Chapel renovation looks curiously theatrical for it lacks an altar. It is, as one historian put it, "difficult to account for there being no altar," especially given the furor over the status of the "rood" or crucifix in the reformed churches and the royal chapels, unless one considers the chair as signaling the use of the space for non-sacred purposes; see St. John Hope, *Windsor Castle,* 267.

83. Shapiro, *Children of the Revels,* "Appendix B: Recorded Court Performances by Children's Troupes, 1559–1613," 257–59; and "Appendix C: Repertories of the Children's Troupes," 263–64 and 266–67.

84. "The Children of the Chapel Stript and Whipt" (1569); cited in Chambers, *The Elizabethan Stage,* 2:34–35.

85. Howard, *Early Tudor Country House,* 114.

86. Westfall, *Patrons and Performance,* 22.

87. Ibid.

88. Ibid., 23.

89. Ibid., 23, 233.

90. Ibid., 24.

91. Ibid., 22, 24.

92. Ibid., 27.

93. Westfall, "'An example of courtesy and liberality,'" 206.

94. Ibid., 214–15.

95. While both "congregation" and "convocation" have a more general application to any type of assembly, both terms are also used for ecclesiastical gatherings. According to the first definition in the *Oxford English Dictionary,* "convocation" is defined as "The act of calling together or assembling by summons" (*OED* 1), but it also has the specific use, "In the Church of England: A provincial synod or assembly of the clergy, constituted by statute and called together to deliberate on ecclesiastical matters" (*OED* 3). References to the third definition dating from 1400, 1472, 1534 appear in the entry.

96. According to White, "In the provinces, moreover, parish naves were turned into

makeshift banqueting halls for church ales and memorial feasts," 135. See also J. H. Bettey, *Church and Community: The Parish Church in English Life* (Bradford-on-Avon, England: Moonraker Press, 1979), 50–53. At St. Edmond's Church in Salisbury, "the clergy sponsored plays, mummers and (morris) dancing . . . inside the church itself"; see Lancashire, *Two Tudor Interludes,* 219n.748.

97. Wasson, "The English Church as Theatrical Space," 30.

98. Ibid., 27.

99. John C. Coldewey, "From Roman to Renaissance in Drama and Theatre," *The Cambridge History of British Theatre: Volume 1, Origins to 1600,* ed. Jane Milling and Peter Thomson (Cambridge: Cambridge University Press, 2004), 3–69.

100. Nelson, *REED: Cambridge,* 1:228.

101. Lancashire, *Two Tudor Interludes,* 18, 22.

102. Ibid., 34.

103. Ibid., 27.

104. *Percy I,* 42, 324–25; cited in Lancashire, *Two Tudor Interludes,* 27, 30, 82n.121.

105. Westfall, *Patrons and Performance,* 15.

106. Ibid., 28, 31.

107. Ibid., 46–47.

108. Percy, *NHB,* 343; cited in Hillebrand, "The Child Actors," 12.

109. Percy, *NHB,* 343; cited in Chambers, *Medieval Stage,* 1:359

110. Westfall, *Patrons and Performance,* 28.

111. Cited in Lancashire, *Two Tudor Interludes,* 29.

112. Ibid., 21, 25–26.

113. Ibid., 25–26.

114. See Bevington, *Mankind to Marlowe,* 68–85. For an example of the argument's application, see Paula Neuss's discussion of doubling in her edition of *Magnificence;* Paula Neuss, ed., *Magnificence,* by John Skelton, Revels Plays Series (Manchester: Manchester University Press, 1980), 43.

115. The title page of the Elizabethan era interlude by Francis Merbury, *Marriage Between Wit and Wisdom,* printed in 1579, for instance, explicitly divides its nineteen parts "for sixe to playe this interlude," while that of the presumably Marian anonymous morality interlude, *Wealth and Health,* advises that "Four may easily play this Play" with its cast of seven characters. *Wealth and Health* in *Recently Discovered "Lost" Tudor Plays with Some Others,* ed. John S. Farmer (London: Early English Drama Society, 1907), 272–309; the title page is reproduced on 272.

116. Streitberger, *Court Revels,* 237.

117. Ibid., 28.

118. Ibid., 253.

119. Ibid., 254.

120. Ibid., 263, 264.

121. Ibid., 261–67.

122. White, *Theatre and Reformation,* 45.

123. Shapiro, *Children of the Revels,* 4.

124. Shapiro, *Children of the Revels,* 4; citing Anthony à Wood, *Athenae Oxoniensis,* 1:35; also see Chambers, *Medieval Stage,* 2:215.

125. For details on this and contemporaneous early Chapel performance records, see Hillebrand, "The Child Actors," 16–17, 40–73; Chambers, *Elizabethan Stage,* 2:29, and passim; and C. W. Wallace, *The Evolution of the English Drama up to Shakespeare, with a History of the First Blackfriars Theatre* (Berlin: Georg Reimer, 1912), 54; Hall, *Hall's Chronicle,* 597; and Walker, *Plays of Persuasion,* 18.

126. Lancashire, *Two Tudor Interludes,* 28.

127. Ibid., 28.

128. Quoted in Lancashire, *Two Tudor Interludes,* 83n.134. Imagination's echo of these lines in *Hick Scorner,* "Huff, huff, huff! Who sent after me? / I am Imagination, full of jollity" (ll. 891–92), is one of the parallels suggesting a link between the two interludes.

129. See Shapiro, *Children of the Revels,* 120–27.

130. Lancashire, *Two Tudor Interludes,* 3.

131. *Catholic Encyclopedia;* here citing Web site, "Inside Your Church," www.kensmen.com/catholic/churchbuilding.html.

132. Lancashire, *Two Tudor Interludes,* 159n.27.

133. Ibid., 228n.864.

134. Ibid., 196n.446.

135. Lancashire, *Two Tudor Interludes,* 168; see note to Pity's critique of "priests" in lines 128–36.

136. Quoted in Mary M. Luke, *Catherine the Queen* (London: Friedrich Muller, 1968), 128.

137. Cited in Shapiro, *Children of the Revels,* 110.

138. William Shakespeare, *Love's Labour's Lost,* The Arden Edition, ed. Richard David (London: Routledge, 1990), 5.1.122–26.

139. Lancashire, *Two Tudor Interludes,* 271, 269.

140. Ibid., 269.

141. Ibid., 269.

142. Ibid., 270.

143. John Heywood, *The Four P's,* ed. L. M. Clopper (Oxford [Oxfordshire]: printed for the Malone Society by David Stanford at the University Press, 1984).

Begging at the Gate: *Jack Straw* and the Acting Out of Popular Rebellion

Stephen Schillinger

THE Life and Death of Jack Straw[1] is a short, anonymous, and rarely read history play from 1593 or 1594.[2] We know nothing of its authorship, little of its performance history, and even less of how audiences reacted to its performance, if it was performed at all. Extant copies of the play are probably incomplete or error-ridden. From a comparison to the various other documents produced by its original printer we can surmise that the play was initially printed with modest profit aspirations and without much concern for the specific content of the text.[3] Even though we have no reason to attribute the text to one person or another, its language either echoes, or is echoed in, other texts from the period.[4] In short, all we know of *Jack Straw* is the result of what we can read in its two alternate versions, and what we can imagine as possible for this play from within its context.

Situating *Jack Straw* in its context is a deeply compelling project as the play represents the most important popular revolt in English history and does so at a time when London was frequently stirring with riots. If ever there was a play in need of reconsideration after the changes in the study of early modern drama, it is *Jack Straw*. In its curious relationship to the actual 1381 uprising, *Jack Straw* departs from its sources and, in its contradictory representation of the rebels and the royalists alike, poses intriguing questions about early modern English culture, riots, popular rebellion, and the reception of early modern plays.

Jack Straw gives voice to the period's most radical ideas about popular revolt and protest, suggesting how the public theater could reflect a sense of significant political unrest in the city. *Jack Straw* represents historical events which themselves were part of the early modern cultural memory in significantly different ways for people at different positions in the social hierarchy. The figure of Jack Straw participates in the Robin Hood tradition, and as such is an important cultural signifier so that his representation cannot easily be contained by royalist or aristocratic readings. Nonetheless, *Jack Straw* has very rarely been studied.[5] The issue is not that *Jack Straw* is literally never read nor mentioned in scholarship, but that its consideration is so profoundly superficial and seemingly secondhand that even very basic aspects of the interactions between characters are entirely lost in scholarship. This most cursory understanding of the play makes it difficult to use the play to develop our knowledge of either the stage or the period. My reading of *Jack Straw* emphasizes the public playhouse as a site in which sentiments of more genuinely radical, common revolt are given articulation. Yet these articulations in the play are almost impossible to see as long as the context of reception is constrained by current models for understanding power and audience reception, and as long as the play is read only in the service of studying Shakespeare.

Jack Straw begins with the rebels presented as sympathetic and ends with the valorization of the royalist position and the valorization of the Lord Mayor. The royalist conclusion is politically inevitable for the printing and performance of the play. So the questions remain: how sympathetically are we to read the rebels after the first scene? Also, how radical are we to perceive the representation of the rebellion throughout the body of the play? The argument of this essay is that the play's royalist-didactic conclusion should be seen as necessarily formulaic and designed to safely contain what is otherwise a generally sympathetic representation of the rebels and the goals of the rebellion. A sympathetic reading of the rebellion emerges by studying not only the formal construction of the play, but from its possible audience reception. Furthermore, the material texts and the adjustments therein are indicative of early modern readers who approved of the rebel position.

There were two printings of *Jack Straw*. The first of these printings occurred in 1593/94 from John Danter. The second, a decade later, was from Thomas Pavyer. From these two printings, *Jack Straw* exists in five copies from the early modern period. None of the five versions from 1593 to –1604 can lay claim to being the true version of the play, nor can any of them be considered secondary copies. The 1604 version seems to be based upon the 1593 copies, but there are good reasons, based on what we know to generally be the case with plays from the period, to not imagine the 1593 copies as especially privileged. The 1604 version does not exist inevitably, but had to emerge for its own specific reasons. If nothing else, the multiple editions of the play suggest a level of popularity over and above the median for the period since under half of all the plays were fortunate enough to see a second printing.[6] Therefore it makes sense to see *Jack Straw* as the two concrete versions of the play, giving precedence to the 1593 version as the primary text in the obvious sense that it emerges first and is the source for the 1604 text. Those moments where the 1604 text differs from the 1593 thus become particularly significant.

Prioritizing the 1604 version is an unorthodox scholarly maneuver. Stephen Longstaffe, while writing in the interest of producing a consistent, readable critical edition, is not especially impressed by the 1604 version. He considers it as "set up very carelessly from Q1 [1593], and thus has no textual interest beyond the occasional plausible correction it introduces" (17). Longstaffe's perspective echoes that of the Malone Society edition in which Kenneth Muir dismisses the 1604 version as "an inaccurate reprint of the first, and is textually worthless" (v). Prioritizing the 1593 version reflects a tradition wherein editorial scholars reason through the production of a text under the assumption of an ideal, intended play, beyond the idiosyncrasies of printers. This is also a model of editing wherein the priority in the study of the documents is to reveal an idealized poetic text where representation is strictly understood as a result of the graphic system—words on the page. In contrast, in the case of studying early modern plays where the relationship between written, printed, and performed plays is especially complicated, it is important to study the plays as concrete, material texts with a range of meaning-producing systems within them.

In the case of *The Life and Death of Jack Straw,* to not give serious consideration to its printing history limits our ability to understand the possible audience responses. Variations in its printed versions are not definitive indicators of how the play was read, but they do indicate how printers approached the play and how they thought it could be presented to a market of possible consumers. While Muir and Longstaffe see their projects as creating readable modern editions, from a critical, historicist perspective it is hard to fathom putting any special emphasis on the 1593 version since it is almost certainly the case that the play that was performed was only loosely adhering to the 1593 text (or vice versa). Thus the first printing has little primacy over the 1604 version. In fact, it is a much more fruitful approach to consider these printings in contrast to one another.

The fundamental differences between the 1593 printing and the 1604 printing are, first, that the 1593 printing comes from John Danter whereas the 1604 version is by Thomas Pavyer/Pavier.[7] There are changes in the layout, typeface, and formatting of the text. Lastly, the two versions have significantly different title pages. An emphasis on the 1593 version ignores evidence that the play was perceived as apologetic to the rebel position, which can be seen, in part, from these changes to the typeface and the changes to the title page. These alterations are partially cosmetic but they nonetheless complicate the royalist reading gleaned from the exclusive emphasis on the 1593 printing.

Increasingly, scholars have come to recognize the interpretive framing function of visual images with early printed texts.[8] Yet there has been essentially no consideration of the importance of the visual signifiers in *Jack Straw,* despite their obvious suggestiveness. A comparison of the Danter and

Pavyer texts indicates that Pavyer (at least) likely identified the audiences and consumers of the play as people who viewed the rebellion sympathetically (see appendixes A and B).

The title page of the 1593 John Danter version of the play reads:

The/ LIFE AND/ Death of Jacke / Straw, A notable Rebell, / in England: / Who was kild in Smithfield/by the Lord Maior of / London. / Printed at London by *John Danter,* and are to be / solde by William Barley at his shop in / Gratious-steet over against/Leaden-Hall, / 1593. (Malone Society xi)

Danter also includes a shield within the middle of the title page.[9] The cover of the 1604 Pavyer edition is similar, with the text reading:

THE / LIFE AND /death of Jacke / Straw, a notable Rebell / in England: / *who was killed in Smithfield, by /* the Lord Mayor of London, / Printed at London for Thomas Pauyer, and are to be / sold at his shop at the entering into the / Exchange 1604. (EEOB / Huntington Library)

Where Danter's title page includes an innocuous shield, Pavyer radically adjusts the title page, including a shield marked with his "T" and "P" initials at the top, with an emblem in the middle.[10] The emblem is a woodcut image of an agricultural worker plowing a field with a village in the background. The seal itself is framed by agricultural tools, including a shovel and a hoe. The emblem is circled by text which reads:

"THOU • SHALT • LABOR • TILL • THOU • RETURN • TO • DUSTE."

Pavyer's invocation of the servitude of the peasants indicates either that he targets the play, or that the play was already perceived, as likely appealing to readers inclined to see the rebels sympathetically. It emphasizes not the heroism of the King and Lord Mayor but the larger structural issue of economic exploitation. To illustrate this, the transition between Danter and Pavyer needs to be understood in the context of their printing histories.

Not surprisingly, much of what we know of Danter is as a result of Shakespeare studies. The records about Danter suggest that he was not above unscrupulous business practices, he was either a careless or unsophisticated reader of the texts he printed, and he was not afraid to print controversial material. David Scott Kastan cites Chambers, Greg, and Carroll who, as a chorus of derision for Danter, see him as "'a stationer of the worst reputation' . . . 'any dramatic quarto with which [Danter] was concerned is necessarily suspect' . . . [and] 'everyone knows of the odor which attaches itself to the name Danter'" (Chambers, Greg, Carroll as cited in Kastan 36). According to Kastan, while Danter had a series of small problems with licensing and minor conflicts with other printers, his greatest crime to posterity was a sloppy printing of *Romeo and Juliet* (36, 37). Kastan observes that "Danter is guilty of printing an imperfect text of one of Shakespeare's plays. [But] There is no reason, of course, to think he knew it imperfect, and the printing itself is unremarkable, except that halfway through the text the type font changes" (36). While this is the crime for which Danter is condemned by the new bibliographers, these curiosities only reveal that Danter was a working printer, vastly more interested in producing a marketable text than historically authoritative versions of plays. Danter was dead by 1600 and apparently destitute at the time of his death (37). Thus Danter was not directly involved in the 1604 printing and Pavyer, for whatever dependence his printing shows to Danter's, printed *Jack Straw* independently.

Pavyer's new printing of the title page appears designed to attract possible readers. In Pavyer, *Jack Straw* has been reframed to suggest a sympathetic reading of the rebels. To assert that "thou shall labor until thou return to dust" is not an especially accurate or specific way of framing the representation of the 1381 uprising, but it does provide enough of a link to early modern circumstances that the inscription can be imagined both as a frame for the rebellion and as one that might speak to Pavyer's market of play buyers. In short, the emblem guides us into the text with a sympathetic perspective on the rebellion, as laboring until you are dead seems a reasonable cause for radical change. Furthermore, this alteration in the title page is especially important to focus upon as many of the critiques of *Jack Straw,* from Tillyard to Patterson, find the recklessness of the rebels to be almost nonsensical. Yet seen from the perspective where the only alternative to the rebellion is servitude until death, the brashness of the rebellion is easier to comprehend.[11]

If the grim image of working until death were the only evidence that the play was targeted toward an audience inclined to read the rebellion sympathetically, we would have only an indication that Pavyer opted for a particular framing. But this frame does not speak to the edition itself: in printing the play, Pavyer also makes important changes from Danter's version. Danter's version of the play is printed in roman script with the King's proclamation in black letter. While it probably only reflects the vagaries of Danter's printing, scholars have seen the King's blackletter proclamation as yet more evidence that the play was a reactionary, royalist text—the play even pounds the rebels through the authority of typeface.[12] Had Danter been more scrupulous about his printing this would be a more compelling argument, but between his haphazard printing practices and the patterns and importance of typeface in printed texts at the turn of the century, Danter's printing of the King's proclamation in blackletter seems less than decisive for how we should imagine audience responses. More important than Danter's initial typesetting is how Pavyer breaks from Danter's precedent in the use of roman and blackletter.

Addressing the patterns of publishing early modern plays, Peter W. M. Blayney points out that the "question of who bought printed plays is yet another about which we know comparatively little" (414). Blayney notes that we have the record of a few private collectors and libraries, but these collections are "atypical." Blayney argues that we need to know not about these exceptional cases or even the names of people who bought plays, but we need to know "what kind of people they were" (414). Blayney argues that:

> During the closing decades of the sixteenth century roman type displaced blackletter as the usual design for books of many kinds, and by 1600 most works still usually printed in blackletter tended toward one of two extremes. The more old-fashioned typography was evidently considered to confer a kind of antiquarian dignity on serious and conservative works such as lawbooks, chronicles and lectern-size Bibles. It was likewise favored for official documents such as proclamations and statues, and the hornbook from which children first learned their alphabet was also customarily printed in blackletter. For fairly obvious reasons, though, roman type (or italic) was preferred for Latin, and the basic Latin school text, Lily's *Grammar,* was therefore printed in roman. This fact apparently led the book trade to associate roman type with a higher level of literacy and education than blackletter. Works aimed at the barely literate—at those who had learned their hornbook but had not graduated to Latin—were usually printed in blackletter: jestbooks, works for the instruction and improvement of the young, certain kinds of sensational news pamphlets, and above all, ballads. (414)

Blayney's research is enormously interesting, as he goes on to observe that

> 1583–1592, nine out of the twenty plays (45 percent) were printed in blackletter, but in 1593–1602 the proportion dropped to ten out of seventy-six (13 percent). One play was printed in blackletter in 1603, another in 1604, and the last three (all printed by William Jaggard for Thomas Pavier) in 1605. For what the evidence is worth, the preference for roman type suggests the publishers of plays were aiming more at the middle class than the working class. That is not to say that they thought of plays as appealing *only* to the educated reader; the significance is more that they did *not* perceive them as belonging to the same market as jestbooks and ballads. (415)

Blayney's research supports the notion that, in Danter's printing, the adjustment of the King's proclamation was in the interest of lending it an official appearance, while the rest of the play, printed in roman type, could be seen as targeting this educated middle class of readers. It is also probable, as Longstaffe argues, that Danter's printing reflects the way the speech would actually be read on the stage. Thus, the alteration of the typeface sets the lines apart for performance—the printing of the speech is as much stage prop as script.

But vastly more interesting than Danter's printing, which conforms to the turn of the century publishing trends, is the fact that Pavyer's printing is entirely unorthodox based on the pattern Blayney identifies. Not only does Pavyer not follow Danter's typeface, but in changing the play to blackletter throughout, his adjustment counters the normative pattern for plays at the beginning of the seventeenth century and instead is exactly what we would expect if his goal was for the play to be read by artisans, apprentices, and the rest of the spectrum of the lower orders, themselves most likely to be sympathetic to the rebels. Also, the structure that Blayney identifies for early modern plays, and in which I am positioning *Jack Straw,* does not apply to plays alone but is part of a larger pattern for early printed texts.[13] It is certainly revealing that Pavyer is one of the printers who occasionally use blackletter. And while there is no way to account for Pavyer's intention, the larger pattern, and its inversion in *Jack Straw,* suggests that not only was Pavyer targeting a lower class audience for the play, but in doing so he was printing the play for an audience he had already established with other publications.[14]

This material evidence is, at best, circumstantial, suggesting readers and audiences who, based on their own conditions, would likely see the rebels sympathetically. Additional evidence in this vein is the fact that Danter's initial printing of the text apparently straddles the New Year. Danter's title page is dated 1593 and the colophon is dated 1594. The disparity may only indicate Danter's sloppy printing practices, and it may have no direct relationship to the calendar for when the play was performed, printed, or sold. But if these dates are accurate for the printing and indicate the possibility that Danter was trying to quickly capitalize on a play recently on stage, these dates become especially important. As Ann Cook observes, "too much evidence supports the presence of ordinary folk at the large public playhouses to suggest that they seldom attended. They came in droves on holidays, when everyone had liberty from work . . ." (317). In the Julian calendar the New Year occurred on March 25, and marked the Lady Day/Assumption holiday. Thus, it is suggestive to imagine that Danter's date discrepancy indicates his desire to capitalize on the moment when the poorest members of the theatergoing population were likely spending their money on plays and thus would be compelled by a play representing a revolt against their economic exploitation.[15]

The forthcoming argument for reading the rebellion as presented sympathetically in *Jack Straw* is based on two foundational positions with respect to the formal construction of the play: first, the rebels themselves are not all of the same mind. The play's royalist, didactic conclusion may be formulaic, but it is not inevitable; rather the play represents the rebellion as failing, in part, because of its internal subversion. If the play is didactic then it is as much a morality drama about the evils of breaking community and class solidarity as it is a warning about the evils of popular revolt. The character of Nobs is fundamental here: he is not, as some critics suggest, the rebellion's conscience, but rather the subversive, royalist undermining figure within the rebellion. Albeit imperfectly constructed and not Aristotelian, the tragedy within the rebellion lies in the failure of solidarity and the failure to see this almost Iagoesque figure within their midst. Second, the play represents the rebels not as irrational or brazen, but rather as participants in a tradition of rural, popular radicalism that remains sympathetic despite the final outcome in the play. In its final outcome, the conservatism of the text is compromised, in part, because the conclusion leaves unresolved the duplicity of the King and his party. The conclusion is also compromised by the constancy of the rebels and by the way the King and Lord Mayor are mocked, with their triumph presented as itself more painful than the gallows.

These positions do not indicate that the play is simply radicalized or advocating mass revolt. If this were so the play would never have appeared on the stage, let alone have been reprinted. Clearly the later parts of the play, the comparative lack of brutality in the defeat of the rebels, and the play's final royalist conclusion do matter and are not merely tacked on to create ideological cover for the more radical, *real* position in the text. Rather, the point is that the play is actually *complex*. While scholars have seen it as formally, aesthetically, and ideologically simple, the play is actually quite complicated. Consequently, the containment of possible readings under the concluding triumph of the King and the Lord Mayor is overly reductive. Despite the conclusion, the King is represented as shallow, cowardly, and hypocritical. At the same time, while the rebellion is largely positioned sympathetically, the rebels are still structured as politically naïve, disorganized, and easily broken apart and deceived in the end.

The Life and Death of Jack Straw begins with a sexual violation and quickly moves to the murder that serves to coalesce the rebels in their common cause. The play opens with the King's Collector on the stage, likely alone, speaking to us and speaking to himself.[16] The play lacks a prologue or any other framing device to indicate what is to happen, why we are here, and what we, as the audience, should use as the lens to gaze upon the action. Certainly the play does not require such a device, but the speed with which the Collector is killed and the lack of development for the cause of his murder suggests an assumption that everyone knows the events depicted. The monarch's representative is presented as villainous, as the Collector appears exasperated by the "murmering" that has risen "upon so trifling a thing" (I.1). The Collector declares that "Tyler and his wife are in a great rage, Affirming their daughter to be under age" (I.4–5). The Collector is astonished that Tyler and his wife would be bothered by his normal practice of groping prepubescent girls to see if they are old enough to count for taxation purposes. Straw then enters, asking if this person is "the Collector of the Kings taske?" (6) to which the collector replies, "I am Tyler why dost thou aske?" (7). These lines reveal some of the textual difficulties we encounter with *Jack Straw* insofar as it is not clear why the Collector is addressing Tyler. And yet, the confusion of Tyler and Straw is potentially not confusion at all but, following Thomas Pettit's argument, an indication of the way Tyler, Straw, and the rebels are not so much clearly individuated characters but archetypes. This moment may mark a lineage to the way "Jack Straw" was a pseudonym taken on by Tyler and other rebels and subsequently became used throughout England in seasonal festivals as a way of performing and representing popular revolts.[17] If we read this opening "mistake" as the trace of a popular tradition the play hails, it teaches us how to understand the characters in the first scene.[18] It is also no longer a problem that when Tyler does enter the scene he appears to have absolutely no special regard for the fact that Straw has just killed the Collector, in part, for his sake.

After Straw does kill the Collector the rest of the rebel group arrives, including Parson Ball, Tyler, Tom Miller, and Nobs. This opening interaction establishes the cause of the rebellion and introduces its leaders. It is not only the most closely related to the legitimate grievance against the Collector, but in the egalitarianism of Ball's speech and in its railing against the abuse of the poor, it is the most sympathetic moment from a modern, liberal reading perspective. It is also the moment in the play that most directly invokes the language of popular rebellion that was commonly known throughout early modern England—Ball's speech, for all its radicalism, is also quite cliché.[19]

While the rebels are given reasonable, known grievances, the opening scene also introduces the separation between Nobs and the rest of the rebels. After Straw kills the King's tax collector, dramatic realism falls away and the narrative unfolds with the political framework for the rebellion established aside carnivalesque humor.[20] The key development in the scene is Nobs's attempt to steer the rebellion to a level of reckless revenge. Ball—who in Holinshed is represented as a raving lunatic, wandering the landscape preaching radicalism—does not begin by suggesting the overthrow of the entire social order, but instead suggests that Straw has done his country a service.

> *Parson Ball.* Content thee, tis no matter, and *Jacke Strawe* godamercie,
> Herein thou hast done good service to thy country:
> Were all inhumaine slaves so served as he,
> England would be civill, and from all such dealings free.

Without even responding to Ball, and without eliciting a response himself, Nobs significantly escalates the stakes of the budding rebellion.

> *Nobs.* By gogs bloud my maisters, we will not put up this so quietly,
> We owe God a death and we can but die:
> And though the fairest end of a Rebell is the gallowes,
> Yet if you will be ruled by mee,[21]
> Wele so deale of ourselves as wele revenge this villainy,

Straw appears to cut off Nobs in mid sentence, but in so doing responds to Ball, saying:

> *Jacke Strawe.* The king God wot knows not whats done by such poore men as we,
> But wele make him know it, if you will be ruled by me.
> Her's Parson *Ball* an honest Priest, and telles us that in charitie,
> We may sticke together in such quarrels honestly.
>
> (I 29–41)

Initially, Straw is not a revolutionary. Rather, he is only reacting to a local injustice that he hopes to rectify. The rashness of the conversation comes from Nobs. Until Nobs speaks there is no talk of dead bodies and it is Nobs who invokes both revenge and a sense that the rebellion should go until the rebels are in the gallows. Even after Nobs's speech, Straw's tone reverts the conversation back to "honesty" and "charity" in the way the poor should stick together. Also, where Straw indicates that he will make the King know what is done to the poor, his comments are not a confirmation of Nobs's desire to take things right to the gallows. Rather, he goes on to echo Ball's more egalitarian perspective. At this point in the conversation none of the characters are responding or paying attention to Nobs. Although the meter and rhyme continue from Nobs's speech, when Straw begins speaking after Nobs's call for revenge he seems to ignore him, referring back to Ball.

The scene continues with the clown, Tom Miller, mocking Ball, asking:

> Tom Miller.
> What is he an honest man? The devil he is, he is the
> Parson of the Towne,
> You thinke ther's no knaverie hid under a black gowne,
> Find him a pulpit but twise in the year,
> And Ile find him fortie times in the ale-house tasting strong beare.
>
> (I 42–45)

Miller's humorous critique of Ball's drinking serves at least two purposes. The clown undermines Ball's legitimacy by providing the preface to Ball's forthcoming utopian fantasies. While the play performs the historical rebellion about which we all know the end result, Miller's joking about Ball—and Parsons generally—only serves to confirm the obvious point that Ball is a utopian dreamer who is possibly intoxicated and corrupt. Since we all know that the rebellion is not successful, Miller's joking allows us to maintain our skepticism as Ball reaches the conclusion of his utopian vision. At the same time, Miller positions the parson within the tradition of rural alehouse radicalism and within a normative, important public space in rural communities. Walter Magagna argues that:

> At the center of a community ritual stood the alehouse and the church, two institutions that formed popular identity and focused local discourse . . . The alehouse also offered a natural forum for the articulation of local opinion and a meeting place for the making of decisions. . . . [T]he alehouse was an important source of seditious rumors and potential plots against elite power. More important, alehouse discourse reinforced the boundaries of community by articulating a folklore of place that encompassed a collective memory of key events and personalities. (Magagna 99)[22]

The alehouse location does not necessarily suggest that this tradition of political radicalism is simply drunken bravado. Instead, Miller's image places Ball's desires within a popular, traditional space for the development of political discourse where radicalism was both commonplace and accepted, despite its limited success. In short, the clown does not so much delegitimize Ball as make him familiar.

Despite the clown's skepticism, Ball concludes his utopian image, suggesting that we

> But follow the counsel of John Ball . . .
> And make division equally,
> Of each mans goods indifferently,
> And rightly may you follow Armes,
> To rid you from these civill harmes.
>
> I 73, 75–78)

Straw and Tyler respond with similar rhetoric, but in organizing the rebellion they begin to lose the sympathy of some modern critics, as they start to overreach their station:

> *Jacke Straw.* Well said Parson so may I bee,
> As wee purpose to preferred thee:
> We will have all the Rich men displaste
> And all the braverie of them defase,
> And as rightly as I am *Jacke Strawe,*
> In spight of all the men of Law,
> Make thee Archbishop of Caunterberie,

	And Chauncellor of England or Ile die.
	How saist thou Wat, shall it bee so?
Wat Tyler.	I *Jacke Strawe,* or else Ile bide any fowle blow.
	It shall bee no other but hee,
	That thus favours the Communaltie,
	Stay wee no longer prating here,
	But let us roundly to this geare,
	Wele be Lords my Maisters everyone.

(I 79–94)

The scene soon comes to a close, leaving Nobs alone on the stage speaking to the audience. But before moving to Nobs's role at the end of the opening scene, this interaction between Tyler and Straw is important to analyze given the radicalism of the conversation. It is not just that they are advocating defacing the rich of their bravery, spiting the law, and recreating the commonwealth in an egalitarian fashion, but they appear to be—paradoxically—seizing power so they can be lords and masters themselves.[23] This rhetoric is, in part, a reflection of the chronicle historians' framing of the rebellion.[24] If we find here only a nefarious desire to seize power for themselves, the rebels look to be little more than bold overreachers and any vision of egalitarianism is just cynical rhetoric.

At stake is how we should understand the usage of "masters and lords" and the limits on the available language for considering an egalitarian community in a play where there are significant limits to the expression of "equality" or "equity" and the desire to "equalize" in the construction of rebellion. Central to the critique of the limited political radicalism within the representation of *Jack Straw,* and central to the assumption that the commons' radical energies inevitably dissolve into tyranny, are problematic assumptions about the conceptual importance of both a "commonweal" and the sense of community in the uprising. When Straw, Wat Tyler, or Parson Ball position themselves and the leaders of the uprising in such a way that they imagine themselves as future "lords" and "masters" it is assumed that their interests have dissolved into a power grab, thus the play is inherently reactionary and serves the ideological interest of the crown, the Lord Mayor, and the aristocracy more generally. By prioritizing this language within the play the rebels seem only self-interested and their successes are tyrannical and chaotic rather than egalitarian.[25]

Such readings are problematic in various ways. Seeing Tyler, Ball, and Straw as tyrannical neglects the primary injustice of the hierarchical system they rebel against. It is an odd way of reading the potentially tyrannical nature of the rebellion not to begin with the acknowledgment that, as a matter of interpretive positions and the political ethics of interpretation, there is little reason to be more disturbed by the change in power if the rebels get their way. To be especially disturbed by the rebels' potential for simply grasping hold of the systems of power in their own interest is to read with an especially paternal, royalist gaze, in which the critic accommodates the actual tyranny of the monarch and the entrenched hierarchy of power. The issue of anachronistic historical reading here is absolutely central. In a certain respect, imposing a humanist equivalency between the rebels and the King and Lord Mayor is deeply anachronistic, for the hierarchy within the body politic was not just imaginary but had concrete consequences in that it was profoundly part of the cultural, national, and political psychology. But more importantly, the whole point in the representation of the rebellion in this play is to see the way in which the rebels are constructed as resistant to the in-place regime and to see the way the rebellion is designed to redraw the lines in the interest of local, community, or regional control. The rebellion is resonant not because of a humanist egalitarianism but because it represents resistance to a nationalist, absolutist agenda using an ancient, ready-made vocabulary of community control.[26]

Furthermore, in their use of this ready-made vocabulary, the rebels invoke a wider politics of commonwealth responsibility only marginally more radical than Robert Crowley's 1548 petition to parliament in which he argues that "the whole earth therefore (by birth right) belongeth to the children of men, They are the inheritors thereof indifferently by nature . . ." (156).[27] As a parliamentary speech, Crowley's position emerges inside official political culture, but next to *Jack Straw* we can see how the play participates in a larger discourse of "commonweale" equality which, paradoxically, does not always mean the elimination of social hierarchy so much as it invokes a tradition of common responsibility.

The point is not that the rebellion is not a critique of social hierarchy, but that the language of political subjectivity and political agency that exists in the 1590s is not our own. Beyond *Jack Straw,* this is a serious conceptual difficulty in the general study of rebellions and their representation in the early modern period. There is a difference in what seem contradictory values within a rebellion for readers with modern expectations for progressively acquired rights or citizenry. Imagining revolution as something other than a *return* is to impose a modern understanding of radicalism onto earlier periods. Therefore, historically approaching the representation of the 1381 rebellion in *Jack Straw* depends upon developing a more nuanced sense of the discourse of rebellion in the play. In particular, this includes recognizing that any rebellion is marked by a sense of returning to a bygone ideal order. This includes the return to a bygone era in which political exploitation was avoided by the fairness of Lords and Masters, and not their absence altogether.

Consider as both part of the popular tradition in which Straw is situated and as a rather contemporary exercise in rebellion, the case of the Kett rebellion and the complexity of the interests and motives behind it. As Stephen Land describes the 1549 Norfolk uprising, although we know very little about its leader, we do know that he was "the advocate of a modified feudal society from which all potentially disturbing economic and social forces would be rigorously excluded by imposition of legal controls. Kett appears to have led a rebellion not against but for a firmly fixed and hierarchical social structure" (150). Kett is represented as and (in a mythographic sense) is similar to Straw. This is partly because Straw is an imaginary everyman, potentially preceding the 1381 uprising and entering the early modern period as more a trope than an actually existent historical subject. In any case, by a modern understanding of rebellion and radicalism, Kett is not a rebel at all. Indeed, Kett is not a rebel but a conservative in that, as Land's work argues, the notion of rebellion within the Norfolk uprising is conditional upon the assumption that the goal of the rebellion is the restoration of a bygone just order which would include lords and masters. If we do not recognize the rebellion as an attempt to restore a bygone biblical political order that is both stable and just, we cannot properly read the relationship between egalitarian desires and the apparent desire for power that is articulated throughout the play.

Additionally, in a literal sense, Wat's claim that "everyone" will be a lord and master is nonsensical insofar as it is impossible for everyone in this rebellion to become "Lords and Masters"—even within the grammar of his own speech the use of "everyone" is structurally ambiguous if we assume the desire to be lords and masters means that the rebels are only after the acquisition of their own power. Also, while this language of lord and master is important to the rebels, it is noticeably different than the language of hierarchy that Ball rails against. For Ball, the problem in England is that "rich men triumph" (I 59) and there was not a "Gentleman" in the Bible as there is England (I 53). Ball is also railing against the rent of landlords. Ball's ideal community is a community where there is "division equally" (I 75) but this is in contrast not to the current world of social hierarchy but to economic abuse and exploitation. The desire to be lords and masters marks political agency in an ideological world of subjectivity—rather than individuality—where to be a gentleman, in particular, is to be someone who does nothing but lives off the exploitation of others. In contrast, theoretically, to be a lord or master only indicates power, it does not indicate corruption or being unjust. To be a gentleman, in the way it is framed in *Jack Straw,* is by definition exploitive. The point here is not nostalgically to suggest that there were the good-old-days of unexploitative rents and just, paternalistic lords. Rather, that in the way the rebels imagine the terms of political exploitation and abuse, it is not hypocritical for them to suggest that they become master and lords. It fits within, as Magagna argues, the traditional models of rural rebellion in which the sense of political solidarity in the rebellion facilitates the strategic imposition of vertical power structures within the localized community, even if these power structures superficially appear to be anything but egalitarian.[28] The desire to be lords and masters does not indicate that the play represents the rebels as tyrants so much as it represents the rebels as engaging in a normative, pragmatic political reorganization in the larger interest of the community. Recognizing this point within the framework of the first scene is essential as the phrase repeats itself throughout the play and becomes incomprehensible unless situated inside an alternative discourse of political agency.

But if we accept the rebellion as legitimate, the first scene's conclusion with Nobs alone appears to compromise its rationale. In fact, where the rebels are significantly unsympathetic they are so because of the way their individual motives and actions are indiscriminately lumped together as inexorably a consequence of their singular lust for power. This fundamental misreading of the play reflects an inability to imagine the rebels as capable of thinking as anything other than a singular, unruly mass, and misses the distinction and importance of Nobs within the dramaturgy. If we focus our attention on the role Nobs plays in the developing rebellion and emphasize the special role he plays in speaking to the audience, we see that he is not the lesser, child rebel among the band of revolutionaries but rather he is an insidious force in the progression of the play and in the rebellion, functioning as a self-interested climber who is the conscience of the rebels as much as Iago is the conscience of Othello.[29]

While Nobs does not have many lines, he often speaks with nobody else on the stage, or if in dialogue with others he notably increases the stakes for the rebellion by thrusting upon the rebellion the recklessness that proves to be so problematic by the end of the play. Also, Nobs is the most significant figure in the play who is purely a product of the drama—unlike Straw, King Richard, Parson Ball, and nearly all of the other characters in the play, Nobs does not exist in the chronicle histories or in any of the principal historical documents describing the rebellion and listing the rebels.[30] As such, Nobs is the most directly literary and imaginary character constructed in the play, with no relation to a "real" historical figure.

In the first scene the contrast between the solidarity of the rebels expressed by Straw and the recklessness of Nobs is illustrated not only by the escalation of revenge that Nobs attempts to introduce into the conversation, but more importantly, by Nobs's deliberate distance from his fellow rebels' goals. At the end of the scene Nobs is alone on the stage confiding in the audience, and thus the distinction between his motives and the rest of the rebels' is clarified. Functioning like an aside in which the inner psychology and motives of the character are revealed to the audience, Nobs speaks to us and does so expressing neither the political solidarity exhibited by the other rebels nor any sense that the rebellion should happen for any reason beyond his own death wish. Furthermore, in speaking of the other rebels he specifically misunderstands

102 STEPHEN SCHILLINGER

the very conversation he has just witnessed and is most concerned with guaranteeing his own welfare should the rebellion fail. At the same time he will conceal his lack of solidarity in the unlikely event that the rebellion succeeds.

Since we already know the conclusion of the forthcoming rebellion, Nobs begins by asking us an especially empty rhetorical question:

> *Nobs.* Heres even worke towards for the Hangman, did you ever see such a crue,
> After so bad a beginning, whats like to insue?
> Faith even the common reward for Rebels, Swingledome Swangledome, you know as well as I,
> But what care they, yee heare them say they owe God a death, and they can but die:
> Tis dishonor for such as they to dye in their bed,
> And credit to caper under the Gallowes all save the head
> And yet by my Fay the beginning of this Riot,
> May chaunce cost many a mans life before all be at quiet:
> And I faith Ile be amongst them as forward as the best.
> And if ought fall out but wel, I shall shift amongst the rest,
> And being but a boy, may hide me in the throng,
> Tyborn stand fast, I feare you will be loden ere it be long.
>
> (I 106–17)

This is a fascinating speech in various ways and understanding how this speech frames our reading of the rebels and how it establishes how we should separate Nobs (as he separates himself) is important for seeing the complexity of the relationship between the audience and its developing sympathies.

While the rest of the rebels envision a utopian future with a rebel army gathered from around England, Nobs simply ignores that aspect of the preceding discussion (which is a curious omission since it occupies virtually the entire conversation). Rather, for Nobs, the emphasis is on the inevitability of the rebels meeting the "hangman," even though it is only he who seemed especially concerned about this fate. Here the foreboding in asking "whats like to insue?" foreshadows aspects of the historical events known to the audience, but Nobs's sense that a rebellion has to result in everyone hanging ("swingledome swangledome") is his own, not the product of the preceding decisions about making more equal the distribution of goods across the land. From here, Nobs's speech becomes especially curious as he claims that we heard "them say they owe God a death, and they can but die" and yet while Nobs was all but silent throughout the conversation, it is this line, in particular, that is his contribution and this is noticeably a contribution that is ignored in the direction Straw takes immediately after Nobs's speech. Nobs's repeating this line in his speech to the audience clarifies his lack of credibility—his version of the events we have just witnessed is clearly inaccurate. Furthermore, this speech, with Nobs's attribution of his own reckless bloodlust to the larger group of rebels, calls into question the legitimacy of his intentions and solidarity with the other rebels and begins to show him as nefarious.

As the speech continues Nobs reveals his own opportunism—he will be "amongst them as forward as the best" until things turn against the rebellion when he will "shift among the rest" for his own protection. Nobs, therefore, marks himself as not interested in the rebellion at all so much as he is interested in making sure *he* gets what he can and avoids the "swingledom-swangledom" that might be forthcoming. In short, he will be the fastest to abandon the rebellion when things begin to go poorly. Furthermore, Nobs's language performs an important reformulation of the terms of the rebellion. While Ball, Tyler, and Straw participate in a long tradition of biblical egalitarianism and a traditional rhetoric of commonwealth responsibility which positions the rebellion (and even the desire to be "lords") on a traditional footing, Nobs reduces the rebellion to its most reckless components.[31] In so doing, he marks himself as not a rebel at all, but as a traitor reproducing the language of the aristocratic position. Pointedly, Nobs's position here has been historically and consistently misread as confirming the conservatism of the play, when in fact it really serves to mark the character so that audiences can see his duplicity.

Nobs's speech frames his own exit from the rebellion as he plots to abandon Tyler, Ball, and Straw. Yet it also invokes the rich polyvalence in the character's name, clarifying his duplicity and self-interest, of which the rest of the rebels are apparently unaware.[32] The etymology and use of "nob" is complicated and diverse.[33] There are multiple, related, and important definitions for the use of "nob" and because the early modern period lacks regularized pronunciation and spelling, the *OED* lists "nab" and "knob" as relevant forms as well. A nob is both a signifier of a person of "wealth and distinction" and also slang for a "head" along the lines of a door [k]"nob." Nobs, in declaring that the entire rebellion will "caper under the Gallowes all save the head" is literally engaging in gallows humor—your head does not "caper" when you hang from your neck—and suggesting that he is not actually among the rebels. As the nob/head he is "saved," for, insofar as he is a nob/gentleman, he is not a rebel at all.

Additional important definitions of nob/nab/knob include an array of terms that suggest a protrusion—something that sticks up or sticks out. This includes "nab" as a welt, as well as includes "knob" and "nob" as boxing terms for hitting someone in the head. But a "nab" or "nob" is also a coxcomb, a fop, or a dandy—presumably related to its gentleman/noble definition. A "nab" or "nob" can be someone who catches, arrest or "nabs" other people, as does a police officer. A "nob" or "nab" can also be a cheat. A "nob" is also a card playing term, first for someone who cheats at cards, but also for the nob-card. This still exists in games such as cribbage, specifically referring to the jack. A nob is also someone who collects money. Lastly, a "nob" or a "knob" or "knobstick" is what is now called a "scab" in a labor strike or lockout.

Not all of these definitions are solidified in early modern usage, but they are all conceptually similar and suggest that a "nob" is disreputable, undesirable, or duplicitous. A nob is a person who cheats and sticks out, often in the interest of entrenched power. This sense of a "nob" even applies in playing cribbage where the nob-card is worth points in a fashion dissimilar to how points are acquired throughout the rest of the game. Nonetheless, there is a possible problem of anachronism in how we read "Nobs." And yet, we know that the sixteenth and seventeenth centuries are marked by enormous mutability in usage and pronunciation. We also know that exactly at this moment where it would be valuable to have documentation of local and plebian variations in usage, "the expurgation of traces of local dialects in both writing and speaking was an imperative of formal education. The enormous expansion of grammar schools clearly had a significant effect in helping homogenize the speech of the social elite and in organizing a self-conscious attempt to distance the language of the learned gentility from that of the lower order" (Fox 60). The impact of this homogenization in trying to understand a word such as "nob" is that we are bound within the vagaries of seventeenth-century antiquarian documentation (Fox 60–61) and within the faux-voyeurism of early modern rogue literature. The canting dictionaries are obviously limited as etymological sources in that they reduce vulgar/common language definitions to criminal language. This is especially problematic for a word such as nob, for which both peasant labor and criminal activity are at stake.[34] Thus, while the problem of documentation in oral and common culture limits the ability to know definitively the range for "Nobs," we can imagine it as being a polyvalent noun, adjective, and verb. The character "Nobs" can conservatively be understood as a head, a noble or fop, a reference to card playing, and a cheat. The construction of his character also suggests his being something of a spy or turncoat in the interest of authority.

After this first scene establishes the sense of common good in the rebellion and introduces us to the duplicitous perspective of Nobs, the second scene[35] offers a short, contrasting perspective: the King's party, annoyed by the budding uprising, attribute it to the "ungrateful" "common sort" (I. 126,129). The Archbishop is incredulous that the commons do not want to pay for the King's war. He is genuinely baffled that the commons fail to understand that ". . . all do live but for a Common weale, / Which Common weale in other termes, is the Kings" (I. 159,160). This scene clarifies the audience's interpretive position: if we see the issue of "commonweale" to be unproblematically a "Kings two Bodies" structure, then the rebels are, by definition, acting without reason. But since in the first scene the rebels do the work of clarifying the terms of their complaints, and the Archbishop and Secretary are presented as simply dumbfounded, the second scene does little to move us against the rebellion. This scene also begins the work of marking the King as both "but young of age" (I. 134) and enough of an adult to rule the country. This is important since the historical King Richard II was only fourteen years old at the time of the rebellion. So while we are informed that the King is "so well ruled by divers of his Pieres" (I 236), he is not presented as a child. As the play proceeds he is presented as enough of an adult to negotiate with the rebels and the issue of his adolescence does not emerge—what problems are presented by the King do not appear age related, except possibly insofar as they contribute to the final heroism of the Lord Mayor.

The third scene reverts to the rebels, without Parson Ball but with Hob Carter emerging. The scene opens with Straw and Tyler complimenting one another and joking that if you "Search me all England and find fower such Captaines, and by gogs blood Ill be hanged" (I 185). Nobs replies, saying, "So you will nevertheless I stand in great doubt" (I 186). This is a joke but nevertheless continues Nobs's eager forecasting of the rebels' failure. From here Hob Carter, as the new rebel, boldly claims that his Essex men "will never yield, but kill else be slaine . . ." (I 189). Carter's boldness is formulaic and unremarkable except that as the play continues this brazenness proves lacking. As the scene progresses it duly covers important information about the capturing of Morton and notes the fifty thousand men in the field. The scene ends with Tyler observing that "Gogs bloud, *Jacke* have we the cards in our hands? / Lets take it upon us while we have it." (I 206). After the rebels have left, Nobs—the card—remains alone, observing, "I marrie, for you know not how long you shall hold it . . . if we hand together as fast some of us shall repent it" (I 209). At this point Nobs's attitude primarily reflects skepticism about the success of the rebellion, but as the play continues the contradictions in his conduct increase.

In the pattern of alternating scenes, the fourth scene introduces the King at the strategic moment when he attempts to contain the rebellion. In this scene the Queen Mother is advised by Salisburie that:

> For though your sonne my Lord the King be young,
> Yet he will see so well unto him selfe,
> That he will make the prowdest Rebell know,
> What tis to moove or to displease a King,
> And though his looks bewray such lenitie,
> Yet at advantage hee can use extremitie . . .
> A King sometimes will make a show of curtesie,
> Onely to fit a following pollicie . . .
>
> (I 220–25, 231–32)

As this conversation develops the young King plans to meet the rebels and hear their grievances, promising that if they have "evill sustaind" (I 316) he will rectify the problem. In the opening scenes the King is represented not as a young Machiavellian but as something of a child bumbler, with his advisers planning the destruction of the rebellion and his mother shocked by the "unnatural" impropriety of it all.

The second act opens with the clown, Tom Miller, on stage with a goose observing that

> ... as long as this Goose lasts wele not starve:
> And as many good fellows as will come to the eating of
> Her, come and welcome,
> For in faith I came lightly by her,
> And lightly come lightly gone,
> We Captaines are Lords within ourselves,
> And if the world hold out we shal be Kings shortly,
>
> (II 2–7)

While Miller is delivering this speech Nobs enters the stage and cuts the goose at the throat, leaving Miller with the useless head. As he exits Miller is left, saying: "Whats the Goose flowne away without her head" (12). This is a moment of great physical humor, and it marks the transition for the first to the second act. The goose incident also allows the rebellion to unfold within a framework that is not entirely grim—the humor moderates the magnitude of what is being performed. And yet, since Nobs is the one stealing the goose, the scene is also a concrete example of Nobs undermining the rebellion—it is hard to overtake a country without food. Indeed, the goose reappears a few scenes later as the rebels are storming the gates of London. After Tyler warns the "porter" that if he loves his own life he will stop resisting and let them in, Miller concludes the portion of the scene saying, "You have a certaine spare Goose came in to bee rosted, / Shee is inough by this" (II 80–81). Beyond Miller's humorous attempt to get the gates open, these lines nonetheless suggest that we should see the stolen goose as delivered to the other side, thus providing some concrete evidence that Nobs is acting against the rebellion.

Nobs emerges next in the following scene with the "Flemming." This scene is the most xenophobic, gruesome component of the rebellion depicted in the play. Within the long textual history of unsympathetic renditions documenting the madness of the rebellion—from Walsingham to Chaucer to Gower to Holinshed—this particular episode is used in various degrees (alternating body counts) to clarify the ruthlessness and pointlessness of the rebel position.[36] Even though it is not specially cited in the scholarship, as a particularly violent act against a mass of people, the inclusion of this episode in the play presumably would serve scholars seeking strong evidence that the play provides only the most reactionary perspective on the rebellion.[37] But in fact, if *Jack Straw* were designed to make the rebels seem especially ruthless, this scene would make much more sense with more than just Nobs on the stage and would be especially problematic were Tyler or Straw involved. Instead, none of the other rebels participate in this murdering spree—it is only Nobs. Scholars incapable of separating Nobs from the rest of the rebels face the problem that it makes little sense for Nobs to be on his own here—if you are including the murder of the Flemish to clarify the madness of the rebels then it makes sense for Straw and Tyler to participate and not the character identified as seeing the recklessness of the rebellion. By recognizing Nobs as nefarious we perceive the place of the scene within the larger text. In separating this action from the other rebels and sloughing it off on Nobs, *Jack Straw* takes what is among the more disturbing parts of the historical narrative and, within a few lines, reframes it as a rogue act by the destructive element within the rebellion.

Furthermore, the brutality of this scene is juxtaposed with the initial conversation after the murder of the Flemish, in which the Lord Mayor declares that

> The greatest wrong this rowt hath done your Grace,
> Amongst a many wicked parts,
> Is in frighting your worthie Lady Mother, . . .
>
> (II 18–20)

While the Lord Mayor does continue on to observe larger crimes committed by the rebels, this is a moment of excessive sycophancy in which the inner circle around the King subordinates the welfare of the country to the indignity of the lack of decorum in the rebellion, which, in its greatest damage, has frightened the Queen Mother.

After the conversation between the Lord Mayor and the King there is a second attempted meeting between the rebels and the King. This meeting between the rebels and the King begins the downfall of the rebellion and lends especially to the rebels seeming ruthless and without concern for the commonwealth, as they initially claim. The scene is framed by the earlier moment wherein the rebels wait in vain for the King. In his frustration, Straw describes it thus:

> Heres a sturre more than needs,
> What means the King thus to abuse us?
> And make us runne about his pleasure, and to no end.
> He promised us to meete us on the water,
> And by Ladie as soone as we came at the water side,

> Hee faire and flat turnes his Barge and away hee goes to
> London.
>
> (II 13–18)

While the rebels take this as the King's refusal to speak with them, we learn that for the King, the rebel presence on the riverbank was just too "unorderly" and "ungently" to be entertained (II 40, 43). After the King leaves the room, his men—Spencer and Newton—discuss how the King really left out of fear. Newton observes that the rebels

> ... fild the Aire with cries and fearfull noise,
> And from the water did an echo rise.
> That pearst the eares of our renowned king,
> Affrighting so his heart with strong conceit,
> Of some unhappy grievous stratigene,
> That trust me with my eares I heard him say,
> He thought they would have all like Spaniels,
> Tane water despertly and borded him.
> So did they all yfare like franticke men,
> That time he thought to speed away apace, ...
>
> (II 55–64)

Spencer's reply is to sympathize with the frightened King, saying

> Indeed I could not greatly blame his Majestie,
> My selfe was not so scarde this seven yeare:
>
> (II 66–67)

The key to this scene is in the disparity between Straw's perception of the King's action and the perception of the rebels by the King. To the rebels, the King has broken his word. To the King, the rebels appear as a ruthless, many-headed monster.

In the second interaction between the rebels and the King, Straw demands wealth and liberty. The King, despite the Lord Mayor, is increasingly magnanimous without actually granting the rebels anything to ameliorate their exploitation. The King grants the rebels "liberty and pardon all . . ." (III 70). But the rebels persist, crying still that they want wealth and liberty. Tyler responds to the King, asserting:

> Ere wele be pincht with povertie,
> To dig our meate and vittels from the ground,
> That are as worthie of good maintenance,
> As any Gentleman your grace doth keepe,

> We will be Kings and Lords within our selves.
> And not abide the pride of tyrannie.
>
> (III 72–77)

The King responds to Tyler, seemingly astonished by his accent, asking "what countryman art thou?" Essential to this dialogue is that while the King appears to present himself as magnanimous, the main charge of exploitation is never met. The King is willing to eliminate the bondage, but not actually engage with the larger economic issue. Furthermore, while Tyler boldly claims that they will be kings and lords, the thrust of the assertion is that they will be so "within our selves"—that to be a king or lord here is a mark of political agency and liberty in contrast to the pride of tyranny in the following line.

The scene develops with the Lord Mayor and King chastising Tyler for his manners (III 81) while the crowd continues to demand both wealth and liberty. Richard grants all the rebels a pardon and repeats the granting of their "libertie" (III 84) but he consistently refuses to engage on the wealth issue. Tyler's railing against tyranny is the last we hear of either Tyler or Straw in this negotiation process. The turning point in the scene comes a few short speeches later when Hob Carter interjects. Carter—who has said nothing throughout the scene and not been part of these negotiations—responds to the King, seemingly craving any opportunity to end his participation in the rebellion saying, "Marrie I thanke your Grace, Hob Carter and the Essex / men will home againe, and we take your word" (III 95–99). The King leaves immediately after Carter's response, accepting Carter's word as definitive for the entire rebellion. This is a very curious moment in the scene and for the development of the outcome of the rebellion since throughout the play Carter's only lines previously had been in the interest of confirming his radical bravado to fight until victory or death. Here that radicalism is nowhere to be found. Instead, in interjecting his acceptance of the King's terms, Carter is neither following the cry of the mass of rebels—who have not come away from their "wealth and liberty" stance—nor is he adequately engaging in the pressing concern for "tyranny" that Tyler has introduced. Hob Carter abandons the rebellion and therefore the King leaves the scene before the rest of the rebels have time to respond. Problematically, although Carter undercuts the rebellion, the King takes him as the representative for the entire rebellion and uses Carter's words as a rationale for his eventual killing of the rebels.

After the King (and presumably Carter as well, although the stage directions are nonexistent) has left the stage, Straw, Tyler, and Ball seem dumbfounded that the rebellion has been foiled so quickly. They resolve to keep fighting even if it means the gallows. In this conversation Nobs interjects, saying "Trust not his [the King's] pardon for you die everie Mothers sonne. / But Captaines, goe forward as we have be gone" (III 106–7). Nobs's persistent comments about pushing the rebellion to the gallows make no sense as a caution. They are, rather, duplicitous provocations. Like an agitator intent on undermining the legitimacy of the rebels, Nobs pushes them to keep on for no apparent reason.[38] After Nobs convinces the remaining rebels to stick together (despite the dire circumstances), the scene shifts to Tom Miller. Miller is preparing to burn more records, having already engaged in a spree of destruction at the Inns of Court and Guild-Hall. Nobs, having just convinced Straw and Tyler to keep on, implores Miller "to looke to / your selfe, for I will looke to myself" (III 121–22). The contrast between the two conversations is striking: Nobs first stimulates the leaders of the rebellion to an almost certain death but then implores the unimportant clown to stop his actual damage to the records of power and abandon the rebels as well.

The remainder of the play is increasingly hard on the rebels but is also, in part, gallows humor. After giving up on the rebellion, Tom Miller finds himself in the presence of the Queen Mother, attempting to fake knowledge of the neck verse to keep himself alive. The ham-handed and inaccurate performance of what Miller hopes will be the neck verse makes explicit the relationship between literacy, cultural power, and the ability "literally" to stay alive.[39] As the clown, Miller also diffuses the inevitable downfall of the rebels that is immediately forthcoming.

After Miller extricates himself from the Queen Mother, the remaining rebels enter the scene. As Straw enters he is convinced of the King's duplicity because of the first attempted meeting at which the King refused to come ashore.

> The King and is Nobls thinke they may sleepe in quiet,
> Now they have given us a little holy water at the Court,
> But thers no such matter, we be no such fooles,
> To be bobd out with words and after come to hanging . . .
>
> (III 162–64)

Straw's position is that the King cannot be trusted and the rebels, as they were earlier when waiting for the King to meet them, should not be deceived by the King's lies—"bobd out." As the King emerges, it is clear that the conflict will be played out as a crisis of legitimacy; Straw sees the King trying to bob-out the rebels and the King declares that the rebels, by virtue of not following Hob Carter's hasty surrender, "stand not to their words" (III 188). In this scene Straw and the other rebels are on stage as the King, Newton, and the Lord Mayor confront them, focusing on Straw. Straw is quickly stabbed, causing the rebels to disband.

From here until the conclusion of the play the Christian goodness of the King is emphasized, the King and the Lord Mayor are triumphant, and as a result of the King's final pardon, all but Ball and Tyler are spared. In the final act Nobs is conspicuously absent despite having been responsible for the single act of mass violence explicitly mentioned in the play. Yet, while the last act emphasizes the triumphalism of the Lord Mayor and King, it is compromised by the obstinacy of Ball and Tyler and the persistence of gallows humor from Tyler. At the conclusion of the King's pardon, Tyler asks to be "powlde first" (i.e., have his head on a pole) (IV 141) rather than listen to Morton go on anymore. While humorously ready to be "powled," Ball and Tyler are pointedly not represented as seeking forgiveness or as acknowledging the errors of their ways. Rather, their concluding dialogue is revealing as it indicates that not only would they do it again, they understand their failure as tactical (rather than acknowledging the greatness of the King or their own evilness).

> *Wat Tyler.* Well then we know the worst,
> He can but hang us, and that is all,
> Were Jacke Strawe a live againe,
> And I in as good possibility as ever I was,
> I would lay a surer trumpe,
> Ere I would lose so faire a tricke.
> *Parson Ball.* And what I said in time of our business I repent not,
> And if it were to speake againe,
> Everie word should be a whole sermon,
> So much I repent me.
>
> (IV 125–34)

Historically, the rebels were known for their dying obstinacy.[40] More importantly, Ball and Tyler's persistence and humor compromise the final authority of the royalist triumph. Their lack of regret for rebelling and the identification of their failure as tactical and rhetorical—rather than somehow wrongheaded—leaves the rationale for the rebellion uninterrogated, intact and as legitimate as it had been previously. For Ball the problem was an issue of spreading the word more—he repents not speaking enough. For Tyler the regret is purely on the issue of execution and, marked within the language of card-play and going back to the etymology for "nob," this speech marks the moment of awareness of Nobs's role in undermining the rebellion—to "lay a surer trump" than the untrustworthy Nob(s)-card would have led to a successful rebellion.

In reading the play in this fashion—as a text which represents the rebellion sympathetically and interrogates the vulnerability of a mass revolt being undermined from within—we have a more consistent way of approaching the construction of the narrative. By reading the rebellion as undermined by its own internal complications but also philosophically and politically intact, we have, first, a stronger explanation for why so much energy in the text is devoted to the legitimacy of the rebels and, in contrast, to the court's disconnection from social reality. We also understand the construction of the rebel characters' relationships to one another as manipulated by Nobs.

Lastly, a reading strategy that looks at *The Life and Death of Jack Straw* as formally constructed around the duplicitousness of Nobs and with a sympathetic view of the rebels provides us with a way of making comprehensible the single piece of evidence we have not only of *Jack Straw* being performed, but of how audiences reacted to its performance. Simon Forman's 1611 *Book of Plaies* contains the one piece of possible evidence that *Jack Straw* was in fact performed. And if the notation is to be believed, it suggests that the play was viable nearly twenty years after Danter's first printing. Forman's comments on the play are included in E. K. Chambers's *William Shakespeare: A Study of Facts and Problems*. Forman observes:

> Remember therin howe Jack Straw by his overmuch boldnes, not being politick nor suspecting Anye thinge: was Soddenly at Smithfield Bars stabbed by Walworth the major of London, & soe he and his wholle Army was overthrown. Therefore in such a case or the like, never admit any party, without a bar between, for A man cannot be to wise, nor kepe him selfe to safe. (Forman, in Chambers 339)

In their interest in Shakespeare and in their lack of emphasis on *Jack Straw,* scholars have either ignored or been flummoxed by Forman's note for the simple reason that it counters the assumption that the rebels are unsympathetic. Forman assumes our concern is for Straw, but from a conservative reading, the moment of Straw's death is triumphant rather than cautionary in the way Forman presents it. Even Longstaffe, who is writing the most sympathetic reading of the play within all of academic scholarship, does not see this as especially compelling material in one way or another.[41] And indeed, isolating Forman as a definitive marker of early modern audience response is potentially treacherous because there is no absolute way to know what he refers to.

But if we assume the rebels are not villainous, Forman's rendition of the conclusion suggests how audiences might have read the rebels as sympathetic. If we are not reading the play with a sense that the rebellion is undermined from someone such as Nobs who they "admit" to the "party" Forman's comment is either not about this play or not an accurate reading of Straw's perspective in the conversation where he is murdered. Straw's whole point in the conversation about the sword is that he does not trust anyone and we know from beforehand that he will not be "bobd with words" by the King. So Forman's seeing Straw's flaw as that of being too trusting only makes sense if what Forman perceived in the play was a character within Straw's own party as part of his undermining.[42]

In trying to construct a framework for understanding how audiences would perceive the representation of rebellion in *The Life and Death of Jack Straw,* we discover that not only is the one indication of an audience response dependent upon seeing Straw sympathetically, it is so through this issue of the rebellion being undermined not by the heroism of the King or the Lord Mayor, but by its internal subversion. And furthermore, this one shred is itself only comprehensible if we read the play as having this complex construction in which the rebellion is both legitimized but undermined from within.

The goal of this essay has been to reclaim *The Life and Death of Jack Straw* from its marginalization and to see the play as speaking to and evidence of a popular, more genuinely politicized plebian audience, aware of the exigencies of power and not just overwhelmed by its monarchical performance. As both literary and cultural history, the goal of the essay has been to engage in a practice of historicism which examines the dramatic text while aware of its place on the margins of literacy and oralism. *Jack Straw* is part of a hybrid playing culture, marking the infusion of popular folklore and plebian politics within the public playhouses. In emphasizing careful, close historical reading, where the rationale for that close reading is historicist itself, I seek to participate in a larger discussion about the politics of popular self-identity, solidarity, and resistance to power as evidenced in the privileged discourse of theatrical representation. The point is not just to evaluate literary representation, but to see literary representation as a way to understand plebian political subjectivity, radicalism, and anxieties about social change in early modern England. Lastly, in thinking about theatrical representation as a site for early modern cultural scholarship, theatrical texts should be privileged precisely because—as *Jack Straw* demonstrates—they are best understood as amalgams of diverse cultural practices, comprehensible within the matrix of oral, manuscript, and print cultures.

Notes

1. While the spelling of the title is regularized throughout the essay, as it is inconsistent between the versions of the play, I maintain in-text spelling and punctuation as it emerges in the 1593 Danter edition.

2. Muir notes that the play was "printed by Danter at the turn of the year, the title page bearing the date 1593 and the colophon 1594" (v).

3. Probably in contrast to Pavyer, there is no reason to think that Danter's profit motive also suggests that he was targeting a niche market of radicalized readers.

4. I am aware of the scholarship attributing the text to one playwright or another, including Shakespeare, but there is noticeably little convincing evidence for the attribution of the play to one person. The supposition that the play is from a single writer assumes a model of early modern play production that is theoretically problematic. In any case, for this project, the authorship question is beside the point since it was not relevant enough for the printers to attach to the title page.

5. It is important to acknowledge that, historically, the play was considered poten-

tially a mayoral pageant and, despite all the renewed historical energy devoted to the study of early modern plays, this impression persists into recent scholarship such as Lawrence Manley's *Literature and Culture in Early Modern London*. Manley cites early twentieth-century scholars but does not interrogate their arguments at all (129, 273). Yet even the most superficial reading of the play should call into question this basic interpretation since there is a very clear formal problem with reading the play in this fashion. The play is essentially too focused upon the rebels, gives the rebels too much space within the text, for good or bad. And Walworth, for a play celebrating his position, is an exceptionally marginal character. While there are representations of the rebellion which celebrate Walworth's triumph, this seems either not to be one, or if it is it is so as an especially sardonic rendition. The second, more recent position on the play is to read it as carnivalesque. While Helgerson (209–13) and Hunt point to the humor of the play, and Hunt even positions it within the tradition of carnivalesque, in part, it is Longstaffe who advocates this most strongly. But even in trying to position the play as carnivalesque Longstaffe partially resorts to misappropriating lines from his own edition (121) and describing a character as a clown when, in contrast to the actual clown, there is no evidence that the character occupies such a role. The argument for the play being carnivalesque is either similar to reading the play as a pageant—in that it is not sustained by really carefully reading the play where a small percentage of the text is devoted to the kind of action that would fit Bakhtin's argument—or it depends upon a misreading of Bakhtin. To read the play as carnivalesque misreads Bakhtin in the sense that if you imagine this play as carnivalesque you must then imagine all instance of humor in the early modern period as fitting the definition and thus the idea of the "carnivalesque" loses any meaningful specificity. But the real problem with reading the play as carnivalesque is that it blocks us from seeing the formal construction of the play which is both historically and politically revealing for the radical potential for how audiences would perceive the dramaturgy. If we are bound by a carnivalesque reading the play becomes *merely* carnivalesque, inherently contained and without any political potential beyond the contained remnants of festive laughter. Between these two polarities, studies of *Jack Straw* are notably few and where they do exist there is a disappointingly thin record of analysis and research. The play has very recently been reproduced in a scholarly edition, there are a few essays in folklore studies that mention the play, and there are occasional "notes" about the play related to its authorship or its textual similarities to other plays from the period. In the increasing accumulation of bibliographic studies of the history of the stage, the play emerges as part of comprehensive indexes of the Elizabethan and Jacobean drama. Lastly, there is the predominant pattern of scholarship whereby literary critics will briefly write about the play either in the service of reading another play, or scholars will cite the play anecdotally in the service of developing a particular argument about the genre or the period itself. In the vast majority of these cases the study of the play is hardly a study or analysis at all if by analysis what is meant is that a reading of the content of the play is put forth in a fashion so as to argue something about the play itself. Rather, citations to the play mostly consist of brief, general assertions that are not even argued so much as declared, or the play is described through the reference to other scholars and scholarly consensus—which consist of citing a series of remarkably brief comments as that consensus. In short, the study of *Jack*

Straw is an example of Robert Hume's problem of scholarly "deference." Lacking a serious reconsideration of the actual play and needing only to develop an understanding of the play as far as it can be used to facilitate the study of something else altogether, scholars have fixed *The Life and Death of Jack Straw* as a deeply reactionary, conservative text without any recent, substantive consideration of the play itself. (The one exception to this pattern is the Longstaffe critical edition of the play, which in including a "critical essay" constitutes the single most significant work on the play in four hundred years.)

6. Longstaffe makes the observation regarding the relative popularity of the play with respect to its second printing (2). Also, see Blayney who observes that in the period of *Jack Straw's* first printing only 48 percent of plays saw a second printing within the next twenty-five years (387).

7. Longstaffe claims "after his death in October 1599, [Danter's] widow assigned the play to Thomas Pavyer" (2). Also, see Muir (V).

8. Chartier and Cavallo argue recent scholarship indicates that given "the territory available to them, readers took command of books (and other printed objects), gave them meaning, and invested them with their own expectations. That appropriation was not without its own rules and limitations. Some of these arose out of strategies inherent in the text itself, which was intended to produce certain effects, dictate a posture, and condition the reader. The snares laid for readers, and into which they fell without even realizing it, were as clever as the rebel inventiveness they are supposed to have possessed. The image contained equally constrained and equally subversive reading codes. Often used to accompany a printed text, images set up a protocol for reading that was intended either to present the same message as the one formulated in the written text, using a different sign language but an identical grammar, or else to present, in a language specific to the image, what logical discourse was powerless to express. In either case (and the two indicate quite different functional relationships between the text and the image), when illustrations were given the task of guiding interpretation, they might instead bear an 'other' reading, detached from the letter of the text and cap able of creating a space of its own"(Cavallo, Chartier 34–35).

9. See appendix A: Danter Title Page, 40.

10. See appendix B: Pavyer Title Page, 41.

11. The seal added by Pavyer is clearly a rich and suggestive device for framing the play, but it is also an especially complicated one given that after *The Life and Death of Jack Straw* Pavyer uses the peasant laborer seal for the next year, including it on other title pages until 1605. (It did not, however, emerge before *Straw*). Part of what is strange about the use of the seal is that in each of the other cases where Pavyer uses the seal after *Straw* the use of the seal appears nonsensical with respect to the content of the play. One possible way of interpreting this would be to see that Pavyer's continued use of the seal suggest some intitial success from *Straw* that he hoped to capitalize on with the printing of other plays.

12. See Simon Shepherd, *Marlowe and the Politics of Elizabethan Theater* (10, 95).

13. Introducing a general consensus for the recent developments in the study of the history of reading and the study of scribal and early printed texts, Cavallo and Chartier observe that ". . . the form of a publication transmits how the person who created

that text or that book perceived the readers' abilities; second, that same form dictates a way of reading the text and of creating comprehension and controlling interpretation. Formal and material differences on several levels exist in both manuscript and print texts" (Cavallo, Chartier 35).

14. Blayney does not list the plays he uses for this study. Pavyer published at least one other play in the period in blackletter, but just an anecdotal on-line database search of the primary archives of early modern texts indicates that he predominately printed in roman (see *EEBOL*).

15. Beyond the scope of this project, but clearly a relevant direction in the study of early modern culture through theatrical representation, would be focused studies of particular printers. Accepting the basic premise that authorship, while important, is not the single relevant piece of historical information for understanding an early modern text should lead to important considerations of other guiding signifiers for framing audience responses. Printers, in their special position as final arbiters of the texts and in their often marginal position within the social hierarchy and tenuous position within the economy, may provide an especially revealing access point for looking at the culture and the stage in the period.

16. The Collector is probably alone because the content of his opening speech suggests that Straw does not arrive on the stage until the scene ends. There is no stage direction one way or another.

17. For the initial modern argument that Straw and Tyler are one and the same, see F. W. D. Brie (106–11). For a recent reconsideration of the problem, see Alistair Dunn (62–63). For an account of Tyler and Straw's position as archetypes within popular, folkloric oral history see Thomas Pettit (8–9).

18. In *Unediting the Renaissance,* Leah Marcus assumes that the "shape and format of a given book are finally not separable from its contents; literary works are not universal in any useful sense of the term, but local and locally specific, existing in an array of concrete forms that need to be studied as an important part of their meaning" (28). What this means is that texts have to be taken as concrete material objects in which the New Bibliography's desire to clarify and clean texts is a problematic Platonic exercise in which scholars "locate the 'reality' of a given literary creation outside its extant material embodiments" (29). In this case there is a clear practical value to this approach because it prevents us from either trying to "fix" the text in accordance to Holinshed—in which case we would lose Straw altogether here—or in accordance to our own sense of "common sense" for the passage, where we would lose the slide that exist between Straw and Tyler as archetypes rather than particular historical individuals being represented.

19. Ball's speech echoes and is echoed in the middle of the sixteenth century in Kett's Rebellion, and also in the seventeenth century with the Levellers. For a tracing of this usage, see Alistair Dunn's *The Great Rising of 1381* (152).

20. Both Hunt and Longstaffe are invested in seeing the play within traditional carnivalesque rituals. While there are these moments that suggest carnival-like humor, the limitation of this reading is that there are only a few, precise moments in the text that suggest the carnivalesque.

21. Longstaffe notes this phrase as conventional for drama in the period, indicating simply "if you will listen to me" (130).

22. For more on the relevance of ale houses as a place of popular political activity and organization see Keith Wrightson, "Alehouses, Order, and Reformation in Rural England, 1590–1660" and Buchanan Sharpe (41–42). Also, for the relationship between early print and the oral transmission of political information among the common people, see Adam Fox (140).

23. For examples of scholars especially bothered by the language of the rebels that appears to suggest they are not egalitarian at all, but just rogues, see Adams (83) in early twentieth-century scholarship. For a relatively lengthy (and especially excited) version of this thinking, see Bevington (236–37). For recent, post new historicism versions of this perception see Carroll (148–49) and Hunter (208–9).

24. It is important to my argument that the written, chronicle histories from the early modern period are not given primacy in thinking about the range of available perspectives on the rebellion in the sixteenth and seventeenth centuries, but it is worth noting in this case that the rebels in the play are notably less assertive than their representation in Holinshed. The difference clearly marks a case where on a simple comparative level (regardless of intent) the final result in the play is that even for unsympathetic readers the play's rebels are less tyrannical than they are in Holinshed.

25. See Bevington, Ribner (74–75). Recently, see Hunt.

26. After the scholarly energy devoted to making Elizabethan hegemony seem absolute in its saturation into the political imagination this claim appears bolder than it actually is. There is a wealth of information about rebellions, assassination attempts, and regional uprising that the bold assumption is in thinking the performance of Elizabethan nationhood is both deep and widespread in its effectiveness.

27. Quoted from the excerpt in Kate Aughterson's *The English Renaissance: An Anthology and Sources and Documents*. Crowley argues "If the possessioners would consider themselves to be but stewards, and not lords over their possessions, this oppression would soon be redressed. But so long as the persuasion sticketh in their minds: *it is mine own: who shall warn me to do with mine own as me self listeth?* it shall not be possible to have any redress at all" (154). But despite Crowley's apparent radicalism, he explicitly warns to "Take me not here that I should go about by these words to persuade men to make all things common: for if you do you mistake me. For I take God to witness I mean no such thing" (154). Crowley's anxiety about being misunderstood suggest that, in fact, he would be misunderstood because his language was so similar to current sentiments to do just this work of making "all things common."

28. In *Communities of Grain* Magagna's central argument is that community "is the most obvious alternative to class as a basis for interpreting the logic of rural institutions" (12). Within this model of reading rebellion through a community logic we can see that "institutional inequalities can be a source of cohesion and solidarity, and the types of hierarchy that facilitate group discipline cannot be reduced to simple class categories. Rural communities almost always display deeply rooted distinctions between the more and less advantaged. Yet those distinctions and divisions allow the community as a whole to mobilize itself for collective action by projecting the advantaged into natural leadership roles" (16). Magagna's position is less at odds with a Marxist sense of the primacy of class than it might seem. Even if it is structurally accurate to analyze historical processes through the lens of class it does not therefore

follow that in the localized cases there are not other more immediate and important conceptual models being employed for one reason or another.

29. Tillyard is the one scholar appreciative of the importance of Nobs but this reflects less Tillyard devoting careful attention to the play than it reflects the ease with which Nobs's lines can be appropriated as marking the "evils" of rebellion. Tillyard comments that "The *Life and Death of Jack Straw* is conventionally sound on the evils of rebellion, the doctrine being put in the mouth not only of those in authority but in that of Nobs, who, though one of the rebels, comments chronically on their excesses" (106). What is amazing about Tillyard's reading is that while he is correct to focus on Nobs, he seems to almost brazenly misread the most explicit component of Nobs's construction as a character in that Nobs does not conventionally comment on the evils of rebellion at all, he promotes the greatest excesses of that rebellion and is responsible for the one explicit act of mass murder in the play.

30. Based on Dobson's edited collection of documents related to the revolt.

31. See John Walter's "Public Transcripts, Popular Agency and the Politics of Subsistence in Early Modern England" where it is observed that the commons or the 'ruled' subjects in early modern England maintained a consistent pattern of just this type of rhetorical practice. Walter observes that of "the texts of these [commoner] appeals [that] have survived they reveal a remarkable ability of the commoners to couch their criticisms in terms of key categories within the public transcript of commonwealth: neighborliness and the moral community, the good lord and the good king, the responsibility of office" (134).

32. Strangely, the claim that this speech is designed to serve as an explicit signifier to the audience that Nobs is self serving and is the insidious mole in the rebellion is apparently lost on essentially every reader of the play. In fact, the circumstances of this speech tend to be ignored and for a scholar like Tillyard it is these moments with Nobs that are taken as the conscience of the rebellion.

33. The following is copied directly from the *OED* but edited down to the usage patterns that contribute to how we could understand the character here. Also included is usage that, even if not occurring in the sixteenth century, is valuable for tracing the development of the word.

Nob . . . Slang . . . A person of some wealth or social distinction. . . .

α**1676** *Minute Bk. Inverness Tailors* 10 Oct., The said John Baillie..resolved..that the most discreet and sound nabbs of the freemen should join with him in council. **1755** R. FORBES *Shop-bill* in tr. Ovid *Ajax* 37 Doughty geer That either knabbs or lairds may weer. **1796** J. LAUDERDALE *Poems* 75 A' the fat nabs through the countra. **1819** J. THOMSON *Poems* 29 (E.D.D.), The nabs will say, that duddy soul Shall no sit near, nor taste our bowl. **1892** J. LUMSDEN *Sheep-head* 62 Upo' her back the wauchty creels, She thraws as eithly in a spell; As yon 'half-nabs' do their mantels. **1917** T. W. PATERSON *Wyse-Sayin's* xxi. 22 A wyse man speels ower the tap o' a toon-fu' o' knabbs, An' gies their upsettin silly consait an unco ding ower. . . .

β**1809** *MS Lett. of W. Fowler,* My Drawings and Engravings..have recommended me to the notice of the first Nobbs of this Kingdom. **1825** C. M. WESTMACOTT *Eng. Spy* I. 255 Nob or big wig. **1832** B. HALL *Frag. Voy. & Trav.* 2nd Ser. I. 117 They [*sc.* the passengers] fall under the description of what Jack calls "Knobs." **1836** B. DISRAELI *Henrietta Temple* V. xviii, The little waiter who began to think Ferdinand was not such a nob as he had imagined. **1872** *Punch* 3 Feb. 47/1 Why don't your nobs and swells get up poor's schools of their own? **1938** P. KAVANAGH *Green Fool* ii. 24 The children of the nobs called their white bread 'lunch' and nibbled at it with aristocratic finger-tips. **1962** J. B. KEANE *Hut 42* 31 When a Paddy tries to come the nob, that's the limit, that is! **1993** *Times Lit. Suppl.* 4 June 31/1 In the unending British civil war of Yobs vs Nobs, Ritchie is decidedly on the side of the Yobs. . . .

Nob, n 3.

Simple uses. **1. a.** orig. *cant.* The head. Also *fig.* Cf. KNOB *n.* 4a, *ginger-nob* s.v. GINGER *n.* 7. Now *colloq.* and somewhat *arch.*

bob a nob: see BOB *n.*⁸ 2.

1699 B. E. *New Dict. Canting Crew, Nob,* a Head. **1725** *New Canting Dict., Knob,* the Head or Skull. **1733** K. O'HARA *Tom Thumb* I. iv 12 Do pop up your nob again, And egad I'll crack your crown. **1759** *Compl. Let.-writer* (ed. 6) 220 Miss Bennet had apparel'd her nob in a frightful Fanny Murry Cap. **1782** G. PARKER *Humorous Sketches* 155 Here no despotic power shews Oppression's haughty nob. **1819** *Sporting Mag.* 4 237 A tremendous lunging blow on his nob. *a*1845 T. HOOD *Public Dinner* 17 A little dark spare man, With bald shining nob. **1888** M. ROBERTSON *Lombard St. Myst.* xvi, It were s'posed the guilty deed were one too much for 'is knob. **1894** G. MEREDITH *Ld. Ormont* i, Matey's sure aim..relieving J. Masner of a foremost assailant with a spanker on the nob. **1899** R. WHITEING *No. 5 John St.* xxvii, They invariably . . . 'ketch it in the knob' in the form of bilious headache. **1910** C. E. MONTAGUE *Hind let Loose* i. 12 Brumby got one for his nob . . . Bellona's other bridegroom took it on the boko [*sc.* nose]. **1938** T. H. WHITE *Sword in Stone* vii. 116 "Take that!" cried Sir Grummore, giving the unfortunate monarch a two-handed swipe on the nob. **1997** T. PYNCHON *Mason & Dixon* 494 Wearily Mason pulls on Oil-cloths, tugs his Service-Grade Beaver of his Nob, and emerges.

†**b.** *Boxing slang.* A blow to the head. *Obs.*

1812 *Sporting Mag.* **39** 153 By flush-hits, and nobs and fibs Who crack'd the jaw and broke the ribs Of fearless Thomas Molineux.

I. 2. *Cribbage.* A jack of the same suit as the card turned up by the dealer, scoring one to its holder; esp. in *one for his* (also *her*) *nob* (or *nobs*). Cf. HEEL *n.*¹ 1d.

1821 C. LAMB *Mrs. Battle* in *London Mag.* Feb. 163/2 There was nothing silly in it, like the nob in cribbage. **1834** DICKENS *Sketches by Boz* (1836) 1st Ser. I. 208 'One for his nob!' said Gobler. **1844** J. T. J. HEWLETT *Parsons & Widows* III. liv. 278 Fifteen two, and a pair's four, and his nob's five. **1870** F. HARDY & J. R. WARE *Mod. Hoyle, Cribbage* 18 If you hold in your hand or crib a knave of the same suit as the card turned up you peg one. In the familiar phrase, you take 'one for his nob'. **1882** *Society* 11 Nov. 9/1 In cribbage parlance, it was one for her nob and two for her heels. **1969** R. C. BELL *Board & Table Games* II. viii. 119 For the Knave of the exposed card, 'his nobs' 1 point. **1979** *Official World Encycl. Sports & Games* 113/3 If a player holds a jack of the same suit as the start, he scores 'one for his nob'.

II. Compounds. **3.** †**nob-thatch** *slang Obs.,* hair. †**nob thatcher** *slang Obs.,* a wigmaker; a hatter.

1846 J. SHEPPARD *Let.* in *Littell's Living Age* 17 Oct. 139 Mr Chesterton's "nick" is yet fearfully visible among my hair, whence a great paucity of *nob-thatch. **1866** E. YATES *Land at Last* vii, You've got a paucity of nob-thatch, and what 'air you 'ave is . . . gray.

1793 F. GROSE *Dict. Vulgar Tongue* (ed. 3), **Nob thatcher,* a peruke maker. **1823** "W. T. MONCRIEFF" *Tom & Jerry* I. v, Some of our dashing straw-chippers and nob-thatchers in Burlington Arcade. **1846** *Swell's Night Guide* 126/2 *Nob thatcher,* a hat maker.

nob, n. = <u>KNOBSTICK</u> *n.* 2a.

1825 *Scots Mag.* Oct. 495 There have of late been several cases of assault upon the workmen termed "nobs" in Messrs. Dunlop's mill. **1870** J. K. HUNTER *Life Stud. Char.* xix. 136 They ha'e a strong society,..and hate nobs such as me. **1886** D. MACLEOD *Clyde District Dumbartonsh.* I. 22 The "nobs" and their protectors proceeded to the works. **1895** J. NICHOLSON *Kilwuddie* 174 Nae mercy for the nobs, the blackleg crew.

Knobstick n.

1. A stick, cane, or club, having a rounded knob for its head; a knobbed stick.

1824 [see b]. **1867** *Crim. Chronol. York Castle* 190 Beating him over the head with knobsticks. **1887** JESSOPP *Arcady* vii. 192 With the knob sticks of the mob.

b. Such a stick used as a weapon; a knobkerrie.

1824 W. J. BURCHELL *Trav. S. Afr.* I. 354 A keeri..(a short knobstick) in his hand. **1859** BURTON *Centr. Afr.* in *Jrnl. Geog. Soc.* XXIX. 266 Terrifying the enemy with maniacal gestures, while stones and knobsticks fly through the air. **1894** B. MITFORD *Curse Clement Waynflete* vii. 241 The warrior's heavy knobstick, hurled with deadly precision.

2. A name given, by workmen, to one who during a strike or lock-out continues to work on the master's terms; a black-leg. (See also quot. 1892.) Also *attrib.*

1826 *Examiner* 663/2 Skirmishes..between the turn-outs and those whom they call 'knobsticks'. **1826** *Ann. Reg.* 151/2 One man, a weaver, was accused of being 'a knobstick spinner'. **1848** MRS. GASKELL *Mary Barton* xvi, Taken up last week for throwing vitriol in a knob-stick's face. **1892** *Labour Commission Gloss.*, A *knobstick* is one who takes the work of an operative on strike, or refuses to go out on strike along with his fellow-workmen . . . Workmen..who are not members of a trade union are frequently called knobsticks by the unionist workmen. The term is also applied to men who work at a trade to which they served no apprenticeship.

b. A master who employs men on terms not recognized by a trade-union.

1851–61 MAYHEW *Lond. Labour* III. 220 (Hoppe), I next went to work at a underpriced hatter's termed a "knob~stick's".

34. See Janet Sorensen. "Vulgar Tongues: Canting Dictionaries and the Language of the People in Eighteenth-Century Britain" *Eighteenth-Century Studies* 37.3(2004): 435–55.

35. The scenes are not textually marked and thus line numbers continue upward inside the particular acts.

36. For the diversity of renditions of the murder of the Flemish, see Dobson (162, 175, 188–89, 201, 206, 210, 387).

37. For the importance of the historical use of the murder of the Flemish within the history of delegitimizing the rebellion, see Justice (72). It is especially noteworthy that this episode does not receive more scholarly attention from people looking to illustrate the reactionary representation of the rebellion. It may indicate, paradoxically, the problem of scholarly deference, but in this case scholars are not so much

getting it wrong, but not bothering to expand past the few points already within the general discussion about history plays.

38. While it is rarely considered by scholars, this scene contains the single most problematic line for reading the rebels in a semi-heroic position as Straw, in his frustration, declares that he "came for spoile and spoile Ile have" (606). This line confirms a reading of the rebels as the worst kind of tyrannical rogues, but it is a single line in a speech marking the frustration of the rebellion being undermined by Carter.

39. As an isolated moment in the play, the scene does appear to perform the sense of the political importance of literacy and the disproportionate access to power literacy facilitates—in the case of the neck verse "literature could bring man back from the grave" (3 Greenblatt 464).

40. Especially for Ball's persistence as both explanation and cause for his being eventually drawn and quartered, see Justice (26).

41. Longstaffe quotes from Chambers and observes that the 1611 citation suggest, at "the very least, the fact that a new version of Straw's death was still being staged twenty years after the first performance of *Jack Straw* [and this] shows that history plays were not, . . . unwriteable after 1600" (15). Longstaffe's rendition of the value of these citations is indeed the very least since simply perusing the play-list from those first two decades of the seventeenth century indicates that history plays were performed after 1603.

42. I recognize that reading Forman's perspective as an impression of the staging of Straw's death presents a textual/performance problem in that Nobs, while on the stage, is not active at this point in the scene. But given the limited stage directions, the mutability of early modern play-texts and the variability between what was performed and what was written for plays in the period, along with the inconsistencies in Danter's printing, this is far less of a problem than the simple fact that Straw is suspicious in this scene. Thus Forman, if he is referring to this play, has to be referring to someone in Straw's rebel party since he suspects everyone else.

Bibliography

Adams, Henry Hitch. *English Domestic or, Homiletic Tragedy: 1575 to 1642*. New York: Columbia University Press, 1943.

Andersen, Jennifer Lotte, Elizabeth Sauer, and Stephen Orgel. *Books and Readers in Early Modern England : Material Studies.* Material Texts. Philadelphia: University of Pennsylvania Press, 2002.

Archer, Ian W. *The Pursuit of Stability: Social Relations in Elizabethan London.* Cambridge: Cambridge University Press, 1991.

Aughterson, Kate, ed. *The English Renaissance: An Anthology of Sources and Documents.* New York: Routledge, 1998.

Bakhtin, M. M.. *Rabelais and his World.* Ed. Helene Iswolsky. Bloomington: Indiana University Press, 1984.

Bevington, David. *Tudor Drama and Politics: A Critical Approach to Topical Meaning.* Cambridge: Harvard University Press, 1968.

Blayney, Peter. W. M. "The Publication of Playbooks." In *A New History of Early*

English Drama, edited by John Cox and David Scott Kastan. New York: Columbia University Press, 1997. 383–422.

Bradbrook, M. C. *The Rise of the Common Player: A Study of Actors and Society in Shakespeare's England.* London: Chatto & Windus, 1962.

Breight, Curtis. *Surveillance, Militarism and Drama in Elizabethan England.* New York: St. Martin's Press, 1996.

Brie, F. W. D. "Wat Tyler and Jack Straw." *HER.* 21. (1906): 106–11.

Bristol, Michael. *Carnival and Theater: Plebian Culture and the Structure of Authority in Renaissance England.* New York: Methuen, 1985.

Brooke, C. F. Tucker. *The Tudor Drama.* New York: Houghton Mifflin, 1911.

Bruster, Douglas. *Drama and the Market in the Age of Shakespeare.* Cambridge: Cambridge University Press, 1992.

Burnett, Mark Thornton. *Masters and Servants in English Renaissance Culture.* New York: St. Martin's, 1997.

Carroll, William C. *Fat King, Lean Beggar: Representations of Poverty in the Age of Shakespeare.* Ithaca: Cornell University Press, 1996.

Chambers, E. K. *The Elizabethan Stage.* 4 vols. Oxford: Clarendon, 1923.

———. *William Shakespeare: A Study of Facts and Problems.* Vol. 2. Oxford: Clarendon, 1930.

Chartier, Roger. *Cultural History: Between Practices and Representations.* Trans. Lydia G. Cochrane. Cambridge: Blackwell, 1988.

———. *Publishing Drama in Early Modern Europe.* London: British Library, 1999.

Chartier, Roger and Guglielmo Cavallo. "Introduction." In *A History of Reading in the West,* trans. Lydia Cochrane, ed. Amherst: University of Massachusetts Press, 1997. 1–36.

Cohen, Walter. *Drama of a Nation: Public Theater in Renaissance England and Spain.* Ithaca: Cornell University Press, 1985.

Coleman, Julie. *A History of Cant and Slang Dictionaries,* Vol 1, *1567–1784.* New York: Oxford University Press, 2004.

Cook, Ann. "Audiences: Investigation, Interpretation, Invention.'" In *A New History of Early English Drama,* edited by John Cox and David Scott Kastan. New York: Columbia University Press, 1997. 305–20.

Cooper, J. P. D. *Propaganda and the Tudor State : Political Culture in the Westcountry.* Oxford Historical Monographs. Oxford: Clarendon; New York: Oxford University Press, 2003.

Cox, John D., and David Scott Kastan. *A New History of Early English Drama.* New York: Columbia University Press, 1997.

Cressy, David. *Literacy and the Social Order: Reading and Writing in Tudor and Stuart England.* Cambridge: Cambridge University Press, 1980.

Dobson, R. B. *The Peasants' Revolt of 1381.* New York: St Martin's, 1970.

Dolan, Frances. *Dangerous Familiars: Representations of Domestic Crime in England, 1550–1700.* Ithaca: Cornell University Press, 1994.

Dunn, Alistair. *The Great Rising of 1381.* Charleston S.C.: Tempus Publishing, 2002.

Dutton, Richard. *Licensing, Censorship and Authorship in Early Modern England.* New York: Palgrave, 2000.

England, Sovereign, et al. *Tudor Royal Proclamations.* New Haven: Yale University Press, 1964.

Finlay, Roger. *Population and Metropolis: The Demography of London, 1580–1650.* Cambridge: Cambridge University Press, 1979.

Fleay, Fredrick Gard. *A Biographical Chronicle of the English Drama 1559–1642.* Vol 2. London: Reeves and Turner, 1891.

Fletcher, Anthony. *Tudor Rebellions,* 3rd ed. Harlow, Essex England: Longman, 1983.

Fletcher, Anthony, and John Stevenson, eds. *Order and Disorder in Early Modern England, 1580–1800.* New Haven: Yale University Press, 1995.

Fox, Adam. *Oral and Literate Culture in England: 1500–1700.* Oxford: Clarendon, 2000.

Ginzburg, Carlo. *Wooden Eyes: Nine Reflections on Distance.* Trans. Martin Ryle, Kate Soper. New York: Columbia University Press, 2003.

Greenblatt, Stephen. "What is the History of Literature?" *Critical Inquiry* (Spring 1987): 460–85.

Greg, W. W., ed. *Dramatic Documents from the Elizabethan Playhouses: Stage Plots; Actors Parts; Prompt Books.* 2 vols. Oxford: Oxford University Press, 1931.

Gurr, Andrew. *The Shakespearean Stage, 1574–1642.* 3rd ed. Cambridge: Cambridge University Press, 1992.

———. *Playgoing in Shakespeare's London.* Cambridge: Cambridge University Press, 1987.

Hazlitt, W. Carew. *A Select Collection of Old English Plays.* London: Reeves and Turner, 1874. Vols. 1–5.

Helgerson, Richard. *Forms of Nationhood.* Chicago: University of Chicago Press, 1992.

Hirst, Derek. *Authority and Conflict: England, 1603–1658.* Cambridge: Harvard University Press, 1986.

Holinshed, Raphael. *Holinshed's Chronicles of England, Scotland, and Ireland.* 6 vols, 1808. London: New York: AMS, 1965.

Hume, Robert B. *Reconstructing Contexts.* Oxford: Oxford University Press, 1999.

Hunt, Simon. "'Leaving Out the Insurrection': Carnival Rebellion, English History Plays, and a Hermeneutics of Advocacy." In *Renaissance Culture and the Everyday,* ed. Patricia Fumerton and Simon Hunt. Philadelphia: University of Pennsylvania Press, 1999. 299–314.

Hunter, G. K. *English Drama: 1586–1642.* Vol. 4. Oxford: Clarendon, 1997.

Johns, Adrian. *The Nature of the Book.* Chicago: University of Chicago Press, 1998.

Justice, Steven. *Writing and Rebellion: England in 1381.* New Historicism; 27. Berkeley: University of California Press, 1994.

Kastan, David Scott, and Peter Stallybrass, eds. *Staging the Renaissance: Reinterpretations of Elizabethan and Jacobean Drama.* New York: Routledge, 1991.

Land, Stephen. *Kett's Rebellion: The Norfolk Rising of 1549.* Totowa, N.J.: Boydell Press, 1977.

The Life and Death of Jack Straw. 1593. In *A Selected Collection of Old English Plays,* 4th ed, ed. W. Carew Hazlitt. London: Reeves and Turner, 1874.

The Life and Death of Jack Straw. 1593. Early English Books Online. June 1, 2005. http://eebo.chadwyck.com/search. Reproduction of the original in the British Library.

The Life and Death of Jack Straw. 1604. Early English Books Online. June 1, 2005.

http://eebo.chadwyck.com/search. Reproduction of the original in the Henry E. Huntington Library and Art Gallery.

The Life and Death of Jack Straw. 1594. Ed. F. P. Wilson. Oxford: Oxford University Press, The Malone Society Reprints, 1957.

The Life and Death of Jack Straw: The Old English Student Facsimile Editon. 1593. 1911.

Longstaffe, Stephen, ed. *A Critical Edition of The Life and Death of Jack Straw.* 1593. Lewiston, N.Y.: Edwin Mellen, 2002.

Magana, Victor V. *Communities of Grain: Rural Rebellion in Comparative Perspective.* Ithaca: Cornell University Press, 1991.

Manley, Lawrence. *Literature and Culture in Early Modern London.* Cambridge: Cambridge University Press, 1995.

Manning, Roger B. *Village Revolts: Social Protest and Popular Disturbances in England, 1509–1640.* Oxford: Clarendon, 1988.

Marcus, Leah. *Unediting the Renaissance: Shakespeare, Marlowe, Milton.* New York: Routledge, 1996.

Marwick, Arthur. *The New Nature of History: Knowledge, Evidence, Language.* London: Palgrave, 2001.

Mullaney, Steven. *The Place of the Stage: Liscence, Play and Power in Renaissance England.* Chicago: University of Chicago Press, 1987.

North, Marcy L. *The Anonymous Renaissance.* Chicago: University of Chicago Press, 2003.

Oxford English Dictionary. Oxford: Oxford University Press, 2005. http://dictionary.oed.com/.

Patterson, Annabel. *Reading Holinshed's Chronicles.* Chicago: University of Chicago Press, 1994.

———. *Shakespeare and the Popular Voice.* Cambridge, Mass.: Blackwell, 1989.

Pettitt, Thomas. "'Here Comes I, Jack Straw': English Folk Drama and Social Revolt." *Folklore* 95 (1984): 3–20.

Ribner, Irving. *The English History Play in the Age of Shakespeare.* Princeton: Princeton University Press, 1957.

Rose, Mary Beth. *The Expense of Spirit: Love and Sexuality in English Renaissance Drama.* Ithaca: Cornell University Press, 1988.

———. "Foreword" to *Literary History as Cultural History: Essays from the Pages Of Renaissance Drama.* Chicago: Northwestern University Press, 1987. v–vi.

Sharp, Buchanan. *In Contempt of All Authority : Rural Artisans and Riot in the West of England, 1586–1660.* Berkeley: University of California Press, 1980.

Sharpe, J. A. *Crime in Seventeenth-Century England: A Country Study.* Cambridge: Cambridge University Press, 1983.

———. *Early Modern England: A Social History 1550–1760.* New York: Arnold, 1987.

Sharpe, Kevin, and P. Lake, eds. *Culture and Politics in Early Stuart England.* Stanford: Stanford University Press, 1991.

Sharpe, Kevin, and Steven N. Zwicker. *Reading, Society, and Politics in Early Modern England.* Cambridge, U.K.; New York: Cambridge University Press, 2003.

Shepherd, Simon. *Marlowe and the Politics of Elizabethan Theater.* New York: St. Martin's, 1986.

Slack, Paul. *The Impact of Plague in Tudor and Stuart England.* London: Routledge & Kegan Paul, 1985.

———., ed. *Rebellion, Popular Protest and the Social Order in Early Modern England.* Cambridge: Cambridge University Press, 1984.

Tillyard, E. W. *The Elizabethan World Picture.* New York: Random House, 1944.

———. *Shakespeare's History Plays.* New York: Macmillan, 1947.

Underdown, David. *Revel, Riot and Rebellion: Popular Politics and Culture in England, 1603–1660.* Oxford: Clarendon, 1985.

Wall, Wendy. *The Imprint of Gender: Authorship and Publication in the English Renaissance.* Ithaca: Cornell University Press, 1993.

Walter, John. "Public Transcripts, Popular Agency and the Politics of Subsistence in Early Modern England." In *Negotiating Power in Early Modern Society: Order, Hierarchy and Subordination in Britain and Ireland,* ed. Michael J. Braddick and John Walter. Cambridge: Cambridge University Press, 2001. 123–48.

Weimann, Robert. *Shakespeare and the Popular Tradition in the Theater: Studies in the Social Dimension of Dramatic Form and Function.* Ed. Robert Schwartz. Baltimore: John Hopkins University Press, 1978.

———. *Structure and Society in Literary History: Studies in the History and Theory of Historical Criticism.* Charlottesville: University Press of Virginia, 1976.

Wrightson, Keith. *English Society, 1580–1680.* London: Hutchinson Press, 1982.

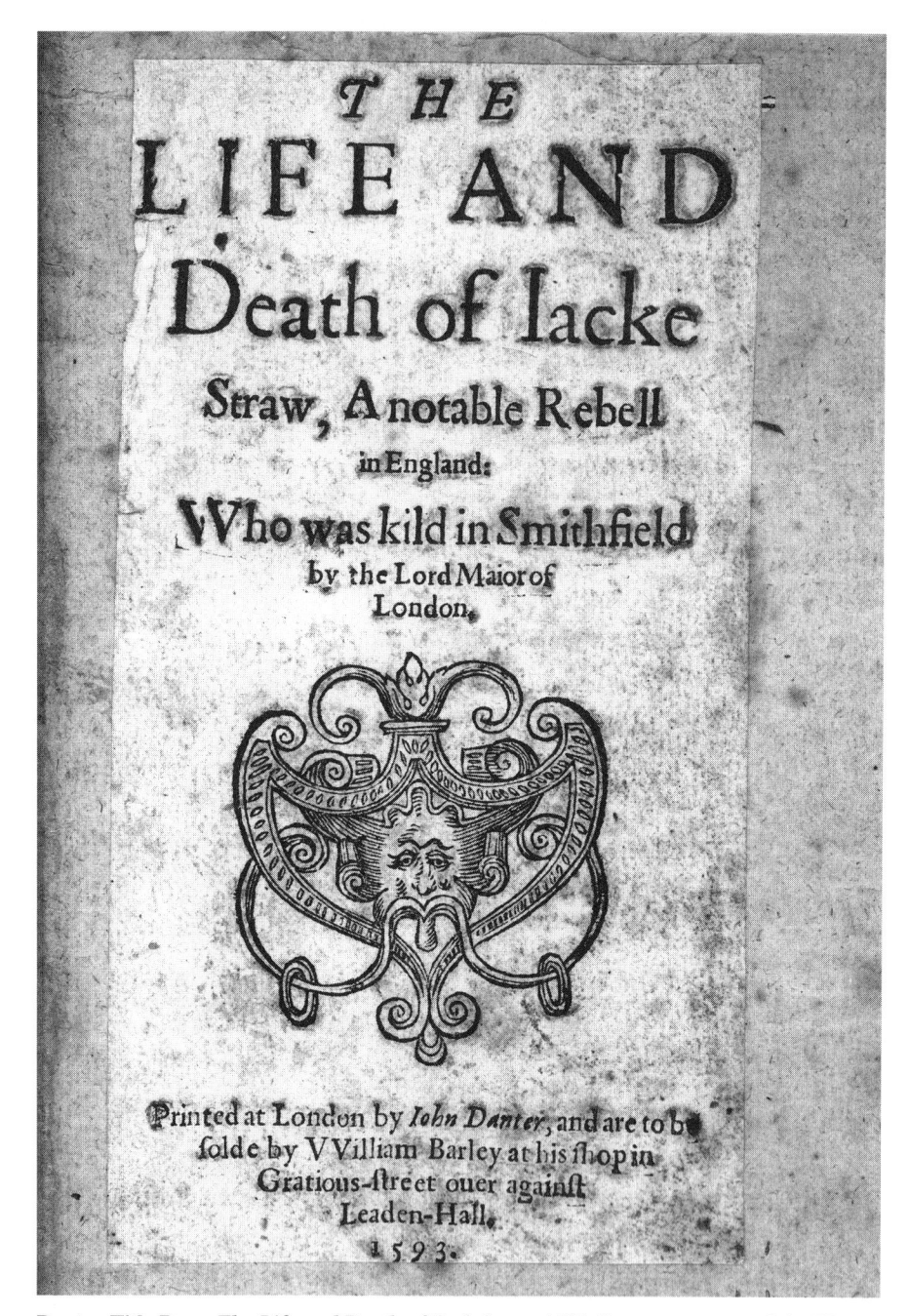

Danter Title Page. *The Life and Death of Jack Straw,* 1593. Image courtesy of the Henry K. Huntington Library and Art Gallery.

Pavyer Title Page. *The Life and Death of Jack Straw,* 1604. Image courtesy of the Henry E. Huntington Library and Art Gallery.

Foul Papers, Promptbooks, and Thomas Heywood's *The Captives*

James Purkis

THE British Library catalogue describes folios 52 to 73 of MS Egerton 1994 as a "[p]lay in five acts, without title, in which the characters are Raphael, Treadway, Ashburne, Lord and Lady Averne, an abbat, *etc.* Apparently *autograph;* with corrections and passages marked for omission." Since its identification by A. H. Bullen in 1885, the manuscript has been recognized widely as a text of Thomas Heywood's *The Captives,* a play written for The Lady Elizabeth's Men for performance at the Cockpit Theatre and granted license by Sir Henry Herbert on September 3, 1624.[1] But exactly what kind of text of Heywood's play the manuscript represents is less clear. The document has proven resistant to scholars' suppositions of what a theatrical manuscript should look like and remains the object of critical contention.[2] As a consequence, much of what the manuscript might tell us about the revision of early modern theatrical texts has been overlooked.

This essay seeks to better understand this troubling and important manuscript by offering a detailed analysis of the document's composition and annotation informed by a consideration of the practical demands of early modern theatrical performance. The following study thus makes available for readers the valuable picture of textual revision in the theater that the manuscript affords and casts light upon aspects of seventeenth-century theater practice. But this essay also seeks to make a general intervention within current editorial and textual studies as the field moves onto a critical terrain after the New Bibliography. The reception of dramatic manuscripts has been dominated by W. W. Greg's categorization of documents into "foul papers" and "prompt books," the former category representing rough authorial drafts that are assumed to contain "contradictions and uncertainties of action and unresolved textual tangles," and the latter, theatrical manuscripts subject to the "ordered levelling" of a bookkeeper, expected to show a degree of textual regularization and tidying as well as specification of performance details.[3] While many of Greg's methods and assumptions have been placed in doubt, scholars in different areas of early modern theater study continue to depend on New Bibliographical assumptions.[4] A recent description of the "making" of Shakespeare, for example, while explicitly aligning itself with post–New Bibliographical work and seeking to situate the Shakespearean text firmly in the Renaissance theater, includes a decidedly Gregian image of the "prompter," adding to the text "any missing entrances and exits," being "specific where the author is vague" and "likely to specify the number of spare people he can muster."[5] The continued operation of New Bibliographical assumptions is nowhere more apparent than in the reception of *The Captives*.

Extant playhouse documents, however, do not uniformly show the thorough and systematic revision posited by accounts that follow Greg.[6] William B. Long's study of the manuscript of Anthony Munday's *John a Kent and John a Cumber,* for instance, shows that in addition to six small cuts, Munday's autograph manuscript has been marked by only six annotations, each a simple repetition of an authorial cue.[7] Contrary to expectations, there is no extensive "tidying" of textual tangles in the document, and the author's indefinite and permissive stage directions are not supplemented with specific details of production. Long's important work has revealed the *occasional* nature of playhouse textual revision, in the sense that annotations tend to be made only in response to particular problems for theatrical production.

However, despite the undoubted importance of his studies of, in particular, Munday's text and the manuscript of *Thomas of Woodstock,* there is a danger that any study of an individual playbook (the term that Long prefers to avoid anachronistic associations expected of the "prompt-book") is taken to be representative of all playhouse revision.[8] Unlike Munday's text, *The Captives* shows extensive annotation, including the resolution of several textual problems, even if, as I shall argue, the principles behind its annotation are more consistent with the marking of *John a Kent* than they might at first appear. This essay is offered as a further micro-narrative of early modern theatrical revision to supplement existing work that advocates a rethinking of the reception of early modern dramatic manuscripts. In the closing section, I shall argue that this reading of *The Captives* as a further story of textual revision challenges a number of assumptions that the New Bibliographical "metanarrative" has occasioned concerning the revision and use of the period's theatrical documents.[9] In pointing toward a plurality of playhouse manuscripts of the same play, the following account also raises fundamental questions about the identity of the theatrical text.

The original text of the play, which includes numerous corrections apparently made *currente calamo,* is written by Heywood in a hand that has been described as "exceedingly rough," "vile," "execrable," "difficult," and as a "villainous scrawl."[10] Throughout this stage of writing, Heywood used an ink or inks that vary from almost black to a medium brown, but which consistently have a brownish tone. The manuscript has undergone subsequent revision in two different hands in two different inks. One reviser is evidently Heywood himself, who went through the manuscript after its initial writing making several alterations in a medium brown ink that for the most part is readily distinguishable from the ink(s) of the original, although making a distinction between later revision and changes made *currente calamo* becomes uncertain where the original text is of a medium tone. Of those alterations that may be identified confidently with this second stage of composition are a small number of verbal changes and corrections, "none of them of great significance" according to Arthur Brown, the editor of the Malone Society Reprints edition of the play.[11] Examples of such revisions are the replacement of "in heaven" by "elcewheare," the addition of the metrically disruptive, interlined "stands" in the phrase "and in my ffyxt thoughts stands Irreproovable," and the passage of the villain of the play, the bawd Mildew, from a "ffrenshe monsier" to an "Italian" and then a "Neopolitane Seignor" (ll. 1351, 1360, 75).[12] We may also surmise that on one folio Heywood added parentheses to clarify the sense and dramatic context of a couple of speeches (ll. 378, 388–89). The most extensive form of revisions that the author made are cuts. In his edition of the play, on the grounds of ink Paul Merchant identifies around 190 lines cut from dialogue by Heywood in revising his text, while a further forty are lost through the author's cutting of two of the original play's three songs.[13]

The second revising hand—which for convenience and convention's sake I shall call that of the bookkeeper—is described by Greg as being "almost as bad as the text."[14] This agent has been very busy, making a little over 110 annotations, in addition to several cuts, which I shall address in the first instance. In all the bookkeeper has canceled around fifty lines of Heywood's text through deletions that vary in length from one line to seventeen lines; so doing, he has also reassigned one line. The cuts are apparently shaped by a number of different, and at times coinciding, theatrical exigencies: the demands of censorship, the limitations of the company's resources, requirements for the play's length, and, perhaps, dramatic tightening.

The longest of the bookkeeper's cuts are to speeches by the young women of the play. Nineteen lines of the lament that Palestra delivers on having been shipwrecked and (she fears) having lost her companion, Scribonia, are canceled, perhaps, as Merchant suggests, because her complaint that "wee poore sowles wreches. / are punishe ffor his [Mildew's] grosse Impietyes" may have run foul of the censor on religious grounds (ll. 674–75).[15] However, later lines of the speech are also cut by Heywood, and the annotator may be taking his lead from Heywood's dramatic priorities to trim expendable lines. Nine lines of Scribonia's anxious words on seeing Mildew and his companion, Sarlebois, are also cut in what appears to be theatrical tightening as again the bookkeeper's deletion connects with a cut that Heywood has made, this time to the speech that follows (ll. 1072–80). Scribonia's speech at the sight of the villains of the piece functions to allow Godfrey time to exit and fill a pail of water before returning to find Scribonia gone; with Heywood's cutting of Godfrey's return, much of Scribonia's speech is no longer required and it has been trimmed. Beyond Palestra's lament, perhaps another instance of self-censorship accounts for the loss of the final six lines of John's fantasizing about Lady D'Averne, as he implies that he is doing the devil's work (ll. 897–902). The same folio sees the fisherman lose five lines of reflection upon the lot of the poor, which may also have interested Herbert (ll. 921–25). One other minor cut, the reason for which is unclear, sees the cancellation of one line from Lady D'Averne voicing her difference in age from her spouse (l. 1294). The bookkeeper has also tidied Heywood's cutting of a short aside from Richard by striking out the last two words that Heywood missed (ll. 360–61). He has in addition tidied other authorial cuts by crossing out the speech headings for deleted passages (ll. 2111–14, 2123–25). The annotator has further crossed out Heywood's call for music (l. 880).

The most extensive series of cancellations is found in the play's final and most populous scene, where Sarlabois and Isabel, Palestra's mother, are cut, presumably in response to the demands that casting this scene posed to the company. To excise these characters, an initial conversation between Mildew and Sarlabois is transformed into a soliloquy for the bawd by cutting all seven of Sarlabois's lines and a further three of Mildew's lines, as well as crossing out Sarlebois from the entrance that he originally shared with Mildew (ll. 2832–35, 2844–49, 2828). Along with her name at a group entrance, one of Isabel's two lines is deleted and the other reassigned to her husband (ll. 2984, 3024, 3059). A further change to Thomas Ashburne's line addressed to Isabel is also required, and provided by the bookkeeper's simple replacement of "syster" with "Brother," changing the recipient of the comment to John Ashburne (l. 3073).

The play's length must further inform understanding of the cuts made by both the bookkeeper and Heywood. As work by Lukas Erne has argued, "there is considerable evidence suggesting that any playtext of a length exceeding approximately 2,800 lines would have been subject to abridgement."[16] Before cutting, the manuscript runs to around three thousand lines, a similar length to the roughly contemporaneous quarto of John Webster's *The Duchess of Malfi,* which was described on its title page as too long for theatrical "Presentment" in its entirety.[17] The deletions made by Heywood and the bookkeeper reduce the text to around 2,750 lines. *The Captives* thus seems to give an insight into a collaborative process of abridgement between Heywood and the company's bookkeeper to make the play fit (for) production. The circumstances surrounding this joint cutting of the play may only be conjectured, and complicate the identification of agency behind each cut.

Heywood's experience of composing for the stage, as well as all of the other theatrical roles that his previous position as a playing sharer in The Queen Anne's Players will have enforced upon him, may well have made him aware that his text required cutting, and he may have made revisions independently before the manuscript reached the players. Alternatively, the players may have requested cuts from Heywood either on first reading or hearing the play, or later as it was readied for production. While the cuts seem to make sense if it is assumed that Heywood's cancellations preceded those of the bookkeeper, there is no certainty that all cuts were made in this order, and a complex relationship between the two agents in the play's abridgement is possible.

If the cuts demonstrate a pragmatic attitude on the part of the play's author and reviser, the theatrical annotator's treatment of stage directions is perhaps even more revealing of the practical nature of playhouse textual supplementation. On five occasions where Heywood calls for offstage sounds, the bookkeeper has made a terse duplication of the authorial direction: "Thunder" instead of the authorial "Enter after a greate Tempestuous storme" (ll. 456–57), "Bell Rung" rather than "The bell ringes to mattens" (ll. 867, 869), "Noise" in the place of Heywood's hardly elaborate "Noyse Wᵗhin" (l. 2033), "Noise within" replacing "Enter after a noyse or tmult" (ll. 2036–37), and "Trampling noise" replacing "A Noyse wᵗhin Trampling off Horses" (ll. 2743–45). As Heywood's placement of each required sound effect in the text is impeccable, the bookkeeper's notations seemingly serve to make the direction readily visible.[18] These supplementations, offering a "succincter duplication" of an authorial direction, are not inconsistent with aspects of Greg's descriptions of the bookkeeper's work in his studies of the extant documents.[19] But crucially, each duplication is concerned with coordinating offstage and onstage actions, and so marks a crucial point for theatrical timing supporting the emphasis placed upon the practical and occasional nature of playhouse annotation recognized by critics that challenge the New Bibliography. The functional concerns of these markings, however, might not end at ensuring correct timing. Perhaps significantly, with one exception, the duplicated sound effects involve the use of machinery or props. The annotations thus also, or perhaps even primarily, serve to make more immediately visible which pieces of backstage equipment would be required for production.[20]

In addition to the duplications of authorial calls for offstage sounds, the bookkeeper has also introduced several cues for sound effects that have no authorial equivalents. The manuscript sees the bookkeeper representing the continuation of the storm by adding "Thund:" (l. 469), "Storme contynewed" (l. 651), and "Tempeste" and "Thunder" (ll. 901, 903). He also notes a marginal "Trample" later on to denote horses offstage as both the dead Friar John (El Cid-like, with the help of D'Averne and Dennis) and Friar

Richard are about to take to the saddle (l. 2723). In these cases the authorial text perhaps invites these supplementary sound effects in performance, but these effects seem more cases of theatrical choices than something apparently demanded by the text. All of the added stage noises involve the use of the same equipment established by the duplications of Heywood's directions.

The manuscript sees a number of other markings performed by the bookkeeper to make authorial directions more readily legible. The annotator frequently places a marginal star next to Heywood's entrance directions, often connected to the direction by a line, and at times he also draws a line above entrances or interposes small vertical lines between the listed names to make clearer at a glance which characters are to enter (for example, ll. 67, 137, 485). On thirteen occasions the bookkeeper rewrites an authorial entrance alongside the authorial cue, listing only the names of those figures that are to enter (for example, ll. 455, 1497, 1584), or, occasionally, he supplements his rewriting of the characters' names with a terse "Ent" (for example, ll. 1068–70, 1300–1303).

Other duplications of entrances are different in form, but display the same tendency toward making the directions more readily visible. A concern with immediate legibility is evident on the couple of occasions when an authorial entrance situated within, or at the end of, a canceled section of text has been rewritten by the bookkeeper at the top of the cut passage to obviate the need to trawl through deleted text for directions (ll. 662, 1581–83). Both instances also save the need to turn the leaf to find the direction. The second such example involves the double repetition of the direction, both duplications emphasized by lines drawn both above and below the direction, as well as a marginal star, making the annotator's concern with the direction's visibility clear. In a similar vein, at the foot of fol. 61a the bookkeeper has written a terse "Noise wthin Clo: Ash: godf." (l. 1428), duplicating the authorial direction "Enter after a great noyse wth in: The Clowne meetinge wth Ashburne and god-ffrey" (ll. 1429–30) that appears at the head of the following folio. The duplication is evidently made to allow a complex entrance, accompanied by offstage sounds, to be discernible in good time as locating the authorial direction at the head of the verso side entails the turning of a leaf and cannot be glanced at in advance. The same verso page sees the only anticipatory duplication of an entrance cue that appears on the same page as the authorial original (ll. 1464–67). This duplication is apparently brought about by the specific theatrical needs of a group entry that included, one assumes, a figure that made only occasional appearances onstage, as one of the "Coontry ffellowes" due to enter is played by a stage keeper, identified marginally as "Stage" (l. 1492).[21] Again, backstage noise preceding the entrance is also called for, perhaps requiring further action on the bookkeeper's part.

On one occasion, the annotations appear not to be concerned with effecting authorial directions, but introduce a change of staging. This instance is made slightly unclear because the original entrance has not been deleted: Heywood's "Enter Att one Doore L Averne. and Dennis wth the ffryar Armed at the other ffryar Richard and the Baker" is only supplemented by the addition of a star and lines to increase its legibility (ll. 2726–27). Yet it is evident that through a second phase of theatrical revision (perhaps separated from the initial supplementation by seconds, perhaps by weeks) a scene involving two different groups of characters envisaged by Heywood as taking place on different sides of the stage at least in part simultaneously is split in two temporally. After the first three speeches following this group entrance are shared by D'Averne and Dennis, the Baker and Richard are given the next thirteen lines while D'Averne and Dennis remain silent for the rest of the scene. Opposite the fourth line of dialogue between Richard and the Baker, the bookkeeper has marked an entrance for them, indicating that a separate and later entrance for these characters is to take place, although presumably not at this precise point (l. 2736). As Dennis and D'Averne must exit at some point before they perform an entrance written for them by Heywood immediately following the exchange between the Baker and Richard (l. 2746), and Heywood has not given them an exit at any point, the bookkeeper's splitting of the entrance probably reflects a decision to place the pairs on stage sequentially rather than simultaneously, with D'Averne and Dennis making their exit while or before the Baker and Richard converse.[22]

Heywood's entrance directions have occasioned further attention in another form resembling the sort of textual tidying that one might associate with an editor today, and which New Bibliographical orthodoxy suggests would be the customary work of the bookkeeper. The annotator has made corrections to two entrance directions where Heywood has seemingly erred, first by interlining "Dennis" with a caret among the other characters in a group entrance where the author has overlooked him, and then by writing "Thom" over the top of Heywood's "Ihon" to identify the correct Ashburne brother in a later group entrance (ll. 1721, 2985). The reviser also adds an entrance for Richard where the author has not provided one (l. 790), and he marks both a couple of exits not specified by the author (ll. 962, 2099), and four exeunts at the end of scenes (ll. 1427, 1719, 2573, 2724).

The annotator resolves further textual problems by noting as speaking "within" both the Baker and Dennis where Heywood has provided lines but no entrance for the characters (ll. 2492, 2584–86). The added direction for the Baker sees the annotator mark the character's first speech as occurring "within" twice, once, to the right with the addition of "Bak: wthin," and more clearly in the left margin with the direction "wthin Baker," both directions over- and underlined for visibility (ll. 2584, 2586). The Baker has a further two speeches in this short dialogue with Friar Richard that are evidently still spoken from "within," as in his final speech the character explains that, with the action taking place early in the morning, he is yet to "ryse" (l. 2587). The bookkeeper has not marked these speeches as taking place "within," however, presumably because staging was clear.

The instance of Dennis's speech from "within" is less straightforward. Only the first of his three speeches is marked as happening "within," although like the Baker's speeches it is likely that all three speeches in his dialogue with D'Averne are delivered from offstage.[23] However, the bookkeeper has also added Dennis to the opening stage direction of the scene, twenty-seven lines earlier (l. 2465). Mariko Ichikawa notes that a number of other theatrical texts, in both manuscript and print, mark entrances for characters that remain "within," and that on occasions characters marked as "within" may have been visible, located "above" or in the discovery space at the back of the stage; it is possible that this is the bookkeeper's intention for this entrance.[24] It seems equally likely, however, that the addition of the entrance results from an earlier revision, made before the annotator thought through the scene's staging and established that Dennis is to remain offstage throughout his conversation with D'Averne. Like the duplicated entrance at line 2736, the bookkeeper evidently did not think it necessary to strike out the earlier direction, perhaps because it occurs on the same folio and the direction for speech "within" is easily visible; the earlier entrance may even have served as a useful reminder of Dennis's imminent involvement. Finally, the annotator makes a further note for a speech "within" by duplicating Heywood's call for an offstage voice, marking both sides of the dialogue the speech as "wthin" (ll. 2774–75). We shall never know, of course, whether the bookkeeper's added directions conform with what Heywood had in mind, but the possible problems over Dennis's speaking "within" after entering notwithstanding, the supplementations provide neat, practical solutions to the problems occasioned by Heywood's text.

Beyond his work to supplement authorial entrances, *The Captives*' bookkeeper exhibits further, and at times elaborate, concerns with the traffic of actors upon the stage. This concern is evident in the unusual use of the annotation "cleare" to mark an empty stage (used fourteen times, for example at ll. 293, 454, 1248, 1428), in the addition of constructions such as "to ye clown," "to them," and "to him" to authorial entrances (see, for example, ll. 2530, 2850, 2861, 2985), as well as in occasional marking of "manet" for characters left on the stage following the exit of other characters (ll. 437, 885, 2099).[25] The frequency of annotations marking either an empty stage or an entrance to another character or characters gestures toward a systematic approach; nevertheless, there remain more entrances "to" other characters that are untouched by the bookkeeper than directions that he has supplemented, and several occasions when the stage is cleared are not marked, so his work is far from comprehensive.

If there is something almost systematic about the bookkeeper's notations of the "cleare" stage, then other annotations regarding player traffic are plainly tied to particular circumstances of production. Four supplementations of authorial stage directions denote the personnel involved. At the beginning of scene 2, "Iack: Gibsen" is added to Heywood's group entrance direction for the first friary scene (l. 297);[26] the "Coontry ffellowes" of a later group entrance are identified marginally as "Gib: Stage: Taylo^r" (l. 1492); the busy "Gibson" is later identified either as John Ashburne or, perhaps, his factor (ll. 2605–6);[27] and in the final scene, with the resources of the company stretched by the congregation of characters from both main plot and subplots, the annotator has added "Stagekeepers as a guard" to Heywood's "Enter The Abbott the baker ffryar Richad prisoner and guarded, etc." (ll. 2804–5).

The most remarkable series of annotations concerning movements on the stage involve the complicated murder(s) of Friar John and the farcical action surrounding the disposal of his body. The play presents the murder of John by D'Averne and Dennis, who, in order to conceal their guilt, decide to dispose of the body in the friary from which D'Averne's house is separated only by a wall. Having climbed the dividing wall with the dead friar on his back, Dennis deposits the body on the friary's privy and exits just as Richard enters to find his adversary blocking his urgently needed access. Taking John's refusal to stir as a deliberate mocking of his "loose" condition (l. 2428), Richard strikes him twice, believes that he has killed his enemy, and in desperation hatches the plan to dispose of the body at the neighboring house. Using the ladder left by Dennis, Richard succeeds in depositing the body on D'Averne's porch where Dennis enters to find the dead friar returned, "com ffrom hell. / on earthe to cry vindicta" (ll. 2528–29). Annotations in the manuscript indicate the bookkeeper's particular interest in the staging of this complex sequence of events.

In the scene in which John is murdered for the first time, as D'Averne and Dennis await him on stage, the bookkeeper supplements Heywood's vague direction "Enter the ffryar wth a letter" by writing alongside it "Iohn to them" (l. 1759). A marginal "Fry: strangled" is added around fifty lines later, next to D'Averne's call for Dennis to "strangle him / wth all his sinnes about him" (ll. 1811–12). It is with the subsequent events, however, that the bookkeeper's concerns with staging are most apparent. As Dennis enters the friary "wth the ffryar vpon his backe" according to the authorial direction, the bookkeeper adds "from aboue," apparently referring to use of an upper level to represent his trip over the wall (ll. 2395–96).[28] There is no stage direction for the setting down of John's body—a couple of lines in the original text, probably deleted by Heywood, that read "wee. have our parts / heare on this seate. (nay hold your head upp Ihon, / lyke a goodd boy,) ffrely dischardgd our selffes" makes clear this action (ll. 2407–9)—but on the following leaf, shortly after Richard encounters John, the bookkeeper has again attended to stage business, locating the corpse's position on the stage by adding "Fry: Io: Arras," and then, on second thoughts, deleting "Arras" and replacing it with "Post:" (ll. 2429–30). At the end of the scene, as Richard resolves to transport John's body back to the D'Averne residence, the bookkeeper has added "carry him vp," suggesting that John will exit in a manner similar to that in which he made his entrance (l. 2462). After Richard emerges at D'Averne's porch a couple of scenes later "wth ffryar Ihon vpon his backe" according to Heywood, the bookkeeper makes the note "Fryer sett vp & left.," completing the stage business required for Dennis's entry to find his victim apparently returned from the dead seeking vengeance (ll. 2506, 2512). The annotator's concern with the bodies on stage for this episode concludes with the added "Exeunt," supplemented with "clere wth yᵉ Fryer," as D'Averne and Dennis head off to dispose of the body once more (ll. 2572–73).

The treatment of stage directions by the bookkeeper in *The Captives* manuscript thus exhibits textual supplementation on a very different scale from the additions that Long describes in his analysis of Munday's *John a Kent;* and the additions to the text take diverse forms. In its attention to the "cleare" stage, the work of the reviser offers something resembling a systematic, if far from comprehensive, approach to textual annotation. By way of contrast, other markings—such as those that denote the theatrical personnel involved in an entrance, as well as those that duplicate authorial entrances to accommodate either problems of staging or difficulties on the page—are more obviously occasioned by specific concerns for the text's use in production. Significantly for our understanding both of the bookkeeper's work and for theatrical textual revision more generally, many of these annotations do perform a degree of textual "tidying." In the correction of entrances in particular, we may see in the manuscript several instances of the resolution of minor "textual tangles" that a New Bibliographical understanding of a "promptbook" (or even "something antecedent to it," as Greg proposed was the case with *The Captives*) would lead us to expect.[29]

Other work by the bookkeeper beyond his treatment of stage directions performs similar rectification of textual problems. On three occasions the annotator has revised a speech heading given by the author where it appears to him that Heywood's text is deficient. In the first scene, the bookkeeper has amended what appears to be a clear mistake by reassigning to Sarlebois a speech arguing for Mildew's trustworthiness that Heywood's text gives to Mildew himself (l. 172). In the following scene, during an exchange between the Abbott, Friar John, and Friar Richard, Heywood has left one speaker indeterminate by writing the speech heading "ffryar," and the bookkeeper has determined the speaker by adding "Rich" (l. 346; there are other, nameless friars on stage to whom the line might be assigned, but the revision makes sense). Two scenes later, Heywood's text is similarly indeterminate, and the bookkeeper has made what appears a straightforward identification of the "ffryar" to speak a couple of lines by appending "Iohn" to the heading (l. 806; this designation is complicated by a ruled line separating John's speech into two, but again, the bookkeeper's intervention appears correct). However, any sense of the bookkeeper's textual "tidying" that we might wish to infer from the manuscript—or, indeed, any conclusions that we may be tempted to draw from his sporadically systematic tendencies—must be qualified carefully. Recognition of these limitations has important consequences for New Bibliographical conceptions of the bookkeeper's work, and for our comprehension of the nature of textual socialization in the early modern playhouse.

First of all, on a couple of occasions textual tidying is the opposite of what is achieved by the bookkeeper's contributions to the manuscript. For the added entrance for Richard and the Baker discussed above, the bookkeeper's annotations are plainly concerned with theatrical choice rather than correction of error, and his supplementations have *introduced* what an editor would identify as a textual tangle through the duplication of an entrance. The addition of both a "within" direction and an entrance for Dennis might also fall short of textual tidying, introducing one textual problem for another. But most importantly, even where "tidying" does take place, such as in the emendation of entrances, it appears that the bookkeeper's work remains guided by a sense of practical theatrical concerns rather than any notion of "perfecting" the text. This is to say that some textual "tangles" raise theatrical problems and others do not, and the bookkeeper tends to respond only to the former where textual and theatrical problems coincide. In this regard, like the annotation of the *John a Kent* manuscript, *The Captives*' supplementations respond to problems for production. It is just that Heywood's manuscript, through its poor penmanship, the dialogue's sprawl to the right-hand side of the leaf, the play's more demanding dramaturgy, and the presence of a number of errors and problematic indeterminacies, has occasioned much more extensive supplementation than Munday's text.

The corrected speech headings that I have mentioned above, for example, resolve theatrical questions as well as problems that we may see as intrinsic to the text (ll. 172, 346, 806). The two indeterminate speeches must be given to a character, they must be copied and given to a player as lines in his part, while the reassignment of Mildew's speech makes (better) dramatic sense of the line. On other occasions, where the speaker is clear (or at least was clear to the bookkeeper) but the designation is textually inconsistent, no alteration is made. One character transforms from "ffisher" to "Grip" or "gripus" and back again in speech headings and stage directions, appearing as "ffisher" and "Gripus" in the same scene within six lines when a sudden and temporary transformation to individuality takes place (ll. 2353, 2359). Another character is similarly multiply designated in speech headings as "woman" (ll. 2039–83), and "Wyffe" or "Wyff" (ll. 2319–49), as well as in entrance directions by "Ashburne, his wyffe" (l. 2037), "the wyff" (l. 2316), and "Isabel," the last of which has been deleted only because her presence in the scene has been cut (l. 2984). And an aberrant speech heading denotes as

"Madam" (l. 1284) a character otherwise designated in speech headings as "Mayde" or "Myde" (for example, ll. 1254, 1754), and as Lady D'Averne's "mayde," "maid Millesant," and "the wytinge myde" in stage directions (ll. 1252, 3212, 1721). None of these inconsistencies is tidied by the bookkeeper because, one assumes, none of them mattered for the play's production. A consideration of what else the bookkeeper has not "corrected" or seen fit to add to the text makes more evident his practical, occasional concerns with making what we might call a text "sufficient" for playhouse use, rather than a text either "complete" by modern editorial standards, or that conforms to New Bibliographical assumptions of the appearance of "a properly constructed prompt book."[30]

Despite the bookkeeper's significant attention to entrances, and in a more constrained sense to speech headings—as well as to the annotations that accompany the murder of John and the farcical adventures of his body, which take on an almost "editorial" appearance by making the staging intelligible—by modern standards of textual completeness the stage directions supplied by both the author and the annotator of *The Captives* remain woefully deficient. If we focus upon entrances and exits for a moment—features that Stanley Wells identifies as "essentials" for modern readers[31]—the "deficiency" of *The Captives*' stage directions becomes clear. In the scene in which John is murdered for the first time, for instance, even as the bookkeeper has supplemented Heywood's entrance direction for John and added a note of his strangulation, he has not added an exit for Lady D'Averne where Heywood has not provided one, nor has he supplied an exit for the maid who lets John into the house and evidently leaves the stage after a short conversation with the Friar (ll. 1746, 1793). The bookkeeper has also not added an "exeunt" at the end of the scene, although his note that the stage is "clere" demonstrates his interest in stage traffic (l. 1891).

The scene of John's first murder is far from exceptional in the inattention to exits on the part of both author and annotator. In all, Brown's commentary notes twenty-two exits that are missing from the text, but he does not attend to any absent exits or exeunts at the end of scenes or where the stage is cleared (perhaps inadvertently alerting us to the fact that such exits are not "essential" after all). Merchant's edition, which edits the "authorial" text rather than the text as revised by the bookkeeper, adds thirty-five exits, a number which matches my own calculations for the revised text. Given the evident attention that the bookkeeper has paid to entrances—which, with a single exception that I discuss later, seem complete, if overdetermined in the two instances described above—it becomes difficult to ascribe the absence within the text of so many exits to the bookkeeper's carelessness; rather, it would appear that the text was simply not seen by its annotator as deficient at these points.

The existence of such "deficiencies" becomes explicable if we re-situate the playbook within the playhouse. Gary Taylor introduces in evocative terms the important matter of what was involved in the staging of Shakespeare's plays that did not involve textual inscription. He asserts that Shakespeare could rely upon the players

> to bring to their reading [of the play text] much specialist knowledge about the conditions and working practices of the contemporary theater, and the circumstances of the specific company to which they and he belonged. The written text of any such manuscript thus depended upon an unwritten para-text which always accompanied it: an invisible life-support system of stage directions, which Shakespeare could either expect his first readers to supply, or which those first readers would expect Shakespeare himself to supply orally.[32]

We know little of rehearsal practices in the early modern playhouse, and of the manner in which this "para-text" would have been composed and communicated.[33] No doubt the arrangements would have varied from company to company, player to player, and playwright to playwright. Contrary to Taylor's emphasis upon an "unwritten para-text," some of the supplementary instructions would have taken an inscribed form in the players' parts and in the plot located backstage. But importantly, most of what Taylor refers to as an unwritten "para-text" would already have been in place *before* the play was written, and would have informed not only the use, but the composition and revision, of the theatrical manuscript itself.

The theatrical custom of the player's acquaintance with the play coming primarily through his individual part, and the consequence that production "would certainly have required an adherence to the shorthand of established staging conventions" to coordinate players who had little if any opportunity for group rehearsal, evidently informed the textual marking of entrances and exits in playbooks.[34] With players perhaps unfamiliar with some elements of the play, the careful organization of entrances was vital to make clear when, and to whom, a character was to enter; and as we have seen in *The Captives*, the bookkeeper has paid careful attention to characters entering the stage. Exits were a different matter. Antony Hammond, remarking upon the relatively "casual" treatment of exit directions in playbooks, points to the practical redundancy of marked exits: "once the actor was on stage, there wasn't much the prompter could do to get him off again."[35] Indeed, as Hammond continues, "what an actor did on stage was his professional business, and was out of the prompter's control anyway."[36] An actor's "professional business" in performing his part seemingly involved a number of conventions and responsibilities, such as positioning himself in large formal scenes according to precedence and taking responsibility for personal props. Here, we might note that only three props are noted by the bookkeeper of *The Captives*, none of which would fall to the individual player's responsibility. Annotations are made for a "Chaire" and a "Barre" (the latter is deleted), neither of which is tied to an individual character (ll. 295, 2834). The third instance of annotation for properties—a marginal "Ink: paper ready" (l. 1341) and the addition of "wth Inke & paper" to the entry of Dennis (l. 1361)—signifies props that must be readied backstage because the actor is onstage and cannot at that point be responsible for them.

The player's "professional business" also appears to have extended to performing exits when the actor's part in a scene was finished. And we can see a number of the manuscript's "missing" exits are marked in *The Captives* in an alternative manner, more useful under the circumstances of theatrical production. The manuscript shows Heywood—by 1624 a very experienced man of the theater—responding to the demands of early modern playhouse practice by making many of the exits clear in the dialogue both for the actors that are to perform them *and* for the other players on stage who may have had scant familiarity with the other parts. In the scene of John's strangulation, for example, the two "omitted" exits that I mentioned previously are accompanied by lines that make clear that the speaking character is to exit the stage. The first instance sees Lady D'Averne respond to her husband's "Lett mee advyse you lyke-wyse instantly / retyre in to your chamber without noyse . . ." with a simple "Syr good night" (ll. 1741–42, 1746). Later, with a metatheatrical nod, the maid leaves Friar John to the devices of Dennis and D'Averne with the lines "my sceanes doon / the next act lyes amongst them" (ll. 1792–93). Under these circumstances of theatrical production it appears that marked exits were often simply not deemed to be necessary components of the playbook. Indeed, that *The Captives'* bookkeeper has sometimes marked "cleare" but left the accompanying exit or exeunt unmarked is evidence that his practical concerns over stage business did not coincide with the careful marking of such directions.

Significantly, the priorities over entrances, exits, and props exhibited by the annotator of *The Captives* are mirrored in the work of his counterparts that marked for performance a quarto of *The Two Merry Milkmaids* now held at The Folger Shakespeare Library.[37] Commenting on the annotations for entrances and exits that the quarto's two early seventeenth-century bookkeepers have made, Leslie Thomson notes that "[a]s logic dictates and these annotations attest, entrances are far more important to a bookkeeper than exits."[38] Likewise, the annotations for stage properties in this quarto are restricted to props that, in Thomson's words, are "large and/or the responsibility of no single actor." None of the personal, hand-held props that an individual actor would bring on stage himself receive attention from the bookkeepers.[39]

Within this framework of convention-heavy theatrical practice we may find an explanation for the careful annotations surrounding the double murder of John and the disposal of his body. The relatively detailed annotations that chart John's posthumous adventures are exceptional, as, indeed, is the staging of this episode. The stage business with John's corpse would be beyond the usual conventions shaping performance, and so a particular attention to staging was evidently required. Whether the annotations show the action being worked out by the bookkeeper or the company, or whether they record Heywood's unwritten paratextual instructions, is impossible to know.

The reliance upon an actor's professional craft also suggests a possible explanation for the manuscript's one "missing" entrance. In the scene in which Palestra's true parentage is revealed, John Ashburne gives the instruction: "call in the damsels / Intreate them ffayrely heather say wee' hope / wee shall have good newes ffor them," (ll. 2153–55). The demand is surely too explicit to be accommodated by a call off stage and must therefore be addressed to a character on stage; but according to the text as it stands, Ashburne is accompanied by just the Fisherman and the Clown, neither of whom respond to this order. Nevertheless, thirteen lines later, evidently in compliance with his master's command, Godfrey, Ashburne's man, enters "vsheringe in Palestra and Scribonia" (l. 2168). Merchant, in accord with a suggestion from Brown, concludes that Godfrey must have entered the playing area in time to receive Ashburne's instructions, and adds the required entrance immediately preceding Ashburne's speech.[40] According to both Brown and Merchant, Godfrey exits as soon as he has received this command and then reenters thirteen lines later with the women. Attending to the professional demands of the convention-reliant theater, one may posit an explanation for the absence of this entrance direction from the manuscript, as other parts of the text point toward the entry of Godfrey in time to receive instruction from his master.

Earlier in the same scene, Ashburne, Isabel, Palestra, Scribonia, and Godfrey are given a joint entrance by Heywood, in which they remain aloof from the Clown and the Fisherman who are already on stage (ll. 2037–38). After Isabel accuses the young women of being "strompetts" and threatens them—"I'l washe your paintinges off / and wth hott skaldinge water: Instantly"—she is given an exit by Heywood (ll. 2063, 2082–83). Fearing for the women's safety, Ashburne issues an instruction that, while it is unspecified in the text, must be addressed to Godfrey: "you syrrah vsher them vnto the ffryeary. / whence none dares fforce them" (ll. 2093–94). Once Scribonia assents to Ashburne's plan, Ashburne specifies in a further address (evidently but not explicitly) to his man that he is to "leave them theire. / to safety then returne" (ll. 2098–99). Heywood provides no exit direction, but the bookkeeper, making sense of the exit for Godfrey, Scribonia, and Palestra that is implied by Heywood's dialogue, adds the direction "Ex^t ma: Ashb:" (l. 2099). The manet direction clearly applies only to the Ashburne party, as the Clown and Fisherman remain on stage and introduce themselves to Ashburne straight after the other characters exit. The next stage direction that the text gives is Godfrey's entrance ushering back the young women at the request of Ashburne. However, the "missing" entrance and exit for Godfrey that comes between his initial exit and his return with the women, is, *perhaps,* already present in the text, embedded in the dialogue. Unspecified in terms of stage directions, Godfrey's swift reentry is scripted in Ashburne's previous command: "leave them theire. / to safety then returne," which is not only an exit direction for Godfrey of the type that we have seen given to Lady D'Averne by her husband, but also a command to reenter the stage after a suitable—and perhaps conventionally, perhaps paratextually, determined—period of time. Once Godfrey is on stage again, having reentered according to his initial command to "returne" in time to receive further orders, his exit in response to Ashburne's command to fetch the women back again is obvious and requires no explicit annotation. This instance gives us a possible insight into how far theatrical convention shaped textual inscription. The bookkeeper has marked with a star Heywood's initial entrance for Godfrey with the women and Ashburne, ensuring that the player is on stage for the scene, and he has also worked out and annotated a complex group exit that requires clarification as the dialogue requires some deciphering; but Godfrey's other movements have been left to the implicit directions of the dialogue and the player's professionalism.

As a final comment upon the bookkeeper's treatment of Heywood's stage directions, we should note that *The Captives* exhibits a number of "indeterminate" authorial directions of the type that it is traditionally assumed would be made specific in a prompt book by the bookkeeper. In the scene of John's "second" death, Richard's attack upon the friar's body is marked by Heywood's famously indeterminate stage direction "Eather strykes him wth a staffe or Casts a stone" (ll. 2432–34). In a scene where, as we have seen, the bookkeeper has been busy with the annotation of aspects of staging, he has neither altered nor supplemented the direction, leaving the text unclear on the manner of John's "second" death at this point. Several other indefinite stage directions occur through Heywood's occasional ending of entrance directions with "etc." (ll. 3, 870, 2805), or by his offering indeterminate directions such as "Enter An abbot wth his Covent off ffryars," "Enter the Abbot wth other ffryars," "Enter the Lord de Averne, wth som ffollowers: his mā Denis," "enter att one, doore, godffrey wth Coontry ffellowes," and "Enter . . . ffryar Richad prisoner and guarded, etc." (ll. 295, 809, 1306, 1496–97, 2804–5). On none of these occasions has the bookkeeper supplemented the direction with something more determinate; indeed, he has duplicated three of these directions with similar language: "Fryers," "Lo : Den : followers," ">bs : Cont : ffellowes" (ll. 809, 1307, 1497).

The indefinite directions of *The Captives* are far from unique among extant theatrical manuscripts. As I have suggested, *John a Kent* contains a number of such directions that have not been made more specific by the bookkeeper. *The Second Maiden's Tragedy* also exhibits a number of similarly unsupplemented indeterminate directions, such as "Enter the Tyrant with Sophonirius

Memphonius and other Nobles," "Enter Tirant wondrous discontentedly: / Nobles afarr of," and "Enter Gouianus with Seruauntes."[41] On one occasion this manuscript's bookkeeper has been similarly indeterminate in making a duplication, writing "*Enter soldiers wth the Ladye*" for his shorter version of an authorial direction (ll. 2221–22, 2225–29). That the bookkeeper of *The Captives* has duplicated some of the original indeterminate directions without introducing further specification suggests that the annotator neither required nor wanted anything more specific; the cases where he has specified actors thus appear as exceptional instances requiring clarification. That the experienced Heywood has used such indeterminate terms probably also reveals that openness in directions was, if anything, preferred to prescriptive and precise demands. Again, returning the text to the playhouse makes sense of these apparent textual "deficiencies." The same play might be performed in different venues, perhaps with different personnel, where the details of staging and of player availability would need to be determined anew and could be established in the plot.

Three further features of the manuscript's revision remain to be noted before I turn to examine what these supplementations mean for our understanding of the theatrical text and its revision. Firstly, the annotator has duplicated Heywood's act divisions for the beginning of acts 2, 3, and 4 in the left-hand margin, making the act break more prominent in the text (ll. 651, 1249, 1892), while the beginning of act 5 is marked with an asterisk (2828; whether this marking is specifically tied to the act break is unclear but unlikely).[42] These annotations are probably concerned with more than the marking of a formal aspect of the text, and again may be traced to practical theatrical matters. As Gary Taylor has argued, by the time of *The Captives*' first production intervals at act divisions were integral parts of the theatrical experience, offering a musical interlude as well as an opportunity for candles to be trimmed in indoor theaters such as the Cockpit.[43] The identification of act breaks would therefore be important for the running of the production. Again, the work of *The Captives*' annotator coincides with revisions in the marked-up copy of *The Two Merry Milkmaids;* each new act in the quarto is marked by the bookkeepers, who have even added anticipatory directions for the act breaks.[44]

The bookkeeper has also made some minor adjustments to Heywood's dialogue. He has rewritten the word "suite," presumably on the grounds of legibility, and replaced the author's confused "twharted" with "thwarted" (ll. 2995, 2621). It is probably also the bookkeeper's hand that has replaced "liberty" with "lyvery," and that has amended Scribonia's original statement that she craves water "ffor god-sake" to "ffor heaven = sake," presumably with the censor's demands in mind (ll. 2521, 1042). Finally, in the play's first reconciliation scene, in which Palestra's personal history reveals her to be the daughter of John Ashburne, it is probably also the bookkeeper that has changed Palestra's date of birth from 1600 to 1530, in a single annotation transposing the play from the present to the past (l. 2227).[45] Why and by whom this new temporal setting was chosen invites, but eludes, explanation.

So far, I have described in detail the revision of *The Captives* in the playhouse, seeking to understand the annotations that have and have not been made through an understanding of textual "sufficiency" within the practices of early modern theatrical performance. But what these annotations may tell us about the forms of socialization and revision that the theatrical text underwent in part depends upon the function that the manuscript fulfilled in the playhouse, as well as any further forms of revision that one supposes that the text would have undergone. Here we must turn to the categorization manuscripts, and *The Captives*' apparent resistance to dominant scholarly expectations. Over the final pages of this essay I shall argue that the manuscript's resistance to New Bibliographical suppositions forces a rethinking of traditional conceptions of the revision and use of the early modern theatrical text, and of the identification of the play with a particular manuscript or even a single verbal structure.

The manuscript's troubling status is evident throughout Greg's work, destabilizing the central distinction between "foul papers" and "prompt books."[46] *Dramatic Documents from the Elizabethan Playhouses,* Greg's early and most extensive work on the manuscripts, categorizes *The Captives* among the "prompt books proper."[47] Yet in his general discussion of the "prompt books," Greg saw the need to comment upon its "remarkable" nature, distancing the text from the class in which he had placed it.[48] While he acknowledged that the text "shows no more 'blotting', interlining, or alteration than many which we naturally accept as fair copies," what Greg saw as the "almost illegible" nature of Heywood's hand, allied with the "almost equally careless" script of the annotator and the absence of Herbert's allowance, led him to express doubts whether the manuscript was "a prompt book properly speaking, and not rather . . . something antecedent to it."[49] Seeking to explain the aberrant text, Greg proposed that the manuscript was an authorial draft annotated by the bookkeeper prior to the transcription of a finished "Book [i.e., prompt book] ready alike for allowance and prompting."[50]

Eleven years later, in *The Editorial Problem in Shakespeare,* Greg presented an almost identical analysis of the text; again he noted that it contained little alteration and elaborate cutting and annotation for performance, and again he offered the same reservations against its identification as a "promptbook." This time, however, he concluded that, as the play represented a draft that would have undergone transcription, "the manuscript would fall technically into the category of foul papers."[51] Greg's *The Shakespeare First Folio,* published a further thirteen years later, placed *The Captives* in the same category, but the manuscript's resistance to his assumptions over the nature of "foul papers" meant that it remained peripheral to the volume's general discussion of documents of this type, even though the manuscript is identified as the only extant complete instance of "foul papers."[52] When the document does reappear in the volume, it is introduced as a unique exception to suppositions that "warnings," or anticipatory directions, are only to be found in "prompt-books." Again, it proves resistant to Greg's expectations of dramatic manuscripts.[53]

Subsequent critical work on the manuscript has seen the repeated invocation of Greg's arguments against *The Captives*' status as a "prompt-book," as well as the introduction of arguments against its theatrical use founded upon its stage directions. But the manuscript's resistant nature is only reconfirmed by examination of its later reception. Brown followed *Editorial Problem*'s analysis closely in categorizing the manuscript as marked-up "foul papers," "annotated by the bookkeeper for the guidance of the scribe by whom the official 'book' was to be prepared."[54] Against the manuscript's identification as a "prompt-book," Brown cited the same reservations as Greg, and added in support of his identification of the text as "foul papers" that although the annotator "has supplied a number of directions omitted by the author, a number of exits have been overlooked."[55] E. A. J. Honigmann subsequently made a forceful case against the designation of the text as "foul papers," at least as he interpreted Greg's category.[56] But while he identified the manuscript as a "fair copy," pointing to the "remarkable cleanness" of the document, Honigmann also suggested that subsequent transcription would have taken place for the production of the "prompt-book."[57]

Merchant endorses Honigmann's analysis of the manuscript as a fouled transcript, and he follows Greg and Brown in insisting that the authorial manuscript was handed to the bookkeeper, "who annotated it carefully for performance, leaving it (though untidy) ready for transcription as a prompt-copy."[58] And like Brown, while summarizing "the extensive annotations of a bookkeeper preparing the play for performance," Merchant too supports his understanding of the text by asserting that further revision would have been required for the finished playbook. The annotated manuscript, he states, was left "needing only minor improvements, notably the addition of other exits and entrances" for the text's transcription into "a clean fair copy by a scribe for use in performance."[59]

Most recently, Grace Ioppolo has argued for *The Captives*' status as "a foul-paper text" against Honigmann's description, but similarly proposes that the manuscript required transcription and further revision for the production of the prompt book.[60] Ioppolo's argument for the manuscript's status is founded in part upon a reading of the manuscript's simultaneously "descriptive *and* vague stage directions."[61] Referring to the manuscript's opening entrance direction, for example, Ioppolo states that Heywood's "Enter Mr Raphael a yonge Marchant Mr Treadway his companion and ffrend. Etc'" (ll. 2–3) "would be corrected once the manuscript came into the hands of the acting company itself, which needed as much precision as possible in determining which actors enter when (and the annotator has failed to do either)."[62] Elsewhere, following Greg, Ioppolo also remarks that the manuscript "remains often too illegible to have served in the theater."[63]

By way of contrast to these scholars that found their analyses upon New Bibliographical principles, Long asserts that despite the document's untidy appearance "[i]t is abundantly clear that the bookkeeper is planning to use this manuscript as his playbook."[64] Rather than seeing the poor penmanship of its writers and its untidy appearance as disproving its status as a playbook, Long rather sees the manuscript as a "corrective to popular impressions about what playbooks should look like."[65] Unencumbered by New Bibliographical expectations, Bullen, the play's first modern editor, also remarked that the manuscript "bears every appearance of being a play-house copy."[66]

Determining whether the manuscript is an instance of "foul-papers" or a "fair copy" is beyond the scope of this essay. But the arguments against its use as a prompt book, or playbook, are crucial to understanding what the document reveals of the revision, use, and identity of the early modern theatrical text. Study of *The Captives*' supplementation in the playhouse, read in terms of the practical demands of theatrical production, places in doubt arguments for the necessity of further revision founded upon the manuscript's "deficient" stage directions. Emplotted within the narrative of playhouse textual "sufficiency" that I have presented above, the matters of the missing exits that Brown invokes, and the indeterminate or vague stage directions that Ioppolo depends upon, are revealed as a rather less secure means of determining the text's status and use. In fact, despite Merchant's rhetoric that implies that there are multiple missing entrances, the ground for the textual "deficiency" of *The Captives* is reduced to one possible omitted entrance, for which I have offered a tentative explanation. Even if this explanation is not accepted, it is notable that a similar deficiency is visible in the "promptbook" of *The Second Maiden's Tragedy,* where an entrance for two soldiers with whom the Tyrant speaks is not noted, but no argument has ever been made against the manuscript's status on this ground (ll. 1725–27).

Most problematically, arguments against *The Captives*' status as a playbook that appeal to stage directions place a priori—or New Bibliographical—assumptions of textual completeness above the evidence that the manuscript provides. Rather than demonstrating its unsuitability for playhouse use, the bookkeeper's treatment of stage directions shows that the manuscript has indeed been prepared for use in theatrical production. The most plausible explanation for the stars and lines that draw attention to, or clarify, authorial directions, is that they serve to make an at times cramped text more readily usable in the playhouse by the book holder. If the bookkeeper was simply annotating Heywood's text for subsequent transcription there seems no reason why he would spend time making more immediately legible, or duplicating, parts of a text that would cause a scribe no problems in the process of transcription. Most tellingly, there seems no other possible explanation for the anticipatory entrance marked at the foot of fol. 61a, nor for the double duplication of the entrance on fol. 62b at the foot of fol. 62a, than that the annotator is preparing the manuscript for use in production. In *The Shakespeare First Folio* Greg himself observes that the "bookkeeper seems to have annotated exactly as though he were dealing with a prompt-book," but he attempts to explain the supplementations by suggesting that that the duplications are made "as though the transcript were certain to follow the original page for page."[67] The coyness of Greg's expression betrays the implausibility of his explanation. The relineation that inevitably would have come with transcription of such a cramped text, containing so many revisions, would make the duplications unnecessary in the new copy.[68]

If the bookkeeper's annotations point toward the manuscript's use in the playhouse, then the other objections over the hands' legibility and the absence of Herbert's license must also be questioned. Rather than offering evidence that the document was not used in performance, the objections become problems for entrenched suppositions over the theatrical text's use and identity.

Greg, as we have seen, stated that the manuscript "is written in a vile hand that must, one would suppose, have made it useless to the prompter," an argument echoed explicitly by Brown and Ioppolo.[69] He further asserted both that the annotator's work was "almost as bad as the text" and, by the writing of *Shakespeare First Folio,* that "no attempt is made to distinguish" the annotations from Heywood's text.[70] Both of these objections must now be reevaluated. To address the revising hand first, the bookkeeper's fine pen and thin gray-black ink mean that many of his annotations are not always as immediately conspicuous as one might expect, but their difference in color does make them stand out on the page; moreover, a number of the annotations are marked with stars or lines which are evidently designed to make them more readily visible. His hand, contrary to Greg's suggestions, is clearly legible throughout.

Turning to Heywood's contribution, the author's hand undoubtedly gives the manuscript an untidy appearance, and compares unfavorably in terms both of ease of use and of aesthetic appeal with the authorial and scribal hands of the other manuscripts with which *The Captives* is bound in the BL MS Egerton 1994 volume.[71] Yet whether the manuscript is "often too illegible to have served in the theater," as Ioppolo contends, is far from certain.[72] Heywood's hand is perhaps not as illegible as is claimed by several critics. Richard Proudfoot, for example, considers that "Heywood's hand is perfectly

FOUL PAPERS, PROMPTBOOKS, AND THOMAS HEYWOOD'S *THE CAPTIVES* 149

legible, with practice," while we might note that one implication of arguments that the manuscript is marked up "foul papers" awaiting transcription is that the text must have been legible both to the postulated transcriber and to the bookkeeper himself, who could read the text well enough to make the annotations in the first place, albeit at greater leisure than would be afforded to the book holder in production.[73]

But of greater importance for our understanding of the theatrical text, though, are the assumptions concerning the playbook's use in the playhouse that lie behind Greg's argument. The supposition that the manuscript of *The Captives* was too illegible for use in the theater seems more than anything founded upon the persistence of an ideal of the "prompt book" as a tidy, directorial document that the prompter would follow word for word. Brown remarks that the manuscript would have been "impossible to prompt from";[74] but if we recognize that "early seventeenth-century bookkeepers were not prompters in the post-Restoration sense of the word," as Leslie Thomson urges us to do, and that bookkeepers were principally concerned with "synchronizing backstage happenings with those onstage" and coordinating the players' entrances, as Long argues, then the manuscript (again) appears perfectly "sufficient" for use as a playbook.[75] Heywood's hand may or may not have been too "difficult" for the book holder of The Lady Elizabeth's Men to decipher word by word during a performance, but Heywood's script is certainly legible enough for the book holder to orient himself within the text to identify the places of entrances, the (very occasional) need for attention to stage properties, and the timing of sound effects.

The other key argument against *The Captives*' status as a playbook that now becomes open to reinterpretation is the absence of Herbert's license. The identification of *The Captives* derives from its association with a play granted license in 1624. If the manuscript is indeed a text of this play, then orthodoxy would lead us to expect the "prompt book" to bear the Master of the Revels' endorsement, but the manuscript shows no sign of the censor's hand. The apparent preparation of this manuscript for use in production raises fundamental questions for current thinking over the identity of "the theatrical text" that has been the object of recent editorial attention. If texts other than those that went before the censor were used in the playhouse for performance, which appears to be the case with the extant manuscript of *The Captives,* then the reassuring fixity promised by the licensed promptbook—the established and singular theatrical text, authorized by the censor's hand in a particular document—is placed in question.

Further study of extant playbooks suggests that *The Captives* is far from unusual in not exhibiting the censor's license. By 1955 Greg himself conceded that the absence of Herbert's license was "[n]ot in itself a very weighty objection" to *The Captives*' status as a "prompt-book," and he noted that "out of fifteen supposed prompt-books at least four appear not to have borne a licence."[76] Of the four "normal autograph promptbooks" that Greg identified in *Editorial Problem*—the category in which *The Captives* might now be placed—not one carries the allowance of the Master of the Revels.[77] Indeed, as Paul Werstine points out, only five of the fifteen manuscripts that Greg categorized as "prompt books proper" in *Dramatic Documents* possess licenses on their final pages.[78]

Andrew Gurr has argued for the "inherent difference" between the allowed text bearing the license of the Master of the Revels and the text that the players performed.[79] He proposes that the licensed text "was designed from the outset to be an idealized text," serving a dual function as, on the one hand, the "maximal" text from which performance texts would derive, "trimmed and modified, in varying degrees of substantiality," and on the other hand, as the authorizing document allowing the company "to perform the play in London or anywhere else in England."[80] Gurr's account is too totalizing as a narrative to account for the particularities of the early modern theater; after all, not every play could expect a prolonged theatrical life that would require such care over its licensed form, while other plays may have undergone little or no significant alteration for the stage, depending upon an individual play's length, the circumstances of production, and its stage run. Yet Gurr's account does point toward one possible way of understanding the extant manuscript of *The Captives*.

Given the absence of a license, it appears probable, or at least we may speculate, that Heywood's manuscript of *The Captives* would have been transcribed and submitted to the censor as Greg indeed maintained. In this sense, Greg would be right that the extant manuscript *was* a text prepared for transcription. But crucially, the document was *also* prepared for use as a playbook. The transcribed copy, in the terms of Gurr's account, would have been the company's "allowed booke" of the play, the official licensed text that authorized and (to a degree) constrained performance.[81] The licensed transcript itself may or may not have been used as a playbook on other occasions of the company performing the play. But for whatever reason—whether it was to preserve the allowed book, as Gurr's narrative implies, or other reasons that we do not at present, and may never, know—it is apparent that The Lady Elizabeth's Men chose to use Heywood's autograph text as the playbook for at least one, and possibly many more, productions of the play. Critical projects that seek to present early modern drama as it was originally performed are thus faced with the challenge that there may have been no single form of the play, no single "theatrical text" identifiable with a particular manuscript.

The (postulated) transcribed text that was submitted to the censor inevitably would have differed from the manuscript that has survived, although we cannot know how or by how much. The transcribed copy of *The Captives* may or may not have included some or all of the cut or revised passages that are visible in the extant manuscript. The transcriber may or may not have taken the opportunity to bring in further revisions. However, it is likely that the censor's allowance would limit the difference between the two manuscripts, as it would have been "perilous" for the company not to have brought Heywood's manuscript into accordance with any "Reformations" that Herbert had demanded.[82] One may speculate as a consequence that what appear as instances of self-censorship in the manuscript may, in fact, derive from Herbert's demands, the bookkeeper collating the extant document against, and bringing it in line with, the allowed book.

To recognize *The Captives* as a manuscript prepared for use in production forces a rethinking of a number of assumptions that continue to shape critical work on the drama of Shakespeare and his contemporaries: the extent of playhouse revision, the "completeness" of theatrical manuscripts, the textual specification of production details, and even the identification of the performance text with a single document. Inevitably, the reading of the manuscript that I have offered in this essay, seeking to understand the text's supplementation in terms of textual "sufficiency" within the playhouse, is itself nothing more than an alternative explanatory narrative. But it is a narrative that responds to the particular story that this manuscript tells, and which brings into question the dominant New Bibliographical explanations that are often too sweeping to account for the particularities of the early modern theater. The analysis of *The Captives* that this essay has presented should thus be seen as a single story of playhouse revision, just one of many provisional micronarratives upon which new understandings of early modern dramatic texts might be founded as textual criticism moves onto new questions, and takes new forms, after the New Bibliography.

Notes

1. A. H. Bullen, *A Collection of Old English Plays,* 4 vols. (1882–89; repr. New York: Benjamin Blom, 1964), 4:99.

2. In the identification of extant playbooks I follow those enumerated in William B. Long, "'Precious Few': English Manuscript Playbooks," in *A Companion to Shakespeare,* ed. David Scott Kastan (Oxford: Blackwell, 1999), 414–33.

3. W. W. Greg, *The Editorial Problem in Shakespeare: A Survey of the Foundations of the Text* (Oxford: Clarendon, 1942), ix.

4. See, for example, Paul Werstine, "Narratives About Printed Shakespeare Texts: 'Foul Papers' and 'Bad' Quartos," *Shakespeare Quarterly* 41 (1990): 65–86; Margreta de Grazia, "The Essential Shakespeare and the Material Book," *Textual Practice* 2 (1988): 69–86; and Marion Trousdale, "Diachronic and Synchronic: Critical Bibliography and the Acting of Plays," in *Shakespeare: Text, Language, Criticism: Essays in Honour of Marvin Spevack,* ed. Bernhard Fabian and Kurt Tetzeli von Rosador (Hildesheim: Olms-Weidmann, 1987), 304–14.

5. Tiffany Stern, *Making Shakespeare: From Stage to Page* (London: Routledge, 2004), 144.

6. See in particular, Long, "'Precious Few,'" and Paul Werstine, "Plays in Manuscript," in *A New History of Early English Drama*, ed. John D. Cox and David Scott Kastan (New York: Columbia University Press, 1997), 481–97.

7. William B. Long, "*John a Kent and John a Cumber:* An Elizabethan Playbook and Its Implications," in *Shakespeare and Dramatic Tradition: Essays in Honor of S. F. Johnson*, ed. W. R. Elton and William B. Long (Newark: University of Delaware Press, 1989), 125–43.

8. William B. Long, "'A bed / for woodstock': A Warning for the Unwary," *Medieval and Renaissance Drama in England* 2 (1985): 91–118.

9. I take the application of the Lyotardian term "metanarrative" to New Bibliographical work from Paul Werstine, "Post-Theory Problems in Shakespeare Editing," *Yearbook of English Studies*, 29 (1999): 103–17 (103).

10. Descriptions of Heywood's hand come from W. W. Greg, *Dramatic Documents from the Elizabethan Playhouses: Stage Plots, Actors' Parts, Prompt Books*, 2 vols. (Oxford: Clarendon, 1931), 1:284; W. W. Greg, *The Shakespeare First Folio: Its Bibliographical and Textual History* (Oxford: Clarendon, 1955), 109; Richard Rowland, "*The Captives:* Thomas Heywood's 'Whole Monopoly off Mischeiff,'" *Modern Language Review* 90 (1995): 585–602 (585); Thomas Heywood, *The Exemplary Lives and Memorable Acts of Nine the Most Worthy Women of the World* (London, 1640), sig. Ff4v; Bullen, *Old English Plays 3:v. Descriptions of the manuscript are found in Arthur Brown, ed., Thomas Heywood, The Captives* (Oxford: The Malone Society, 1953), v–xii, and Greg, *Dramatic Documents*, 1:284–85.

11. Brown, ed., *The Captives*, x.

12. All line references to the play cite Brown, ed., *The Captives*.

13. Thomas Heywood, *Three Marriage Plays: The Wise-Woman of Hogsdon, The English Traveller, The Captives*, ed. by Paul Merchant (Manchester: Manchester University Press, 1996), 266–75.

14. Greg, *The Shakespeare First Folio*, 109.

15. Merchant, ed., *Three Marriage Plays*, offers a discussion of these cuts (20).

16. Lukas Erne, *Shakespeare as Literary Dramatist* (Cambridge: Cambridge University Press, 2003), 173.

17. John Webster, *The Works of John Webster: An Old-Spelling Critical Edition*, ed. David Gunby, David Carnegie, Antony Hammond, and Doreen DelVecchio, 2/3 vols. (Cambridge: Cambridge University Press, 1995–), 1:467.

18. That not all of these duplications are written in the left-hand margin, and the bookkeeper's pen is extremely fine, means that these duplications do not stand out on the page as clearly as those in the *John a Kent* manuscript. The direction on line 867 is to the right-hand side of the dialogue, but it is clearly visible since it is marked with a cross and with a line drawn both above and below the duplication. The duplication at line 2036, squeezed in above a centred stage direction is harder to see, although it also has a line drawn above it that distinguishes it from the authorial text and makes it more visible on the page.

19. Greg, *Dramatic Documents*, 1:213; Greg offers a survey of bookkeepers' treatment of stage directions on pages 213 to 221.

20. In one instance, rather than offering a duplication of the author's call for offstage sounds, the annotator has crossed out Heywood's call for music (l. 880).

21. If the use of a stage keeper as an extra player is unusual, it is not unique. The manuscript of *The Two Noble Ladies*, which may have been annotated by the same bookkeeper as *The Captives*, twice calls upon a "Stage k" to enter (MS Egerton, 1994, ff. 228b, 233a).

22. Merchant's edition, which is founded upon Heywood's final intentions and so preserves the common entrance, inserts an exit for D'Averne and Dennis at this point (*Three Marriage Plays*, 253); Brown notes a similar exeunt in the commentary to his edition (*The Captives*, 109).

23. While the dialogue's subject matter—the disposal of John's body—makes for a surprising topic to be discussed between different rooms in the fictional space of the D'Averne residence, Dennis's confidence in his plan to rid the murderers of the body, as well as the suggestion that he is, like the Baker, still in bed, make Dennis's continued absence from the stage likely. Heywood gives Dennis an entrance shortly afterwards "halff vnredy" as if he has just risen (l. 2512). Merchant's edition marks all three of Dennis's speeches as occurring "within" (*Three Marriage Plays*, 246). Brown, confusingly, notes an exit for Dennis after his final speech (l. 2502), implying that Dennis is to enter at the beginning of the scene as the bookkeeper's supplementation indicates, but makes no comment on the notation that his first speech occurs "within" (*The Captives*, 99).

24. Mariko Ichikawa, "'*Maluolio within*': Acting on the hreshold between Onstage and Offstage Spaces," *Medieval and Renaissance Drama in England* 18 (2005): 123–45. See also Ichikawa's *Shakespearean Entrances* (Basingstoke: Palgrave Macmillan, 2002), 129–31.

25. Alan C. Dessen and Leslie Thomson note in *A Dictionary of Stage Directions in English Drama, 1580–1642* that the direction "clear" is found only in three playtexts, one of which is *The Captives* (Cambridge: Cambridge University Press, 1999; repr. 2000).

26. Greg speculates that it is possible that this annotation identifies two actors playing friars, but considers it more likely that they are noted to set up the chair which is also called for (*The Shakespeare First Folio: Its Bibliographical and Textual History* (Oxford: Clarendon, 1955), 118.

27. The annotation "Fact: Gibson" that accompanies Heywood's direction "Enter Thomas Ashburne the yonger brother to Ihon A merchant wth one of his factors" is ambiguous (ll. 2605–6). Merchant suggests that Gibson is to play the factor (*Three Marriage Plays*, 20).

28. For a discussion of the staging of this scene, see David Bradley, *From Text to Performance in the Elizabethan Theatre: Preparing the Play for the Stage* (Cambridge: Cambridge University Press, 1992), 30–31.

29. Greg, *Dramatic Documents*, 1:203.

30. Greg, *Editorial Problem*, 156.

31. Stanley Wells, *Re-Editing Shakespeare for the Modern Reader* (Oxford: Clarendon, 1984), 75.

32. Stanley Wells and Gary Taylor, with John Jowett and William Montgomery, *William Shakespeare: A Textual Companion* (Oxford: Clarendon, 1987; repr. London: Norton, 1997), 2.

33. "Nothing," according to Peter Thomson in *Shakespeare's Professional Career* (Cambridge: Cambridge University Press, 1992), 92; see also Tiffany Stern, *Rehearsal from Shakespeare to Sheridan* (Oxford: Clarendon, 2000), Gerald Eades Bentley, *The Profession of Player in Shakespeare's Time, 1590–1642* (Princeton: Princeton University Press, 1984), and Peter Thomson, "Rogues and Rhetoricians: Acting Styles in Early English Drama," in *A New History of Early English Drama*, ed. John D. Cox and David Scott Kastan (New York: Columbia University Press, 1997), 321–35 (323–25).

34. Thomson, "Rogues and Rhetoricians," 324.

35. Antony Hammond, "Encounters of the Third Kind in Stage-Directions in Elizabethan and Jacobean Drama," *Studies in Philology* 89 (1992): 71–99 (79).

36. Hammond, "Encounters of the Third Kind," 79.

37. J. C., *The Two Merry Milke-Maids; or The Best Words Wear the Garland* (1620), Folger copy 2. See Leslie Thomson, "A Quarto 'Marked for Performance': Evidence of What?" *Medieval and Renaissance Drama in England*, 8 (1996): 176–210.

38. Leslie Thomson, "A Quarto," 184. But see also Charles Read Baskervill, "A Prompt-Copy of *A Looking Glass for London and England*," *Modern* Philology 30 (1932–33): 29–51, a discussion of a marked-up copy of *A Looking Glass for London and England* held at the University of Chicago in which missing exits have been provided in manuscript. Baskervill notes, however, that "[w]hereas exits are marked in manuscript only when there is no printed SD, manuscript SDs for entrances, which are more important for the prompter, frequently occur in addition to the printed ones" (47).

39. Leslie Thomson, "A Quarto," 198.

40. Merchant, ed., *Three Marriage Plays*, 238. Brown notes that the command is "[p]resumably addressed to Godfrey, who must have re-entered," but does not note an exit for Godfrey before his re-entrance on line 2168 (*The Captives*, (85). Bullen does not add an entrance for Godfrey at any point in the scene, whether by accident or design (*Old English Plays*, vol. 4, 179).

41. W. W. Greg, ed., *The Second Maiden's Tragedy* (Oxford: The Malone Society, 1909; repr. 1964), ll. 1026–27, 1655–56, 2162. Subsequent references given parenthetically in the text.

42. It seems likely that the asterisk is drawn to emphasize the entrance direction at the beginning of the scene as a later entrance on the same page is marked in the same manner (l. 2642).

43. Gary Taylor and John Jowett, *Shakespeare Reshaped, 1606–1623* (Oxford: Clarendon, 1993), 3–50.

44. J. C., *The Two Merry Milke-Maids,* Folger copy 2, sigs. E2r, H1v, K2v, K3r, N3v, N4r.

45. Brown, ed., *The Captives,* 88; Merchant, ed., *Three Marriage Plays,* 240.

46. For a discussion of *The Captives*' resistance to Greg's categorization see Werstine, "Plays in Manuscript," 489–90.

47. Greg, *Dramatic Documents,* 1:191.

48. Ibid., 1:203.

49. Ibid., 1:202–3.

50. Ibid., 1:203. Heywood's claim to have written, at least in part, 220 plays appears in the letter "To the Reader" that prefaces *The English Traveller* (Merchant, ed.), *Three Marriage Plays,* 108.

51. Greg, *Editorial Problem,* 30.

52. Greg, *The Shakespeare First Folio,* 108–9.

53. Ibid., 141.

54. Brown, ed., *The Captives,* xii.

55. Ibid.

56. E. A. J. Honigmann, *The Stability of Shakespeare's Text* (London: Edward Arnold, 1965), 206.

57. Ibid.

58. Merchant, ed., *Three Marriage Plays,* 28, 29.

59. Ibid., 20.

60. Grace Ioppolo, "'The Foule Sheet and ye Fayr': Henslowe, Daborne, Heywood and the Nature of Foul-Paper and Fair-Copy Dramatic Manuscripts," *English Manuscript Studies 1100–1700,* 11 (2002): 132–53, (43, 145, 144–45). Ioppolo restates this argument in a shorter form in *Dramatists and their Manuscripts in the Age of Shakespeare, Jonson, Middleton and Heywood: Authorship, Authority and the Playhouse* (London: Routledge, 2006), 94–99.

61. Ioppolo, "'The Foule Sheet and ye Fayr,'" 146.

62. Ibid., 148.

63. Ibid., 145.

64. Long, "'Precious Few,'" 428.

65. Ibid.

66. Bullen, *Old English Plays,* 4:101.

67. Greg, *The Shakespeare First Folio,* 141.

68. This argument is made by D. Nicole Campbell, "Material Adventures: The Production and Reproduction of Early Modern Dramatic Manuscripts" (Ph.D. diss., University of Western Ontario, 2001).

69. Greg, *The Shakespeare First Folio,* 109; Brown, ed., *The Captives,* xii; Ioppolo, "'The Foule Sheet and ye Fayr,'" 145.

70. Greg, *The Shakespeare First Folio,* 109.

71. MS. Egerton 1994 includes *Charlemagne, Dick of Devonshire, Edmond Ironside, The Lady Mother, The Launching of the Mary, The Two Noble Ladies,* and *The First Part of the Reign of Richard II, or Thomas of Woodstock.*

72. Ioppolo, "'The Foule Sheet and ye Fayr,'" 145.

73. Richard Proudfoot, "Richard Johnson's *Tom a' Lincoln* Dramatized: A Jacobean Play in British Library MS. Add. 61745," in *New Ways of Looking at Old Texts: Papers of the Renaissance English Text Society, 1985–1991,* ed. W. Speed Hill (Binghamton: Medieval and Renaissance Texts and Studies in conjunction with Renaissance English Text Society, 1993), 75–101 (98). At least for his earlier work for Henslowe, Ioppolo assumes that the scribe would have worked with Heywood in the preparation of a fair copy ("'The Foule Sheet and ye Fayr,'" 150).

74. Brown, ed., *The Captives,* xii.

75. Leslie Thomson, "A Quarto," 179. William B. Long, "Perspective on Provenance: The Context of Varying Speech-heads," in *Shakespeare's Speech-Headings,*

ed. George Walton Williams (Newark: University of Delaware Press, 1997), 21–44 (24).

76. Greg, *The Shakespeare First Folio,* 109, n. 2.

77. There are probably no traces of the censor's attention and there is certainly no license in *The Two Noble Ladies* or *John a Kent* (although the last page of the latter, where, presumably, license would have been noted, has been lost). The hand of George Buc, acting as censor, is present in the manuscript of *Charlemagne,* but the manuscript bears no license. The "original" text of *Sir Thomas More* bears many signs of censorship, but rather than granting license, Tilney demanded extensive changes.

78. Werstine, "Plays in Manuscript," 496, n. 8.

79. Andrew Gurr, "Maximal and Minimal Texts: Shakespeare v. the Globe," *Shakespeare Survey* 52 (1999): 68–87 (70).

80. Gurr, "Maximal and Minimal Texts," 70, 71.

81. Ibid., 76.

82. I take the term from Herbert's license for Walter Mountford, *The Launching of the Mary,* ed. John Henry Walter (Oxford: Malone Society Reprints, 1933), fol. 349 b. "[P]erilous" alludes to Tilney's warning to the players of *Sir Thomas More,* ed. W. W. Greg, rev. by Harold Jenkins (Oxford: The Malone Society, 1961), fol. 3a.

Women and Crowds at the Theater

Andrew Gurr and Karoline Szatek

AUDIENCES at the early modern theaters from Shakespeare's time up to the closure of 1642 were different from modern spectators in two distinct ways. First, they behaved as crowds, not as individuals, and second the female element in their composition influenced their behavior more strongly than the witnesses of the time were prepared to admit. The prejudice behind the early testimonies, and the effect of spectator behavior and female presences, need a careful and a cautious examination.

The chief problem with the available testimonies is that so much of it is obviously prejudiced. A great deal throughout the period was written by men about how plays could so easily corrupt women. As early as 1577 John Northbrook, after targeting the newly built Theatre and Curtain playhouses (82), wrote the following in his eloquently titled pamphlet *A Treatise wherein Dicing, Daunicing, Vaine playes, or Enterluds, with other idle pastimes, &c., commonly used on the Sabbath day, are reproved by the Authorities of the word of God and the auntient writers:* "If you will learne howe to be false and deceyve your husbandes . . . howe to playe the harlottes, to obtayne one's love . . . shall you not learne then, at such enterludes howe to practise them" (92). Anthony Munday wrote a similar diatribe in 1580.

That men and women went to plays for sex was a constant sneer. It became enough of a cliché to be repeated to Thomas Platter, who, in his *Travels in England* (1599), noted of whores that "although close watch is kept on them, great swarms of these women haunt the town in the taverns and playhouses" (175). So Dekker in *Lanthorne and Candlelight,* 1608: "Pay thy two-pence to a *Player,* in his gallerie maist thou sitte by a harlot." Men expected all married women seen at plays to be corrupted or at least corruptible. John Lane (*Tom Tell-Troths Message,* 1600, sig.F3r), Henry Fitzgeoffrey (*Satyres*, 1617, sig.E8v), Robert Anton (*The Philosophers Satyrs,* 1617, sig.I3v), Richard Brathwaite (*Anniversaries Continued,* 1635, sig.A6v), and Thomas Cranley (*Amanda,* 1635, sig.F2r) all made such claims. Of course, in a crowd the attention of the men hunting for a whore is unlikely to be supported by the play. The women, on the other hand, both before and after they brought themselves to their customer's notice, could afford to concentrate on the story.

Male fear of the moon-like changeability of women featured in versifying through the 1630s to 1642 and after. But Thomas Brande, in a letter about recent events in London dated November 8, 1629, showed the more basic male fear, the one that in 1642 helped to secure the closure of all playhouses for eighteen years. He argued that all women are weak, and those who show themselves in audiences or on the stage itself, as Moll Frith did in the Fortune's *Roaring Girl,* proved the women's vulnerability. Now the Blackfriars had actually put women on its stage. And despite the favorable audience reaction to women on stage, Brande wrote that "certaine vagrant French players, who had beene expelled from their owne contrey, and those women, did attempt, thereby giving just offence to all vertuous and well-disposed persons in this town, to act a certain lacivious and unchaste comedye, in the French tonge at the Blackfryers" (Bentley I.25). Brande and Prynne after him in *Histromastix* claimed that London was corrupted by foreign women exhibiting themselves on stage. The King's Men used to move from playing at the Globe to the Blackfriars in winter, so giving it to a French company in November was a concession to their French queen and her French visitors.

Curiously, after William Prynne lost his ears and his freedom for attacking women on stage, a later visit by a French company was better received. On February 15, 1635, a French company performed for Henrietta Maria at Denmark House, and two days later at her invitation for the king and court in Whitehall. Although it was Lent, when plays were banned, the players then transferred the company to Beeston's indoor Cockpit. In any the event they played in London for most of the year, even using a riding school in Drury Lane near the Cockpit, then they performed at court the next Christmas.[1] Henrietta Maria was a major social force at the indoor playhouses, but she was far from alone in influencing crowds.

Ample evidence for the power of women in crowds can be found in the society of the time. Women played major entrepreneurial roles in the everyday world of Renaissance England, particularly in capitalist ventures. According to Alice Clark, for instance, they became, at least for a time, more independent than their menfolk, and more influential, so much so that women led both men and women to riot, "particularly against enclosures and for common rights" (Davis, *Women,* 183, n. 38).[2] Another Alice Clark, a.k.a. "Captain," headed a mixed-gendered mob of weavers in Essex in 1629 in a demonstration for better earnings. The female weavers wore their conventional dresses; the men, in accord with Clark's bidding, wore the same, while Clark donned a codpiece (this practice of women dressing and behaving as men calls for further comment below). In Lincolnshire the 1603 siphoning of fens that were essential for watering cattle caused at least two hundred women to rebel. Later, in 1642, Anne Stagge, heading four hundred women, petitioned both the House of Lords and Commons to save their businesses and to help them meet their financial obligations. Stagge claimed that the queen's absence affected the economic downturn and lobbied for Parliament's assistance. One year later and immediately after a smaller demonstration, between two and three thousand "women assembled crying out for 'Peace and our King.'" They "hurled abuse and assaulted the republican members of Parliament, and blocked the exit to the House of Commons." Curiously, in this instance "male demonstrators went unmolested while troops dispersed the women, leaving slashed faces and three or four female demonstrators dead" (Anderson and Zinsser 411).[3] Many women also fought to halt land enclosures; their weapons, pitchforks and scythes.

Alice Clark's codpiece was a striking demonstration of her adoption of a masculine role as leader of the mob of protesters. Women's flouting of patriarchal standards for female fashion and decorum was never more obvious than when they dressed like men. It was the stage that was said to have instigated cross-dressing, since boy players assumed female roles. But Linda Woodbridge has pointed out that James I's own disposition toward homosexual relationships and cross-dressing induced women to wear breeches and to carry pistols. James's own niece Arbella Stuart fled the court disguised as a boy page, sword at side. One woman in particular of James's time who made a show of controlling her own life, financial concerns, and sexuality, and about whom many told tales, was Mary Frith. Nicknamed Moll Cutpurse because of her thieving exploits, highway robbery, and pawnbroking, Mary Frith adopted male behavior, as when she "procured her pardon" out of Newgate "by giving her adversary two thousand pounds" (Newgate Calendar 172). She also influenced crowds as a woman. Her personality, said to have been very much like a boy's, boisterous, disorderly, voluble, fearless, and quarrelsome, could also be quite sociable. She showed herself off in taverns, matching the men in drink and sports, without fear for her maidenhood. The Newgate Calendar records that the Court of Archers once attempted to punish Moll for having worn male clothing by causing her to stand dressed only in a white sheet in front of St. Paul's Cross during a sermon one Sunday. As the Newgate Calendar recounts, the court

> might as soon have shamed a black dog as Moll with any kind of such punishment; for a halfpenny she would have travelled through all the market towns in England with her penitential habit, and been as proud of it as that citizen who rode to his friends in the country in his livery gown and hood. Besides, many of the spectators had little cause to sport themselves then at the sight; for some of her emissaries, without any regard to the sacredness of the place, spoiled a good many clothes, by cutting part of their cloaks and gowns, and sending them home as naked behind as Aesop's crow, when every bird took its own feather from her. (174–75)

Not only did Moll prove she was not a hermaphrodite as many claimed, but like other early modern women she also assumed a liberty that affected early modern domestic, social, cultural, political, and economic life and was an out-and-out threat to the patriarchy, especially when she attended the theater.

No doubt, then, early modern women, the key "elements in the street life of the capital," could sway crowds (Fletcher 261). The two plays that best demonstrate female dominance in crowds at the theater, both at open-air and indoor playhouses, are Heywood's *The Wise-Woman of Hogsdon,* first acted in 1604, and, to be discussed later, Middleton and Dekker's *The Roaring Girl,* produced initially in 1611.

In Heywood's play the most influential character, Wise-woman, dresses in lady's apparel and runs her own business. She offers many services: headache medicine, midwives for unfortunate women, adoption (the distribution and placement of unwanted newborns onto moneyed individuals' doorsteps), prostitution, soothsaying, and marriage ceremonies. The young gallants in this play disparage Wise-woman, calling her "the Witch, the Beldame, the Hagge of Hogsdon" and "Inchantresse, Sorceresse, Shee-devill . . . Madam Hecate, Lady Proserpina" (I. ii. B3^{r,} C1^{r}). These names typify the abusive language and its implications so often pitched at women, particularly those attending the theater. Wise-woman, however, lets the scoundrels have their fun. She knows they will receive their comeuppance in front of their friends at the very end of the play when the characters, like audience members, come together as a crowd and finally comprehend the pivotal role she has played in their lives.

At the opening of act 5 all characters have congregated at Wise-woman's home, constructed of all the theatrical elements she needs to influence her audience. Second Luce, Wise-woman's assistant who has disguised herself as Jack, induced Wise-woman in act 1 to help her teach Young Chartley a lesson and make him return to her, his first wife, rather than his second wife, sempster Luce. Neither character knows that upon Wise-woman's direction, Jack concealed the others in different rooms. Boyster, Sempster, and Luce's father are in two separate chambers while Gratiana, Sir Harry's daughter, and a young woman whom Young Chartley also plans to marry, waits in another room. Sir Harry is sequestered with chair and cushion in "a close chamber" (H4v), while Old Chartley sits with Jack, or Second Luce. Young Chartley has deceived each character and does not expect the people that Wise-woman has tucked away will eventually confront him.

This last act shows Wise-woman's deceiving and manipulating each character to form a crowd she deftly handles. At this point, Wise-woman drops her scheming, but not her cleverness, intuition, or intellect. She uses these attributes and the crowd to disentangle Chartley's stratagems. Such tactics could easily influence a theater crowd to reconsider their own positions on subjects such as antifeminism, which this play strongly undermines. More importantly, Wise-woman represents one kind of woman who watched early modern plays.

Given the evidence we have regarding male/female interactions at the playhouses, gentlemen like Chartley might have attempted to proposition one or more of the respectable women; it is a known fact that early modern men and women of any class expressed themselves more vocally than we—especially at the theater. The women, therefore, would quickly learn of Chartley's indiscretions; they would no doubt complain of his abuse within earshot of reputable men, who would then defend the women's honor. Like the notorious instances when people in a playhouse audience betrayed their guilt; as Hamlet noted, any crowd held in a small space for a long stretch can create an uproar even from a small disturbance.

When we are in a modern crowd, we assume we are individuals. There is something too undifferentiated in belonging to a mob. We resent being viewed as part of a "many-headed multitude," the Hydra that Coriolanus saw in a political crowd.[4] When collected together as audience at a play, we assume individual responses, and engage professional reviewers to give us their opinions, presumably in the expectation that theirs will be, if not better informed, at least sufficiently individual to be worth reading. But there are signs that this self-generated distinction is dissolving under recent experiences and practices in theater. One of the lessons from the reconstruction of the Globe in London is that modern theater audiences, when visible to one another and mostly on their feet, respond much more actively and collectively than they do when sitting in a darkened auditorium. They behave like a crowd, not an aggregation of individuals, as demonstrated in Heywood's play. Crowd psychology in the form of group behavior has returned as a crucial feature of playgoing.

Crowd psychology is a complex, even confused exercise. Classical studies of "collective behavior" as a political force mainly derive from Le Bon's concept of a "group mind," and his "Law of the Mental Unity of Crowds," set out in 1895 in *The Crowd* as a direct consequence of the Paris Commune of 1870–71. In J. S. McClelland's rather abrupt summary, the group mind's workings "did not follow the same laws as the workings of an individual's mind because it was unconscious" (11). Clark McPhail's *Myth of the Madding Crowd,* as its title suggests, rejects yet develops Le Bon's reductive idea through systematic observation of crowd behavior.[5] This has produced a taxonomy of different types of crowds, none of them, regrettably for our purposes, including the relatively docile patterns of theater audience behavior. Outlines of "collective behavior" and the kind of study that belongs to it by, for instance, Gary T. Marx and Douglas McAdam, make that clear. They lay down a methodology that covers what they see as the seven factors in such study: legitimacy of numbers, illusions of unanimity, diffusion of responsibility, anonymity, solidarity, social facilitation, and immediacy. Their chief object is to identify patterns of crowd behavior in political crises (40–42). Of their list, only the second, fourth, and fifth, illusions of unanimity, anonymity, and solidarity, appear to have much significance in theater audience behavior, as exemplified by Mary Shiel and her visit to the British Embassy in Persia in the 1880s.

Sympathy or empathy with a mass show of emotion can arise even in the most alienated situations. While visiting the embassy, Mary Shiel recorded her experience of attending a Persian religious drama. First, the play was a Shiah representation of the slaughter in the desert of "Imam Hoossein" and his family (commonly performed in the month of Moharen), and the audience displayed such real grief at the enacted events that initially Mary, with her Victorian starchiness, was shocked. From behind the purdah screen, where she sat with the other women, she saw several thousand people give vent to their grief "in the style of schoolboys and girls." But, to her confusion, the "contagion," once it had started, spread to her also. "I too felt myself forced, would I or not, to join my tears to those of the Persian women around me," she confessed, "which appeared to give considerable satisfaction to them." It was a model theatrical experience, a classic expression of how crowd emotions even in the nineteenth century could overcome Mary Shiel's stalwart Christian individualism. Her own response, then, also affirms the magnitude of individual female emotion, an experience that applied equally strongly to early modern playgoing audiences as a whole.

Early observations on theater audiences have more force than modern analyses of group psychology. Bacon was thinking of his own experience of theater when in about 1622 he wrote that

> The action of the theatre, though modern states esteem it but ludicrous, unless it be satirical and biting, was carefully watched by the ancients, that it might improve mankind in virtue; and indeed many wise men and great philosophers have thought it to the mind as the bow to the fiddle; and certain it is, though a great secret in nature, that the minds of men in company are more open to affections and impressions than when alone. (*Advancement,* bk. 2, chp. 13)

Group response was dangerous for the new Protestants who shared the principle of salvation by faith alone.[6] Most comments from the time claim a necessary level of individualist detachment from a show that itself suggests how engaged and enthralled the normal spectator was. In our reading early modern theater productions, however, male individualism understates the force of the female presence in the early audiences.

We are beginning to recognize, though, that theater audiences work better as crowds than as isolated modern individuals curled up like eavesdroppers in their comfortable seats in the dark. Yet for obvious practical reasons little has been done to study the psychology of theater audiences as crowds rather than as individuals. Many studies have been made of crowd behavior at sports events, where the great majority of any crowd is male. The recovery of women's voices in early modern England shows, though, that women—even one woman—played a significant role in the forming and/or influencing of a crowd socially, politically, and even theatrically. What is ignored in studies of early modern crowds, and especially its audiences, is that the female presence in crowds affected behavior. There is a mass of evidence that playwriting changed in response to the presence of women in early audiences. Therefore, lumping early modern theater audiences together without considering one of the major components of theater crowds destroys some important distinctions. The companies playing at the open-air playhouses in the 1590s certainly catered chiefly to male audiences with their battle plays, but once Shakespeare's company opened at the Blackfriars in 1609 their repertory shifted its priorities, and within a few years John Fletcher's pro-feminist plays began to rule audience taste. His sequel to Shakespeare's *Shrew, The Tamer Tamed,* was on stage at Blackfriars by 1612. His play introducing a dominant female component into a war play, *Bonduca,* was staged in 1614. By the Caroline period the majority of plays staged at court were feminist, and Fletcher's were featured ten times more often than Shakespeare's.

Concepts of the group nature of behavior by theater audiences, and its powerful impact on performance, do in basic ways acknowledge the experience of the original audiences at the Globe and Blackfriars in London. The two factors need to be run together: first, the behavior of theater audiences as crowds, and second, the influence of the women who formed a major element in these crowds.[7]

The role of women in audiences affected not only Shakespeare's company. Jean E. Howard has studied Heywood's *The Wise Woman of Hogsdon,* written for an open-air playhouse, as a play thematizing "women as spectacle and spectator" (82). Whole families went to the open-air playhouses from the outset, and while it took the writers a while to adapt to the female presence, they certainly did so at the indoor playhouses, as noted. The notorious incident at the Rose in 1587 when a shot from a gun killed "a child, and a woman great with child," confirms the female presence, as does John Taylor the water-poet's verse saying that even beggars could bring their entire family: "yet have I seene a beggar with his many / Come in at a Play-house, all in for one penny" (sig.C4v). Women of different social status prevailed at both types of playhouse, in different ways. John Tatham, *The Fancies Theater* (1640), in a prologue for the Red Bull condemning the Fortune, grouped crowds indiscriminately as a collective ruled by the female voice, bringing in

> . . . a noyse
> Of *Rables, Apple-wives* and Chimney-boyes,
> Whose shrill confused Ecchoes loud doe cry,
> Enlarge your Commons, We hate Privacie
>
> (sig.H2v)

At indoor playhouses like the Blackfriars and the Cockpit it was the poets who had to acknowledge the dominant female presence. That Jonson set four women "gossips" on stage at the Blackfriars in his 1624 *A Staple of News* who speak to each other during the pauses meant that they were a familiar presence, epitomizing his view of a normative audience and its opinions. Only the gossips' decision to sit on the stage, where they were allocated a bench rather than the men's stools, picked them out as in any way a non-familiar presence.

Women certainly dominated audiences all through the Caroline period. In *Microcosmographie* (1628) John Earle wrote cynically of a leading player that "the waiting-women Spectators are over-eares in love with him, and Ladies send for him to act in their Chambers" (sig.H3^v). Queen Henrietta Maria went four times to the Blackfriars to see plays, the first member of any royal family to visit a public playhouse rather than wait for the players to bring their plays to her at court.[8] The dominance of women at the Cockpit was marked by James Shirley, in the prologue spoken by a boy player in *The Coronation*, 1634:

> . . . is there not
> A blush upon my cheekes that I forgot
> The Ladies, and a Female Prologue too?
> Your pardon noble Gentlewomen, you
> Were first within my thoughts, I know you sit
> As free, and high Commissioners of wit.

Plays that targeted the ladies in the audience, particularly those like Shirley's written for an indoor playhouse, became the prevalent mode by the Caroline years of the 1630s.

The privacy of television and video-viewing too easily determines current assumptions about theatre crowds. Richard Sennett noted that "in a study of . . . television watchers, the psychologists Robert Kubey and Mihaly Csikszentmihalyi found that 'people consistently report their experiences with television as being passive, relaxing, and involving relatively little concentration.'"[9] Those experiences largely determine the shape of all modern auditoria, where the two-dimensional alignment, the audience facing the stage, denies the Shakespearean theater's three dimensions, with the audience completely surrounding the stage. In such a situation, audiences could not behave like the passive eavesdroppers modern staging expects. Such viewing characteristics only grew with the footlight divide and the stage made into picture frames, with the darkening of auditoria, and finally with the even greater privacy of viewing from one's own room. We need to remember Bacon's comment on the responses of crowds, and even St. Augustine, who, writing before individualism, thought the experience of being in a crowd and sharing the collective emotions was so powerful that it could imperil the soul. In his *Confessions* he admitted that stage plays could draw him away from his devotions. He noted the power of actors to draw tears for a fiction, and the theatrical paradox that "the spectator . . . is not expected to aid the sufferer but merely to grieve for him." This he explained with the point that "a man is more affected by these actions the more he is spuriously involved in these affections. Now, if he should suffer them in his own person, it is the custom to call this 'misery.' But when he suffers with another, then it is called 'compassion.' But what kind of compassion is it that arises from viewing fictitious and unreal sufferings? . . . The more he grieves the more he applauds the actor of these fictions" (book 3, ch. 2, p. 62). Compassion, or pity, is an audience's response to tragedy. What is wrong in modern versions of such situations is its secondariness and its passivity. It calls for no direct action. Augustine was famously hard on himself, and famously skeptical of his own emotions. We have less reason to suspect our own feelings in such situations.

It is quite likely that such feisty attitudes manifested themselves in the playhouses, too. Naturally, this influence spilled into the theater. Tobacco-packed, sword-carrying, masculine-looking Mary Frith frequented early modern theaters. *The Consistory of London Correction Book* (1605) writes of her attending plays through the year of her incarceration. She would appear in

> man's apparel and in her boots and [with] a sword at her syde[.] [S]he told the company then present . . . she thought many of them were of opinion that she was a man, but if any of them would come to her lodging they should finde she is a woman, and some other immodest and lascivious speaches she also used at [the] time. [She] also sat upon the stage in the public viewe of all the people there present in man's apparel and played upon her lute and sange a song. (*JCS* 6.141)

Mary made such an impact that Middleton and Dekker based their character Moll in the play *The Roaring Girl* on her. This play celebrates Molls, and of course Mary's, control of the men and of the Fortune's audience.

Much of the evidence for public interactions depends on the legal records of female-led affrays, such as those already cited, and on ethnographic readings of plays. Victor Turner refers to them as theater because they are social dramas that function as part of the "anthropology of experience" (13). Turner also argues of these social dramas that "every type of cultural performance, including ritual, ceremony, carnival, theater, and poetry, is an explanation and expectation of life itself" (13). The literary ethnographer seeks narratives that recount and document the lives of individuals involved in a culture to which they are inexorably tied. The ethnographer regards the drama's characters as literary and, more importantly, as cultural informants. Thus, if the literary critic reads early modern plays ethnographically, then he or she can write a "thick" description, using Clifford Geertz's term, of what probably occurred in the actual world the play depicts. Thus, the above reading of *The Wise-Woman of Hogsdon* and the one to follow about Mary Frith suggest but two ways in which playgoing women actually influenced crowd emotion and behavior.

Both female leads, Wise-Woman and Moll Cutpurse, have similar personality traits. Both single, they have proven their ability to support themselves. Moll is less vengeful than Wise-woman though equally self-sufficient. Only she controls "the head now of" herself, and is "man enough for a woman" (II.ii.44–45). Like Wise-woman, Moll states emphatically: "My spirit shall be mistress of this house / As long as I have time in't" (III.I.142–43). Unlike Wise-woman, though, Moll dresses as a man. Other characters in the play comment on her garments, and the stage directions reveal that she wears "a frieze jerkin and a black saveguard" (II.i.38). Because of her "Otherness," the play's male characters label her a "Roaring Girl." But in the play Moll demonstrates her honesty, beneficence, and even virtuousness. As she says, "But being awake, I keep my legs together" (IV.i.130). Moll certainly knows thieves and their practices. As she admits in V.i. she "was apt to stray" when she was young, but she did not cut purses. She offers her experience as a playgoer patterning her behavior now. Then she "sat amongst such adders" in "full playhouses," where she "watch'd" thieves' "quick-diving hands, to bring to shame / Such rogues" (329–34). More than once she raises her sword to defend either herself or someone else from villains. She also prevents the arrest of Sir Davy's son Jack Dapper by the local sergeant, Curtleax, because she understands Jack's youthful scampering will dwindle as he matures. Whenever Moll chooses to favor or oppose another person—Jack, Curtleax, Laxton, and Trapdoor—she alone influences the outcome their situations.

In addition to a quick and ready wit that she exploits throughout the play, Moll's attire enables her to fight. Although Wise-woman dresses according to custom, society marginalizes her as much as Moll. Wise-woman even lives apart from the urban community, which further amplifies her nonconforming nature. When juxtaposed against the men and other female characters, who appear as wenches, maidens, patient wives, gossips, and/or superficial simpletons, both women emerge as self-assured, self-reliant, clever, independent, and altogether equipped to sway individuals' attitudes and actions.

Besides women who conformed to patriarchal demands, "wise-women" and "molls" could be seen in playhouses. Many of these women motivated male responses. Some women frequented the plays alone or with other women. They sometimes ignored, flirted, trifled with, and even solicited individual men, as noted above.

Although somewhat similar, Moll Cutpurse's approach to managing crowds differs from Wise-woman's. Moll does not ordinarily depend on circular logic, manipulation, backbiting, subterfuges, or underhandedness to alter situations, to capture a husband, or to command a crowd. Instead, Moll addresses people, whether individuals or a group, directly, intelligently, logically, and courageously. She demonstrates her adeptness in V.i. Five or six cutpurses, one with a sword, attempt to mug Moll and her companions, Lord Noland, Sir Thomas Long, and Sir Beauteous Ganymede. Immediately, Moll steps forward and commands the three gentlemen to shadow her while she draws her sword and scares off the thieves who happen to reveal her identity. Her companions respond hesitantly and with consternation. Moll initially challenges the remaining three men, then softens and explains how she came to be called Moll Cutpurse.

Moll's stage world, like Wise-woman's, may have appeared fictional, for the theater did indeed depict features of real life. One reality was that fathers did determine whom their children married. Fathers, daughters, sons, cutpurses, and strong women like Moll all attended plays. Opinionated, assertive, and loyal women would have had a commanding presence there and would therefore have been watched by others, since such women tended to be leaders, central power figures, and politically involved (Jenkins 23).

According to Esslin, people tend to be "social animal[s] . . . unable to live in isolation, compelled to form part of a tribe, a clan, a nation . . . deeply dependent on such collective experiences. For the identity of a social group consists, by definition, of a common stock of customs, beliefs, concepts, of its language, its myths, its laws, its rules of conduct" (27).

A good theater audience, states Esslin, "ceases to be an assemblage of isolated individuals; it becomes a collective consciousness" (24). When audience members focus on stage characters or even those around them who warrant observation, we can safely assume that if the play has any potency, "they all have the same thought in their minds . . . and experience something like the same emotion" (24). As the men in Wengrave's house reacted similarly to Moll's rumor and then to Moll's presence, so too, if we can follow Esslin, would audience members have shared their reactions to an independent woman's assertions, demands, requests, questions, and behavior. A large proportion of women representing the different social classes attended plays in court, private, and public venues from Lady Jane May and Lady Smith to maidservants to prostitutes and cutpurses, like Mary Frith. Powerful, influential women came from every socioeconomic class in London, and each, in her own manner, affected those around her. The theater was one space where women could most readily determine the collective response. The thick descriptions of women's behavior in crowds, allied to the actions of women on stage, confirm the view that women could dominate theater audiences as often in the open-air playhouses as on the Fletcher-dominated stages of the indoor theaters.

Notes

1. Sophie Tomlinson, "She that Plays the King: Henrietta Maria and the Threat of the Actress in Caroline Culture," in *The Politics of Tragicomedy. Shakespeare and After,* ed. Gordon McMullan and Jonathan Hope (London: Routledge, 1992), 189–207, gives a clear account of how deeply Henrietta Maria influenced audience culture and play fashions, directing playwrights' attention to the ladies in the audiences in the 1630s, and commanding respect for her own preference to show the social values of love through stories echoing her own concept of platonic love.

2. This Alice Clark wrote in the twentieth century, not to be confused with her namesake and rioter who lived in early modern England.

3. See also E. A. McArthur's "Women Petitioners and the Long Parliament," *English Historical Review* vol. 24 (1909): 698–709.

4. Versions of this term were used widely to summarize the dangers of democracy in the years leading up to the English Civil War. See Christopher Hill, "The Many-Headed Monster," in *From the Renaissance to the Counter-Reformation, Essays in Honor of Garrett Mattingly,* ed. C. H. Carter (New York: Random House, 1965), republished in Hill, *Change and Continuity.*

5. Richard Sennett has some illuminating comments in his study of crowds and political debate in *Flesh and Stone. The Body and the City in Western Civilization* (New York: W. W. Norton, 1994). The political origin of this topic is most evident in George Rudé's *The Crowd in the French Revolution,* and the publications of Elias Canetti.

6. Thomas Cartelli, *Marlowe, Shakespeare and the Economy of Theatrical Experience,* argues (20–22) that it was no mystery, but he does not explain why Bacon called it one.

7. Richard Levin has emphasized the high proportion of women in early modern playhouses in "Women in the Renaissance Theatre Audience," *Shakespeare Quarterly* 40 (1989): 165–74.

8. See Michael Neill, "'Wits most accomplished Senate': The Audience of the Caroline Private Theaters," *SEL* 18 (1978): 341–60. A good overview of women in playhouse audiences, and the prejudice built into the comments on them, is Kathleen McLuskie, *Renaissance Dramatists, Feminist Readings* (Hemel Hempstead: Harvester Wheatsheaf, 1989), chapter 4.

9. *Flesh and Stone. The Body and the City in Western Civilization* (New York: W. W. Norton, 1994): 17, quoting *Television and the Quality of Life: How Viewing Shapes Everyday Experience* (Hillside, NJ: Lawrence Erlbaum, 1990): 175.

Works Cited

Anderson, Bonnie S., and Judith P. Zinsser. *A History of Their Own: Women in Europe from Prehistory to the Present.* 1988. 2 vols. New York: Harper & Row, 1989. I:411.

Archer, Ian W. "Shakespeare's London." *A Companion to Shakespeare.* Ed. David Scott Kastan. Oxford: Blackwell, 1999. 43–56.

Augustine. *Confessions.* Vol. VI. 8. *Augustine: Confessions and Enchridion.* Trans. Albert C. Outler. London: SCM Press, 1955.

Bacon, Francis. *The Advancement of Learning.* Revised edition, 1622. Bk. 2, ch. 3.

Bem, Sandra Lipitz. *The Lenses of Gender: Transforming the Debate on Sexual Inequality.* New Haven: Yale University Press, 1993.

Bentley, Gerald Eades. *The Jacobean and Caroline Stage.* 7 vols. Oxford: Clarendon Press, 1956.

Briggs, Julia. *This Stage-Play World: Texts and Contexts, 1580–1625.* 2nd ed. Oxford: Oxford University Press, 1997.

Cartelli, Thomas. *Marlowe, Shakespeare and the Economy of Theatrical Experience.* Philadelphia: University of Pennsylvania Press, 1991.

Clark, Alice. *Working Life of Women in the Seventeenth Century.* 1919. Introduction by Miranda Chaytor and Jane Lewis. London: Routledge & Kegan Paul, 1982.

Davis, Natalie Zemon. *Fiction in the Archives: Pardon Tales and their Tellers in Sixteenth-Century France.* Cambridge: Cambridge University Press, 1988.

———. "Women on Top." *Feminism and Renaissance Studies.* Ed. Lorna Hutson. Oxford: Oxford University Press, 1999. 156–85.

Esslin, Martin. *An Anatomy of Drama.* New York: Hill and Wang, 1976.

Fletcher, Anthony. *Gender, Sex and Subordination in England 1500–1800.* New Haven: Yale University Press, 1995.

Heywood, Thomas. *The Wise-woman of Hogsdon.* 1638.

Howard, Jean E. *The Stage and Social Struggle in Early Modern England.* London: Routledge, 1994.

Hickman, Katie. *Daughters of Britannia: The Lives and Times of Diplomatic Wives.* London: HarperCollins, 2000.

Jenkins, Richard. *Social Identity.* 1996. Key Ideas. London: Routledge, 1999.

Marx, Gary T., and Douglas McAdam. *Collective Behavior and Social Movements: Process and Structure.* Englewood Cliffs: Prentice Hall, 1994.

MARY FRITH OTHERWISE MOLL CUTPURSE: A famous Master-Thief and an Ugly, who dressed like a Man, and died in 1663. The Complete Newgate Calendar. 5 vols. London, Navarre Society Ltd., 1926. I:169–79. Tarlton Law Library—The Law in Popular Culture Collection. E-Texts. http://www.law.utexas.edu/lpop/etext/newgate/frith.htm.

McClelland, J. S. *The Crowd and the Mob: From Plato to Canetti.* London: Unwin, 1989.

McPhail, Clark. *The Myth of the Madding Crowd.* New York: De Gruyter, 1991.

Middleton, Thomas, and Thomas Dekker. *The Roaring Girl or Moll Cut-Purse.* 1611. *The Works of Thomas Middleton.* Ed. A. H. Bullen. 8 vols. New York: AMS Press, 1964. 4:7–152.

Platter, Thomas. *Travels in England 1599.* Trans. Clare Williams. London: Jonathan Cape, 1937, 175.

Taylor, John. *The praise, antiquity, and commodity of beggery, beggers and begging,* London, 1628.

Turner, Victor. *From Ritual to Theatre: The Human Seriousness of Play.* Performance Studies Series. New York: Performing Arts Journal, 1982.

Woodbridge, Linda. *Women and the English Renaissance: Literature and the Nature of Womankind, 1540–1620.* Urbana: University of Illinois Press, 19.

"Follow the Money":
Sex, Murder, Print, and Domestic Tragedy

Peter Berek

"FOLLOW the money," said the whistle-blower who helped Bob Woodward and Carl Bernstein unravel the Watergate story—or at least he did so in the movie version, *All the President's Men*. And the nickname the reporters gave to the tipster (eventually revealed as FBI official Mark Felt) displays, no doubt unintentionally, how readily transgressions become sexualized. "Deep Throat" took his code name from a notorious pornographic movie named for the sex act it celebrated.

In this essay I "follow the money" through a cluster of plays about transgressions performed and printed between about 1590 and 1607, plays since the nineteenth century usually called by the name "domestic." All of these plays share a concern with wealth and social mobility, most of them are based on true stories about murder, and most proclaim themselves "tragedy" on their title pages. The earliest, *Arden of Faversham* (printed in 1592), sexualizes transgressive social mobility. Female sexual avidity becomes a screen narrative that largely effaces what could have been a story of how Thomas Arden rose in the world by gaining new wealth. *Arden* scarcely speaks of money. A decade later, money becomes more speakable in tragic plays about nonaristocratic life. Female sexual avidity seems less necessary as a substitute threat to obscure anxiety about social mobility. But as money becomes more speakable, women lose their voices. Instead of powerful, murderous Alice Arden, we find versions of Griselda such as the wife in *A Yorkshire Tragedy* and Anne Frankford in Heywood's *A Woman Killed with Kindness* (printed 1607).

Definitions of domestic tragedy have been as fluid as the term has been persistent.[1] Moreover, the meaning of the word "tragedy" on a title page is in flux in the 1590s and the early years of the next century. I accept the judgment of writers since Collier that there are meaningful connections among the group of plays called "domestic." What can we infer from the fact that playwrights and printers present some of these plays as tragedies, and not others? Can this apparent anomaly illuminate changes in the marketing implications of generic categories in the years between *Arden* (first printed in

1592) at one end of the series and *A Woman Killed With Kindness, The Miseries of Enforced Marriage* (both printed 1607), and *A Yorkshire Tragedy* (printed 1608)? That genre matters to these plays is suggested by the way some of them—*Two Lamentable Tragedies, A Yorkshire Tragedy*—make the promise of a generically defined experience virtually the whole of their titles. *A Warning for Fair Women* makes an elaborate, extensive debate among Comedy, History, and Tragedy both its prologue and its choruses. A curious foregrounding of the generic as well as the homiletic is part of the way these plays both use morality-play techniques to assert meaning and simultaneously evade closure. The way these plays both deploy and repress issues of wealth, social mobility, and female sexuality is linked to evolving meanings for the word "tragedy" on title pages.

I

Theatrical tragedies printed in the early 1590s are often plays about heroic social mobility. The two parts of *Tamburlaine* (1590, reprinted 1592) virtually define glamorous but destructive rising in the world; so do the anonymous *The True Tragedy of Richard III* (printed 1594) and Shakespeare's play about that monarch (performed earlier, but not printed until 1597). Even *The Spanish Tragedy* (first printed 1592) represents anxieties about social mobility as Horatio, son of legal official Hieronimo, becomes embroiled in the marital and dynastic ambitions of Spain and Portugal. Unlike these, the story of *Arden of Faversham* is "but a private matter, and therefore as it were impertinent to this history," as Holinshed says in apparent apology for including the story of Arden's murder in his chronicle.[2] Leah Cowen Orlin's research shows that despite Arden's relatively modest circumstances, his "private" story exemplifies the social mobility, and attendant social disruptions, enabled by the dissolution of the monasteries. For nonaristocratic theatergoers or book buyers, the account in *Arden* of the murder of Faversham's richest citizen could represent in more familiar terms those anxieties *Tamburlaine* figured on the grand scale of empire.

Despite cursory references to Thomas Arden's greed, the play offers surprisingly little information about his rise in social status. Admittedly, Greene complains to Alice about Arden that "Desire of wealth is endless in his mind, / And he is greedy-gaping still for gain."[3] Despite Greene's remark, we learn almost nothing of how Arden achieved the favor of his noble patron or marriage with a woman born to a status much higher than his own. Following the money, we can see the subtext of the play as about Arden's grasping mobility. But the play displaces most anxiety about mobility onto the sexual relationship between Mosby and Alice. Though the play begins with Franklin's news that the Duke of Somerset has given Abbey lands to Arden, Arden almost immediately turns the subject to his wavering wife and berates Mosby for being a social climber. Mosby is

> A botcher, and no better at the first,
> Who, by base brokage getting some small stock,
> Crept into service of a nobleman,
> And by his servile flattery and fawning
> Is now become the steward of his house,
> And bravely jets it in his silken gown.
>
> (i. 25–30)

When they meet, Arden rebukes Mosby for wearing a sword instead of a needle or pressing iron, and Mosby replies, "Measure me what I am, not what I was" (i.321). For Mosby, the link between money and social position is clear. He talks with both rue and ambition about climbing to gold and romance:

> My golden time was when I had no gold;
> Though then I wanted, yet I slept secure;
> My daily toil begat me night's repose;
> My night's repose made daylight fresh to me.
> But, since I climbed the top bough of the tree
> And sought to build my nest among the clouds,
> Each gentle starry gale doth shake my bed
> And makes me dread my downfall to the earth.
>
> (viii.11–18)

Mosby's soliloquy rejects going back; he vows to pursue his way to "Arden's seat" (viii.31) in which he will be "sole ruler of mine own" (viii.36). Mosby's climb, not Arden's remains the focus of the play, and Mosby's climb (unlike Arden's) links desire for gold with desire for Alice. True, Arden himself comes in for further criticism for his greed when Dick Reede complains about how Arden robbed him of his plot of ground—the very plot where Arden's body eventually lies. But by the end of the play, Alice's and Mosby's adulterous behavior gets far more attention than Arden's past misconduct.

In other words, *Arden of Faversham* manages to suppress the most interesting story it might have told about money; deep, throaty, erotic passion deflects attention from the story of how new men destabilized relationships of power. Instead of speaking of control of land and wealth, the play emphasizes male control of women's bodies. And the title page of the 1592 edition focuses only on Alice Arden's crime; her husband appears as the victim of a wicked wife who assumes control, not as a high-flying subject whose wings were clipped. The 1592 title page reads, "THE LAMENTABLE AND TRUE TRAGEDIE OF M. ARDEN OF FEVERSHAM IN KENT. Who was most wickedlye murdered, by the meanes of his disloyall and wanton wyfe, who for the love she bare to one Mosbie, hyred two desperate ruffins Blackwill and Shakbag, to kill him. Wherin is shewed the great mallice and discimulation of a wicked woman, the unsatiable desire of filthie lust and the shamefull end of all murderers."[4] The title page offers a clear meaning for the Arden story, a meaning that above all condemns the malicious deceptiveness of a woman driven by "filthie lust." Now, *Arden* is not a tightly constructed play, and almost any briefly asserted moral would omit some possible implications of the story. But given the importance of money in the play, it seems especially strange that when the title page mentions the "desperate ruffins Blackwill and Shakbag" it makes no mention of their expectation of payment. That is just as strange as the way the title page ignores the epilogue, which by mentioning that Arden's body lay on land that had belonged to Reede, implies a prophetic power to Reede's earlier cursing Arden for his greed. Perhaps most notably, the *Arden* title page suppresses the name of Alice—a powerful woman appears on the title page only as Arden's wife.

We cannot know what audiences in the theater thought about *Arden*. (Indeed, we know nothing about who performed the play, or where, or when.) But when the play reaches print, Holinshed's "private matter" becomes even more private. The title page edits out of the story issues of social change that may have made Thomas Arden's life and death seem worth noting to the people of Faversham and to the maker of the chronicle of England. Arden's greedy ambition gets translated into Alice's murderous sexual irregularity. Female sexual avidity functions as a weapon of myth construction; instead of feeling anxious about social change, men in the audience can merely keep control of their women. In a way perhaps painfully familiar, controlling women's sexuality offers an acceptable outlet for expressing a culture's anxiety about the way its economy and structures of power are changing.

Arden appears again in 1599 with a virtually identical title page. (Reissues of plays almost always copy the title page of the previous edition, even when newer plays show that the fashion in title pages is changing.) The re-issue of *Arden* may be associated with a surge of interest in the late nineties in plays about domestic murder: from Henslowe's diary and other sources we know of lost plays in those years such as *Cox of Collumpton* and *Page of Plymouth*.[5] In the year 1599 *A Warning for Fair Women* appears, and *Two Lamentable Tragedies* appears in 1601. Like *Arden, Warning for Fair Women* and *Two Lamentable Tragedies* are both plays about murder; like *Arden,* both clearly want to moralize their spectacles. But in comparison to *Arden,* both plays foreground their own theatricality. Some of the machinery of their prologues, epilogues, and dumb shows is homiletic, and in many ways similar to the personifications of the hybrid moralities popular earlier in the century. Frances Dolan has argued that hybrid moralities such as *A Warning* and *Two Lamentable Tragedies* reveal a culture's unease about issues of gender and agency.[6] By the late nineties there are more plays in print, and the allegorical machinery of *A Warning* and *Two Lamentable Tragedies* suggests that printed tragedies by the end of the nineties associate themselves more strongly with theater than did *Arden.* Women remain an absent problem on title pages. *A Warning,* a play with very important and assertive female characters, acknowledges "women" in its title, but only as members of the audience, not as agents in its action.

The induction to *A Warning* (acted by the Lord Chamberlain's Men) brings on stage personifications of Tragedy, Comedy, and History to debate who will have charge of today's performance. All are gendered female. The three taunt one another about the stagy props they carry—History has a drum, Tragedy a knife and a whip. (Comedy asks Tragedy if she plans to skin someone's dead mare.) Comedy has some of the best lines, and she defines stage tragedy as though she were a sixteenth-century Italian critic who had read Seneca, Kyd, and the *ur-Hamlet:*

> How some damnd tyrant, to obtaine a crowne,
> Stabs, hangs, impoysons, smothers, cutteth throats,
> And then a Chorus too comes howling in,
> And tells us of the worrying of a cat,
> Then of a filthie whining ghost,
> Lapt in some fowle sheete, or a leather pelch,
> Comes skreaming like a pigge halfe stickt,
> And cries *Vindicta,* revenge, revenge.
>
> (induction, 50–57)[7]

Comedy's speech invites the reader—and perhaps the auditor—to see the play in relationship to stage hits of the nineties, not the texts of other printed books. This is the case even though *A Warning* includes plentiful examples of the entanglements of sin, the power of Providence, and the importance of deathbed repentances. There is an uneasy disconnect between the earnestness of much of the action in *A Warning* and the generic jokiness of the induction. It's as though the play were uncertain about whether the term "tragedy" proclaimed affinities with Kyd or with moralizing.

The induction to *A Warning* reveals one peculiarity; the dumb shows later in the play reveal others. Tragedy is not merely a narrator, but an actor in the first dumb show: she carries a bowl of blood into which either she or Murder dips the hands of the characters embracing wickedness.[8] Tragedy is the name of a genre, not of a moral category or action, yet she interacts with characters on the same footing as more conventional stage personifications. (Revenge, in *The Spanish Tragedy,* doesn't interact with the revengers whose actions he and the ghost of Don Andrea observe.) And we can't explain away the peculiarity by describing "tragedy" as a synonym for death or murder; Tragedy speaks of murder as distinct from her own person.

The play itself is a clunky, highly moralized retelling of a celebrated 1573 murder. One source, a narrative of the event written by Arthur Golding, includes elaborate sermonizing about the lessons to be drawn from the murder. (Accounts of the murder in Stow's *Annals* and Holinshed's *Chronicles* omit most of the sermonizing.) With the aid of Ann Drury and her servant, "trusty Roger," Captain George Browne wins the love of Ann Sanders and murders her husband, a prosperous merchant. While killing Sanders Browne also fatally wounds a comic servant, John Bean, who remains alive just long enough to incriminate Browne with wounds that bleed afresh in Browne's presence. All the wicked characters repent of their crimes before being hanged. Browne is conscience-stricken immediately after killing Sanders, but he continues nonetheless to reap the fruits of his murder, and goes lying to his death trying to protect Anne Sanders. Anne Drury and Trusty Roger confess their crimes; Anne Sanders denies her guilt until she knows Anne Drury has implicated her, and then launches into a long scene of confession and repentance. (Though such repentances may not be to the taste of modern audiences, they seem to have been part of the pleasure as well as the instruction offered by domestic tragedies.)

A Warning is less explicit than *Arden* about social mobility. An outsider in the mercantile world of the play, George Brown visits the court at Greenwich after the murder. Richard Helgerson suggests that military figures in Dutch genre paintings represent royal power; perhaps Browne's rank of "captain" and court visit similarly represents the intrusion of court authority or values into the domestic space of the Sanders household.[9] Yet in a play in which motivations and explanations are sometimes obscure, and sometimes rendered only through allegorical machinery, money matters. Anne Drury assures Trusty Roger that she will milk George Browne and Anne Sanders of enough money to provide a handsome dowry for her daughter—enough to marry her "to some rich Atturney, or Gentleman" (l. 466). Browne offers her a hundred pounds. Even more tellingly, George and Anne Sanders quarrel when George refuses to honor his wife's commitment to paying a draper and a milliner. Because George Sanders needs his ready money to discharge bills upon the exchange, he has his man tell Anne she will have to delay paying her creditors. Anne is irate that she must "curtesie to my man: / And he must be purse-bearer, when I neede" (ll. 619–20). Though the draper and milliner are perfectly happy to extend credit, Anne Sanders sends them home with both a tip and their merchandise and continues her complaint:

> I am a woman, and in that respect,
> Am well content my husband shal controule me,
> But that my man should over-awe me too,
> And in the sight of strangers, mistris *Drurie*,
> I tell you true, do's grieve me to the heart.

(ll. 655–59)

Anne Sanders's anger at her husband's perceived slight becomes a resource Anne Drury uses to soften up her friend for Browne's advances. Female unruliness about money, like Mistress Drury's self-proclaimed status as a "wise woman," seems to function as a symptom of moral weakness.

A Warning moves down the social scale from *Arden.* Its London world, with shrewd wives, tricky servants, and a courting captain, could be the world of city comedy—a world very far away from tragedy. Even more "domestic," and less concerned than *Arden* with power, *A Warning* does not repress concerns about money. Like *Arden,* it is quick to shift its explanations of misconduct to female sexual rapacity, even though the play's only overt sexual pursuer, and only murderer, is George Browne. *A Warning* is more self-consciously theatrical than *Arden,* and flamboyantly deploys on stage generic claims that in *Arden* are largely confined to print. Tragedy's language is frequently theatrical; she speaks, for example, of "scenes." The theatrical can include the homiletic, as when *A Warning* recounts the story—familiar to modern scholars from Heywood's 1612 *Apology for Actors*—of the woman at Lynn who confessed to having murdered her husband after seeing murder represented in a stage play. But *A Warning* doesn't tidy up its own apparent unease about its potential contradictions. In the epilogue, Tragedy addresses the audience directly—she has done so before—and seems to be expressing some concerns about the theatrical representation over which she has been presiding:

> Here are the launces that have sluic'd forth sinne,
> And ript the venom'd ulcer of foule lust,
> Which being by due vengeance qualified,
> Here *Tragedie* of force must needes conclude.
> Perhaps it may seeme strange unto you al,
> That one hath not revengde anothers death,
> After the observation of such course:
> The reason is, that now of truth I sing,
> And should I adde, or else diminish aught,
> Many of these spectators then could say,
> I have committed error in my play.
> Beare with this true and home-borne Tragedie,
> Yeelding so slender argument and scope,
> To build a matter of importance on,
> And in such forme as happly you expected.
> What now hath faild, to morrow you shall see,
> Perform'd by *Hystorie* or *Comedie.*
>
> (2718–34)

Is the claim of "truth" an acknowledgment, or suppression, of the issues of money and gender we have been discussing? Does tragedy, as a theatrical term, harmonize with, or conflict with, the edifying presumptions of tracts and tragicall histories?

Two Lamentable Tragedies differs from *A Warning* because it pays no attention to sexual relationships, and it differs from *Arden* because it is much more explicit about money. The English plot of *Two Lamentable Tragedies* is a tale of greed and murder far down the social scale from any of the other domestic plays. Perhaps pushing greed down the social scale to alehouse keepers and chandlers is itself a way of displacing anxiety about money and social change; even more likely is that *Two Lamentable Tragedies* displaces social anxieties by making murder, not mobility, its central theme. Like Tragedy in *A Warning, Two Lamentable Tragedies* could say, "Of truth I sing." Its London plot is based on the true London story of the murder of a chandler, Master Beech, and his boy by an alehouse keeper, Thomas Merry. The other "tragedy" is the tale of a murder for money in Italy. The allegorical figures of Homicide and Avarice (often called Murder and Covetousness) appear, along with Truth, who functions as a presenter. Truth seems sometimes to serve as an earnest of veracity, sometimes (like Tragedy in *A Warning*) as a commentator on staging.

Thomas Merry, serving in his alehouse, hears a customer, Thomas Beech, talking cheerfully about how fortunate he is to have a score of pounds in savings. Merry vows to invent some "stratagem, / To bring his coyne to my possession" (sig. A4v). Aided in a variety of ways by his sister, Rachel, and his servant, Harry Williams, Merry kills Beech and his boy and steals Beech's money. The Italian plot moves up the social scale, but is equally about money and murder. A dying couple, Pandino and Armenia, bequeath four hundred pounds a year, plus two thousand in "money, Jewels, Plate and houshold stuffe" (sig. B1r) to their little son Pertillo, asking Pandino's brother Falleria to hold the estate in trust until their son comes of age. Once he has control of the money, Falleria hires murderers to slay Pertillo so the money can come to his own son, Allenso. Despite the fact that Allenso loves Pertillo and struggles to protect him, Falleria urges Allenso to "advance thyselfe / Above the height of all thine Auncestours" (sig. C2r). But Allenso replies, "I would not have him dye, / Might I enjoy the *Soldans* Emperie" (sig. C2r). In this Italian murder story, Allenso describes seeking social mobility by wealth in the heroic rhetoric of plays of the early 1590s. But instead of figuring anxiety about wealth and social mobility by tales of foreign conquest or domestic royal usurpation, now such concerns are domesticated into stories of greed and murder.

Truth reminds the audience at the end of the play of the commonalities among the Merry and Fallerio stories: "See here the end of lucre and desire / Of riches, gotten by unlawfull meanes" (sig. K2v). Murder and Covetousness can never prevail "Where faire *Eliza* Prince of pietie, / Doth weare the peace adorned Diadem" (sig. K3r). Truth, rather than Tragedy, has the last word in

Two Lamentable Tragedies. But this play, like *A Warning,* is more self-aware about its status as a work of theater than *Arden of Faversham.* The Fallerio plot resolves itself in a game of disguises, which like any scene of disguise foregrounds the play's theatricality. Even more so, in mid-play, after Merry dismembers Beech's body on stage, Truth directly addresses the audience as "the sad spectators of this Acte" and asks, "Why shed you teares, this deede is but a playe" (sig. E2v). Whereas *Arden* in 1592 implied its links to printed tracts and tragicall histories, *Two Lamentable Tragedies* is very much a printed book of a play.

Most intriguingly, while *Two Lamentable Tragedies* is forthright about money and adumbrates some concern for mobility, it raises no issues—or deploys no screen stories—of sexuality or gender. Are issues that seemed too anxiety-producing for explicit acknowledgment in the early nineties now visible on stage? Yes, in a sense. But in a world where relationships among rank, wealth, and power—to say nothing of gender—are in flux, *Two Lamentable Tragedies* defines the social problem as murder and greed. The play, like *A Warning,* domesticates social change into a "private matter." And it besmirches the idea of change with vivid stage images of butchered bodies and axes in living skulls. The politics of our own time often project anxiety about change onto a racialized "other," or drugs, or street crime, or youthful sexual promiscuity, or homosexuality. Like murder, these objects of projection are real and important. But like murder, they can be "weapons of myth construction" that displace more central matters with ones on the periphery, causes with symptoms, real problems with ideological distractions. Affirming one's hostility to murder in 1600 can momentarily efface an audience's anxiety about new men, new wealth, urbanization, economic change, religious change. And calling a story that serves these purposes a "tragedy" lends dignity to the strategy of obscuring an anxiety by pushing it downward on the social scale.

The three surviving domestic tragedies of the 1590s use the tension between the connotations of the generic term and the actuality of each play's setting to both dramatize and contain anxieties about social mobility. The three plays don't all work in the same way. *Arden* takes a potentially vivid story of rising in society and instead of following the money deflects the story's energies toward claims about sexual avidity, especially female. Doing so, the printed play stays within the frame of the "tragicall history." *A Warning* uses the putative dignity of stage tragedy to elevate the importance of anxieties about domestic instability and clever manipulative women. The money matters in large part because women want to have some control of it. That the wrong people seize control of the money (in some ways, not a bad metaphor for social mobility) is the theme of *Two Lamentable Tragedies,* but the "wrong people" are so far down the scale of rank, or so safely Italian, that anxiety about economic and social change can be effaced by the moral, "thou shalt not kill." All three plays take true stories of murder and make them more like other models of artful narrative, whether in print or on stage. And all three make important use of the word "tragedy" on their title pages. Doing so, they make the stories simultaneously mirror and deflect important concerns of late Elizabethan society.

III

But something changes in the uses of the domestic after 1600. Money, murder, women, and tragedy seem to figure in different ways in *A Yorkshire Tragedy, The Miseries of Enforced Marriage,* and *A Woman Killed with Kindness.* To start with, only one of these plays is called a tragedy on its title page. Like *A Warning, A Yorkshire Tragedy* is a Chamberlain's Men–King's Men play, and like *Two Lamentable Tragedies* it appears to have been part of a play with multiple narratives. The head title of the 1608 quarto reads "ALL'S ONE; *OR,* One of the foure Plaies in one, called a *York-shire* Tragedy*:* as it was plaid by the Kings Majesties Players." We cannot know what the other plays were like, but *Yorkshire* is very much about the intersection of power, money, and marriage, and (unlike *Miseries*) very much about murder.

Both *Yorkshire* and *Miseries* are based on the same story of extravagance and murder. The story, whose veracity is confirmed by legal records, first appears in print in a 1605 pamphlet, *Two most unnaturall and bloodie Murthers: The one by Maister Caverley, a Yorkshire Gentleman, practised upon his wife, and committed uppon his two Children, the three and twentie of April 1605. The other, by Mistris Browne, and her servant Peter, upon her husband, who were executed in Lent last past in at Bury in Suffolke. 1605.*[10] Forced by his guardian, the Yorkshire gentleman abandons the woman to whom he is betrothed and marries the guardian's niece instead. Once married, he spends his money on gambling, drink, and bad companions, impoverishes his family, traduces his wife as a whore and his children as bastards, and wounds his wife while stabbing his children to death. Unlike the pamphlet, *A Yorkshire Tragedy* makes no mention of the guardian's interference in the betrothal, though its first scene reports the protagonist's betrayal of his first betrothed. The murder of the children is vividly present on stage. *Miseries* retains the pamphlet story of the first betrothal and intrusive guardian, but omits the murders. Though both plays are about marriage, neither represents sexual desire. Both plays treat money as a key signifier of family status and stability. But (unlike the plays of the 1590s), now money figures anxiety about downward mobility among the gentry, not upward mobility among the middling or lower sorts.

Women matter in both Yorkshire plays only as an occasion for male behavior, whether good or ill. The wife in *A Yorkshire Tragedy,* astonishingly passive, bears all her trials with patience, including the butchery of her children. Her patience and forgiveness ultimately bring the husband to his senses and enable him to die repentant. *Miseries,* a full-length play, gives more attention to the story of the betrothal, and gives the protagonist the family name of Scarborrow. Unlike *Yorkshire, Miseries* also includes a comic Butler, a long-time servant of Scarborrow's family, whose role has much in common with Adam's in *As You Like It.* The Butler represents the stability and respect for rank Scarborrow has abandoned. This loyal servant and Scarborrow's loyal wife bring about the happy resolution. At the play's penultimate moment Scarborrow rebukes the Doctor who married him to his wife for letting the Doctor's,desire for promotion motivate a bigamous marriage he should have scorned. With his wife and children on stage, Scarborrow threatens them and the Doctor with death. But tragical vengeance is not to be. The audience knows that the death of Clare, Scarborrow's first betrothed, made legitimate this marriage and its children. Furthermore, the devoted Butler arrives with Scarborrow's brothers, sister, and uncle. They bring the news that his guardian is dead and has left the family enough money to remedy all Scarborrow's profligacy and (apparently) all the family's suffering. The tragical gives way to a happy comic reconciliation.

Tragic *Yorkshire* ends with the Husband and his children dead; *Miseries* sacrifices Clare, but leaves the Scarborrow family alive and happy. Though "enforced marriage" is the ostensible theme of both plays, their real focus is how want of money can drag a gentry family down from its previous status. Both plays could have pursued the linkages among women's behavior, money, and social status that *Arden of Faversham* partly initiates and partially suppresses, but instead they focus on the money and turn women into unthreatening representations of obedience. Male agents work out financial and family relationships for good or for ill; women have the power only to efface their desires and by doing so to promote male happiness. And perhaps most centrally: social mobility exists largely as a threat of decline. No one—except perhaps the doctor of divinity—desires advancement; happiness is restoring the status quo. No longer the prize of climbing, women are counters pushed around by men in men's conflicts. Their only power is the reassuring power to obey and suffer patiently. By 1605 or 1606, domestic tragedy has rid itself of unruly women like Alice Arden, Anne Saunders, and Anne Drury; in the plays about the Yorkshire murders, women are as safely obedient as men could wish. Domestic unrest is created not by sexual desire, but by money, and not so much by desire for money as by its profligate display and expense. And while taming its women, these domestic tales begin to shed the term "tragedy" in their titles.

IV

Neither title page, head title, nor running title describes Thomas Heywood's *A Woman Killed with Kindness* (1607) as a tragedy, nor is it listed as a tragedy in the Stationer's Register. Unlike the other works I have been discussing, this play makes no fuss about genre. If *A Woman Killed* belongs in a discussion of domestic tragedy—as I think it does—it is because Heywood's play deploys materials we find in other domestic plays. But Heywood's play decouples sexual and financial transgressions, and offers little challenge to established social order. Though Anne Frankford dies "killed with kindness," other deaths are unpremeditated. The play neither explores the aspirations of stage tragedy of the early nineties, nor insists in its title materials on generic classification.[11] Perhaps the status of printed plays is secure enough not to need decking out in generic emblems of merit. As the reading of playbooks becomes more established as a phenomenon in its own right, perhaps printers feel less need to link plays to the old tradition of tragical histories.

Like *Arden* and *A Warning*, *A Woman Killed* is a play about adultery punished. And like the Yorkshire plays, *A Woman Killed* displays and condemns profligacy with money. But female sexual unruliness occupies the main plot, and money the subplot. They coexist, but barely intersect. Multiple plots function in a new way. In *Two Lamentable Tragedies,* the two plots are thematically identical: both emphasize the destructive impact of desire for money. But in *A Woman Killed,* the Frankford plot poses and claims to resolve a problem in male friendship and female fidelity, while the subplot story of Sir Francis Acton (Anne's brother) and Sir Charles Mountford is about competition for status based on hawks, money, swordplay, and litigation about land—all accoutrements of rank. The penalty for Sir Charles's murderous transgression is loss of wealth and social position.[12] While Anne Frankford is, to be sure, a sexually unruly woman, her unruliness has nothing to do with money and barely shakes the stable fabric of her husband's gentry household. Found out, Anne becomes passive and repentant. By self-abnegation, sexual virtue, and obedience—an obvious foil to Anne's yielding to her own desires—Susan Mountford revives her family's fortunes. Recklessness with money can tear the gentry down; female virtue and obedience heals the community. As she starves herself to death, Anne, "killed with kindness," restores honor to her family and (Frankford asserts) to herself. Rebecca Ann Bach asks what domestic tragedy imagines about the sex-gender system in early modern England, and answers, "In that system, as represented in the play, women function to bind men to one another, to cement kinship alliances in a teetering world where such alliances are threatened by a love of money dissociated from rank."[13] I agree with Bach about *A Woman Killed,* but in this respect, contrary to what Bach argues, the play is unlike most domestic tragedies. Emphasizing homosocial bonds is one of the ways in which Heywood diminishes the female agency we saw in *Arden* and *A Warning.*

Upward mobility—rising in the world—barely exists as a possibility in *A Woman Killed.* Only Wendoll, fleeing overseas at the end of the play, imagines a future when "My worth and parts being by some great man prais'd, /

At my return I may in court be raised" (sc. xvi, 135–36). Downward mobility is the punishment of the profligate and the careless; upward mobility beyond the status of one's birth is the lure of the wicked and sexually avid man. But money is the theme of the second plot. At the wedding of Anne and Frankford, Sir Francis and Sir Charles wager hundreds of pounds on their dogs and hawks. When the two knights quarrel about whose hawks have triumphed, Sir Charles kills two of Sir Francis's followers. Money, in this play, has little to do with either greed or aspiration to power; rather, money tempts the rich man to ostentatious display and profligate behavior. Immediately repentant about the killings, Charles refuses to preserve himself by flying from "my country and my father's patrimony" (sc. iii, 91) and his sister Susan watches him carried off to prison. "Patrimony"—family name and family lands—figures the stability Heywood's play celebrates. But, unlike *Arden,* the play makes little effort to recast its anxieties about stability into anxieties about women's sexuality. Though Susan and Charles are reduced to a status far below their gentle birth, Susan remains loyal and obedient in Charles's efforts to restore their patrimony. Even when her obedience makes her into sexual bait to end the Mountfords' vengeful persecution by Sir Francis Acton, Susan assures the audience she will die rather than sexually transgress.

The play's most unequivocally wicked character, Shafton, puts "in suit" (sc. vii, 33) the bond Mountford gave on the meager remnant of his family lands. Not unlike the historical Thomas Arden, Shafton wants Mountford's property to fill out the boundaries of an estate he has newly acquired. He jails Sir Charles because he cannot pay the debt. Smitten by love of Susan, Sir Francis pays her brother's debts and releases him from prison. Feeling doubly dishonored because he now owes an unpayable debt of money and gratitude to his enemy Acton, Mountford plots to restore his honor by giving Susan to Acton, even though both he and his sister will die upon the consummation of the transaction. Susan is being treated as a medium of exchange between men, but not (as Bach argued about Frankford and Wendoll) within the framework of homosocial desire. Susan, as a chaste and obedient woman, can repair a world made worse by money. And Acton, taking Susan as wife and Charles as brother, repays kindness with kindness and completes the healing. Money, the sign of modernity and threatener of social stability, gets put in its place by honor and by love.

This sentimental turn in the plot brings the domestic full circle. *Arden of Faversham* initiates domestic tragedy by using female sexual avidity as a screen story for what could have been a narrative about men rising in wealth and rising in status. To the extent that *Arden* acknowledges ambition to rise, the play locates that ambition in the lower-status Mosby. By 1607, money is no longer unmentionable and is an acknowledged threat to a stable society. But as in the Yorkshire plays, the chief threat is that gentry will decline, not because of meaningful economic activity, but because of profligacy. Women matter in the Acton-Mountford plot, not as a screen for money, but as an ultimate reassurance that an honor culture can survive in a world of money so long as women are chaste. Chastity, not sexual avidity, is the screen story. Now, it may seem peculiar to treat a notorious play about adultery punished as a celebration of female chastity. Frankford's "kindness" kills unfaithful Anne; the wronged husband achieves vengeance on the woman who defiles household and marriage bed. But the play gives much more attention to Anne as submissive than to Anne as transgressive. Yes, Anne yields to Wendoll, but the play makes it hard to figure out why. Even at the moment of yielding, Anne says, "This maze I am in / I fear will prove the labyrinth of sin" (sc. vi, 160–61). Her repentance is immediate; her death self-inflicted and serene; Frankford himself testifies that she dies "honest in heart" (sc. xvii, 120). The play seems eager to hold harmless those who fail in conduct, as indeed is usually the case in comedy.

I am not suggesting that *A Woman Killed* is "really" a comedy—as I said above, the play's traditional grouping among domestic tragedies makes as much sense as the category "domestic tragedy" itself. But *A Woman Killed* creates a different kind of relationship among social mobility, wealth, and sexual conduct than *Arden*. Through the late 1590s and the early years of the next century, wealth—"the money"—becomes more speakable in "tragic" plays about nonaristocratic life. Female sexual avidity seems less necessary as a screen, a substitute threat for the threat of social mobility. But as though to enable a new forthrightness about Elizabethan social change, women lose their voices, or at least their power to assert themselves and survive. What most clearly unites *A Woman Killed* with the two Yorkshire plays is female suffering. It is as though the suffering and often the death of a woman helps preserve an ideal of stable rank and hierarchy in society, even as the actualities of received hierarchies grow more tenuous. By enduring suffering caused by a man, a woman teaches all observers the value of obedience in a hierarchical world. Curiously, *A Woman Killed* is the first of these domestic plays to identify a female character in its title. But the title safely presents the woman as both harmless and dead.

V

A Woman Killed and the Yorkshire plays embrace the theme of the social power of self-effacing women. One recognizes, of course, the topos of Griselda, as old as Petrarch and Boccaccio. This troubling story of noble Walter's wedding and then tormenting a poor but virtuous wife over the centuries serves multiple parabolic or allegorical functions, but always invites our questions about why a culture chooses a patiently suffering woman to figure values the culture ostensibly admires. The two early modern Griselda plays use the old story in very different ways; a brief look at what these plays do with female suffering can sharpen our understanding of domestic tragedy. Though the two plays are different from one another, both name Griselda in their titles.

John Phillip's *The Commodye of Pacient and Meeke Grissell* appears in print without a date, but a Stationer's Register entry suggests 1565.[14] Appearing during the decade in which tragicall histories were much in vogue, in its emphasis on obedience of children to parents, as well as of wives to husbands, *Patient Grissell* seems a comic counterpoise to Arthur Brooke's *Tragicall Historye of Romeus and Juliet* (1562). (When Grissell agrees to marry Marquis Gautier, they sing a duet in which Gautier compares himself to Romeo in fidelity.) But the play is above all an intervention in debate about royal marriage—clearly an important topic in the early years of Elizabeth's reign.[15] Grissell and her father, Janicle, figure by their obedience a subject's appropriate relationship to a prince. But the vice, Politic Persuasion, tries to stir up trouble by telling Gautier the common people disapprove of his choice of wife. To preserve his rule, Gautier has to make unpalatable choices, such as killing or banishing his own child. Despite believing she has lost her children, by her patience and constancy (both allegorically represented on stage) Grissell preserves the Marquis's rule and earns acceptance from Nobilitie (also a character) of her elevation in social status, and of her father's elevation as well. A woman's suffering, patience, and constancy demonstrate the rightness of letting a ruler make his own choice of spouse. Or, to underscore this play's somewhat paradoxical implications, the suffering of an implausibly self-effacing and submissive woman, Grissell, serves to ratify the legitimate authority of the Queen whom her husband figures.

One could argue that *Patient Grissell* wittingly or unwittingly represents a conflicted attitude toward female rule as well as toward social mobility. Perhaps audiences took a certain delight in hearing Politic Persuasion deride the upward mobility of Grissell's family as well as the willful choice of a ruler. However, the *Patient Grissil* of Dekker, Chettle, and Haughton (probably performed in 1600, and printed in 1603) seems hardly concerned at all with matters of rule; its sphere is more domestic. The play acknowledges the possibility of social mobility; Grissil's brother Laureo returns home after nine years at university, complaining that a scholar can't earn a living. But his father, Janicola, and his sister urge him to be content with the family's traditional trade of basket making. Though the Grissil-Gwalter story unfolds in more or less its usual way, additions to the story, including Janiculo's clownish servant Babulo, emphasize the virtues of both obedience and contentment with one's lot. Moreover, Dekker, Chettle, and Haughton add a subplot about a comic Welsh knight, Sir Owen Ap Meredith, who is married to a Welsh widow, Gwenthyan, cousin to Gwalter by her first marriage. Feisty Gwenthyan tries to rule her husband; she is recognizably kin to Katherine in *The*

Taming of the Shrew. Like Katherine, Gwenthyan is tamed by the end of the play, but instead of the violence of Petruchio, *Patient Grissil* gives us the patience of Sir Owen. Indeed, the subplot reinforces a theme of the main plot: as Grissil teaches Gwalter patience by her obedience, so Sir Owen does the same to Gwenthyan.

Whereas Phillip's play used the Griselda story to make a point about the ruler's freedom to make his own match as well as the subject's obligation to obey, Dekker and his colleagues use a story of Grissil's patient suffering to praise contentment with the station in life to which one is born. Instead of the tragic quest for gold and power, *Patient Grissil* gives us the golden slumber of the contented laboring poor (see I.ii.92ff.). But in the overtly comic mode of this play, the suffering Grissil can be doubled by the henpecked Sir Owen. With no money at stake, *Patient Grissil* seems not to need a permanently afflicted woman; no children die in this play. Nor does the play need to blame marital discontent on one sex or the other, as *Arden* and *A Warning* blame women and the Yorkshire plays blame men. When we follow the money, we see gender and rank collide painfully, even tragically, with social mobility. When one of these elements is removed, comedy becomes possible.

I am not trying to claim that money never matters in comedies about marriage. Petruchio, after all, comes to wive it wealthily in Padua; Orlando regains his inheritance as well as gaining Rosalind. City comedy, in some ways the successor to domestic tragedy, plays many games with greed as well as with marriage among those not of gentle birth. What, then, happens to domestic tragedy in the years around 1600, and how does whatever happens relate to the evolving uses of the word "tragedy" on title pages? In its initial world of performance, *Arden* takes the story of Thomas Arden's successful gentry rapacity and makes it into a homily about a social climbing tailor and an adulterous, sexually avid and murderous wife. For the anxiety about social change visible in other stage tragedies of the 1590s, *Arden* substitutes an apparently less threatening anxiety about female sexuality. In doing so *Arden* makes the tale of Thomas Arden's death less like other stage tragedies and more like *novelle* transformed to "tragical histories." And in its printed form, the term "tragedy" on *Arden*'s 1592 title page signals to the book buyer a potential affinity with the translated *novelle* of Brooke, Painter, and their successors. A racy tale of transgression will be turned into a moral homily.

A Warning for Fair Women and *Two Lamentable Tragedies* thrust the linkages between domestic murder and social mobility even further down the scale of rank at the end of the 1590s. But veils come off money, that medium by which men can rise and fall. *A Warning* acknowledges more than *Arden* links between sexual transgression and the desire for money and power. *Two Lamentable Tragedies* dispenses with sexuality entirely as it sermonizes against murder and greed. Both plays domesticate more than *Arden* issues of social change. And much more than *Arden,* both plays foreground their theatricality. Though *A Warning* and *Two Lamentable Tragedies* incorporate elements every bit as homiletic as those of "tragicall histories," the plays, both on stage and in print, market themselves as theatrical events. Or, to put the same point differently, printed plays seem now to be fulfilling the desires of book buyers who once bought prose narratives.

Though derived from a pamphlet about a murder, and though just as "true" as their domestic precursors, the two Yorkshire plays make money a vehicle for gentry profligacy, not social climbing by the lower or middle sorts. *A Yorkshire Tragedy* and *Miseries of Enforced Marriage* are concerned with status, as most early modern plays are concerned with status. But they are anxious about falling, not rising. And women in these plays could scarcely be more different from Alice Arden, Anne Sanders, or Anne Drury. The wives in the Yorkshire plays are loyal and obedient; their sexuality is apparently purely reproductive. Passive, obedient women figure the stability that evades *Yorkshire* but that *Miseries* achieves. The title-page marketing of the Yorkshire plays seems to have little connection to the world of prose *novelle;* plays stand on their own as commodities in the world of print. And generic terms such as "tragedy" seem to have lost their utility as a reassurance of a moralized spectacle: *Miseries,* with no generic marking, is at least as homiletic as *Yorkshire.*

One can speculate—I will speculate—that in the early and middle 1590s domestic plays in print and on stage played a role in containing social anxiety about new wealth and men rising in the world by participating in a screen narrative in which the pressing issues were women's sexual desires and their links to murder. For a brief time in the theater, and in print, assertive women worked their will on stage. Profligacy with money and concern for status survive as issues, but *A Woman Killed with Kindness* returns to the old model of the Griselda tale. Like the play by Dekker, Chettle, and Haughton, Heywood's play doubles its plot to reinforce its message about the saving powers of patience and obedience. Anne Frankford dies, but needs no tragic genre to teach her lessons.

Notes

1. J. Payne Collier appears to have invented the category "domestic tragedy" in the nineteenth century in discussions of the apocryphal *Arden of Faversham* and *A Yorkshire Tragedy.* The middling social class of characters in *Arden* and *Yorkshire,* and the plays' sordid accounts of marital murders, puzzled scholars who admired "*tragedia cothurnata,* fitting kings," and no doubt contributed to skepticism about crediting Shakespeare's name on the *Yorkshire* title page and both plays' appearance in the 1664 folio. In 1943, Henry Hitch Adams rescued one version of importance for these plays by arguing for their homiletic power and dependence on Elizabethan reli-

gious morality (*English Domestic or Homiletic Tragedy, 1575 to 1642* [New York: Columbia University Press, 1943]). The Elizabethan World Picture nicely framed domestic tragedy. Less concerned than Adams with celebrating Elizabethan orthodoxies or a nineteenth century version of theatrical realism, more recent critics such as Orlin, Dolan, Comensoli and Helgerson rightly see in these plays exciting possibilities for tracing Early Modern ideas about gender, class and an emerging concept of private life. See Lena Cowen Orlin, *Private Matters and Public Culture in Post-Reformation England* (Ithaca: Cornell University Press, 1994); Frances E. Dolan, *Dangerous Familiars: Representations of Domestic Crime in England, 1550–1700* (Ithaca: Cornell University Press, 1994); Viviana Comensoli, *"Household Business": Domestic Plays of Early Modern England* (Toronto: University of Toronto Press, 1996), and Richard Helgerson, *Adulterous Alliances: Home, State and History in Early Modern European Drama and Painting* (Chicago: University of Chicago Press, 2000). Orlin's book in particular extends the analysis of Arden's sources into a study of matters unexpressed in the play that are rich in their revelations about the intersections of patronage, class, wealth and marriage in the years immediately after the dissolution of the monasteries by Henry VIII. For useful lists of plays and sources, see Andrew Clark, "An Annotated List of Sources and Related Material for Elizabethan Domestic Tragedy, 1591–1625," *RORD* 17 (1974): 25–33, and Clark, "An Annotated List of Lost Domestic Plays, 1578–1624," *RORD* 18 (1975): 29–44.

2. Orlin, *Private Matters,* 16.

3. *The Tragedy of Master Arden of Faversham,* ed. M. L. Wine, *The Revels Plays* (London: Methuen, 1973), scene 1, lines 474–75. Future references will appear in the text.

4. Scolar Press facsimile, Menston, Yorkshire, 1971. I retain capitalization but otherwise normalize fonts and lineation.

5. See Adams, appendix A, 195–199.

6. Frances E. Dolan, "Gender, Moral Agency and Dramatic Form in *A Warning for Fair Women,*" *SEL* 29 (1989): 201–18.

7. *A Warning for Fair Women: A Critical Edition,* ed. Charles Dale Cannon (The Hague: Mouton, 1975).

8. The 1599 quarto says "Murder" dips their hands; editor Charles Cannon emends to "Tragedy," arguing that Murder doesn't otherwise appear as a character. Dolan disagrees with the emendation, and may well be correct.

9. See Helgerson, *Adulterous Alliances,* 29–31 and 79–119.

10. *A Yorkshire Tragedy,* ed. A. C. Cawley and Barry Gaines, *The Revels Plays* (Manchester: Manchester University Press, 1986), 95. The family name, "Caverly," is completely suppressed in *Yorkshire,* where the protagonist is simply called "Husband," and is changed to "Scarborrow" in *Miseries.*

11. *A Woman Killed* uses a tale from Painter as source for its subplot, and may also rely on Painter for the main plot. See *A Woman Killed with Kindness,* ed. R. W. Van Fossen, *The Revels Plays* (Cambridge: Harvard University Press, 1961), xvii–xxvii. Future citations are to this edition. David Atkinson explains that the stories in Painter show a very different attitude to adultery than *A Woman Killed.* See David Atkinson, "An Approach to the Main Plot of Thomas Heywood's A Woman Killed with Kindness." *English Studies: A Journal of English Language and Literature* 70, no. 1 (February 1989): 15–27.

12. For a useful summary of the debate about the unity of the two plots, see Laura G. Bromley, "Domestic Conduct in *A Woman Killed with Kindness, SEL* 26 (1986): 259–76. Citing early modern manuals of conduct, Bromley argues that lack of moderation causes the crises in both plots.

13. Rebecca Ann Bach, "The Homosocial Imaginary of *A Woman Killed with Kindness,*" *Textual Practice* 12, no. 3 (1998): 516–17.

14. All citations refer to John Phillip, *The Play of Patient Grissell,* ed. Ronald B. McKerrow and W. W. Greg (Chiswick: The Malone Society, 1909). The play is also reprinted in Faith Gildenhuys, ed., *A Gathering of Griseldas: Three Sixteenth Century Texts* (Ottowa: Dovehouse Editions, 1996). Gildenhuys also reprints a ballad and a prose narrative that are not pertinent to my argument.

15. See Louis B. Wright, "A Political Reflection in Phillip's Patient Grissell," *Review of English Studies* 4, no. 16 (October 1928): 424–28.

Notes and Documents

An Illustration of Traveling Players in Franz Hartmann's Early Modern *Album amicorum*

June Schlueter

THE *album amicorum* flourished in German- (and Dutch-) speaking Europe during the sixteenth and seventeenth centuries. Begun in German universities, where students collected autographs of fellow students and professors, friendship albums, now in archives throughout Europe, stand as a *Who's Who* of the early modern period. Typically, a contributor, at the album owner's invitation, would inscribe a motto, a dedication, and a signature, along with date and place, and, often, have his coat of arms painted on the page. As the form evolved, watercolors of emblems, costumes, objects, and scenes, reflecting personal interests and travel, were commissioned by album owners and contributors. The album of Michael van Meer, for example, who was born in Antwerp, lived most of his life in Hamburg, and visited London for a year and a half in 1614–15, gives us the familiar painting of a cock fight, with King James and others waging bets; a skiff crossing the Thames at London Bridge; King James on horseback riding to Parliament; a St. George's Day procession; and an American Indian on display in St. James's Park.[1] Often, album owners added to their albums for years—at least thirty-five in van Meer's case—resulting in a compendium of continental and British autographs as well as a pictorial scrapbook of the times.

A number of *alba amicorum* hold special interest for theater historians. Johannes de Witt, whose ca. 1596 sketch of the Swan theater has proven to be valuable and vexing, signed his friend Aernout van Buchell's album in 1585 with a dedication in Latin and a painting of a lily, symbolizing their lifelong friendship.[2] An album owned by Francis Segar, an Englishman who spent much of his career in Kassel, Germany, and who accompanied the Hessian Landgrave Moritz's son Otto to London in 1611 when the prince was a hopeful for the hand of James' daughter, contains the signature of Ben Jonson on one page, with a dedication in Latin, and that of Inigo Jones on another, with a motto in Italian.[3] A number of *commedia dell'arte* figures appear in friendship albums as well, and an album at the Staatsbibliothek Bamberg pictures a late sixteenth-/early seventeenth-century outdoor stage with five actors/musicians.[4]

Such pages are not abundant: aside from the *commedia* figures, I have come across only a handful of theater-related entries in the fifteen hundred or so albums I have thus far examined. But there is one watercolor that is, to say the least, intriguing (see figure 1). It appears on f. 25 of the early modern album of Franz Hartmann of Frankfurt an der Oder, Germany.[5] Painted with colors that remain bright, the illustration depicts six figures, in costume, on a cobblestone pavement, against a blue sky. Three—in pink, green, and blue robes, white ruffs, and helmets with plumes matching the colors of their robes—carry, respectively, a falcon, a model of a church, and a model of a boat; one—in red robe, white ruff, and golden crown atop long flowing hair—carries a flaming heart or ball. The four ride horses, while two—in doublets, ruffs, and bird masks, carrying torches—walk.

The painting, of course, could be allegorical, as at least two other paintings in the Hartmann album are. One, on f. 7, is of a young man straddling the ball of Fortune as he is pulled by contending forces: on one side, a man with bags of gold and silver; on the other, an attractive young woman. Another, on f. 137, shows the figure of a prince against a mountainous landscape, with

A watercolor painting, c. 1605–6, from the album of Franz Hartmann. Permission of British Library.

a vertically divided male figure on either side: one is half bishop, half man in loincloth with oil lamp; the other is half scholar, book in arm, half military man in armor with pike. Both illustrations represent common tropes in German albums. The subject painting, though unique among album paintings I have seen, also contains allegorical features: the objects the figures on horseback carry represent the four elements, with air designated by the falcon, earth by the church on a plot of land, water by the boat, and fire by the flaming heart or ball. Moreover, the two figures on foot, in rooster and owl masks, round out the conventional display as Night and Day.[6] Indeed, the scene is much like that in a 1564 print after Maarten van Heemskerck (see figure 2), in which figures on a processional car are associated with similar representations of the sister elements, with Night and Day—cutouts of a moon and a sun atop winged horses' heads—leading the way.[7]

But the album painting and the van Heemskerck print show marked differences as well. Van Heemskerck's depiction of the processional car, like those in the other album paintings, is unmistakably allegorical. Each of the four figures on the car, as well as a fifth, the coachman, representing Time, may have been performers in the 1561 Circumcision Procession in Antwerp on

The Triumph of Mundus, after a 1564 print by Maarten van Heemskerck. Permission of Rijksprentenkabinet, Amsterdam.

which the illustration is based. But the inclusion of the four Winds, to complete the cosmic portrait, confirms the print's allegorical nature, as does its place in the *Circulus vicissitudinis rerum humanarum,* a series of eight prints designed to present a moral lesson (pointed in Latin verses).[8] The van Heemskerck print combines the historical moment of the ceremonial procession with the moral significance of the Triumph of Mundus, embellishing, stylizing, and idealizing what a spectator would have seen.

The album painting, by contrast, is unmistakably realistic: the scene we see is the scene a person standing at the roadside would have seen. The objects the figures carry do represent the four elements, but the allegory here is neither coherent nor sustained. Compare the headgear of the four elements on the car in the van Heemskerck print with the plumed helmets and crown of those on horseback in the album painting. In the print, each wears a further token of her allegorical status; in the album, neither the headgear nor the costumes contribute to or even complement the allegorical message. Indeed, in the album painting, it would appear that the significance of the objects is embodied not in the present moment but in an anticipated one. Clearly, there is a performance element to the painting, but the performance is not yet realized. Instead, there is a sense of anticipation, with a future event promising to actualize all the objects: falcon, church, boat, flame, helmets, crown, long flowing hair, and masks. In short, a person along the roadside and a current-day reader of the painting would see not an allegorical procession but a troupe of traveling players, with objects and gear that attract attention along the way and serve as stage properties at a future time.

Where, though, might Hartmann have seen a troupe of traveling players? And who might these players be?

Reconstructing the chronology of *alba amicorum* is a knotty task, for except for the early leaves of the album, which are conventionally reserved for princes of high estate (King James, Frederick V, the Landgraves of Germany, for example), signature pages were selected arbitrarily: even when two people were asked to sign on the same occasion, one might choose f. 120, the other f. 45v. Moreover, while many contributors inscribe both the date and place of signing, just as many do not, and watercolor illustrations are often undated and unidentified. Still, by mapping the chronology of an album, one can establish context and often infer where and when an illustration was done. In the case of the Hartmann album, entries span twenty years, from 1597 to 1617.[9] Those that indicate place fall into two time frames: 1605–7, with numerous entries from Marburg (1605–6) and a few from Giessen, Tübingen, and Hamburg (1606–7), and 1614–17, with entries from Strasbourg (Argentoratum) (1614–15), Paris (Lutetia Parisiorum) (1615), Angers (1615–16), England (1616), and Paris again (1616–17). Dedications to Hartmann indicate that he was a degree candidate at Marburg, which means he kept his album while a university student there. In or before 1614, Hartmann traveled to France, then to England, album in hand. (Indeed, although there are only four entries identifying England as the place of inscription, Hartmann secured the earliest of these on a date of some import to Shakespeareans: April 23, 1616.)

Aside from coats of arms and a number of paintings on pages signed by contributors, the Hartmann album contains at least eight watercolors, including the traveling players, that appear to have been done by the same hand. One of these is dated Marburg 1605; another is sited Marburg but bears no date: the album's chronology, however, implies that it, too, is from 1605–6. Indeed, stylistic and technical similarities among these paintings—particularly the positioning of four of them, including the traveling players, sideways on the page—suggest that most or all were from Hartmann's university years.

But what of the figures in the Hartmann album? Other historical paintings in the album are of courtship and tavern scenes, perhaps particular to Marburg. What in 1605–6 Marburg might have prompted this more exotic illustration? The question, though almost certainly unanswerable, is nonetheless seductive, for what we know about traveling players in Germany suggests that a German could have seen such a troupe in 1605–6 Marburg. And—even more provocative—the actors could have been English.

Much of what follows, of course, is conjectural: we cannot know what prompted the illustration. But we do know a fair amount about traveling players in Germany. And we know that Marburg and the Academia Marpurgensis, where Hartmann studied, was in a line of theatrical activity associated with the Landgrave Moritz, who not only kept English actors at court in Kassel but regularly lent the actors to others, endorsed their appearance at the Frankfurt am Main fair, and, in 1604–6, built the English-style Ottoneum theater.[10] As the halfway point between Kassel and Frankfurt am Main—a journey of ninety-odd miles—and as the site of the university begun by the Landgrave Moritz's grandfather, Philipp der Großmütige, in 1527, Marburg was likely to have seen English actors, in performance or on their way to and from the fair.

Records of the Frankfurt fair indicate that English actors from the Kassel court regularly performed there, both at Easter and in the fall, from 1600 to 1613. In an informative 1978 Heidelberg University master's thesis, Peter Brand[11] traces the travels of the best-known of the continental actor-managers, Robert Browne, whose association with the Landgrave Moritz dates back at least to 1595. In 1605–6, the Landgrave's troupe of English actors, having returned from France and spent the winter in Kassel, were given a letter from their patron commending them to the Frankfurt officials. Twice in 1606, the troupe of fourteen to seventeen players traveled to the Frankfurt fair. They performed at the Easter fair in April, after which they returned to Kassel. In June, they were in Strasbourg, in early August in Ulm. In late August, fifteen persons, including Robert Browne, John Green, Robert Ledbetter,[12] and other players from Moritz's court, were, once again, at the Frankfurt fair, after which they returned to Kassel.[13] The journey (of six days?) would likely have taken them to—or at least through—Marburg.

The scenario, though grounded in archival materials, is imaginary, for there is no known record of the English actors in Marburg in 1605–6. Nonetheless, it is not unlikely. Two letters from 1597 establish a connection between the Landgrave Moritz and theatrical activity in Marburg. The first indicates that Moritz lent Landgrave Ludwig of Marburg costumes and properties in order that the comedy of the Old Potentates might be performed; it was a performance that Moritz himself hoped to attend. The second records Ludwig's return of the costumes and properties to Moritz following a performance that was seen by Grave Hans Ernest von Solms.[14] Alternatively, Hartmann could have seen the actors in Kassel, at the Frankfurt fair, or elsewhere; sufficiently intrigued, he could have had the players painted in his album. Albums, after all, were not only records of one's circle of acquaintances and one's travels, prompted by motives similar to those of modern-day autograph seekers and vacation photographers; they were also acts of self-representation, designed to draw attention to the album owner as a man of experience and learning: perhaps the album owner here wished to show his knowledge of something his friends may not have seen. Or perhaps he was still excited over having seen the players perform. For despite Fynes Moryson's disdain for the English actors he saw at the Frankfurt fair in 1592, the English traveler did remark on the undiscriminating German audience, who "flocked wonderfully to see theire gesture and Action."[15] And Balthasar Baumgartner the Younger, of Nuremberg, who also saw the players at the Frankfurt fair in 1592, reported in a letter to his wife that he was greatly impressed with the English comedians' music and their talents at leaping and dancing. (He also mentioned that they were "khöstlich herrlich wol geklayded"—wonderfully splendidly dressed.)[16] Either way, Hartmann's *album amicorum* offered him an opportunity to create a pictorial record of the traveling troupe.

But what of the painting itself? What can we learn from the figures on the horses and the two masked figures that lead them? Of immediate interest is the representation of gender: clearly the crowned player in red, with flowing hair, is intended to be a princess or queen. But what of the figure who brings up the rear? Is this a boy actor, dressed in a woman's skirt? (Note that neither he/she nor the princess/queen is riding sidesaddle.) And what of the other two, in green and blue? Are they, too, in skirts, or are they in men's robes? (The horses' heads obscure the line of the fabric.) Three of the players on horseback wear plumed helmets: what should we make of their headgear? And what of the properties they carry? The falcon that sits on one player's fist may or may not be alive, but it is clearly outfitted for hawking, with hood, jesses, and bell. Might we learn something of the character from the bird? The August 13 entry in R. Chambers's *Book of Days* observes that "the grade of the hawk-bearer was known also by the bird he bore": a gerfalcon (for a king), a falcon-gentle (for a prince), a falcon of the rock (for a duke), a peregrine-falcon (for an earl), a merlin (for a lady), a goshawk (for a yeoman), a nobby (for a young man), a kestrel (for the ordinary servingman).[17] Two other players carry a model church and a model boat: do these represent larger sets the troupe would have carted with them—or did traveling players use economical, "Brechtian" indicators in production? Moryson, who saw the same performers as Baumgartner, observes that they had "nether a Complete number of Actours, nor any good Appareil, nor any ornament of the Stage."[18] But that was in 1592; once the actors were under the patronage of the Landgrave Moritz, did the circumstances of their performance change? Or did such properties, along with the falcon, church, boat, and flame, function allegorically in performance? And what of the two masked figures at the front? Are they part of a performance involving the four elements, or are they costumed for a masque or an *entre-act?* Is the rooster related to the cock of classical mime, the Chanticleer of medieval fabliaux, the Cucurucu of the *commedia?* And, finally, is the painting generic, or are these particular players costumed for a particular play?

Some months after the English actors returned to Kassel for the winter of 1606–7, Johann Eckel, an official at the Kassel court, informed the Landgrave Moritz of the actors' dissatisfaction with their compensation; if it did not improve, their last performance at Kassel would be the *Comoedia vom Konig auß England ud Schottland wie die beide gegen einand kreig führten, da der eine des Andern Sohn d Ander des Andern tochter gefangn hatte* [*The Play of the King of England and Scotland, how the two waged war against each other, where the one takes the Other's Son and the Other the Other's daughter prisoner*].[19] Might the players have performed this six-character play at the Frankfurt fair, just prior to their return to Kassel? If the Hartmann painting is of a particular troupe, could the player in red have been the captive princess, the player with the falcon the captive prince? Or could they have performed the *Tragedy of Julius and Hyppolita,* another six-character play in the repertory of the English actors? The characters in that play, involving the marriage of one brother and the departure of the other, are a prince, a princess, two Roman brothers, and two servants.[20]

German records identify a number of plays that were performed by English actors on the continent, some carried there by Robert Browne. Those known to have been presented by the Kassel actors include (by title or description) *Comedy of Abraham and Lot and of the destruction of Sodom and Gomorrah; Of a King of England who fell in love with a goldsmith's wife and abducted her; Comedy of the prodigal son; Of a pious woman of Antwerp; Of a duke of Florence who fell in love with a nobleman's daughter; Of Nobody and*

Somebody; Of the two brothers King Ludwig and King Frederick of Hungary. King Frederick had all stabbed and murdered; Of a King of Khipern, of a Duke of Venice;[21] *Of a rich man and of Lazarus; Comedy of Amadis;*[22] and three that may be versions of Marlowe plays: *Fortunatus, Von dem Doctor Faustus,* and *Vom dem Jude.*

Clearly, the painting of the traveling players poses more questions than it answers. The album context has yielded a time and a place, but as yet we know of no archival documents that can, with authority, fill in the narrative. Yet like the de Witt sketch of the Swan theater—extant through the copy made by van Buchell—and the Peacham drawing of *Titus Andronicus*—or a German version of the play—the Hartmann illustration claims a unique place in the early modern theatrical record.

Notes

An earlier version of this essay was presented at the theater history seminar at the Shakespeare Association of America conference in Philadelphia, April 13–15, 2006.

1. Edinburgh University Library, La.III.283. See my "Michael van Meer's *Album Amicorum,* with Illustrations of London, 1614–15," *The Huntington Library Quarterly* 69.2 (2006): 301–13.

2. Kunstbibliothek Berlin, Lipp 0Z3.

3. Huntington Library, HM 743. See my "His Great-Granduncle's *Album amicorum*: Francis Segar and the International Network of Early Modern Englishmen," forthcoming.

4. See, among others, the albums of Gervasius Fabricius of Salzburg (1603–37), British Library, Add 17025, and Frederic de Botnia of Saumur (1616–18), British Library, Add 16889. The Bamberg illustration, I Qc 75, is reproduced in Werner Taegert, *Edler Schatz holden Erinnerns: Bilder in Stammbüchern der Staatsbibliothek Bamberg aus vier Jahrhunderten* (Bamberg: Staatsbibliothek Bamberg, 1995), 67.

5. British Library, Eg 1222.

6. I am grateful to David Landman for pointing out the allegorical features of the painting.

7. I am grateful to John Astington for drawing my attention to the van Heemskerck print.

8. The text for the lead car, The Triumph of the World, identifies the figures and ends with this comment: "How swiftly do immutable laws on earth engender the rotary motion which reveals everything in its turn." Ilja M. Veldman, *Maarten van Heemskerck and Dutch Humanism in the Sixteenth Century* (Maarssen: Gary Schwartz, 1977), 137. Although these "after Heemskerck" prints have been attributed to Dirck Coornhert, Veldman suggests they were done by Cornelis Cort. See Veldman, 133–41, for a discussion of the print series.

9. One of four 1597 entries is sited Frankfurt an der Oder. These entries are the oldest in the album, which does not start in earnest until 1605.

10. See my "English Actors in Kassel, Germany, during Shakespeare's Time," *Medieval and Renaissance Drama in England* 10 (1998): 238–61.

11. Peter Brand, "Der englische Komödiant Robert Browne, (1563-ca. 1621/39)" (master's thesis, Heidelberg University 1978).

12. John Green's name appears frequently in continental records. Those that place him with Browne include June 1606 Strasbourg and the 1606 fall Frankfurt fair. Robert Ledbetter is on record with Browne in 1599 and 1601, as well as 1606. The "Johan Le Peter" in a 1606 letter regarding the Frankfurt Easter fair from "Robert Browne, Johan Le Peter, and other Hessische commediens" may be an elision of John Green (Johan Grün) and Robert Ledbetter.

13. An October 1606 record indicates they played in Nuremberg: they may have stopped there after Frankfurt or made the trip after returning to Kassel.

14. Christoph von Rommel, *Geschichte von Hessen* 6 (Cassel: Frederich Perthes, 1837), 402n, offers a modernized transcript of Landgrave Moritz's letter, which he says is to an unidentified princely person. Hans Hartleb, *Deutschlands erster Theaterbau: Eine Geschichte des Theaterlebens und der englischen Komödianten unter Landgraf Moritz dem Gelehrten von Hessen-Cassel* (Berlin and Leipzig: Walter de Gruyter, 1936), 53, relying on the manuscript in the Hessisches Staatsarchiv Marburg, "Correspondenz L. Moritz mit landgr. Ludwig IV. 1597," identifies the addressee as Landgrave Ludwig IV of Hessen-Marburg and fixes the date as February 1597. Both Rommel, 401f, and Hartleb, 30–31, refer to Landgrave Ludwig's return of the borrowed items after Grave Hans Ernst von Solms and his company saw the performance.

15. *Shakespeare's Europe: A Survey of the Condition of Europe at the end of the 16th century. Being unpublished chapters of Fynes Moryson's Itinerary (1617).* With an Introduction and an Account of Fynes Moryson's Career by Charles Hughes, 2d ed. (1903; New York: Benjamin Blom, 1967), 304.

16. Georg Steinhausen, ed., *Briefwechsel Balthasar Baumgartners des Jüngeren mit seiner Gattin Magdalena, geb. Behaim (1582–1598)* (Tübingen: Litterarischer Verein in Stuttgart, 1895), 176.

17. R. Chambers, ed., *The Book of Days: A Miscellany of Popular Antiquities in Connection with the Calendar including Anecdote, Biography, and History, Curiosities of Literature, and Oddities of Human Life and Character,* vol. 2 (Philadelphia: J. B. Lippincott, 1899), 211.

18. *Shakespeare's Europe,* 304.

19. Hartleb, *Deutschlands erster Theaterbau,* 53.

20. The texts of *Eine Schöne Lustig Triumphirende Comœdia von Eines Königes Sohne auss Engellandt und des Königes Tochter auss Schottlandt* and *Tragœdia von Julio und Hyppolita* may be found in *Spieltexte der Wanderbühne,* ed. Manfred Brauneck, vol. 1 (Berlin: Walter de Gruyter, 1970), 211–68 and 427–59.

21. *Of a King of Khipern, a Duke of Venice* may be related to *Othello,* with "Khipern" a German version of Kypros (Greek) or Kibris (Turkish) for Cyprus.

22. The records also provide titles or descriptions of plays that were "probably" or "perhaps" in the Kassel actors' repertory. Identified as such by Christiane Engelbrecht, Wilfried Brennecke, Franz Uhlendorff, and Hans Joachim Schaefer, *Theater in Kassel: Aus der Geschichte des Staatstheaters Kassel von den Anfängen bis zur Gegenwart* (Kassel: Bärenreiter, 1959), 7–8, these include *Comoedia Otto Schutz*

[*Comedy Otto Schutz* (written by the Landgrave Moritz)]; *Die Belohnung der Gottesfurcht* [*The Reward of the Godfearing*]; *Ariodante und Ginevra; Komedia von Tarquinio und Lukretia; Speculum aistheticum* ("probably"); *Vincentius Ladislaus, Satrap von Mantua* (written by Heinrich Julius of Braunschweig); *Romeo und Julia; Viel Lärm um Nichts* [*Much Ado About Nothing*]; *Komödie der Irrungen* [*Comedy of Errors*]; *Spanish Tragedy; Sidonia und Theagenes; Julius und Hypolita;* and *Titus Andronicus* ("perhaps").

German titles or descriptions of the plays that were surely performed by the Kassel actors are *Comoedia von Abraham und Loth und vom Untergang von Sodom und Gomorra; Fortunatus; Von einem König aus England, der sich in eines Goldschmidts Weib verliebte und sie enführte; Comoedie vom verlorenen Sohn; Von einer frommen Frauen von Antworf; Von dem doctor Faustus; Von ein Herzog von Florenz, der sich in sines Edelmanns Tochter verliebt hat; Von Niemandts und Jemand; Von dem Jude; Von den zwei Brüder König Ludwig und König Friedrich von Ungarn. Hats der König Friedrich als errstocher und ermordet; Von ein Konig Friedrich von ein Herzog von Venedig; Von dem reichen Mann und von dem Lazarus;* and *Comoedi aus dem Amadi.*

Review Essay

Perspectives on Shakespeare and 1599

A Year in the Life of William Shakespeare: 1599, James Shapiro. xxiv + 429. London and New York: HarperCollins, 2005. Pp. xxiv + 429. Cloth $27.95. Paperback: New York: Harper Perennial, 2006, $14.95.

Reviewer: WILLIAM B. LONG

James Shapiro's *A Year in the Life of William Shakespeare: 1599* [British title: *1599: A Year in the Life of William Shakespeare*] is not a scholarly study and should not be confused with one. Unfortunately, this volume is basically a house of cards. From a distance, the edifice is interesting and even pleasing. But a push here and there collapses the structure. Incorrect facts and unsupportable suppositions do not provide firm bases for supporting Shapiro's contentions. He gets off to a bad start in the "Preface" where he reveals to the naive and unlearned but hopefully awed and duly impressed readers that: "In search of answers I was fortunate to have access to the archives where the literary treasures of Elizabethan England have been preserved—especially the Folger Shakespeare Library in Washington, DC, the Huntington Library in San Marino, California, and the British Library (at both its old and new London addresses)" (xxii). How is this supposed to set Shapiro off from the sea of readers who also have used these magnificent collections? Any qualified scholar can "have access" to these libraries and thousands upon thousands have. Particularly amusing is Shapiro's need to tell the masses that he has used The British Library "at both its old and new addresses." Is this wonderful and so distinctive and unusual revelation supposed to make what he says more trustworthy? Will it overwhelm any doubts that might surface?

Albeit written by an English professor at a leading research university, this book is basically just another entry in the seemingly endless parade of "biographies" of Shakespeare chasing after the seemingly endless flow of cash spent for such volumes and clearly aimed at that nebulous, much-sought-after although much-abused creature: the general reader. Even the title itself follows a recently popular pattern: an eye-catching date followed by the rest of the title that explains the subject matter of the book. Andrew Bridgeford's *1066: The Hidden History in the Bayeaux Tapestry,* Gavin Menzies's *1421: The Year China Discovered America,* and Charles C. Mann's *1491: New Revelations of the Americas before Columbus* are similarly titled works, brought out by trade houses, that also pursue the perhaps not so elusive general reader. Choosing a title, of course, is a problem: how to attract the maximum number of buyers while appearing to be "scholarly" but without seeming to court the *hoi polloi*. Thus a title more closely conforming to the subject matter of the book, such as "The Intellectual and Artistic Development of William Shakespeare in His Social and Political Contexts with Special Reference to the Year 1599" would seem to gather dust even as it is read. Similarly, something along the line of "Shakespeare Confronts the Perils of '99" would slide much too far the other way.

There is, however, one glaring difference between this group of "date-titled" studies and *1599;* unfortunately in sharp contrast to these others, Shapiro's volume contains neither footnotes nor endnotes. If this decision was the publisher's, it is both financially and intellectually indefensible. If this decision was the author's, it is unprofessional and reprehensible. The reader, yes, even that shaggy beast of a general reader, deserves to know exactly where an author is getting his/her quotations and other information. How an author can defend his choices is paramount in any historical study. If *1599* were a novel, such standards need not be invoked. Shapiro attempts to evade the problem by issuing a "global qualification" about his use of sources: "[r]ather than awkwardly littering the pages . . . with words such as 'perhaps' . . . [or] . . . 'probably,'" he passes off as assurance that "Readers interested in the historical sources on which I rely will find them in the bibliographical essay at the end of the book" (xxiii). But such an "explanation" is not a license to play fast and loose with "facts" and to introduce unfettered imaginings. Thus instead of specific, traceable notes, Shapiro appends this "Bibliographical Essay"; although for one who spends some time discussing Montaigne, he surely must realize that this is no essay. Both for the book in general and for each chapter, Shapiro lists a series of books and articles, occasionally accompanied by comments, that he claims to have used and which are intended "as a guide for those interested in consulting my sources directly" (375). But this arrangement is entirely unsatisfactory for anyone attempting to use it. For scholars checking any particular topic, it is woefully inadequate. For the general reader, such a listing is overwhelming, confusing, and certainly not geared to help. For everyone, only works are given, never the specific place in the work. For this reader, such actions are obscurantism and simple chicanery.

This entire "Bibliographical Essay" is basically a thirty-nine-page blurb, a kind of heraldic blazon meant to display the author's scholarly heritage, thus saying to the unsuspecting reader: "Look at all I have read!" and thus: "Trust me, I know." The problem is that most readers, even reviewers in the popular press, do not know; and they do not possess the tools with which to explore and to judge what the writer claims. Shapiro prints many "facts" which are patently not true and accepts as true many things which cannot be proved; he makes numerous declarations which are merely surmises; thus without specific references, the ordinary reader cannot know when the author can document his statements and defend his assertions and when he cannot, or perhaps more directly: when Shapiro can be trusted and when he cannot. In 1934, the distinguished Elizabethan historian, J. E. Neale, published what many still consider to be the best biography of Queen Elizabeth although it is surprisingly absent from Shapiro's "Bibliographical Essay." Neale, for whatever reasons, also published his study without notes, for which, and for many years, he endured rejections by his peers ranging from highly arched eyebrows to vitriolic comments.

A more than cursory glance at the "Bibliographical Essay" reveals both its very uneven nature and the many places where Shapiro's knowledge is not equal to the task. Everything a writer finds does not deserve inclusion in a bibliography. One cannot just pile up previous works on a topic; they must be sorted out and evaluated. And this means that the evaluator must have the knowledge to do so, a situation by no means always evident here. A few examples will do. On page 380, Shapiro pretentiously declares that "Any discussion of Shakespeare in print begins with A. W. Pollard and G. R. Redgrave, eds., *Short-Title Catalogue of Books*. . . ." This work is undeniably of great importance (and Peter Blayney's new edition is eagerly awaited), but one is tempted to ask exactly how many academic investigators of "Shakespeare in print" ever touched finger to page. Why is the general reader sent here? What would he/she make of it? Shapiro's assertion leads one to be wary of his understanding of printing practices (of which, more later). On page 388, Shapiro announces that "The standard authorities on Elizabethan censorship are Richard Dutton's . . . *Mastering the Revels* . . . and Janet Clare, '*Art made tongue-tied by authority*' . . ."; however, the nonspecialist reader is not told that Dutton's work both opposes and demolishes Clare's. Thus, one might ask: why list the latter? How is the reader helped? Or perhaps more to the unpleasant point: has Shapiro read either? On the design of the Globe, the hapless reader is initially referred to John Cranford Adams's *The Globe Playhouse* . . . (1942), a work destroyed by Richard Hosley in 1957. Why is Adams listed at all? And where are poor Hosley's articles?

On page 395, the reader (seemingly soberly) is instructed: "On textual issues and censorship, see Annabel Patterson 'Back by Popular Demand: The Two Versions of *Henry V*' . . ." even though this article was blown out of the water by Paul Werstine shortly after its publication. On pages 396–97, the reader is sent to a book on building practices published in 1663, assured that this is "a richly informative account of early modern building practices." But this publication is sixty-four years—two generations—after the building of the First Globe. Exactly how relevant is it to 1599? If Shapiro had not hidden behind that meaningless and deliberately vague and obfuscating term "early modern," he might not have hobbled himself. No scholar can be expected to know everything; but then, no one should pretend to. In spite of its seemingly limited scope, "*1599: A Year . . .,*" this book actually encompasses a very large number of topics that developed over many years; and therein lie a number of the problems with this volume which are revealed in so humble a place as the end of the book.

Enough of wandering in the Antipodes; the narrative itself demands attention. It seems that the purpose of this book (other than making money) is to advance the thesis that 1599 is not only a very important year in the history of England and of the history of the theater in England, but also (and most importantly) that 1599 was Shakespeare's *annus mirabilis,* a time of great artistic achievement and an important turning point in his career. There is nothing wrong with such a thesis; but establishing proof for any of the three legs of it can be difficult, making the whole structure wobbly.

Essentially, Shapiro sketches out major historical problems of the year and attempts to show how Shakespeare fitted into them and to demonstrate how he, in his work, responded to them. This means that Shapiro delivers 373 pages of mostly history enlivened by the interacting presence of William Shakespeare. The book *1599* is not a biography, but rather bits of biography and supposed biography and artistic development fitted into an historical context. Again, there is nothing wrong with such a plan; the success or failure lies in how it is accomplished. Thus the reader, general or otherwise, must decide the validity of Shapiro's assumptions and claims.

Like most years, 1599 visited many problems on England, none of them new. There was another serious threat of a new Spanish Armada, but these occurred with agonizing regularity. Queen Elizabeth grew ever older causing concomitantly rising anxiety about succession in courtier and commoner alike. She was not to die until 1603 at the (for that time) quite advanced age of seventy, although, of course, no one could know that in 1599. She could have died at any moment. (Shakespeare himself died at fifty-two, but no one at that time seems to have thought that he died untimely early [although Shapiro does, presumably working from early twenty-first-century actuarial tables, asserting that Shakespeare "died prematurely" (373)]; two generations earlier, Erasmus at fifty had complained that nearly all of his contemporaries were dead.) The Irish problems had been festering for years and continue to do so. Although quite serious, the problems of Armada and succession and Ireland were neither new nor unique to 1599; this year, however, did mark the addition of the addle-pated Earl of Essex as a major mixer in this volatile brew. But discussions of these three acutely worrisome issues could be constructed for any year in the 1590s.

Nonetheless, Shapiro shapes *1599* around these problems, presumably because that also was the year of the building of the First Globe and that no other year fit so well his notion of Shakespeare's artistic maturation. Appropriately enough for a book about a year, the book is divided into four sections: "Winter," "Spring," "Summer," and "Autumn" and attempts to deal with problems as they occurred chronologically, not always so easy when a number of crucial dates pertaining to Shakespeare are unknown. And fitting Shakespeare into all this history, into all that existed in his time, presents numerous difficulties. It necessarily asks: "Did Shakespeare know about this, see that, hear about something else? How did he react to all these things?" But what if he did not know about them, or did not care, or did not choose to work them into his plays? One could be tempted to fasten upon an historical happening and then search through Shakespeare's texts to see how one might wrench an "influence" or a "reference." If due caution is not administered, such a nebulous situation as placing a figure in history can tempt an author to place his "hero" (a quite vague word that Shapiro uses with some regularity but consistently refuses to define) into unlikely situations and making decisions and responses that he, in fact, never may have made. Asserting that Shakespeare had been born "too late" (271), Shapiro pictures Shakespeare's political preferences much involved with nostalgia for past times including at least facets of Catholicism, the old nobility, and the passing of feudalism.

"The reformist effort to do away with the distracting rituals of Catholic worship resulted in a kind of sensory deprivation, for the rush to reform had overlooked the extent to which people craved the sights and sounds of the old communal celebration" (170–71). No doubt some did, but percentages are hard to establish. Here and elsewhere Shapiro and his Shakespeare long at least for elements of "the good old days" without Shapiro's acknowledging that many, many people in Britain were enthusiastic supporters of varying degrees of ecclesiastical reform. Shapiro then proceeds to unite Essex with "chivalry" and to claim that Shakespeare's supposed nostalgia also extended to the "passing" of chivalry. Armed with this whole series of assumptions, Shapiro finds no difficulty in asserting that "Shakespeare would have found Essex's *Apology* fascinating both as a character study and as a daring political tract" (54). Shapiro's romanticism, his nostalgia for "chivalry," and his failure to see the danger to life, limb, and the stability of the state threatened by allowing loose cannons like Essex to do as they pleased, produces statements such as "Essex had done his best to embody this chivalric code" (55) and "During this anxious time, when England badly needed his leadership, Essex withdrew from the court in a sulk" (56). Although Shapiro does not say so because it would not fit into his view of Essex and Shakespeare, the obvious parallel with Essex at this point is the withdrawal of Achilles.

In studying the life of anyone living in the late sixteenth and early seventeenth centuries who was not a major governmental figure or at least a wealthy holder of estates from which detailed records survive, there is precious little material with which to construct a life. Even though more is known about the life of William Shakespeare than that of any other Elizabethan-Jacobean playwright except Ben Jonson, documented records are few and far between. Consequently anyone attempting to reconstruct any portion of Shakespeare's life is forced to construct a narrative using whatever is available. The problem is to use events that happened and to create situations that very well could have happened and to label everything carefully. In a work professing to be historically accurate, an author cannot just invent what fits into his general pattern for the book or his notion of the character he/she is studying.

Readers, general or otherwise, most likely will be pleased to find that Shapiro is not an anti-Stratfordian and that his Shakespeare, in contrast to the figure presented in several recent over-publicized and grotesquely overrated "biographies" of Shakespeare, is not a Roman Catholic (secret or otherwise) although he does seem (as noted) to possess some nostalgia for older forms of celebration and rituals, and is neither a Marxist nor an unwavering monarchist; but Shapiro's Shakespeare does turn out to have desires to be at court, to influence courtiers, and to be valued and appreciated by them. "Shakespeare knew that his plays were valued differently at court, where he was recognized as a dramatist alert to the factional world of contemporary politics" (19). Shapiro's Shakespeare is a man ". . . who mingles easily with princes and paupers . . ." (105). "Shakespeare had had unparalleled success in pleasing both courtly and popular audiences over the past few years—but these admirers weren't [sic] necessarily drawn to the same things in his plays" (16).

The book *1599* is filled with statements that either are patently not true or might be true but are very unlikely to be so, given many other facts that are known about this historical time. Sometimes "Shapiro-facts" are dropped on the unsuspecting reader in "throwaway" portions of sentences with rather the air of "I in my great knowledge am reminding you ignorant readers of something all us scholars know." Thus Shapiro assures his nonspecialist readers that "Shakespeare kept close at hand a sheaf of forty or more folded sheets, each sheet with four writing sides, covered with sonnets in various stages of composition (it wasn't [sic] until the early seventeenth century that writers began using single sheets of paper)" (223). Neither Shapiro nor anyone else knows how Shakespeare composed or stored his sonnets; this half of his sentence is novelistic froth. The second half is far worse; *whatever* is Shapiro talking about with his "single sheets of paper"? There were many different sizes of paper available in Shakespeare's England, and large ones could be (and were) cut into smaller pieces if occasion demanded; and even a popular size, for instance, the one approximately 16 by 24 inches, folded once becomes a folio, twice a quarto, thrice an octavo, but all of them began and remain a single sheet of paper. What was the point of throwing in that meaningless parenthetical sentence? What is the poor general reader expected to do with such a combination of imagination and misinformation and confusion?

A few further instances of mangled facts and suppositions are worth noting here. Shapiro pointedly asserts that "The Globe was the first London theater built by actors for actors . . ." (131). This wildly erroneous statement drastically reduces the number of known purpose-built theaters. Certainly the Globe was built with a large portion of the funds advanced by players, but even general readers may wonder for whom the Red Lion, the Theatre, the Curtain, the Rose, and the Swan were built previous to the Globe. Sheep, perhaps. On page 123, readers are told unequivocally that the Globe had a diameter of seventy-two feet, a dimension known to no one but James Shapiro. And unless he has been doing some illegal archeological tunneling and secreting his findings from the public, he does not know it either. Henslowe's 1587 Rose did have such a diameter, an ascertainable and documented fact: the Rose foundation has been excavated, measured, photographed, and published. But except for a very small portion, the Globe foundation is not yet available for exploration; thus the diameter and nearly every other specific dimension are unknown. What is the point of claiming that it is known? When Sam Wanamaker's reproduction of a generic Elizabethan theater (also named The Globe) was being planned, the diameter of the building was the focus of a crucial debate. Those favoring a hundred-foot diameter won, and the theater was so constructed. This dimension matters very much if one is considering the size of the stage, the proximity of the players to various members of the audience, sight lines, acoustics, and to deciding how many persons the theater could hold. It is well to note that an entire seventy-two-foot theater could be placed within the inner ring (that is, the pit and the stage) of a hundred-foot one.

Setting the scene—the historical context—is important in both novels and biographies; but again, the author has an obligation in a nonfiction work to place the figure discussed into situations that were likely or probable, and perhaps occasionally, possible. One cannot assume that merely because a place or situation existed contemporaneously, that his featured figure participated in it. But Shakespeare, neither a menial servant cleaning up after his masters nor a courtier nor an honored guest, is imagined to have been allowed to roam unsupervised through state and private rooms in Whitehall Palace (29–31). Such an imaginary peregrination allows Shapiro to describe the rooms, but does not add veracity to his vision of Shakespeare's place in this world or his knowledge of it. As a member of the King's Men (but not yet so in 1599, of course), he would have been styled a "Gentleman," but this is very far down in the courtly pecking order, hardly a place from which to get cozy with the great and powerful, nor is it a place from which they necessarily would value his craft, let alone his political observations. By contrast, Philip Henslowe was for many years a "Groom of the Chamber" then moving up to being a "Sewer of the Chamber," both positions worlds away from Shakespeare's. In stark contrast to Shakespeare's few visits to court, Henslowe spent the vast majority of his days there. But Shapiro's description is part and parcel of his notion of Shakespeare (and his creation Hamlet) as "straddling worlds and struggling to reconcile past and present" (322). How noble! How romantic! (Shapiro would label it the ever-undefined "heroic.") Such a conception merely romanticizes both Shakespeare's importance to the court as well as the intellectual level of the court and its entertainments.

In attempting to sketch the intellectual milieu of the writing of *Julius Caesar,* Shapiro notes the burning of the satires and feels compelled to list a series of them (153). Would any of his general readers have heard of (or care about) *Virgidemiarum, Skialetheia,* or *Caltha Poetarum,* let alone the more well-known *The Scourge of Villainy?* How does this listing help these readers to understand what was going on and why? Here as elsewhere, such as giving the later stage-history of *As You Like It* (251–52) and the sources of *Hamlet* (319–20), there is a sense of his feeling that he had to stuff in every scrap of information found in doing research—a situation of "No note card left unused." Shapiro further declares without a shred of evidence that plays chosen to be performed at court were judged by the Master of the Revels to be the year's best (363); at another point, it was Shakespeare's "most recent work" that was wanted at court (36). And readers are told that ". . . Spenser was probably eager to see the best plays of the previous year staged at Whitehall . . ." (71). The criteria for choosing plays for court performance are unknown and most likely varied from year to year and with the personalities involved, but plays certainly were not chosen for court performance as an award for "quality." Behind such statements are Shapiro's assumptions both that the court is intellectually interested in drama and that Shakespeare wanted to be (even a minor) force there. This is not proved on either side; both suppositions seem to this reader to be highly unlikely.

But such presumed proximity of Shakespeare with the great (admittedly he occasionally was in the same large, crowded room with a number of them) unfortunately releases a romantic streak in Shapiro which merely compounds the problem by placing the man of the theater in a social position which he could not inhabit: "A monarch [Elizabeth] who wrote every day must have been an especially discriminating critic and perhaps better disposed than most to a playwright who did the same" (31). This is getting very sloppy. All writers are not discriminating critics, then or now. Was Elizabeth similarly disposed to other playwrights who presumably also spent most of their days writing? "By 1598 Shakespeare's relationship with the court had become increasingly reciprocal" (20). Shapiro regularly posits Shakespeare as straddling two worlds, those of the court and the theater: ". . . his play-writing was constrained by the needs of his fellow players as well as the expectations of audiences both at the public playhouse and at court—demands that often pulled him in opposite directions" (8).

If only those naughty players and their uncouth [paying] audiences would have left him alone, Shakespeare could have spent all his time writing poetry and political philosophy for the "court"! Only a romantic inflation of Shakespeare's position in and importance to the court could sustain Shapiro's notion of Shakespeare's place in his world. And, of course, Shakespeare's adventures in the palace must have provided grist for his artistic mill: one of the objects to be seen at Whitehall was "a portrait of Julius Caesar (which surely caught Shakespeare's attention)" (32). Speaking of Shakespeare's work on *impresa,* Shapiro assures his readers that "No doubt when Shakespeare entered the shield gallery his eye was drawn to his own anonymous contributions" (34). Supposition or even possibility is neither fact nor accomplishment. The line simply has disappeared between what might possibly have happened and what most likely occurred (not to mention what actually did or did not happen). In a nonfiction work, this is irresponsibility. Shapiro wants his Shakespeare to have had access to all the facilities that existed and knowledge of all manner of events that happened in his time and place; but just because something existed does not at all mean that Shakespeare necessarily knew about it, much less experienced it or even cared about it.

Early on the nonspecialist reader is pummeled by both inaccuracy and ill-founded supposition. On the very first page, before even beginning the "Prologue," the reader is presented a small, rather dark portion of Wenceslaus Hollar's "Long View of London" (not identified by Shapiro), published in 1647 but drawn some years before the Second Globe was pulled down in 1644, purporting to display "the Globe Theatre"; Shapiro is correct in warning the readers that the labels on the engraving for "The Globe" and "Beere bayting" are incorrectly exchanged. However, he fails to inform his readers that he is supplying them with a picture of the wrong theater; the picture on page 1 of *1599* is that of the Second Globe built in 1614, not that of the First built in 1599 which constitutes one of the legs upon which Shapiro builds his thesis. Or does Shapiro think that they looked the same? But then, none of the pictures at the chapter openings are fully identified; only "The Globe," however, is totally wrong. The captions to the color plates also are erratic and incomplete. When he gets to the writing of plays, Shapiro does not seem to understand that crafting plays was a well-paying way for clever young men to earn quite a rewarding living. This is why even those with university educations were attracted to the theater. Shapiro denigrates playwrights by noting that ". . . a freelance dramatist earned just £6 a play and a day-laborer earned £10 a year" (4). Even if Shapiro's statistics are correct and a laborer managed to earn ten pounds, a single play paid three-fifths of that, did not require over three hundred dawn-to-dusk days of hard physical work, and more than one play could be written in a year. Collaboration, of course, facilitated chunks of even faster cash. And some playwrights were paid more, occasionally to £10.

In trying to trim performance-time to the much-tongued and much-contested "two hours traffic" (he seems not to know of the many references to playing time as being three hours), Shapiro asserts that the sun had set in London by 6:00 P.M. in September (260); at another point the reader is told that the sun sets "in late winter and early autumn around five clock" (339); this sunset schedule was no more true in 1599 than it is today. But when he gets to the Globe's chief carpenter, Peter Street, Shapiro shifts his imagination into high gear.

> The wagons [containing the timbers from the dismantled Theatre] headed through Bishopsgate and south-west to Peter Street's waterfront warehouse near Bridewell Stairs, where the timber was unloaded and safely stored. The popular story of the dismantled frame being drawn across or over the Thames (which was "nigh frozen over") to the future building site is a fantasy; it would have been too risky sledding the heavy load across thin ice and the steep tolls on London Bridge for wheelage and poundage would have been prohibitive; and had the timber been left exposed to the elements through the winter months at the marshy site on the Globe, it could have been warped beyond repair (if not subject to a counter-raid by Giles Allen's friends). (7)

I have quoted at length because this is a particularly egregious example of arrogant ignorance and baseless supposition masking as theater history. There is no evidence that Peter Street ever had a warehouse near Bridewell Stairs nor anywhere else; why would he? Warehouses were not common in Elizabethan London, and one large enough to hold these particular timbers would have had to have been fairly spacious. Why would even a master carpenter possess such an expensive and highly atypical and generally useless building? Shapiro simply has invented this building and this scenario to fit into his notions about when and how the new theater was built. So much for the handling of facts.

It is not known for certain how the timbers were taken across the Thames. No responsible scholar ever has suggested that they were carted over London Bridge. Why does Shapiro make an issue of it? Theater historians who have spent their scholarly lives studying the archeology and genealogy of Elizabethan-Jacobean-Caroline London theaters believe that it is most probable that the timbers either were dragged on sledges over the ice or floated on barges. The problem is: how strong was the ice as well as when and for how long was the river frozen? Certainly the players would have wanted to start building as soon as possible. The land on the south bank was indeed marshy, but it was not unusable; and surely it was not frozen all winter to prevent the digging and laying of footers for the walls. If the players were worried about stacking the timbers on the ground, a temporary raised platform of stones or of disposable wood could have been laid up quickly, easily, and inexpensively. The notion of these timbers being "warped beyond repair" by being "exposed to the elements" is ludicrous. This was not green wood. These timbers already had been "exposed to the elements" since 1576 and, once reassembled, would continue to be "exposed" until 1613. The notion that Allen would try to retrieve the timber—to which he had no legal right—is highly unlikely. Shapiro was unwise to have attacked previous (although of course unnamed) work as "fantasy." A little knowledge of scholarship reveals where the real fantasy lies.

Interpretation of evidence often has more to do with the attitude of the interpreter than with the facts themselves. Because Shapiro proposes (he hardly could know since none of the Globe timbers survive) that different numbers and patterns of slashes marked the proper joinings of timbers in buildings of the time, he concludes that the carpenters were illiterate (130). This is not a valid conclusion because there is no evidence presented. Did he expect that literate carpenters would have written notes? Or perhaps a "'Timberological' Essay"? Whether or not the carpenters were illiterate, matching markings to indicate proper insertions was simply the way things were done and has nothing to do with the ability to read. Such markings were quickly made, could endure abuse in handling and moving, and were infallible guides. Carpenters who most assuredly were literate were still making similarly purposed markings at least to the end of the twentieth century. And what is the point about whether or not the carpenters were illiterate? Since when did craftsmanship necessarily rely on literacy?

Inventions or at least the repeating of others' defenseless suppositions about the functioning of the theaters pepper the text. "The titles of the plays to be performed that afternoon by the Chamberlain's and Lord Admiral's Men—'Printed in play-bills, upon every post'—had already been widely advertised [*sic*] through out the city. Musicians were dispatched to literally drum up business . . ." (97). Such statements make for a colorful picture, but they have no backing in documented fact; in spite of certain recent claims by others, there is no surviving proof either of the printing and distribution of playbills or of roving musicians. Who was to pay for such advertising extravagances? The shareholders for the Chamberlain's and Henslowe for the Admiral's? Printing was expensive, so would have been the distribution, so were musicians. Were the players themselves to save money by taking time and energy from their valuable rehearsal hours to run all over London posting bills? Shapiro's claims have no bases in documented facts, are basically senseless, and do not constitute theater history; they are imaginary scene-painting.

Shapiro also bends the presentation of facts to support his fantasies of Shakespeare's contemporary value and his place in historical England. "It's [*sic*] no surprise that the few references at this time to popular plays performed in aristocrats' homes are limited to Shakespeare's work, typically his histories" (21). Not only does Shapiro not reveal his sources here, but also he does not tell his deliberately misled readers that most references to private productions do not mention even the title of the play, much less the name of the playwright. At best, his "statistic" is basically worthless. But Shapiro relentlessly pushes his favorite author into community with the great. "By 1598 Shakespeare's relationship with the court had become increasingly reciprocal. He was not only a regular presence at court but also shaped how England's leading families in turn gave voice to their political experiences and his words entered court vocabulary as a shorthand for the complicated maneuvering and gossip that defined court life" (20). Such claims are so ludicrously overblown that they probably just should be ignored. Suffice to say that a player appearing before the court even several times a year cannot be labeled as being "at court" in the sense that a nobleman or a valued daily senior attendant such as Philip Henslowe could, and a player hardly was likely to be valued as Shapiro imagines. Someone quoting a line or making an analogy to characters he has seen is by no means necessarily valuing the playwright as a political commentator or philosopher. Such a commenter well might not know the name of the playwright.

When Shapiro turns to the plays themselves, not surprisingly the same problems emerge. Part of the difficulty results from Shapiro's wanting to see the new theater as a kind of at least semi-elite gathering place: at the Globe "Shakespeare could offer plays there that set a new standard and attracted a regular, charmed clientele" (127). Exactly how this audience was or became "charmed" is not elucidated. Facts get changed, ignored, or misinterpreted to fit Shapiro's shapings of his thesis. Shapiro believes that many things, political, personal, and artistic came together in 1599 to change forever Shakespeare, his art, his theater, and even his world. This is a tall order to prove, whatever indications and partial support may exist. Shapiro is convinced that in 1599 Shakespeare completed *Henry V,* entirely wrote *Julius Caesar* and *As You Like It,* and did much work on *Hamlet* (xv). This is an astounding output even for Shakespeare, not impossible but not particularly likely either. But this thesis must be driven because that is what justifies the rest of the book. Shapiro offers no defense for his crowding these plays into this time period or for excluding others, except for the implied one that this arrangement fits his thesis and other chronologies do not.

E. K. Chambers attuned his chronicling of Shakespeare's creations to the law terms which began their years in the autumn, a schedule to which the theatrical companies attached their new seasons (and still do). Shapiro, for whatever reasons, strictly adheres to the January-through-December chronology for his tale. Thus Chambers assigns *Much Ado* and *Henry V* to the theatrical season of 1598–99, *Julius Caesar, As You Like It,* and *Twelfth Night* to the 1599–1600 season, and *Hamlet* and *Merry Wives* to 1600–1601. Chambers was not infallible; but to disagree with him, one needs either to produce new evidence or at least to reevaluate existing evidence to show how Chambers erred. Shapiro offers nothing; he simply declares that Shakespeare wrote certain plays at certain times because that is what fits his proffered arc of

Shakespeare's artistic maturity. In so doing, Shapiro tosses aside *Twelfth Night,* "a formulaic throwback" (369); needless to say, he does not wish to pair the inspiration and creativity of *Hamlet* ("Shakespeare's greatest play" [357]) with *Merry Wives* which he says Shakespeare interrupted *2 Henry IV* to write (20). Shapiro's thesis necessarily must have *Hamlet* written in 1599. Chambers had assigned *1* and *2 Henry IV* to 1597–98. Shapiro gives no date for *Merry Wives,* but it obviously must precede the magic *Hamlet:* "in the course of a little over a year he went from writing *The Merry Wives of Windsor* to writing a play as inspired as *Hamlet*" (xxii). "When Shakespeare was at his most creative, he wrote plays in bunches . . ." (366). Shapiro offers no proof: "Trust me; I know."

Chambers most often had assigned two plays to each regular, theatrical season, a major exception was 1599–1600 with the three short plays. To stitch *Hamlet* onto the fabric of his version of history, Shapiro envisions ". . . *Hamlet,* a play poised midway between a religious past and a secular future" (337). Inhabitants of Shakespeare's religiously contentious England well might have been surprised (or appalled) to be told that they were about to step into "a secular future." Such sweeping, undefined, unqualified outbursts do not strengthen Shapiro's credentials as one competent to deal with history.

Shapiro wants to see Shakespeare use the pair of talented boy players who at least played Portia and Nerissa, Beatrice and Hero, Rosalind and Celia, and Viola and Olivia also as playing Ophelia and Gertrude, Katherine of France and Alice, as well as Portia and Calphurnia—the last pair he describes as "another pair of sterling roles" (127). Shapiro, not unexpectedly, does not bother to define what he means by "sterling," perhaps he just means "short" which also would apply to Katherine and Alice; at least such a meaning would not be risible. Katherine has 59 lines, Alice, 26. Portia has 94 lines including one twenty-line speech; Calphurnia, 27. (All line counts are those of T. J. King.) Any player of middling ability and experience could turn in credible performances of these quite short parts. "Sterling" indeed. Shapiro wants to see these roles as preludes to Rosalind and Celia, but he has nothing to support his contention. Shapiro tells his readers that Shakespeare gave Rosalind "over a quarter of the play's lines [true enough]. Not even Cleopatra would speak so much" (235). King awards the laurels to Cleopatra: 693 lines to 686, but seven lines is not much to quibble about in such exceptionally large female roles. More importantly, Shapiro does not give the source of his information or what edition he used if he did the counting himself. Text does make a difference: King, quite uncontestably, used the First Folio for these plays. That Rosalind is a huge role and of course vitally important to the play is obvious and cannot be disputed, but Shapiro cannot stop there. Here as elsewhere he allows himself to become involved emotionally, and this slops him into sentimentality. Thus Rosalind is the most beloved of Shakespeare's heroines [a very vague term, not defined by Shapiro] and for good reason. It's [*sic*] not just her intelligence and wit that account for this. Rosalind's emotions are close to the surface, and we see—and are able to experience through her—an extraordinary range of feelings, from the exhilaration and pain of love to terror and embarrassment. Like Shakespeare's other great [another very vague term, also never defined] creations—Falstaff, Hamlet, Iago and Cleopatra—Rosalind loves to plot, to banter, to direct and play out scenes; and, like these other unforgettable characters, she begins to take on a life of her own, and in doing so comes close to wresting the play away from her creator.

(241–42)

This is not literary criticism; this is drivel. Shapiro has abandoned his critical and analytical tools to wallow in emotion and vagueness. Later he falls into that classic romantic trap of treating characters in plays as if they were "real" human beings; thus he cannot understand how the player portraying Rosalind also can play the Epilogue.

In the final scene of the play, Shakespeare pulls out all the stops.

... He had taken naturalism [undefined] unusually far in this artificial [also undefined] pastoral.... Once the dance is over and the other characters exit, the young actor who played Rosalind steps forward to interact with the audience directly, in an epilogue. The audience would have been shocked by this....

(253, 255)

Shapiro is the one who is shocked by this because he has forgotten that the play and its characters are not real; they are an authorial creation, an artifact, a dream. Puck had told him that several plays earlier; but Shapiro, befogged by his romanticism and sentimentality, has forgotten, or never understood.

Because he wants to show Shakespeare influenced by the history that envelops him, Shapiro also wants to portray Shakespeare as sensitive to larger issues, to great historical perspectives. Thus "*Hamlet*, born at the crossroads of the death of chivalry and the birth of globalization, is marked by these forces, but, unlike the caustic *Troilus and Cressida*, not deformed by them" (309). It is perhaps not surprising to find bad history and bad criticism cheek-by-jowl in the same sentence. It also is not surprising that the romantic Shapiro dislikes the very unromantic *Troilus*, later dismissed as "too unmoored and too bitter" (370).

Because Shapiro seems averse to water travel—the most popular way of getting around in Elizabethan London and its environs, many of his "historical" re-creations ring false. The "Chamberlain's Men made their way through London's dark and chilly streets to Whitehall Palace" (27). When the Chamberlain's Men travel to Richmond, Shapiro declares "it is likely that they traveled overland rather than by boat up the Thames" (84). Streets were narrow, dark, muddy, filthy, and dangerous; they were to be avoided if at all possible. Shapiro does not even bother to say why his proffered mode of transportation would be used rather than the usual one. Readers are drawn another highly improbable picture: "Henslowe, who had to pass the Globe every day on his walk to his ageing Rose . . ." (130); Henslowe, of course, did not go to the Rose every day, walking or otherwise. He spent the vast majority of his days at court; and when he went to the Rose, he most likely took a boat from whichever palace the court was using at the moment. The usual, certainly the most expeditious, way of travel was to get to the river as quickly and as shortly as possible and then to take a boat. That is why royal palaces, the London residences of bishops and great noblemen, The Tower, the Bankside theaters, and much else were on the river.

As the year 1599 moves on, Shapiro decides that it is time to take Shakespeare to Stratford-upon-Avon since he *must* have traveled there at least occasionally. Readers are told that Shakespeare most likely would have hired a horse which would cost five shillings each way (261). While this means of travel is a possibility, it seems highly unlikely that a man so concerned with investing his spare cash in income-producing properties would be so flagrantly extravagant as to spend the equivalent of at least five hundred 2007 American dollars on such a trip. The usual way for ordinary people to travel anywhere overland was to walk. All manner of persons were traveling Elizabethan roads; it would seem far more likely that Shakespeare walked, and if he tired he could have shared portions of the trip with carters or others at a small fraction of hiring a horse. This is not, admittedly, a very romantic picture of Shapiro's increasingly politically important Shakespeare, but it is far more likely than his hiring a horse.

Once Shapiro gets Shakespeare to Stratford, he claims that the chapel of the Guild of the Holy Cross "had stood at the heart of Stratford's civic and religious life since the thirteenth century" (164). Shapiro would seem to be saying that this chapel opposite the side of New Place was the parish church which it was not then and is not now. Holy Trinity Church was and remains the parish church; it is where Shakespeare was baptized and buried and can be reached by a pleasant stroll of a few minutes from the chapel. Until the religious guilds were dissolved during the Reformation, this chapel held the religious services of the Guild; after the Reformation, it became and remains the chapel of the King Edward VI School which it adjoins. As a student in the school, Shakespeare indeed would have attended services there. But at no time in its existence was the chapel ever the "heart" of religious and civic activity in Stratford.

Hugh Clopton, the builder and original owner of Shakespeare's New Place, would have obtained a crick in his neck trying to see "the beautiful stained-glass windows" (164) of the chapel from his garden. New Place was a fairly large residence extending many yards back from its front on Church [then

Chapel] Street, effectively blocking any good view of the windows from any point in the gardens. One also wonders what Shapiro fantasizes that anyone would have seen by looking from any angle at any stained-glass window from the outside. In natural light, from the outside a stained-glass window is just so many gray and black pieces of glass held in place by stone tracery or lead. The beauty can be realized only by seeing the glass from the inside through the illumination of the Sun (theological implications intended).

When discussing the *Henry IV* plays and later with *As You Like It* and *Hamlet,* Shapiro pushes his undocumented contentions about Will Kemp. That the nature of Shakespeare's clowns changes when Kemp leaves the company and is replaced by Robert Armin is easily demonstrable, but that is about all that is. Shapiro wastes an entire chapter, "A Battle of Wills," concocting an unsubstantiated, and unless new archival material is found, unprovable, tale of an artistic dispute between Kemp and Shakespeare. The narrative produced fits Shapiro's purpose for his book; but his story is an invention, just more of his shaped fantasy. Unfortunately it is presented as if it actually were theatrical and artistic history. It is not.

No one knows why Kemp left the Chamberlain's Men to dance to Norfolk and then over the Alps. Shapiro concocts an intellectual and artistic debate/feud between Shakespeare and Kemp about the role of clowns and dance in plays. The reader is invited to think that Shapiro is reading from the corporate records of the Lord Chamberlain's Men documenting artistic debates. Alas, no such records survive, if they ever existed. No one knows that Shakespeare was dissatisfied with Kemp and wanted him out of the company. No one knows that Kemp did not want to leave. Shapiro defends his notions by quoting Hamlet's quips and instructions about acting without seeming to realize that Hamlet is a very fallible character commenting in very particular situations in a particular play and not the playwright discussing his craft in an essay. Taking the play out of the context of its peers, Shapiro has problems with what he calls "*Hamlet*'s unusual length" (340), but it is not even the longest Shakespearian play. Q2 *Hamlet* is 3680 lines (F1, 3593); Folio *Richard III* is longer at 3731 (Quarto, 3419); others are very close: *Coriolanus* is 3583; Folio *Othello* is 3572, *Antony and Cleopatra,* 3484.

Shapiro has more than a little trouble in distinguishing between Shakespeare and his characters when a character says something that Shapiro wishes Shakespeare had said in a tract about dramaturgy. Thus after dutifully dowsing his readers with all the eighteenth-century hearsay about Shakespeare in the theater, Shapiro supposes, no, he actually tells his beleaguered readers that Shakespeare himself played the Chorus in *Henry V* and personally gave the epilogue at court for *2 Henry IV.* What Shapiro would like to believe—what fits his notion of Shakespeare's artistic development—and what can be proved or even conjectured as probable need to be carefully distinguished.

While not the only writer to assume without warrant that Kemp played Falstaff, Shapiro has no more proof than anyone else. The "logic" seems to be: Kemp played clowns, Falstaff was a clown, therefore Kemp played Falstaff. While Falstaff has some funny lines, he is very far from being a clown; he is a liar, a trickster, a thief, a coward, a glutton, a misleader of youth, a person who endangers the well-being of the state in many ways; he is the residue of the medieval devil who must be rejected. And if Shakespeare were trying to limit Kemp, why would he be allowed to play Falstaff who has the largest role in all three plays in which he appears? Will Kemp was the most famous dancer in England. Audiences paid to see Kemp dance. Then would his fat-suited Falstaff have danced? How could he have avoided it? What did dancing Kemp do in roles where proof exists that he did play: Peter in *Romeo and Juliet* and Dogberry?

Shapiro's grasp of the functioning of theater companies and of dramatic history also is less than secure. He seems to think that there was no stage machinery at The Theatre, thus nothing or no one from above or below, and therefore that such "spectacular" things (flying, traps) were new at The Globe (254). There is no documented proof that there was a sign at The Globe, although there well may have been one. Many have conjectured about a figure on it; but on page 257, Shapiro also dreams up an inscription: "Totus mundus agit histrionem," which he translates for his often-deluded readers as "We are all players"! And this occurs at the end of a chapter where he has spent some time talking about Jaques who had translated this proverb correctly. Shapiro still thinks that John Marston wrote *Histriomastix* (72, 209). He states (of course without evidence) that Shakespeare turned in his completed manuscript plays to the Master of the Revels for approval (132); this was a function of the company bookkeeper, not the playwright; licensing was a situation of legal ownership and playing permission—a company matter, not a personal one.

When Shapiro talks about playwrights' manuscripts and what happens in printing houses, he is clearly out of his depth and thirty-five years behind scholarship. Thus what he has to say about these topics concerning *Henry V* and *Hamlet,* the placing of *Troilus and Cressida* in the First Folio, the printing of epilogues, or the troubled "editor" of the Second Folio is just silly and need not take up space here. Needless to say, the poor general reader cannot rely upon what he or she is told.

When Shapiro settles down to his main purpose, talking about plays—especially *As You Like It* and *Hamlet,* he falls into romanticism and sentimentality which greatly compromises his ability to examine Shakespeare's craft with anything approaching objectivity and even hampers his ability to render intelligent criticism. ". . . Shakespeare found himself moving steadily at this time towards a more naturalistic [undefined] drama in which characters like Rosalind and Hamlet feel real [also undefined] . . ." (46). "As Gravedigger, he [Robert Armin] never competes with Hamlet for our affection" (324). ". . . Shakespeare didn't [*sic*] invent a new sensibility in *Hamlet;* rather, he gave voice to what he and others saw and felt around them—which is why *Hamlet* resonated so powerfully with audiences from the moment it was first staged" (331); *Hamlet* ". . . is so often taken as the ultimate expression of its age" (337). These are extreme statements which have little to support them (and nothing is offered). Shapiro well may *feel* that they are true, but that is quite another matter. One of the chief problems is that performance records for the Lord Chamberlain's / King's Men do not exist; determining popularity is little more than a matter of counting the chance survival of casual references and quarto printings; that is slim support indeed for his comments about *Hamlet* as well as for his claim that "*Henry the Fifth* . . . [had] one of the shortest first runs of any of Shakespeare's plays" (103). Such statements are irresponsible because they can be supported by nothing but supposition.

Some things need to be said about the writing. All readers should be grateful that Shapiro does not hide behind theory, spew cant and jargon, or pen tangled prose. This reader, however, is disturbed by some writing quirks. Unless he simply is adapting his style ("dumbing down" in the current idiom) to a mode supposedly more friendly to his abused "general reader," Shapiro is inordinately fond of contractions which to this reviewer have no place in a formal study, even one geared to general readers. There are more than 250 contractions defacing his pages like so many ugly splotches. In addition, there are over two dozen mis-punctuated compound or complex-compound sentences, a large handful of split verb-phrases, about half as many indefinite antecedents, even more inanimate possessives, a sprinkling of adjectives used instead of adverbs, several indicative verbs which should have been in the subjunctive, and at least two misspelled words. Also, people are or might be "hung" rather than "hanged" (76, 162). A good copyeditor would have eliminated all of these.

The book also could have been strengthened by the removal of a number of colloquialisms, particularly "a lot" used with some frequency (purportedly describing quantity); other offenders include "a great deal," "hit his stride," "nice touch," "upmarket," "scared," "the long and short of it," "two-faced," "end up," "pretty clearly," and "kind of stuff." These items do the book, the author, and his arguments no service. Dumbing down indeed. Shapiro also is prone to falling into using first- and second- person pronouns, perhaps in a misguided attempt to draw in his abused and probably confused readers: ". . . everywhere you turned in London, you could hear . . ." (47); "If you accepted Rome's verdict . . . you could, in good conscience, support the assassination of Elizabeth as a tyrant" (157); "You can see why Shakespeare cuts him off . . ." (350); ". . . we don't know which version he preferred" (356); "We're left with a Hamlet who is confused . . ." (356–57). Such usages do not demonstrate a writer in control.

Seemingly, this review could go on forever; but I shall close with a sentence worthy of James Shapiro: "You get the picture; there's a lot wrong with this book." Shapiro's *1599,* ultimately, seems to this reader to be a botched opportunity. An interesting, perhaps even an exciting, study could have been written about Shakespeare's artistic development in or about 1599; but to do so would have necessitated leaving out the froth and the suppositions, expunging the romanticism and the sentimentality, and concentrating on a more detailed and far more sophisticated examination of the plays, a path Shapiro, for whatever reasons, chose not to follow.

Reviews

Shakespeare's Marlowe: The Influence of Christopher Marlowe on Shakespeare's Artistry, by Robert A. Logan. Aldershot, Hampshire and Burlington, Vermont: Ashgate Publishing Ltd., 2007. Pp. 251. $89.95.

Reviewer: CHARLES R. FORKER

In this outrageously overpriced and somewhat inconveniently presented volume (the extensive footnotes, which need constantly to be consulted, appear only at the end of chapters, besides which the print is uncomfortably small), Professor Logan provides us with a thoughtful, wide-ranging, and careful reconsideration of a subject that has attracted students of the two dramatists for well over a century. Although I have reservations about some of the conclusions reached, as well as about certain of the critical formulations that serve as their premise, I want to begin by praising three of the book's major strengths. First, Logan treats Marlowe and Shakespeare as artists—as dramatists and poets with uniquely individual temperaments, talents, and purposes, rather than as mere producers of "cultural texts" that may serve as fodder for postmodernist harangues on the politics of power struggle in Tudor and Stuart society or for reducing the excitements of great drama to the narrow specialisms of class, race, and gender. Second, Logan's analyses are couched in a lucid and humane style, generally unmarred by jargon, "critspeak," and the ugly, obfuscatory abstractions that have lately become the common parlance of much scholarly discourse. Third, the author has done his homework. One of the exemplary features of *Shakespeare's Marlowe* is its impressive command of scholarship and its assimilation of the daunting accumulation of commentary by multifarious predecessors.

Convincingly, Logan sees the relationship between Marlowe and Shakespeare less as a professional rivalry than as a probably cordial and stimulating colleagueship in the business of producing popular entertainment for similar audiences—a colleagueship from which the less experienced Shakespeare learned self-confidence and that, after Marlowe's murder, spurred him to adopt Marlovian innovations in poetic expression, characterization, and dramaturgy without slavishly imitating his model or uncritically sharing his more pessimistic worldview. Logan assumes, probably correctly, that although the two playwrights were associated with different acting companies, they knew each other well enough to be fully aware of each other's work, and that in 1594 when Shakespeare became part of the Lord Chamberlain's Men, the force of his dead friend's plays began to tell on him in subtle and heterogeneous ways. Properly rejecting Stephen Greenblatt's glib dictum that "source study is . . . the elephants' graveyard of literary history" and Harold Bloom's notion that an "anxiety of influence" (9) could have shaped Shakespeare's reaction to Marlowe, Logan insists that "a study of influences illuminates both the influencing and the influenced work" (14). It is a measure of Logan's critical caution and common sense that he begins by acknowledging the prominent element of subjectivity and speculation that inevitably attends any attempt to assess the nature of Marlowe's impact upon Shakespeare. As he points out, the influence of one dramatist upon another is not only a matter of formidable complexity but one that should never be considered as an end in itself. What this book seeks to accomplish, then, is to gain greater insight into the achievements of both dramatists by setting various of their works in juxtaposition—to point out how a given play or poem by Marlowe that invites comparison to a work by Shakespeare helps to illuminate the latter's fresh development and originality, however unprovable or remote the supposed "influence" might be. Indeed, one of the paradoxes of this investigation is Logan's conclusion that the more generalized and distant the supposed impact of Marlowe's work on Shakespeare, the deeper and more pervasive is its importance. Influence signaled by allusions to Marlowe or by verbal echoes of him, dutifully noted and discussed to be sure, turns out to be a mode of access to grander and more profound issues.

Inevitably Logan pairs works by Marlowe and Shakespeare that approximate comparable genres, subjects, styles, or character types. Thus he gives us chapters in which the Duke of Guise in *The Massacre at Paris* can be seen as a theoretical model for Aaron in *Titus Andronicus* and for the villain-hero of *Richard III*. In the same way *Hero and Leander* becomes an artistic stimulus for *Venus and Adonis, Edward II* for *Richard II, The Jew of Malta* for *The Merchant of Venice,* the two parts of *Tamburlaine* for *Henry V, Dido, Queen of Carthage* for *Antony and Cleopatra,* and *Doctor Faustus* (in different ways) for *Macbeth* and *The Tempest*. When it comes to establishing that Shakespeare knew a work by Marlowe well enough to use it as a springboard for a new creation of his own, Logan can be surprisingly timid. A case in point is the patently close relationship between *Edward II* and *Richard II*. Logan's principle seems irrefragable: "An influence can be reduced to a source when it is as straightforward as a quotation or an allusion that recalls a particular phrase" (15). At least seven times in *Richard II* Shakespeare quotes verbatim or with only minor alteration from Marlowe's play, besides which he borrows obvious imagery, situational details, and effects of staging. Bolingbroke's unsubstantiated charge that Bushy and Green have been homosexually involved with Richard, thereby grieving his queen (nothing in Shakespeare's other sources can explain such a charge), is almost certainly a reminiscence of Marlowe's King Edward, whose favorites, Gaveston and Spencer Jr., have precisely the effect on his queen that Bolingbroke attributes to the analogous characters in Shakespeare. It might be argued indeed that Shakespeare's detail constitutes a covert allusion to the earlier drama.[1] Yet Logan hesitates, unnecessarily qualifying his belief in the connection between the two tragedies: "It seems . . . likely that [Shakespeare] was familiar with . . . *Edward II,* but the proof is less [than] concrete" (14).

In two early chapters on *The Massacre at Paris* and *Hero and Leander,*

Logan initiates his analyses of specific works and establishes his methodology. Aware of the textual and dating complexities of *The Massacre* that make its *direct* impact on *Titus* and *Richard III* open to doubt, he begins with a line in the Marlowe play ("Yet Caesar shall go forth" [xxi..67]) that Shakespeare almost certainly repeats in *Julius Caesar* (1599) at 2.2.28. This connection then allows him to speculate on a probable relationship between Marlowe's Machiavellian Guise and Shakespeare's Aaron and Richard III as more fully imagined, more shockingly assertive versions of the same villainous type. As Logan sees it, the paradoxical union of fertile imagination and destructiveness in such characters can be traced to Marlowe—a combination that triggers in audiences an ambivalent urge both to admire and to condemn. No craven obeisance to Marlowe is evident in Shakespeare's early plays. Rather, Marlowe seems to grant Shakespeare permission to experiment in figures such as Aaron and Gloucester with the theatrical possibilities of creative evil. In stressing imaginative freedom as a component of the magnetism of Richard's character, however, Logan seems to discount the Christian metaphysic in which Richard's fall and death are contextualized. He gives no weight whatever, for instance, to the objective reality of the ghosts of Richard's victims who appear to curse him before the Battle of Bosworth. Guilty projections they may certainly be (as in the case of Banquo's apparition whom no one but Macbeth can see): but Shakespeare's age believed in the actuality of ghosts and did not think of them solely as manifestations of a guilty conscience. One of the pervasive limitations of Logan's analyses is his stress on psychological realism to the exclusion of older conventions of characterization and staging that reflect belief in a world of supernatural presence and judgment. His major point that Marlowe's dramaturgical resourcefulness and daring carry over into Shakespeare is, however, certainly valid.

Since we cannot be sure whether *Hero and Leander* preceded or followed *Venus and Adonis,* the question of the one poet's imitating the other must obviously remain moot. Comparison and contrast of the two epyllions nonetheless help us define the distinctive gifts and "divergent artistic aims" (57) of both authors. Doubtless because of his delineated subject, Logan ignores Chapman's stylistically distinct completion of *Hero and Leander* (no mention of the later poet appears anywhere in the chapter), thus giving the false impression that Marlowe's brilliant fragment is an artistic whole. Whichever poem came first, Marlowe's, according to Logan, is the more adventurous and successful. Whereas Shakespeare subordinates eroticism to the theme of *carpe diem,* Marlowe concentrates on the power of sexual desire. Marlowe, Logan believes, is more comfortable with the artifice and detachment of Ovidian tradition, while Shakespeare's innate tendency to psychologize figures who are usually portrayed as flat, mythic, and cold (Shakespeare even gets inside the skins of animals such as the hare, the snail, and the jennet) pushes him into an emotional engagement with his subject that is foreign to its genre, also betraying him into an unsatisfactory mingle of moral and aesthetic attitudes. Logan's ponderous analysis of the these deliciously lightweight entertainments in terms of Greenblattian "containment and restraint" (68) versus sexual freedom—of "the tension between orthodoxy and heterodoxy" (73) with an emphasis on the "fear of a lack of control, including the consequences" (68)—seems puritanical as well as insufficiently responsive to the comic and satirical elements of both works and smacks at times of breaking a butterfly upon a wheel.

Logan's chapter on *Edward II* and *Richard II*—the first instance among his pairings in which Marlowe's influence on Shakespeare is indisputable—disappoints. Not only does the author slight the numerous verbal, situational, imagistic, plotting, and structural links between the two plays; he also oversimplifies the two protagonists by forcing them into false categories. Logan insists on neatly dividing characters into those "who assume the moral responsibilities their roles imply" and "those who, by giving themselves over to play . . . deny the conventional moral limitations of [such] roles" (88). Logan regards Edward as a king "who often conducts himself as if there were no such thing as a moral frame of reference" (88) and evaluates Richard as a man so "amoral" (89) and so given over to his aesthetic predilections—his "will to play"—that the impulse "easily obliterates whatever moral sense" he has or "might develop" (90). Given such a formulation, Edward's homosexual passion for Gaveston and later dependency on Spencer Jr. constitute nothing less than a culpable refusal to face up to the ethical imperatives of rule. Logan appears to accept Mortimer's term, "wanton humor" (1.4.401), as an objectively reliable summation of Edward's identity, and though defining his fatal flaw as "an uncontrollable will to play" (98), condemns him for not controlling it. This critic wastes little sympathy on Marlowe's appallingly degraded monarch, believing that the dramatist was principally interested in shocking complacent audiences out of their conventional conceptions of manliness. As for Richard, his masochistic self-indulgence in flights of poetic fancy simply encapsulates an alternative form of escape from kingly duty. Both monarchs come to grief because they yield to the "aesthetic" or playful aspects of life's temptations (sexual infatuation, role playing, the pleasures of rhetorical invention, self-pity) and fail to recognize that kingship requires engagement with the harsh political and moral realities of the state. Such pat judgments could almost have been uttered by Mortimer or Bolingbroke. Nor are Edward and Richard so "amoral" as Logan supposes. Edward's romantic faithfulness to the men he loves at the cost of even his life is not without a certain moral fiber, and the lynching of Gaveston kindles him to righteous fury and a devastating vengeance upon enemies. Richard's banishment of Mowbray and Bolingbroke, although unjust, is reluctantly seconded by Gaunt, the weightiest moralist of the play, who clearly accepts his nephew's view that the punishments serve England's greater good. Richard matures enough through his suffering to acknowledge that he has "wasted time" (5.5.49), and his deeply felt commitment to the doctrine of divine right, a religious aspect of his character that Logan mentions only in passing, is presented by Shakespeare as an idea to be taken seriously—certainly not as a merely escapist or chimerical fantasy to be discredited by Richard's emotionalism or Bolingbroke's political success. Logan treats Richard's poignant echo of Faustus's address to the apparition of Helen of Troy—"Was this the face . . . That every day . . . Did keep ten thousand men? (4.1.281–83)—as "parody" (84), thus diminishing the rich complexity of its effect as a melding of wit, vanity, pathos, self-recognition, and the symbolic destruction of anointed monarchy itself. To say simply that "*Doctor Faustus* . . . is twitted in *Richard II*" (162) seems totally inadequate.

Logan's assessment of tone seems more secure in his handling of the parallel (with profound differences including genre) between the Barabas of Marlowe's *Jew* and the Shylock of Shakespeare's *Merchant*. The former's "O girl! O gold" (2.1.54) would seem to be an obvious source for the latter's "My daughter! O my ducats! (2.8.15), but Logan correctly regards the imitation not as parody but as "a catalyst in the heightening of Shakespeare's creative sensibility" (119). He might have said the same for the analogous echo of *Doctor Faustus* in *Richard II*. We can surely agree that Marlowe's influence upon *Merchant* "is both particular and general" (125). In quoting one of Gratiano's speeches in which the character promises to "Talk with respect," "put on a sober habit," "Wear prayer books in my pocket," and "look demurely" (*Merchant of Venice,* 2.2.178–80), Logan overlooks the probable influence of an episode in *Edward II* in which Spencer Jr. mocks the clerkly Baldock for "saying 'truly, an't may please your honour,'" for wearing "a black coat and a little band," for "saying a long grace at a table's end," and for "looking downward with [his] eyelids close" (2.1.33–40). Of course one may question, as Logan does, whether Shakespeare's individualization of character (as evidenced by the transformation of Shylock from a stereotypical grotesque into a complex personality) and the impressive variability of style, adjusted so carefully to particular speakers in particular contexts, can be debited exclusively to Marlowe. But it is hard to dispute Logan's general contention that Shakespeare's technique of creating characters to whom we react with divided or ambiguous responses, characters alien to the social constructs in which they find themselves, probably derives from the dramatist who invented Tamburlaine, Edward II, and Barabas.

Logan's discussions of *Henry V, Antony and Cleopatra, Macbeth,* and *The Tempest* seem to me his worthiest contributions. This may be precisely because he is able to tie these later plays less directly to Marlowe, and because he is freed, generally speaking, from trying to examine the specific indebtedness of particular details and can concentrate on larger matters such as themes, ideological perspectives, complication of character, and stylistic experimentation. By the time he was composing *Henry V* and the plays that followed, Shakespeare had thoroughly internalized Marlowe, subduing artistic consciousness of the latter's achievement to a richer complex of cultural and intellectual forces that allowed his own originality to exfoliate multitudinously.

Everyone knows that blustering Pistol, who appears in both *2 Henry IV* and *Henry V*, nonsensically mangles a few mighty lines from *2 Tamburlaine* in the earlier play, thus presenting himself as a parody of Marlowe's overreacher.[2] Whether this entitles Logan to assert that Tamburlaine may be regarded as a "prototype" (144) of the hero of Agincourt is doubtful, although he takes the allusion as an opportunity to analyze the "mirror of all Christian kings" as a figure, like the Scythian shepherd, who evokes a pattern of positive and negative responses. Quite sensibly, Logan refrains from pushing the comparison much beyond this point, although he sees the grandiloquence of the play's rhetoric, with all its differences, as a child of Marlowe's inspiration. If Marlovian influence can be detected, it is of course "aesthetic" rather than "moral" (148) and consists, in part, in the conflicting public and private images that prevent a single-eyed view of the hero. Logan speaks of the dramatist's "artistic naïveté" (153) in attempting to reconcile Henry's ordinary humanity with his super-stature as a conqueror, apparently forgetting the doctrine of the King's two bodies, mentioned by the character himself, that makes an anointed sovereign a "god" who suffers "mortal griefs" and is so "twin-born" (4.1.234, 241–42).

Logan's treatment of *Antony and Cleopatra*, using Marlowe's *Dido* as the foil, marks a high point of the book. Despite verbal evidence that Shakespeare was familiar with the earlier play, specific stylistic influence counts for little in the analysis. Logan is much concerned with the cool artifice and emotional detachment of the Marlowe drama as contrasted with the more engaged and passionate style of its Shakespearean counterpart—a style that fuses the literary with the realistic in such as way as to produce effects of unmediated human feeling. He writes provocatively on different "modes of perception" (179) in the two tragedies, characterizing Marlowe's as more rationalist, hard-headed, and cynical, Shakespeare's as more romantic and "cheerfully realistic" (179), though not to the exclusion of hard-headedness in the representation of Octavius. He makes the excellent point, regarding the visual and imagistic opulence of Shakespeare's play, that "For the non-rationalist, spectacle is symbolic, a ritual demonstration of genuine feeling," its "importance" lying "in its enduring content" (182). (He might equally have applied the same insight to several scenes in *Richard II*.) Logan also discusses gender roles with acuity. Both Dido and Cleopatra violate conventional expectations of female passivity, although Marlowe finally reaffirms traditional patriarchy by justifying Aeneas's abandonment of Dido as a calling superior to romance. In characterizing Antony, so Logan avers, Shakespeare overrides a moralistic separation of love from lust, as also the so-called manliness of battle as a value higher than sexual fulfillment. Logan makes a good case for Shakespeare's having learned to experiment more freely with flexible conceptions of gender and to "set his priorities" (191) from Marlowe's drama, though he fails to mention that Shakespeare had already toyed with the subject from a different angle in comedies such as *As You Like It* and *Twelfth Night.*

In discussing *Macbeth* and *The Tempest* as possible artistic progeny of *Doctor Faustus,* Logan understandably builds on C. L. Barber and Jonathan Bate. *Macbeth,* like Marlowe's play, explores blasphemy as "a heroic enterprise" (199) while *The Tempest* also follows Marlowe in having as its protagonist a magus who says, "I'll drown my book" (5.1.57), an echo, as Bate thinks, of Faustus's "I'll burn my books" (A-Text, 5.2.123).[3] Logan notes the metadramatic element in both plays—Macbeth as a criminal whose knowing descent into a self-created hell reduces him to the status of a "poor player" on the world's stage, Prospero as a metaphorical playwright whose magical rearrangement of other people's lives is undertaken to promote love and reconciliation. As Logan would be the first to admit, the notion of life as a play is too common to be traceable specifically to Marlowe, but Faustus's commencement as a practitioner of white (or godly) magic before he takes up its demonic counterpart serves as an interesting parallel to Prospero's immersion in the mystic arts. Apart from the concern with witchcraft, the strongest link between *Doctor Faustus* and *Macbeth* is the open-eyed choice of both protagonists to violate their own souls and thus to commit spiritual suicide. What Shakespeare seems to have taken from Marlowe here was the idea of interiorizing such a fatal decision and of powerfully dramatizing its psychological effects. In both plays hell is conceived, not naively as a place, but more terrifyingly as a state of consciousness.

Logan concludes by suggesting that Shakespeare was less taken by Marlowe's radical ideas and heterodox outlook than by his poetic and dramaturgical originality. What he could most fruitfully absorb and transmute from his theatrical predecessor was the latter's verbal dexterity, his flexibility in reconfiguring genres, and his way of creating ambiguity and ambivalence of response to dramatic characters and situations. Since these are significant findings with which it is difficult to disagree, Logan's book is likely to become a standard work on the subject. One could wish that his generally dignified prose had not been marred by occasional lapses into colloquialism and journalese ("strut his stuff," "too cute," "terrible goofiness," "one-upping Marlowe," and the like), but these are minor stumbles and do not lessen the impressiveness of his achievement.

Notes

1. See my Arden edition of *Richard II* (London: Thomson Learning, 2002), 159–64.
2. Pistol also draws upon Peele's *Battle of Alcazar;* see A. R. Humphreys, ed., *2 Henry IV* (London: Methuen, 1966), 73.
3. Barber, *Creating Elizabethan Tragedy: The Theater of Marlowe and Kyd,* ed. Richard. P Wheeler (Chicago: University of Chicago Press, 1988), 14; Bate, *The Genius of Shakespeare* (New York: Oxford University Press, 1998), 129.

Shakespeare and Republicanism, by Andrew Hadfield. Cambridge and New York: Cambridge University Press, 2005. Pp. xiii + 363. Hardback $80.00

Reviewer: GRAHAM HAMMILL

In *Shakespeare and Republicanism* Andrew Hadfield argues two main points. The first is that between the execution of Mary and the accession of James, Elizabethan England witnessed a "republican moment" (210) in which strands of republican thought coalesced—especially but not exclusively on the London stage—to form a point of speculative opposition to a more strictly defined monarchical rule. Following Patrick Collinson's important and controversial work on what he calls Elizabeth's "monarchical republic," Hadfield proposes that the succession question opened the possibility of an interim, quasi-republican oligarchy that could decide the question if Elizabeth died without naming an heir. This possibility, Hadfield argues, led to more general speculation over what forms of government might be better than monarchy. Driven by the execution of Mary, potential republicans learned the lesson that "the conduct of other monarchs might be subject to hostile scrutiny" (146), but stymied by an atmosphere of censorship, they taught this lesson in literature, where writers "could explore their ideas in their chosen forms, as political theorists and historians" (52). The unexpected stability that came with James's accession weakened this moment until, presumably, it was revitalized later in James's rule and after.

Hadfield's second point is that, as a writer sensitive to the public imagination and committed to some degree or another to an antimonarchical position, Shakespeare "[decided] to fashion himself as a republican writer" (100). In this groundbreaking reading, Hadfield emplots Shakespeare's engagement with republicanism by arguing for a career trajectory. That is, Hadfield argues that the publication history of the early plays and poetry tells the story of a writer who wants to be seen and understood as a republican. We learn that Shakespeare positioned himself as a republican writer by promoting the first tetralogy as his *Pharsalia,* (in arguments like Hadfield's, references to and imitation of Lucan's *Pharsalia* being the equivalent of a party card for early modern republicans). Shakespeare opposed the dead-end figure of Elizabeth against the promises of republican Rome in *Venus and Adonis* and *The Rape of Lucrece*. In *Titus Andronicus* Shakespeare argues for limited constitutionalism. And in *Julius Caesar* Shakespeare shows how the attempts to establish a republic inadvertently sow the seeds of the republic's destruction. Hadfield's bold and innovative analysis culminates with a fascinating reading of *Hamlet*. He argues that Shakespeare's early engagement with republicanism comes to a head in *Hamlet*, which combines republican concerns about succession and the rule of law with topical and suppressed references to Scotland in order to ask its audience "how they would act if faced with an unjust and unpalatable succession, leaving them governed by a ruler who has obtained power by nefarious means" (203). Hadfield concludes by arguing that *Measure for Measure* and *Othello* show the waning of Shakespeare's public republicanism as James ascends to the throne, although Hadfield also suggests that Shakespeare remained true to his republican commitments by reading *Antony and Cleopatra* as a cautionary example of the problems of empire.

One of the most interesting quirks of this book is that the argument is strongest when republicanism is waning or when, in the case of Hadfield's reading of *Hamlet*, the political content is "suppressed and disguised" (198). The argument tends to be weakest when republican elements are supposed to be more strongly present. In chapter 3, for instance, to show that the first tetralogy makes up "Shakespeare's *Pharsalia*" (105), Hadfield discusses references to the *Pharsalia* in these plays. The problem is that there aren't any direct references that Hadfield can find. Correctly locating the references to Caesar that run throughout the play in figures like Plutarch and Suetonius, Hadfield then goes on to suggest that generally these references allude to Lucan's *Pharsalia*. We are told that a reference to Nero that comes from Suetonius recalls Lucan because "Nero was the emperor when Lucan wrote *Pharsalia*" (115), and the "mention of Pompey" by Suffolk "was likely to have had the effect of triggering a memory of the *Pharsalia*" (118). The chapter ends with a brilliant reading of Prince Edward's reference to Caesar's *Commentaries* in *Richard III*, when Richard is urging the princes to stay in the Tower for their protection. Noting that given the educational program that Shakespeare and his audiences would have known, Prince Edward would have been too young to have been taught the *Pharsalia* but would have been old enough to have studied the *Commentaries*, Hadfield proposes that at least some members of Shakespeare's audience would have recognized the *Pharsalia* as a suppressed subtext by which to judge Prince Edward's misjudgment and, more broadly, Richard's claims to the throne. In this chapter, we end up with a series of claims about referentiality that constrain a much more interesting reading and reading practice from fully developing. Hadfield wants to say that the first tetralogy is Shakespeare's *Pharsalia*, which would go a long way toward proving that Shakespeare wants to fashion himself as a republican writer. He ends up demonstrating that the first tetralogy stages a complex and unacknowledged relation with the *Pharsalia* in which republican possibilities form a plausible underside or repressed content of the plays. Instead of casting the argument in terms of referentiality, Hadfield needs a more supple argumentative framework to do justice to his insights and their implications.

One reason Hadfield does not develop this framework is that he wants to argue that it was possible to be a republican in late Elizabethan England. That is, he wants to say that republicanism was not just part of the political language of late sixteenth-century England; it was a position a writer could take and argue for. In the introduction, Hadfield pays homage to J. G. A. Pocock and Quentin Skinner, who show that republicanism was "both a language and a system of belief" (13). For Pocock and Skinner, this means showing how the semantic value or values given to a word, phrase, or discursive formation changes over time. But for Hadfield, it means exactly the opposite: how language cements meaning and holds it in place. In the sentence immediately following the one I just quoted, Hadfield collapses the distinction between language and belief, as language becomes a "collection of *topoi* . . . or examples, or triggers" that metonymically "signalled and stood for a larger argument or set of beliefs." Republicanism is, for Hadfield, a firm concept that stands behind the language in which and by which it is expressed. This understanding of language and politics leads Hadfield to read republicanism as a secret history that has been "disappeared" from our understanding of Elizabethan England (1), and it also leads him to read republicanism as a secret intention that gives meaning to the fragmented and unformed nature of its expression in pre–civil war England. People like Blair Worden point to this piecemeal expression in order to say that one could not be a republican in the late sixteenth century, even if republicanism was part of political discourse. Arguing against Worden, Hadfield writes:

> [I]f we are justified in writing about republicanism, we also need to acknowledge its inchoate nature as well as its existence as a series of related, overlapping and sometimes contradictory points. That is, of course, hardly a surprising revelation, given the limited means of expression of republican ideas before the Civil War. . . . Advocates of republican thought could not risk anything as explicit [as interregnum politicians could] in the 1590s, this was their aim; rather, they had to rely on suggestive hints, references, and lavish praise of foreign and historical nations, rarely on outright and sustained expression. This is one reason why republicanism seems to have appealed as much to imaginative writers of literature, who could explore their ideas in their chosen forms, as political theorists and historians. (51–52)

For Hadfield, the inchoate nature of republican discourse is a sign of political repression and not the sign of a developing or changing discourse. He does not prove or discuss in any specific or precise way the mechanisms, institutions, or other mediating forces of this repression; he asserts and assumes it in order to make the claim that the inchoate nature of republican discourse is intentional. A number of years ago, Pocock remarked that while "Shakespeare's *Coriolanus* could only have been played to an audience sensitive to the idea that a balanced republic was necessary to prevent the corruption of civic virtues," nevertheless "they were not in themselves republicans" because in Elizabethan England there was "an excess" of civic consciousness, "more than the available institutional and conceptual schemes could contain."[1] Hadfield tries to say that because Shakespeare's plays could only have been played to the kind of audience that Pocock describes, both Shakespeare and at least some members of his audiences were republicans. The problem is that at his best (which is very good indeed), Hadfield tends to prove Pocock's claim that republicanism was more than Elizabethan conceptual forms could assimilate, instead of proving the thesis he wants to prove, which is that Shakespeare and some of his contemporaries were republicans. It is too bad that Hadfield starts off by rejecting "the problem of subjectivity" which he sees as "at the expense of an analysis of politics" (9). Some attention to political subjectivity may have allowed him more fully to substantiate his broader claims.

This is not at all to say that Hadfield's monograph should not be read and carefully studied. One of the most exciting and important contemporary conversations in early modern literary studies is happening around the problem of Elizabethan republicanism, and Hadfield's monograph significantly deepens the level at which that conversation can now occur. *Shakespeare and Republicanism* is an important and even groundbreaking book, which deserves a great deal of praise for showing how significant and prevalent republican discourses were in the Elizabethan theater and for developing fascinating readings of Shakespeare's early plays. Perhaps most significantly, though, Hadfield's arguments revolve around an unworked relation between political thought, manifest in cultural discourses, and political subjectivity, embodied in readership and spectatorship, forms of address, and rhetorical posturing. Through both what the book does and what it does not do, *Shakespeare and Republicanism* promises to be part of the critical conversation on early modern literature and political thought for some time. Not only does Hadfield offer fresh readings of plays and poems that have received a great deal of interpretation, but also the book's blind spot lays the groundwork for a more historically and theoretically nuanced account of subjectivity, political thought, and the mediation between the two.

Note

1. J. G. A. Pocock, *The Machiavellian Moment: Florentine Political Thought and the Atlantic Republican Tradition* (Princeton: Princeton University Press, 1975), 348–49.

Marvelous Protestantism: Monstrous Births in Post-Reformation England, by Julie Crawford. Baltimore and London: The Johns Hopkins University Press, 2005. Pp. x + 270. Hardcover $50.00.

Reviewer: GRACE TIFFANY

In newly Reformed England, through the sixteenth and seventeenth centuries, the popular printing press birthed a many-bodied, inky monster: hundreds of illustrated pamphlets and books declaring the shocking, prodigious arrivals of strangely deformed babies in the nation's villages and towns. Investigating this low-cultural print phenomenon, Julie Crawford discovers how stories and pictures of the "monstrous births" served a variety of (mostly) Reformed Protestant purposes. Whether the births were real or fictional, their stories and images were turned by the pamphleteers—and by at least one Puritan preacher—into symbols of a moral distemper which their commentators presented as national, social, religious, or all three. Crawford deftly demonstrates that the brunt of these stories' attacks was borne by women, whose alleged lecheries or blasphemies (often both) were thought physically to have imprinted themselves on their offsprings' bodies. Thus "[i]n many popular pamphlets . . . the headless child is both a symbol and a product of its mother's lack of patriarchal guidance" (118). Such pamphlets fused the Pauline instruction to women to submit to their husbands' headship with the frightening quasi-medical suggestion that pregnant women's imaginations and moral behavior could affect their unborn children. "Discreet women, and such as desire to have children, will not give eare unto lamentable and fearefull tales or storyes, nor cast their eyes upon pictures or persons which are uglie or deformed, least the imagination imprint on the child the similitude of the said person or picture," Crawford quotes a French physician as saying in a treatise published in London in 1612.

The cruel irony of such admonitions for women is apparent. No doubt the anxieties of the pregnant were exacerbated in early modern England by pamphlets warning mothers-to-be not to contemplate the monstrous babies and behaviors vividly represented in those very pamphlets. The "imprint" of imagination, indeed! (In her acknowledgments page Crawford lets it be known that she finished the book while pregnant herself, and I admire her nerve.) One wonders about early modern Englishwomen's responses to the pamphlets, as well as about the continuing fortunes of the unlucky babies—some of whom must have really existed and even survived—and the subsequent lives of their parents. Real early modern families, however, are not the subject of Crawford's book, whose critical eye focuses mainly on the monstrous texts themselves, not on those folk whose misfortunes helped inspire them. Thus her study is sensational in two senses of the word. It yields, in lucid and compelling prose, an impeccably researched and fascinating account of an important early modern textual and social phenomenon, and is thus a wonderful work of cultural scholarship. It is, at the same time, a book that reproduces—in verbatim quotations of the pamphlets' "monster" descriptions and in more than forty illustrations, including a big green beast on the cover—the lurid, often apocalyptic warnings of the Reformers whose project it coolly examines. "Most people," Crawford states in her conclusion, "neglect books and stories that are not 'Somewhat antick and extraordinary'" (185). That final sentence implies that *Marvelous Protestantism,* like the writings it dissects, was structured to appeal to the popular appetite for grotesque images and tales.

It does, which is not to say it doesn't also appeal to the intellect. "Antick and extraordinary" though Crawford's book is, its serious informative purpose is not undermined but vitally served by its colorful excursions into over one hundred textual (most can't be called literary) accounts of prodigious births. The titles of these works range from the should-be-shocking (*"The Holy Sister's Conspiracy against their Husbands"* [239]) to the mildly reassuring (*"Dies Novissimus, or, Dooms-day Not so Near as Dreaded"* [238]) to the wonderingly verbose (*"The most strange and wounderfull apperation of blood in poole at Garraton in Leicester-shire, which continued for the space of foure dayes, the rednesse of the colour for the space of those foure dayes every day increasing higher and higher, to the infinet amazement of many hundreds of beholders of all degrees and conditions, who have dipped their handketchers in this bloody poole, . . . As also the true relation of a miraculous and prodigious birth in Shoo-lane, where one Mistris Browne a cuttlers wife was delivered of a monster without a head or feet, and in stead of a head had a hollow out of which a child did proceed, which was little but lovely, perfect in all but very spare and leane. As also the Kings sending to his Parliament for hostage for the security of his person to come unto London and to sit with his parliament for the composing the diffirences in the kingdome"* [241–42]). Reading Crawford's bibliography is an entertainment and an education in itself. Due to their abysmal artistic quality, the woodcut illustrations she reprints don't help her counter a conventional charge to which she objects: that Protestant iconoclasm led to "enormous visual impoverishment" in English culture (the phrase is Margaret Aston's). The pictures do, however, help show "the role of visual imagery in Protestant proselytizing" (7), as Crawford points out. Also, the images' accompanying texts, examined and contextualized by Crawford, become a compelling demonstration of how English religious zealots invented or distorted news of extraordinary births to suit the purposes of Protestant propaganda.

Thus, in her most interesting chapter, Crawford describes how a two-headed monster—what we would call Siamese twins—was identified in 1613 by the Puritan pastor William Leigh not only as fit punishment for its "lewd" parents (101), but as a symbol of general ungodliness in his parish of Standish, which he found damnably Romish (and thus "double-faced," like equivocal Jesuits). To some Protestant moralists the two-headed child represented England itself, which contained recusants whose allegiance was split between two heads, namely James I and the pope. In this particular case "[t]he conjoined monsters served . . . joint purposes of local moral reform and national reprimand—its body a sign of Protestant England's imperfect union, its story a vehicle of dissent," Crawford writes (113). In a subsequent chapter, Crawford describes how the headless babies allegedly born to reputedly uppity females served, in the pamphlets describing them, conservative Protestant didactic purposes. The headless-offspring pamphlets circulated most frequently in the mid-seventeenth century, when the fragmentation of English Protestantism was registered in the increasing numbers of folk who resisted "the dominance of Parliament and its struggling ecclesiastical and ministerial systems" (116). So, in 1642, a mason's wife is punished with a headless child for refusing, before its birth, to have it baptized with the sign of the cross, a ritual then still one of the "laudable and decent ceremon[ies]" of the English Church (122). Thus in an increasingly diverse seventeenth-century Protestant culture, monstrous births might signify punishment either for hidden papistry or for zealous repudiation of a Romish tradition still practiced by the national church.

Crawford is attentive to such complexities, and to the variety of English sins Reformers found punished by different sorts of prodigious births. Perhaps most phenomenal among these unhappy or imaginary offspring is what Crawford calls the "fashion monster" (27): animals and children whose afflicted bodies were said to figure different kinds of sartorial decadence. An early instance was the sixteenth-century "monk calf," "purportedly born [in Europe] with a large flap of skin on its back and a bald spot on its head, deformities resembling the cowl and tonsure of a monk" (28). Luther invoked the monk calf to demonstrate that beneath his habit the Catholic monk was no holier than such a one. His commentary was widely read in later sixteenth-century England, where an additional, native tale of a "ruffed calf" pointed a moralistic teaching against vain "double Ruffes" and supported a statute that forbade such Continental frippery (38). A ruffed child was also described in an English pamphlet. In the 1560s John Hayward wrote of a fleshless child who yet had "a collar of fleshe and skinne, pleighted and foulded like a double ruffe . . . as if nature would upbraide our pride in artificiall braverie, by producing monsters in the same attires" (46). It should be noticed that the monstrous infant whose skin represented "artificiall braverie," like the purportedly headless children of unruly women, was a warning chiefly directed against "womankinde" (47). Crawford likens *The true discripcion of a Childe with Ruffes* (1566) to the slightly earlier Elizabethan "Homilie Against Excess of Apparel," both of which "preached specifically to women"—or, to quote the homily, to "the proude and haughtie . . . daughters of England," whose vanity was seen to court "GODS fearefull vengeance"

(49). Indeed, *Marvelous Protestantism* constructs a plausible connection between the Elizabethan "Childe with Ruffes" and "The Ranters Monster," a pamphlet printed a century later which tells of a headless child born to Mary Adams, a Protestant Independent (one of the "Puritans . . . whose rallying cry was freedom of conscience and freedom of assembly" [164]). Adams, like some other female Independents, preached, and the headless child story applied to Independents like her rebuked not just unruly wives but women who rejected the role of proper feminine silence in Christian assemblies.

Some readers might be surprised that a professor of literature, as is Crawford, would exclude from her discussion the two great Renaissance Protestant literary examples of monstrous births, namely Spenser's Error, who spews Catholic tracts as she suckles her thousand shapeless young (*The Faerie Queene,* 1590), and Milton's Sin, who repeatedly births, swallows, and is inwardly gnawed by her baby-sins (*Paradise Lost,* 1667). I myself initially wondered at both Spenser's and Milton's absence from Crawford's index, but came ultimately to see that Crawford had fixed her gaze resolutely on low-print culture because of the pictorial (as opposed to the literary) images the pamphlets afforded. Unlike Protestant epic poetry, whose iconoclasm was served by what Judith Dundas calls the "narrativizing" of spectacle (293–94),[1] the monstrous-birth pamphlets exploited images. Crawford wants both to disclose this phenomenon—that is, actually to show us the "antick and extraordinary" pictures—and, by means of the disclosure, to challenge received understandings of what early English Protestants believed. She wishes not only to rectify the view that Protestants rejected didactic images in favor of sermons and texts, but also the idea that they disbelieved in miracles, and in what she calls "material religious symbols" (34). Thus an unfortunate cat who was hanged in London in 1554, wearing a priestly garment and holding a mock-Eucharistic wafer, "attest[s] to the trenchant early modern belief in the power of material objects" to achieve "symbolic resonance," despite Protestants' professed disdain for Catholic relics, crosses, and rosaries (34). Likewise, the monstrous births, seen as God's judgments on sin, contradicted "Protestant efforts to discredit . . . miracles," which "were still understood by many"—including the Protestants who exploited the stories—as "revelations of divine will" (12).

There are problems with this thesis. Chief among them is the argument's inattention to what Calvinist-leaning English Protestants meant when they claimed that the age of miracles was over. What the Thirty-Nine Articles of the English Church rejected were miracles of healing performed by saints who intervened in human lives if properly supplicated. While Reformers believed the gospel accounts of apostolic healing, they denied the modern efficacy of the whole apparatus of priests, saints, and chantries which stood between Christians and God in the Catholic scheme, and on which Catholics falsely relied for the effecting of wonders. However, they never denied God's direct work in the world. "Although the Reformation officially discredited Catholic miracles as superstition, Protestantism . . . nevertheless deployed many supernatural beliefs of its own" (12), Crawford writes, but surely it is not news that the Reformers believed in a God and a devil whose work was manifest in human life. Crawford proposes a kind of straw Protestant who denied God's activity in the physical universe, as though Calvinists were Deists. Yet Calvin himself wrote lucidly of God's work in Nature, supposing that a man who "having been tossed by the waves, reaches harbor; [and] miraculously escapes death by a finger's breadth" demonstrated God's salvific power. "[A]nyone who has been taught . . . that all the hairs of his head are numbered [Matt. 10:30] . . . will consider that all events are governed by God's secret plan," Calvin added (198–99).[2] In *Paradise Lost* Milton's Adam tells Eve that "Heaven by . . . mute signs in nature shows/ Forerunners of his purpose" (11:194–95),[3] a Protestant (though also a Catholic) view that was widely propounded, but goes unacknowledged by Crawford. Crawford also misinterprets Protestants' attitude toward material things. Reformers didn't deny objects' didactic power, only their sacral status. They knew they were living in a material world (to adapt the words of our own desacralized Madonna). Because they objected to the fetishistic use of tokens in prayer and to praying to statues and images—that is, they disliked the attribution of sacredness to the profane —Crawford supposes that their instructive use of such objects and images contradicted their own faith and teaching. It was, however, the desacralization of traditional religious objects in early modern England that freed those things for ordinary use, in much the same way as the English formal repudiation of the doctrines of Purgatory and canonization facilitated secular play with both ideas in Renaissance drama and literature.[4] Table instead of altar, flat black cap instead of crowned red one, wafers of bread instead of the ostentatiously displayed Eucharistic Presence, were fit signs—not containers and transmitters—of Godliness in Reformed churches. Likewise, in a parodic register, a dead cat or live calf really or apparently clad in clerical vestments was the fit expression of those vestments' profane quality, whether the sign was fashioned by men or given by God.

Thus Crawford's demonstration that Protestants interpreted monstrous births as divine punishments or warnings does not qualitatively alter our sense of Protestants' relation to the visible, tangible world. Indeed, her book sharpens our understanding of the distinction we know Protestants made (and still make) between the symbolic and the actual presence of God in the concrete things of the world (Calvin's claim that amazing events enact God's will is not a claim that God inhabits the events). It was no contradiction for Protestants to credit what Crawford calls "efficacious materiality," since Reformers never denied the usefulness of things. For many of them the grotesquely misshapen babies were in fact helpful lessons, parodying as they did the holy infant, and pointing to as well as punishing English sins against that Christ.

What is, then, most valuable in Crawford's comprehensive study is not her discussion of Protestants and miracles but her fascinating disclosure of the varieties of sins thought to be chastised through monstrous births, as well as her careful demonstration that Protestant pamphleteers consistently represented women's childbeds and their newborns' bodies as theaters and material witnesses of God's judgment. Thus ancient feminine unruliness was newly "policed" (a word Crawford likes). The motives of the births' commentators were doctrinally mixed—"[p]rodigious births . . . attested to a wide range of [Protestant] voices," as Crawford shows (176)—though the Reformers' varied warnings were almost all directed at sinful women and those men who failed to control them.

For this reason it is odd that, at the close of her book, she criticizes a 1663 work by John Spencer, which derided the monstrous-birth pamphleteers' assumptions that "God's judgments [had] no greater design than 'the service of [men's] little passions and animosities'" (178). Strangely respectful of the horrific treatises which "policed" mothers by characterizing deformed children as "monsters," Crawford chides Spencer for attributing those works to popular ignorance and superstition. Her argument is that in claiming the prodigy stories "never did, never could serve the interest of truth," Spencer overlooked the real use to which such tales were put by "royalist men of God" and the church itself, as well as by Puritan zealots (180). But certainly it is this malignant "real use"—namely, the terrifying of the innocent and the ignorant by anyone, to promote Christian lessons—to which Spencer humanely objects. Crawford charges Spencer with "false[ly]" thinking the writers of monstrous-birth pamphlets "preliterate," as he could not have done, and "superstitious" (180), which they were. (A preachment that recusant wives risk bearing two-headed babies remains sensational, even when rooted in and explicitly connected to an educated consideration of England's religious dividedness.) Spencer's "patronizing" dismissal of admonitory monstrous-birth writings very likely removed them from serious historical consideration for two centuries, as Crawford argues (181). But for Spencer in the early years of the Restoration, these sensational tales weren't quaint and historical, but dangerous and present. They were weapons that threatened to perpetuate the bloody sectarian conflicts of the Interregnum by preying on ignorance and inciting fear.

Most of them, at any rate, were works of this type, if Crawford's explication of them—admittedly far more detailed and nuanced than Spencer's—is representative (and her exhaustive bibliography and careful comparisons of different kinds of pamphlets and stories certainly argue that it is). We can be grateful for the link her book provides between the monster tales and early modern Reformers' serious considerations of doctrinal dangers that threatened England, not to mention New England (which Crawford also discusses, in a fascinating account of how Anne Hutchinson's ejection from the Massachusetts Bay community was accompanied by a charge that she birthed monsters). The Reformers' fear of both Jesuit equivocators and of James I's equivocal position with regard to Catholics; Protestants' discomfort with how the Reformers' validation of individual spiritual witness emboldened some women to speak in church; even pamphlets which, against the norm, presented "mitigating circumstances" of monstrous births which argued for readers' private interpretations of the events and their "sympathy" (66): these and other early modern cultural trends and phenomena are granted ample and intelligent attention in *Marvelous Protestantism.* This "antick and extraordinary" book's virtues far exceed its flaws, and argue for its place not on Spencer's "historical shelf of quaint and vaguely ridiculous superstitions" (181), but in the hands of serious students of English history.

Notes

1. Judith Dundas, "Spenser and the Emblem Books," *Emblematica* 11 (2001): 293–324.

2. John Calvin, *Institutes of the Christian Religion,* 2 vols., ed. John T. McNeill, trans. Ford Lewis Battles (Philadelphia: Westminster, 1960).

3. John Milton, *Paradise Lost,* ed. Scott Elledge (New York: W. W. Norton, 1975).

4. See Stephen Greenblatt, *Hamlet in Purgatory* (Princeton: Princeton University Press, 2001), and Grace Tiffany, *Love's Pilgrimage: The Holy Journey in English Renaissance Literature* (Newark: University of Delaware Press, 2006).

Anthony Munday and the Catholics, 1560–1633, by Donna B. Hamilton. Aldershot: Ashgate, 2005. Pp. xxxvi + 268. Cloth $94.95.

Reviewer: JOHN D. COX

In a work of careful historical reconstruction, Donna Hamilton has written what will surely be the definitive literary biography of Anthony Munday for a long time to come. Munday is principally known as a minor dramatist, writing for the late Elizabethan popular stage from 1590 to 1602. This brief theatrical career brought him tangentially into the orbit of Shakespeare, whose sunlike luster likely made Munday's small planet visible to literary historians in the first place. Both are thought to have contributed to the play called *Sir Thomas More* (unpublished until the nineteenth century), and Munday had a hand in *Sir John Oldcastle,* which was written in response to Shakespeare's *1 Henry IV.* But Munday's writing includes far more than plays. As Hamilton shows, he had an extraordinarily long and prolific literary career in many genres, stretching from 1577 (when he was only seventeen) to 1633, the year of his death.

What is most striking about Hamilton's biography is her argument for Munday's adherence to Catholicism. At a time when the argument for Shakespeare's Catholic adherence is enjoying unprecedented popularity, the careful study of a possible parallel is illuminating and helpful, especially since Munday's Catholicism is not obvious. He published a condemnation of the recusant priest Edmund Campion, when Campion was captured and executed in 1581; Munday dedicated a book to Richard Topcliffe, chief torturer for Elizabeth and James and eager persecutor of recusants; Munday published two sermons by John Calvin; and at least once in his long career Munday took service with the crown as a "pursuivant" or warrant officer, charged to find, inform on, and assist in the apprehension of traitors, especially recusants. Munday's hand in *Sir John Oldcastle* adds to the puzzle, because the play resuscitates the reputation of a Lollard (or proto-Protestant) martyr whom Shakespeare lampooned in the character subsequently known as Falstaff.

Well aware of these difficulties, Hamilton nonetheless makes her case persuasively by means of various kinds of historical evidence together with informed close reading of Munday's daunting corpus. She argues that Munday is what Elizabethans called a "church papist," that is, one who adhered to the government's standards for religious conformity while continuing to believe in Catholic doctrine. This was not an easy stance to maintain. Elizabeth was not only queen of the realm but also head of the English Church, which was independent of the Church of Rome and therefore opposed to papal domination. Depending on the strenuousness of one's belief in Catholic doctrine, conforming to the standards of the English Church was heretical, as recusants maintained, because it necessarily entailed denial of the pope's authority. Munday was clearly not a recusant, or he would not have survived. In what, then, did his Catholicism consist?

Hamilton argues convincingly that even though Munday remained loyal to the crown, he consistently advocated tolerance of Catholics, rather than persecution, and he signaled his Catholic allegiance in a variety of ways. His patronage network was consistently Catholic, for example, as Hamilton shows in detail. He published with printers who were known Catholic sympathizers. He addressed issues that concerned Catholics in particular, and he addressed them in ways that suggest Catholic sympathy. Finally, and here Hamilton's interpretation is boldest and most arresting, Munday frequently spoke through the experience and voices of others in ways that suggest his own position as revealed outside the texts he published. Reading Munday's writing in light of a densely elucidated context is thus essential to Hamilton's strategy and makes it credible.

Regarding Munday's *Brief discourse on the takinge of Edmund Campion, the seditious Jesuit* (1581), for example, Hamilton notes that the tract concludes with a list "of the priests, gentlemen and yeomen now in the Tower, as well as those of the wives and nuns who remained at Lyford," where Campion had been captured (37). While the tract explicitly condemns Campion for disloyalty to the crown, in other words, it also dispenses crucial information that Catholic readers craved about the disposition of their community in the wake of Campion's arrest. This gently subversive tactic was not original with Munday; drawing on the work of Arthur Marotti, Hamilton notes that it was a standard strategy of English Catholics in Reformation England. Citing another strategy, where Munday's publication of romances is concerned, Hamilton argues that his choice "to translate Iberian romances from French translations involved him directly in the importation—smuggling, if you will—of material that carried foreign ideologies" (75). In contrast to staunchly Protestant narratives like John Foxe's or Edmund Spenser's, Munday's translations consistently imagine a world in which noticing "how much is the same becomes more important than noticing what has been changed." His romances thus "helped create a public sphere in which the Catholic perspective remained a competing voice and offered a counter-narrative that represented the larger Catholic world as advantageous to England's safety and identity" (79). That counter-narrative imagined, in short, a different national identity from the one that was being shaped by the Protestant establishment, identified by Richard Helgerson and others as the dominant narrative of early modern England.

In Hamilton's view, Munday walked a tightrope with remarkable dexterity throughout his entire life. Hamilton makes clear the difficulty of maintaining one's position as a church papist in Munday's response to the Gunpower Plot of 1605. Seemingly an unambiguous case of recusant sedition, the plot resulted in a governmental clampdown on Catholic sympathizers, some of whom were compelled to serve as spies and pursuivants to prove their loyalty to the crown. Hamilton reports that Munday again took service with Richard Topcliffe, principal enforcer for the crown, at this time (156), in an apparent attempt to exempt himself from suspicion, and he republished some of his earlier loyalist tracts from the 1580s (157). "It was shrewd and convenient to have Catholics decry the actions of other Catholics," Hamilton observes (157), and Munday's response to this shrewd government policy shows the ambiguities of his position. He took a serious risk in maintaining a dual loyalty, because his temporizing must inevitably have been suspicious to less ambiguous loyalists on both sides.

The documentation Hamilton offers in support of her path-blazing argument is noteworthy. Out of some 286 pages of substantive text, about 106 pages consist of notes, bibliography, and index. Hamilton has compiled three bibliographies: a chronological list of Munday's publications, a bibliography of primary sources, and a bibliography of secondary sources. The last in particular is a mine of sources, both literary and historical, for anyone interested in the topic of Elizabethan and early Stuart Catholicism. Organizing the discussion of so much material, published over the course of more than fifty years, is a challenge for any literary biographer, and Hamilton for the most part follows a chronological scheme. Beginning with two chapters that deal, respectively, with Munday's writing in 1577–80 and 1581–88, she organizes the rest of his career generically, giving a chapter apiece to Munday's translation of Iberian romances, his writing for the popular stage, and his writing for the City of London. Genre is a useful way to organize a large body of writing, but it confuses the chronological scheme, because Munday did not take up and abandon particular genres in succession; he wrote in several of them simultaneously, and attention to his multi-generic writing in a given year or years could conceivably help to strengthen Hamilton's point. This confusion in narrative organization is compounded by infelicities of style and poor copyediting that makes the index difficult to use, sometimes when it is most needed.

Still, this remains an important book, and it should be read by all those who engage in debate about Shakespeare's Catholicism, because it makes a strong case for the Catholic allegiance of a man who was almost Shakespeare's exact contemporary, and who had a much longer writing career. If Shakespeare was himself a church papist or possibly even a secret recusant, as many have argued, then one ought to be able to find at least some parallels between his career and Munday's. Hamilton has herself addressed the issue of Shakespeare's attention to religious issues in an earlier book, *Shakespeare and the Politics of Protestant England* (1992), in which she concludes that Shakespeare's own religion is impossible to determine. Her work on Anthony Munday has not changed her mind. "Shakespeare's religion remains inaccessible," she states unequivocally (xxiv n 3). For those engaged in proving Shakespeare's Catholicism from what he wrote, Hamilton's book on Munday would seem to carry an implicit warning: *caveat lector.*

Shakespeare's History Plays: Performance, Translation and Adaptation in Britain and Abroad, edited by Ton Honselaars. Cambridge: Cambridge University Press, 2004. Pp. xiv + 287. Cloth $80.00.

Reviewer: **Brian Walsh**

Ton Honselaars brings together twelve essays loosely themed around the reception, production, and translation of Shakespeare's histories. While some of the essays do touch on twentieth-century British productions of the history plays, in particular those of John Barton and Peter Hall, the focus is on the fortunes of these plays outside Britain in places as far flung as Bulgaria and Japan. The bulk of the pieces deal with the development of a tradition of staging the histories in such places, as well as strategies for translating the texts and ensuring the material would not be too obscure for non-English playgoers to appreciate.

The first two essays in the collection are the exceptions to this pattern. They do not consider productions or adaptations of the plays outside Britain after Shakespeare's lifetime, but instead present more traditional readings of Shakespeare's playtexts. These pieces by Andrew Murphy and Lisa Hopkins on Ireland and Wales respectively are both essentially New Historicist approaches to how an English nation defines itself, or fails to define itself, against two-thirds of the Celtic fringe in Shakespeare's histories. Murphy for instance argues that the history plays "are significantly informed by the context of the Nine Years' War (1594–1603)," a series of Irish rebellions lead by Hugh O'Neill (42). Murphy's ability to connect this figure to Jack Cade in particular is a strong point in his argument that Ireland is ambiguously positioned by the histories alternately as part of an emerging English nation, and as its threatening "other." Hopkins comes to similar conclusions about Wales and its "simultaneous similarity and estrangement" for early modern English audiences (61). Although not necessarily relevant to the rest of the collection, these are strong contributions to the discussion about the emergence of national consciousness in England, especially in relation to how the people and nations most proximate to England were included, excluded, lauded, and denigrated in productions of its history.

The rest of the essays tend to be a cross between micro-histories and analyses of the Shakespearean history play in various countries. We get fascinating surveys of how the history plays have made their way, usually at a slow pace, into the theatrical repertory of various nations. An overriding concern of the collection is the common perception that history plays are by necessity more parochial than other genres, and will therefore translate less smoothly to contexts outside the country from which they originate. Thus we learn throughout the course of the collection that in Japan, Italy, and Bulgaria, Shakespeare's history plays arrived on the theatrical scene much later than plays like *Hamlet* or *The Merchant of Venice*. Ultimately, the essays tend toward an arc wherein the history plays are eventually taken up by directors and translators as a way to depict universal, perpetually relevant insights about the nature of power, ambition, and state violence. It is not surprising, then, that Jan Kott's reading of the histories and their demonstration of the "Grand Mechanism" of authority from *Shakespeare Our Contemporary* is frequently cited in the book as a major inspiration for postmodern global Shakespeare productions.

In addition to essays that explore the histories in Japan, Italy, Bulgaria, Austria, Spain, and France, there is a worthwhile if somewhat opaque piece on the challenges of translating a "bilingual" text like *Henry V*, as well as a useful essay on the development of the notion of the histories as "cycles." One the volume's strongest essays is by James N. Loehlin, on the influence of Brechtian theater theory on the resurgence of the *Henry VI* plays in the twentieth century. Loehlin makes ingenious connections between Brechtian elements already in the plays—such as an emphasis on the economic factors involved in England's loss of France—and productions of the histories that were directly influenced by Brecht, such as Peter Palitzsch's 1967 German work *Der Krieg der Rosen.*

Although generally speaking the volume addresses current hot-button questions of globalization and cultural appropriation, with the exception of Dominique Goy-Blanquet's tendentious essay on *Henry V* at Avignon, and Honselaars's own piece on a radical adaptation of the histories in Belgium (to which I will return), the essays tend to be modest in their political claims. Several authors do point out how particular productions of the plays could have served as commentary on topical issues. For instance, Mariangela Tempera in "Italian Responses to Shakespeare's Histories" writes about an Italian opera version of *Richard III* in 1859 that "drew a subtextual parallel between Richard's subjects and [Italians] on the eve of the 1860 uprisings which would bring about Italy's independence" (124). But such assertions, here and elsewhere in the volume, tend to paint the relation between such productions and contemporaneous politics in broad strokes.

An exception to that is Honselaar's essay, the last in the collection. Honselaar describes a radical Belgian production of the history plays, *Ten Oorlog* ("To War"), condensed into a trilogy, that combines the storyline of the two tetralogies with an aesthetic that seems highly influenced by German playwright Heiner Müller and British playwright Sarah Kane. The trilogy revels in onstage violence and grotesque spectacle, including a scene in which the Richard III figure, called here Risjaar, eats the corpses of the two murdered princes on stage. Another sensational image from the plays is a feminized Falstaff breastfeeding Hal. Honselaar's article makes sense of these choices through connecting the production to social and political problems in 1990's Belgium, including the "traumatic discovery of a nationwide practice of child abuse, and increasing evidence of the corruption of state justice" (247). Honselaars makes a convincing case for how *Ten Oorlog* addresses topical concerns in a specifically Belgian context. In his thesis that the production was ultimately an act of Shakespearean iconoclasm (again a la Müller) that nonetheless perpetuates Shakespeare as a font of political and social insight, Honselaars delivers the sharpest and most politically charged commentary in the collection on the appropriation of the histories in foreign contexts.

The volume is split into three sections: "Alienating Histories," "The Appropriated Past," and "Stage Adaptations of the Histories." Honselaars's initial introduction to the book does not offer brief descriptions of the essays, as is common for introductions in edited collections; instead, in addition to the longer opening introduction, Honselaars offers a brief introduction to each section. This construction of the collection is its notable weak point.

The three rubrics do not really illustrate the content of the various sections, and it is difficult to tell why they are needed at all. With the exception of the Hopkins and Murphy pieces, the essays of this book are thematically close enough to each other to justify inclusion in one volume, but also sufficiently distinct that the section divisions feel forced, and the additional introductory sections unnecessary. Ultimately, *Shakespeare's History Plays: Performance, Translation and Adaptation in Britain and Abroad* is a somewhat eccentric collection. It lacks a clear sense of aim, but it is filled with essays that deserve to be read and that might not have found their way into print outside of this volume. This book will help to historicize further the breadth of interest in Shakespeare around the globe, and will perhaps open new avenues of interest for readers who will be introduced to exciting Shakespeare traditions of which they were not aware. In particular it is difficult to imagine many Anglo-American scholars who would not learn a great deal of new and interesting information about the development of the Shakespeare industry in other cultures.

Renaissance Drama and the Politics of Publication, by Zachary Lesser. Cambridge: Cambridge University Press, 2004. Pp. xii + 244. Cloth $75.00.

Reviewer: RICHARD PREISS

As the intellectual and professional demands of academics grow increasingly onerous, one cannot help but read *Renaissance Drama and the Politics of Publication* with a double dose of envy: not only of its scholarly originality and elegant exposition, but for how predestined, by virtue of its very subject, such a study seems to have been to attract a commercial publisher. For publishers (early modern ones at least) are the heroes of this book, and by striving to re-materialize their subjectivity—a subjectivity on whose visibility, indeed, Lesser argues they routinely depended—he adds a new, vital dimension to the historical analysis of English Renaissance texts, one that looks to bridge fissures both in and between established critical methodologies. Lesser's principal concern is to consider publication (nominally dramatic, but the thesis must perforce encompass other kinds) as an emphatically interpretive act, a record of literary reception preserved in the social locutions of the material book itself. Nonquantitative histories of reading have heretofore been limited in their political articulation by the irrevocably local nature of the extant documentary evidence: marginalia can be either wildly eccentric or resolutely impersonal, while libraries inventory patterns of individual consumption merely in undifferentiated, retrospective blocks. To recover something of how people read a given text at a specific historical juncture, then, Lesser suggests we turn to the moment at which that text was packaged into the book they were meant to read, a process steeped in the speculative practices and economic constraints of an expanding, rapidly stratifying print marketplace. Since publishers of drama had to judge not only for themselves but for their potential customers the value of a manuscript before investing in it, predicting how and to whom that commodity could be sold, "every play publication is already a piece of literary criticism" (8), an entrepreneurial *poesis* wherein production always bears the trace of a prior consumption that is itself actively trying to determine future ones. The second state of Bonian and Walley's 1609 *Troilus and Cressida,* with its new epistle suddenly hyping the play's satirical urbanity, thus serves as a rare (if also problematic) example of such tactical guesswork caught in dynamic flux.[1] What makes these readings legible in more straightforward cases, however, where a publisher has not left us a sedimentation of their rhetorical fine-tunings—and this is Lesser's crucial premise—is that, viewed as a whole, the corpus of every publisher almost always forms just such a sediment. In a concise, persuasive pair of introductory chapters, he describes the development of "professional" publishing (a free-floating economic position gradually annexed by booksellers instead of printers) not only as a function of disparate regulatory standards within the Stationers' Company, favoring virtual assets over real ones, but subsequently as a history of market specialization. The financial scale of print publication meant that a book had to be bought by just a few hundred people in order to turn a profit—a theatrical performance might require thousands of patrons to do so—meaning in turn that publishers could afford (or could not afford not) to calibrate their products toward relatively small, precise segments of the bookbuying public. Enabling stable relationships with his suppliers of copy, Lesser contends, as well as reinforcing the "brand" identity of his shop (itself often dictated by the shop's location), cultivating a thematic niche keyed to a single demographic was the governing principle of a publisher's business; as a bookseller, he knew the interests of his likely customers, and to customers familiar with his previous wares, his name on a new title would have signaled a continuity with those interests. When applied to the seemingly anomalous items in a publisher's catalogue, like the playbooks around which Lesser's chapters pivot, this deduction can run the risk of hermeneutic circularity, but it is also an intuitively powerful explanatory model, yielding a basis for surrogating the question of "how a play was read," with "why *that* play was published *then*" (16). Plays are radically open-ended as verbal systems, but a play*book* was always embedded in a commercial context—the other books its publisher sold—that lent it a circumstantial coherence, both reflective of an anticipated horizon of reception and prescriptive of it in the process.

Attending to the historical and material totality of a given edition, then—who produced it, when, in what format, and as part of what field of specialty—can yield what Lesser calls the "politics" of its publication, if not as ultimately construed by readers then at least as constructed by those courting them. Lesser may thus be mincing terms when he says that these politics "come into focus only as the authors of plays are decentered" from our inquiry (21), since broadly speaking the "author function" as the privileged origin and delimiting property of a text's cultural meaning is here being performed by the publisher instead of the writer, its moment of activation reset to the manufacture of the book rather than to the composition of the text. But the substitution is still an exciting one, and might perhaps have been more resonant if simply stated as such. Rather than opt for the all-too-easy opposition to the ideological miscarriages of the New Bibliography, which perverted the calls of empiricists like Edward Arber for a recognition of printers and publishers into a forensic fantasy of authorial access fixed solely on the transmission of texts, for Lesser to have argued instead that publishers form a neglected node on a circuit of "authorship" more robustly and materially imagined would have served to throw into sharper relief—albeit in a less-than-fashionable vocabulary—his counterpart observation that the New Historicism has long been in need of such a renovated authorial concept, some limiting function to specify "*which* cultural discourses were engaged by a given text," for and by which historical agents, such that publication becomes the locus of "simultaneously text *and* event or political action" (22, emphasis in original). Lesser is aware (at times even apologetic) of his methodology's tendency to produce "dominant" or "preferred" readings, but this is just what it is designed to do, the maximization of its theoretical potential—especially when the readings it produces so often delightfully reverse our present critical emphases. And we have little to fear from them, since as intended interpretive frames they are themselves already the result of a prior set of readings, with an intrinsic cultural authority always subject to the opportunistic idiosyncrasies of commerce—the limitations of their prescriptive force implied, indeed, by the sheer length of time it has taken for someone to contemplate reconstructing them. A less "politic" sidestepping of the seeming retrogression of this approach, then—to call it "material" authorship, perhaps, an opening salvo in a "New" Old Historicism—would not only avoid confusing moments in Lesser's critical self-situation, such as the instinctual rejection of New Textualism's "remain[ing] focused on authors" (15) (when some of the very publishers he considers, like Bonian, Walley and Walter Burre, show the marketing of an author function to be just one face of the publisher function), but would also underscore, for scholars similarly interested in the hybrid discursivity of booksellers, copyholders, and editors, the fertile yet still materially grounded theoretical intervention that the History of the Book has seemed forever poised to make on traditional "literary" study.

The linchpin of this intervention, in Lesser's case, is of course the central idea of the publisher's "specialty" itself as the economic rationale and sociopolitical grammar of publication—a phenomenon whose most salient examples, at least, he is able to convert into illuminating and richly detailed genealogies between canonical and marginal texts. Chapter 2, the most uniformly dramatic in its orientation, may also explain Lesser's reluctance to label the global thrust of his arguments quasi-authorial (despite its telling title, "Walter Burre's *Knight of the Burning Pestle*"), since it examines Burre's playbook catalogue as an instance of "brand" homogenization effected as much through visual and generic class markers as by means of the playwright's name—which, we are always told, is supposed to be gaining currency as just such a sign in the early seventeenth century. Not so, according to Lesser, for Burre: in spite of (or, perhaps more intriguingly, thanks to) the precedent established by his long publishing record with the most self-textualizing poet of his generation, Ben Jonson, Burre elected in 1613 to publish Beaumont's *Knight of the Burning Pestle* without authorial attribution. The *Knight* thus becomes for Lesser a limit case of authorship's underlying contingency to a publishing strategy that relied instead on creating a freestanding category of "select" drama—culled, as were Jonson's *Every Man In His Humour, Cynthia's Revels, Catiline, Alchemist* and Middleton's *A Mad World My Masters,* mainly from the elitist, satire-driven indoor theaters. What the *Knight*'s anonymity illustrates about the collective commercial identity of these plays—what made it a "Burre" before a Beaumont—is the common emphasis on constructing an exclusive reading audience, through visual features like Latin epigraphy and continuous printing, and through a thematization of "wit" to which the educated gentry and Inns of Court men who frequented the children's playhouses (and anxious of just such a commodification of class signifiers) would have been particularly attuned. Lesser does well to stress that Burre's literary-dramatic project exceeds the genre of city comedy, though the discussion of continuous printing would have benefited from some reference to Douglas Brooks's recent work (2001), which maps similar territory. But the chapter's initial, most fascinating insight—that the majority of these plays were theatrical failures, and boldly advertised that fact in print—is left least satisfactorily integrated into Lesser's otherwise rigorous account. Just as Burre merely translated into print the disdain for popular theater which the plays themselves enunciate, does the valorization of their *own* public disapproval really further a Jonsonian "eras[ure of] the theatrical origins of the play" (63), or suggest that the same heightened performativity of self and taste now governs their private reception as well? Since the audience to whose distinction both the plays and playbooks appeal were roughly the same, a thicker analysis here might actually revise Jonsonian anti-theatricality instead of merely invoke it.

Far more cogent and dynamic a narrative is offered in chapter 3, on Nicholas Vavasour's perplexing publication in 1633 of Marlowe's *Jew of Malta,* some forty-odd years after its debut. Here the gap between performance and print is masterfully exploited to give perhaps the strongest showcase of Lesser's thesis, and produces a deliciously anti-Greenblattian reading of the play's supposed (and even then schizophrenic) heterodoxy. What stands in our way, of course, is Marlowe himself, who for Vavasour's readers in the 1630s, Lesser contends, was a virtual non-factor; far more pertinent to the play's printing was its recent revival for Court, which seems to have suggested to Vavasour, struggling to make a living as the publisher of predominantly Puritan literature, an opportunity to reinvent his specialty as establishmentarian. Analyzing his career in reverse until the hiatus that preceded *Jew*, Lesser argues that it inaugurated a "Laudian" phase for Vavasour—and, alongside other plays like Dekker's *Wonder of a Kingdom* and *The Noble Spanish Soldier*, with it the category of "Laudian drama"— because "Jew" had by now become a (self-applied) code for Puritan, a figure for recalcitrant nonconformity more connotative of domestic schism than of the alien infiltration it had represented in the 1590s; to the extent that this reading remains at all alive to what we consider the moral ambivalence of the play, in the England of Marlowe's Cyprus the Christians are exposed as hypocritical and corrupt only because Barabas's divisiveness has corrupted them. As mentioned, the unabashed flatness of this reading would not in itself be a problem—it is copiously and refreshingly historicized—except for the degree to which Lesser uses the play to impose a narrative on the publishing specialty rather than merely vice versa. As he himself notes, readers could just as easily have interpreted *Jew*'s apparent call for a crusade of doctrinal unity as itself a Machiavellian ploy for popish backsliding (113–14); given the play's pivotal role in Vavasour's professional profile, then, might we not expect its pro-Laudian semiotics to have been more pronounced, other than devolving on a single and ultimately volatile byword? How did Vavasour know the play would be taken as Laudian? How do you *start* a specialty in drama? To ask this—to suppose that he in fact *didn't* know—is to recuperate the play's polysemy on behalf of its retrospectively "dominant" interpretation: perhaps it was just a coin toss, a flag run up to see which way the book-buying wind was blowing strongest. This might explain why Vavasour's edition is so conspicuously free of any paratextual apparatus—making it hard, indeed, even to call it "Vavasour's edition"—save the poet's name, whose lingering notoriety may have served as a sign of just such duplicity. Here Lesser's orbit might truly escape the gravity of the author function: what made *Jew* "Laudian" was not Vavasour but the prevailing judgment of his customers.

A fuller treatment of this ambiguity would form a nice segue to Lesser's suitably complex fourth chapter, which examines Thomas Archer's maintenance of a "dialogic" publishing strategy in another prominent early seventeenth-century cultural debate, the so-called woman question. Reading Archer's dramatic catalogue of citizen plays alongside the seeming paradox of his having printed *both* Joseph Swetnam's raunchy, misogynistic *Arraign-*

ment of Lewd . . . Women as well as Rachel Speght's temperate reply *A Mouzell for Melastomus,* Lesser first contrasts the precedents for this practice (the printer John Wolfe had likewise single-handedly subtended the Nashe/Harvey quarrel until Harvey brought pamphleteering into it) in order to situate the *querelle des femmes* as an intra-discursive question specific to the mercantile class—a problem of marital rule—to whom Archer already catered with books on overseas trade and economic theory. If the analysis of such dialogism inevitably dissolves it, however—Swetnam and Speght together allowed male readers to experience both the ribald misogyny and the enlightened dotage that formed equal parts of the power equation in marriage—it regains force when it moves inside the individual Archer plays Lesser treats, becoming a template for a dramatic structure that produced the same "safe danger" (139) of simultaneously licensed and punished female sexuality. *The Insatiate Countess* thus offers both a tragic and a comic infidelity plot, one real and the other feigned; *The Roaring Girl* achieves this "double gesture of attraction and disavowal" (142) in the single plot of Moll, whose commodified transgressiveness greases the marital economy she can never join; *The White Devil,* finally, embodies it in the central character of Vittoria, her metamorphosis from willful virago to penitent wife tracing another redemptive liberation of female power. Lesser settles the lingering issue of whether Archer had to work to condition these readings at all by pointing out the predigestedness of Moll's self-commodifying woodcut and the typographic demarcation of Vittoria's arraignment—though one wishes he had more to say about Archer's edition of Robert Armin's *The Two Maids of More-clacke,* its frontispiece clearly not about maids but about Armin. In an otherwise well-developed chapter, moreover, it seems partial to conclude that such "armchair" consumption of sexual deviance "functioned differently," as reading matter, "than it did in the theater" (153), since, despite carrying its own erotic charge, the playhouse already represented its women with boys.

The poetics of matrimony likewise permeate Lesser's sprawling last chapter, an immensely erudite placement of Thomas Walkley's publications of *A King and No King* and *Othello* within a complex of monarchic theory, domestic and foreign policy during the onset of Stuart personal rule. Breathing new life into the Old Historicist notion that these plays concern "affairs of state," Lesser reminds us that this would become precisely Walkley's specialty—his bookshop in Britain's Burse by the mid-1620s a premier source of news about parliamentary factions and vicissitudes—and once again asks how (if not why) drama, seemingly, was the genre that established this readership. Making novel and overdue use of Walkley's dedication of *A King and No King* to Henry Neville, James's intercessory MP, Lesser resists the play's titular binary to read it as an allegory of "mixed government" under the literal terms in which James defined it: twinned union, the sibling bond of prerogative and legislation. How the gender-specific demands of drama actually allow the play to overcome the incestuous entanglements of such nuptial rhetoric—the paradoxes by which Arbaces can end up both subject to and a member of the landowning gentry, by which his power can both emanate from and efface Panthea's—thus becomes, like its pendant frontispiece, a *coup-de-theatre* of diplomatic mediation, and a political etiology of tragicomic miracle itself. The chapter's midsection extends Walkley's interest in such "family counseling" to the Spanish match, between whose royal advocates and parliamentary opponents the paternal anxieties of later Fletcher plays like *Philaster* and *Thierry and Theodoret* seem to have staked a more exhortative position. But readers will be especially rewarded by the provocative reading of Walkley's 1622 *Othello* it sets up: the comico-tragic story of another Spanish match, after all, of "mixed government" and mixed marriage gone wrong—here read in the surprising context of seventeenth-century romance, and of contemporary debates about "chivalric Protestantism" and the dangers of mercenary demilitarization—that shows how the publisher's niche might have impressed an entirely different locution upon the play than did the First Folio the following year.

Plentifully illustrated, close to exhaustive in its historical and critical scholarship, and written with lucidity and flair, *Renaissance Drama and the Politics of Publication* is one of those rare studies that plumbs the cavernous depths of cultural meaning stretching beneath and between texts both familiar and arcane, yet uses as its only tool information actually more obvious to early modern consumers than to us, the name at the bottom of a title page. Just how rare it will prove, however, remains this reviewer's only reservation: to the extent that, as mentioned, Lesser's readings stand or fall on the premise of each publisher's coherent, legible market "specialty," one is left wondering how universal and analytically generative this practice really was, or whether Lesser has already tapped all the richest veins. A cursory scan of the ESTC will bear his thesis out—*Hamlet* was not the only book of Nicholas Ling's aimed at "the wiser sort"—but there are limits to its replicability, even in cases where we select only for publishers (as Lesser admits he does) with prolific, sustained careers. Nathaniel Butter is surely one of these, notorious enough as a newsbook hawker by the 1620s for Jonson to parody him, but a glance at his output for 1608 yields little insight on any calculated reception of the quarto *King Lear:* along with Heywood's *If You Know Not Me,* his *Rape of Lucrece,* and George Wilkins's *Painful Adventures of Pericles,* we get Dekker's *Belman of London,* a reprinting of *The Cobler of Caunterburie,* a third run of Henoch Clapham's *Brief of the Bible,* three books of travel and news, and consignments of Withal's Latin/English *Dictionary for Children* and of Arthur Dent's *Sermon of Repentance*—in sum, a miscellany.[2] Specialties were certainly real, but in a still embryonically capitalized book trade they were also organic and took time to establish, sometimes never doing so. Coupled with the professional reinventions Lesser's own subjects perform—constantly switching the codes they hoped to stabilize—such inherent variability only augments the relevance of the new branch of study Lesser launches here, one that explores rather than tries to traverse the interpretive gap between publishing and reading, between producers and users, between texts and books.

Notes

1. Lesser argues that Bonian and Walley's preliminaries read the play as a kind of city comedy in order to assimilate it to the repertoire they were building—works of "wit and classicism" like Jonson's *Masque of Queenes,* Chapman's *Euthymiae Raptus,* Fletcher's *The Faithfull Shepheardesse*—when the classicism of this particular play would not seem to need much massaging. Lesser's claim that "this decision makes much more sense in 1609, after the vogue for satirical city comedies had been cultivated, than in 1603 [the year they first acquired the play]" (3) is slightly suspect, since by 1609 the vogue was already quite over; but more importantly it cannot explain the initial cancel, the reason Bonian and Walley apparently had a mind to change about the play in the first place.

2. A. F. Pollard and G. R. Redgrave, eds., *A Short Title Catalogue of Books Printed in England, Scotland and Ireland* (3 vols.), 2nd ed. (London: Bibliographical Society, 1991), 3:34.

Memory and Forgetting in English Renaissance Drama, by Garrett A. Sullivan, Jr. Cambridge: Cambridge University Press, 2005. Pp. vii + 184. Cloth $75.00

Reviewer: ANTHONY B. DAWSON

A contribution to the growing literature on memory in early modern studies, this book adopts a fresh perspective by focusing on memory's opposite—the propensity to forget and the ethical implications of such forgetfulness. As it turns out, forgetting has multiple dimensions. In many orthodox texts of the period, to forget is to miss the mark either morally or intellectually. Often condemned as a sign of insufficient awareness, it is figured as a kind of spiritual sleepiness, and indeed, as Sullivan shows, is frequently linked physiologically, as well as psychologically, with sleep. But in the hands of writers such as Montaigne, who praises forgetfulness as a necessary precondition for original thought, or Shakespeare, who links forgetting with a subtle and deeply individualized form of subjectivity, a much more positive spin is put on forms of "oblivion." The end result is a double, even at times paradoxical, view of the importance of memory for early modern writers.

Given his interest in the way the drama constructs subjectivity, Sullivan confines his analysis mainly to the role of individual memory, the way that it is understood as a mental faculty, foundational for rational thought and moral behavior. There are occasional forays into collective or cultural forms of memory, but for the most part the focus is on dramatic character and matters that pertain to individual personhood. As is customary in books of this kind, the analysis begins with a general introductory chapter that, in this case, discusses the various orthodoxies of memory theory, plus its physiological basis in anatomical theory, and then moves on to some of the contemporary challenges to received cultural discourses which privilege memory and critique forgetfulness. The conventional views are primarily moralistic and find prominent expression in, for example, anti-theatrical treatises. After laying these out in some detail, Sullivan, in a move that characterizes the book's general strategy, argues at the end of the first chapter that the theater to some extent subverts the orthodoxies, undermining the anti-theatrical critique by valorizing forgetting and showing its *productive* potential—most especially, as he puts it, "forgetfulness is generative of dramatic character" (43). This point is bolstered by a brief but telling analysis of the frontispiece of Raleigh's *History of the World,* a detail of which graces the cover of the book. In the image, Oblivion, who, together with Death, appears squeezed beneath the powerful female figure of *Historia* (the *"Magistra Vitae"*), is not only trodden down by history/memory but is also, Sullivan argues, "foundational" in that he "bears much of the weight of History on his head" (43).

As I indicated, this strategy of inverting the orthodox way of thinking about the opposition between memory and forgetfulness is maintained throughout. The book proceeds, after the first chapter, to an analysis of four plays, Shakespeare's *All's Well that Ends Well* and *Antony and Cleopatra,* Marlowe's *Dr. Faustus,* and Webster's *Duchess of Malfi.* Each of these works is linked with a variety of prose texts from the period that tend to represent both conventional and unorthodox perspectives on the main theme; after presenting the contextual material, Sullivan moves deftly on to show how the play registers some of the complexities of the particular mode of forgetfulness under discussion. For example, in the *All's Well* chapter, the theme is erotic self-forgetting and the issues taken up are drawn from psychological discourse (La Primaudaye and Montaigne representing opposing views about the need to remember). In the discussion of *All's Well,* Montaigne's idea that forgetting is foundational for original thought is transposed to theater and erotic desire. Forgetting oneself in the course of erotic pursuit both threatens identity (leading to dark outcomes in tragedies such as *Romeo and Juliet*) and enables it. In comedy especially, forgetting is necessary to fulfillment of desire, but in the case of *All's Well* (accounting in part for its "problematic" status), a sense of subjection to outside forces is in tension with the development of subjectivity. Bertram's subjection to the King and his extremely hesitant acceptance of Helena are signs of this incomplete identity; the ending especially suggests the ambiguity of forgetting and emphasizes the open-endedness of the play's exploration of it.

This sense of the uncertainties associated with forgetting characterizes the analysis of the three plays discussed in the succeeding three chapters. Forms of forgetting allow for a conventional moral reading: Antony's abandonment of Roman values, Faustus's strategic forgetting of the salutary possibilities offered by the truncated biblical quotations he cites at the outset, the Duchess's obliviousness to expectations of family and noble status. But at the same time, each play offers a way of celebrating the oblivion that it shows to be potentially destructive. If tragedy is one possible outcome of forgetting, so too is the potential for transcendence or at least an individualistic challenge to cultural norms. Thus while the Duchess's choice of erotic fulfillment and domestic happiness over the demands of family and class has devastating effects, it also reconfigures forgetfulness as a form of identity-making. Antony, to cite a more complex example, is remembered in quite different ways by Octavius and by Cleopatra. The former remembers Antony's past heroism, his Roman masculinity, and after his death allows an element of sentiment to color that sense of loss. But such commemoration is inadequate to the figure Antony has become, which is epitomized in Cleopatra's mythic reconstruction of the hero in terms that reach beyond conventional notions of the heroic to a sense of theatricalized identity, one that values multiplicity and instability: "Cleopatra transforms the discontinuities generative of self-forgetting into a prerequisite for heroic masculinity," thus producing an "alternative to Rome's . . . conception of fame" (107). In a move which I wish he had pursued at more length, Sullivan links this kind of creative forgetting/commemoration with the way Shakespeare (and perhaps the drama more generally) confronts the classical past. In other words, a way of construing *Antony and Cleopatra* is to see it as an expression of cultural memory, one that does not simply repeat but refigures and transvalues the past, especially the literary past.

There are hints throughout the book that Sullivan sees the theater in these culturally transvaluative terms, though the focus remains primarily on individual character and identity. In the *Faustus* chapter, he links the subjective self-fashioning of the main character with the allure of the theater itself—i.e., the appeal of Faustus's aspiration is analogous to that of theater, which also induces, and even seems to advocate, self-forgetting. Thus the theater becomes a kind of laboratory in which the creative tensions between memory and oblivion are tested and recombined in energetic new ways.

The book's various readings are handled adroitly and succinctly, and I have little quarrel with any of the conclusions. The only drawback is that they seem relatively familiar; coming at these plays from the standpoint of the tension between memory and forgetting opens up a different avenue, but the new road leads to places we've visited before. On the other hand, there is the advantage that the book provides a set of terms that allows us to approach certain aspects of each play differently. And, perhaps most valuable, the different chapters adduce a wide variety of specific texts and contexts through which to assess the complex ramifications of what Ulysses calls "alms for oblivion."

Shakespeare, Memory and Performance, Peter Holland, ed. Cambridge and New York: Cambridge University Press, 2006. Pp. xx + 367. Cloth $90.00.

Reviewer: R. A. FOAKES

One of my earliest memories of a Shakespeare performance spotlights a stunning treatment of a scene in Glen Byam Shaw's *Macbeth* with Laurence Olivier in the title role in 1955. The Weird Sisters had appeared, as I recall, in customary black robes in the first scene and in 1.3, where they greet Banquo and Macbeth as they return from their victory over rebels. In 3.1, the murder of Duncan accomplished, Macbeth summons the two murderers he has hired to deal with Banquo. He asks them if they have thought about his "speeches" in which he put the blame for their poverty and misfortunes on Banquo. They neither agree nor disagree, but the first murderer responds with the enigmatic "We are men, my liege," which provokes Macbeth into his great lines beginning, "Ay, in the catalogue ye go for men," comparing the variety of men to the various kinds of dogs. This is the speech in which Macbeth, so to speak, lets go, and speaks his mind. The previous exchanges with the murderers serve as an introduction to it. But Shaw and Olivier shaped the scene differently: he stood center stage, and the murderers appeared one on each side downstage, as their dialogue begins. Memory tells me that as the murderers entered Olivier summoned them to him on the next phrase, with a finger gesture to each, as he spoke the words "Well," beckoning one, "then," beckoning the other, "now" bringing both to form a close group with himself at the center. The murderers and Macbeth were cloaked in black, so that they gathered to create a stage image matching the three witches in the opening scene. It was a striking visual parallel that for me added a new perspective into the power of the witches and the power of three in the play.

But is this really how the scene was played? Can memories be trusted? It so happens that two promptbooks for this production by Glen Byam Shaw survive. One, (A), Shaw's outline of his blocking, has been edited in facsimile by Michael Mullin (*Macbeth on Stage,* Columbia: University of Missouri Press, 1976). The other (B) is in the library of the Shakespeare Centre in Stratford-upon-Avon, and appears to be the working promptbook of the stage manager, Jean Roberts, and assistants, showing what in practice was intended. These differ, making a reconstruction even more difficult, and they tell us what the director and stage manager wanted, but not necessarily what happened when I attended a performance, since as the season went by actors may have introduced variations. But my memory blanked out altogether the introduction of the murderers by a servant (Seyton in Shaw's production), and the lines that immediately follow Macbeth's call, "Who's there?" According to promptbook A, Macbeth was to make a "slight move" downstage at this point, and on "till we call" he beckoned "1st. & 2nd. Murds to him." Promptbook B says Macbeth clapped his hands, and Seyton entered right center, followed by the murderers, and then directed one to cross downstage to left of center, "bottom step," the other to cross downstage right of center.

Re-enter [Attendants] Seyton, with two Murderers

Now go to the door, and stay there till we call.
[*Exit Attendant*]
Was it not yesterday we spoke together?
1. *M.* It was, so please your highness.
Mac.   Well then, now
Have you considered of my speeches?

At "Well then, now" Macbeth was to move to center downstage. Seyton then was to exit upstage of the murderers as Macbeth beckons the murderers to him. This is where my memory of the scene cuts in, omitting Seyton's presence altogether.

In the grouping of Macbeth and the murderers as figures costumed in black I saw an image recalling the grouping of the witches in the opening scene. Here again their entry as floating airborne figures in fog disappeared from my memory, as also did their descent to earth "like passengers on a flying bedstead," as one reviewer, Peter Rodford in the *Western Daily Press,* June 9, 1955, rather scathingly described their arrival. And were they in black?— Cecil Wilson, the reviewer in the *Daily Mail,* June 8, saw "grey scrawny witches." Macbeth himself was costumed not in black, but in "a red cloak and a plum velvet drape" (Mullin, 113) for his appearance as King in this scene. It seems that my memory here is highly selective, erroneous in details, and simply fails to record much of what went on in performance. In this instance I have a vivid recall of those elements in the staging that established what was for me a brilliant and novel connection in the grouping, marking visually Macbeth's surrender to the powers of darkness. No review of the production that I have seen commented on this connection, and it was Olivier's "Ay, in the catalogue ye go for men" speech that reviewers like Harold Hobson (*Sunday Times,* June 12) praised, as Macbeth "briefs the murderers with a contempt for their trade which is exceeded by his contempt for himself."

These reflections bear on the question, what are we talking about when we talk about "performance criticism"? A book on *Shakespeare, Memory and Performance* is to be welcomed as having the laudable aim, according to Peter Holland in his introduction, of marking "an inauguration of the study of memory in Shakespeare performance studies as a vital topic of debate." It consists of thirteen essays by different authors divided among five sections. In the fascinating essay that begins the first section, Bruce Smith broods on his memories of three 1990 stage productions of *King Lear,* in effect "a series of isolated moments" that fuse several productions in his mind. In trying to sort these out he "had to rummage through a disorganized box of souvenir programs, go to the library and check three stage history books on *Lear,* order three others on interlibrary loan, click my way through twenty or so screens on the internet, locate a copy of *The Cambridge King Lear CD-ROM,* insert the CD, learn to navigate the program, and move back and forth, up and down, into and out of the CD's three sectors." In this way he was able to reorder his memories: "They're tidier now, but they still don't compose a coherent whole" (25). In the end he is left with "two different sorts of phenomena: (1) a series of visual and aural vignettes and (2) a sense of how I felt—no, how I *feel* about them" (25). But a connective tissue is missing. Memory is selective and performances "constitute moving targets" (25).

Smith goes on to quote Alexander Leggatt's comment after writing his book on *King Lear* for a series on Shakespeare in Performance: "Memory cheats: . . . in researching this book I have been astonished by how often my memory is at odds with the evidence—much of which depends on other people's memories" (36). Memory is selective in relation to performances of long plays, memory cheats, and memory may be affected by other people's memories as recorded in program notes, commentaries, or conversations. Then there is the question of what is remembered of performances. As Smith observes, the actor can communicate emotions by movements, body language, not just through the text. So what he remembers about one actress's performance in *Lear* is "not what she said but how she used her hands" (30). I cannot follow Smith into his conclusion, where he uses the last lines of the play to link memory to the line "Speak what we feel, not what we ought to say." He says "'Ought' and 'feel' shape up as two quite distinct modes of memory" (41): ought he relates to fixed ideas and "the verbal formulations of academic criticism," while feel "takes its cue from subjectivity, from internal experiences of sensation and movement." This makes a neat conclusion, but has little to do with the way these terms recall the opening of the play, where Cordelia is placed in the dilemma that she cannot say what she ought, what obedience and a public ceremonial occasion demand, because it would be false, and cannot heave her heart into her mouth to say what she really feels because that is a private matter between her and her father—so she speaks something of what she feels, but in a way that misleads and falsifies. Ought has to do with duty, as Regan reminds us later in the scene, and I cannot see the connection with academic criticism, which is in the main concerned with the text of a play.

This essay nevertheless is very perceptive in identifying the fluid nature of memory in relation to performances which occupy space and time. Memory records "aural and visual vignettes" involving movement, such as my recall of Olivier beckoning the murderers to come to him. I would add, as far as my own experience is relevant, that such vignettes often remain in the memory because they embody an interpretation of action and/or text in the play that struck me as exciting or innovatory. Such was Olivier's grouping in *Macbeth,* 3.1, and such was his entry in *Othello,* 1.2, holding and smelling a rose, business for which there is no hint in the text of this scene, but which brilliantly identified Othello's peaceful concern with marriage and anticipated his perception of Desdemona as a rose at the end when he prepares to kill her:

> When I have plucked the rose
> I cannot give it vital growth again,
> It needs must wither. I'll smell thee on the tree;
> O balmy breath . . .
>
> (5.2.13)

Performance memories may thus have little to do with the text, but remain vivid because they show how an actor or director reinvigorates the staging of a play by business or movements that make unexpected connections within the play or open up possibilities for interesting and novel interpretations of the action.

The topic of memory in relation to performance, however, has many dimensions, which are dealt with in other essays in *Shakespeare, Memory and Performance.* Anthony B. Dawson writes about what he calls "memorial repetition" in plays by Marlowe and Shakespeare, beginning with Marlowe's echoes of Virgil in his *Dido and Aeneas,* and going on to comment on Shakespeare's recall of Virgil's *Aeneid* in *Hamlet, The Tempest, Troilus and Cressida,* and elsewhere. He is concerned especially with grief and loss, and the way "the theatre is responding to the sense of belatedness that accompanied a return to the classics" (82), and he claims "that the uncertainty and ambivalence about remembering performance registers a widespread ambivalence about performative memorial in the culture, which in turn is connected to the profound sense of loss, along with the equally powerful hope about the building of England, that arose out of the trauma of the Reformation" (83). This suggests an interesting connection, but one that has more to do with the literary remembrances embedded in the plays than with performance, and I'm not sure what "performative memorial" means. All Renaissance drama, however, is belated in building on what earlier writers and dramatists had achieved, and Dawson shows how Shakespeare's deployment of his memories of the classics enriches his plays.

Another section of the book consists of two essays on editing and memory. In one Michael Cordner raps two notable editors of *Macbeth* (A. R. Braunmuller for the Oxford and Nicholas Brooke for the Cambridge editions) over the knuckles for not doing enough in their commentaries to suggest ways of performing the play. Cordner's ideal seems to be something on the scale of Marvin Rosenberg's exhaustive treatment of staging in *The Masks of Macbeth*. In his edition, Braunmuller describes Henry Irving's mode of leaving the stage very slowly in 2.1 on his way to murder Duncan. Cordner comments that "Highlighting Irving's interpretation in this way seems in the end merely anecdotal. If Irving is to be invoked, why not also tell us about the handling of this exit by David Garrick and by Laurence Olivier, by Ian McKellen and by Edmund Kean, and so on, until, at the very least, a representative sampling of different staging options has been laid before the reader?" (95). Do readers need to be advised that actors may make different choices about how to exit at this point? Cordner thinks we "urgently need" editions fashioned from curiosity about the "performance record." But that record consists of memories which may not be reliable, and would such editions be merely bewildering to many users? In her companion essay Margaret Jane Kidnie begins by reminding readers that performance "is ephemeral" (117), and can only be relived as memory and communicated through forms of storytelling. Archives about stage performances are "limited and partial" (122) and may mislead. So, "in the case of unrecorded changes to a production made during previews, after press night, or over the course of a long run, the official documents can lend authority to moments and memories shared by few, if any audience members" (122). Kidnie illustrates how, from personal experience, she generated a "pragmatic notion of a play constructed from a series of plausible memories—some textual, some theatrical and filmic—that come to stand for *Hamlet*" (126). A canon of theatrical production is formed in that "process of recovering certain stories of memory from the past."

Precisely. And what makes particular memories significant while others fade? Cordner seems to want editions to include as complete a register of staging as possible, but the result may be no more than a catalogue of memories, useful only for finding out what various actors were said to have done. My memory of Olivier's encounter with the murderers in *Macbeth* is close to that of Gareth Lloyd Evans, who records in his commentary on Stratford productions, 1946–80, in *Focus on Macbeth* (ed. John Russell Brown [London: Routledge, 1982], 99) a more nuanced impression of what happened:

> Visually the scene's pattern was of Macbeth restlessly advancing towards them and their disposition to back away. But with "well, then, now", that pattern was broken. Olivier stopped in his hypnotic movements, eyed them mockingly, lifted up his arms and with each index finger pointing at a murderer said "well" questioningly. Each finger then crooked as, after a pause, he said "then" and the movement and

tone suggested he wanted them to move nearer to him. They remained still, however, and his "now", after another pause, was a commanding and frightening imperative. This verbal equation which produced fissionable material out of apparently verbal rubble, produced a silence in the audience that beggars description.

Lloyd Evans also found this scene sensational, but did not, apparently, see it in symbolic terms as related to the grouping of the witches in earlier scenes. Most reviewers paid little if any attention to the staging here, but Marvin Rosenberg's detailed survey of performances in *The Masks of Macbeth* (Newark: University of Delaware Press, 1978, 400–401) cites the notice in *Theatre Quarterly* which registers a somewhat different impression after Olivier "crooked the index finger of each hand in terrible invitation, and made 'well' into a question. He paused. The murderers looked at one another. The index fingers swept downwards and pointed straight at the floor on each side of him. He said 'then' as a command. They moved slowly towards him like frightened stoats. Almost humorously, but with an edge of impatience, he said 'now' and an act of hypnosis was completed." The director, Glen Byam Shaw, had envisaged this Macbeth as having an "almost hypnotic personality" (Rosenberg, 105), and this is what caught the reviewer's attention.

Cordner wants editors to note what all major actors did, but as the example of *Macbeth,* 3.1, shows, it would be an impossible project. In the first place, each spectator sees what happens differently, and the actor's performance may change from day to day. Secondly, what a spectator notices is likely to be colored by her interpretation of the action. So, for me the grouping of the murderers was striking as repeating the grouping of the witches; for Gareth Lloyd Evans Olivier's brilliance in exerting a psychological domination over the murderers by exploiting a seemingly trivial phrase was paramount; and Marvin Rosenberg and the reviewer in *Theatre Quarterly* were most impressed by the hypnotic power of Olivier's acting. What an actor does in much of a performance may often not be of great interest, as there is always a range of possible ways to stage any action; but some find ways to reveal new relationships or resonances, so that a particular way of playing one moment or one scene may expand our sense of the play's potential for meaning. Ideally an edition might strive to identify and record these, if only there were reliable witnesses and space and time enough. Kidnie's skepticism appeals to me more than Cordner's desire to attend "properly to all that the multifarious stage history can tell us about the line-by-line intricacies of potential signification in a play like *Macbeth*" (116). As she says, "the search for the play, as distinct from its one or many texts, always comes back to the individual spectator" (126).

The most entertaining section of the book (partly so because of the excellent illustrations) begins with an essay by Barbara Hodgdon based on a visit to the costume archive of the Royal Shakespeare Company in Stratford-upon-Avon. She meditates on the evocative nature of the costumes from old productions she studied and photographed, Ian Holm's boots for Richard III in 1963–64, Richard Burton's costume as Henry V in 1951, and a number more. Such costumes can reanimate a memory of performance, whereas professional photographers of productions tend to offer an "invented pose" rather than a performance image (151). Costumes also affect the nature of a performance. Hodgdon contrasts the costume worn by Vivien Leigh as Lady Macbeth in 1955, an elaborate cloak, ornaments and crown, with the bare shift worn by Judi Dench in 1977: Leigh's costume for her part weighed twelve pounds appropriate to a "statuesque" representation, while Dench's weighed twenty-one pounds, enabling the latter to "assert a remarkable physical performance" (153). Carol Chillington Rutter then considers the "materials of memory" in what she calls "an essay in gossip" (169) culled from memories of performances. She is concerned mainly with he way actors "depend on objects" (181) used on stage,—the book held by Alan Howard playing the king in *Henry VI,* Part 3, 3.1, which was not the prayer book called for by the stage direction, but a copy of *Coriolanus,* in which he was to play the title role later in the 1978 season; or the scarf used by Emrys James in various roles as "a mnemonic that ties him to the book, both fetish and prophylaxis: it's how he remembers his lines how he wards off forgetting" (174). Moving on to objects required in the plays, she ascribes to properties a "power' to "remember the histories they've accumulated" (182). So the skull in *Hamlet* "remembers the professional man who played it and remembers his name" (183). This is pushing too far, leading to the claim that "the skull fashions the Prince" (184). The skull "could sing once," as Hamlet says of the first one thrown up by the gravedigger, but now reflects the memories attributed to it, and we only have his word that it belonged to Yorick: the gravedigger and the Prince in fact fashion the skull as a repository of memories. Rutter concludes her chapter with a brilliant analysis of the uses and treatment of the handkerchief in recent productions of *Othello,* and shows how this trifle light as air floats as an image in productions, in posters and on the cover of the Arden edition of the play, working "like a designer label" to provide instant brand recognition (200). The current emphasis on the handkerchief no doubt has to do with increasing openness about sexual activities, and Rutter ends with her assessment of Declan Donnellan's Cheek by Jowl production of the play in 2004: "Making spectators look, up close, at the sex that Shakespeare's play-text puts somewhere else, out of sight; making them see the handkerchief as a sex toy used to play out, for post-adolescent kicks, a deeply-clichéd jealousy/punishment scenario, Cheek by Jowl invented for the object a whole new career path that forgot Iago's 'trifle'. And remembered instead a 'thing' of darkness, violence, and pain" (206).

Rutter earlier cites approvingly W. B. Worthen's statement that the text "becomes significant only as embodied in the changing conventions of its performance" (179). But the Cheek by Jowl production "invented" a use for the handkerchief that has nothing to do with Shakespeare's text. Worthen's statement is understandable as part of an effort to establish the importance of performance criticism, but in performances that seem compelling to critics the text may be altered, abandoned, or reworked in ways that have little to do with what the playwright actually wrote. In his essay on memory and forgetting Peter Holland illustrates another problem for criticism, that performance lives in memory that is "partial and fragmentary," and in recalling the experience "we create constructs of memory" (211). What's more, "the show is never the same two nights running" (213). He is thinking especially of the Royal Shakespeare company, whose productions he reviewed for years in *Shakespeare Survey*. He cites Laurie Maguire's demonstration that in six BBC television productions of plays by Shakespeare the actors introduced many errors, both small and substantial in kind, and additions, as well as "garbled transpositions and major omissions" (223). Add to this Holland's reminder that "what is heard and seen as well as what is remembered is uncontrollably individual" (211), and we seem to have a tangle of difficult questions to resolve in writing about performance, adding to those raised by the enjoyable and informative accounts by Hodgdon and Rutter of specific uses of costumes and objects in various productions.

The next section of the book is concerned with reconstructing performances, as Russell Jackson explores accounts of Elisabeth Bergner as Rosalind in a 1936 film of *As You Like It,* and Michael Dobson investigates the ideological significance of the "vogue for outdoor production" (277) of plays by Shakespeare in the period before World War II. The final section brings a splendid essay by W. B. Worthen on the impact of new technologies on filmed Shakespeare as we move into a digital age. He analyzes the use of devices like cellphones, laptops, videos, and recorders in Michael Almereyda's *Hamlet* to establish the "central conceit, that Hamlet uses video recording and digital editing throughout the film as a means of reflection" (289). He reduces all information to "data bits that are indistinguishable and susceptible to being reconfigured in a range of signifying environments" (299). The noise and frenzy of images "displace the more leisurely contemplation of Shakespeare's text" (299), so again the question of the relation of performance to text becomes an issue, even as we may agree with Worthen's observation that our understanding of "ourselves, and how dramatic action represents us, speaks to and for us" (304) is changed by the media. Robert Shaughnessy then considers the reconstructed Globe theater in London as a center of "digitized resources," in respect of its educational outreach, "virtual tours and videoconferencing" (308). However, in relation to the way popular theater in general "increasingly models itself on television and film" (311), he perceives "the stages of the Royal Shakespeare Theatre and the Globe" as "technologically destitute—and proudly so" (314). He is anxious about the effect of the "overpowering imperatives of the media system" on the staging of Shakespeare, as they may "diminish or interrogate the capacity of the live to function normally in its own terms" and also "call into question what those terms are" (319). This essay adds a cautionary note to Worthen's, and is further supplemented by Dennis Kennedy's closing consideration of festivals and museums as repositories of cultural memory. This leads him to reflect on the impossibility of codifying memories of performance, since they belong to the individual consciousness: "The job of performance history is to understand and give meaning to the event through social and aesthetic analysis, not to be the sum of the audience's experiences" (337).

A gathering of essays is almost bound to result in a mixed bag, and this collection is no exception, but it does lay the groundwork for further and more focused study of some basic and very important issues. This collection deals with many aspects of memory and performance criticism, returning frequently to the problem that performances are always in the past and recollected in the memories of individuals. Is it possible to establish parameters of performance criticism? And how does it relate to the texts and verbal meanings of the plays? I began with a memory of Olivier as Macbeth. What stands out in my memory, as in that of Gareth Lloyd Evans and in Marvin Rosenberg's account, is the force with which Olivier seemed to draw the murderers to him in 3.1. We were all impressed by the way Olivier seemed by force of personality to compel the murderers to move to him. Richard David, on the other hand, also praising the performance in *Shakespeare Survey* 9 (1956), was struck by Olivier's constant motion, noting how the murderers shrank back every time Macbeth approached them "in a swirl of robes, while he, pacing the stage between and around them" dazzled them (*Shakespeare Survey* 9 [1956]: 130). As individuals we each see things differently, or see different things. But here, it seems, is where performance criticism inevitably begins.

Horrid Spectacle: Violation in the Theater of Early Modern England, by Deborah G. Burks. Pittsburgh, PA: Duquesne University Press, 2004. Pp. viii + 456. Hardcover $60.00.

Reviewer: EMILY DETMER-GOEBEL

Violation is a concept that has recently appeared in the title of several works concerning early modern English drama. Alexander Leggatt's most recent book, *Shakespeare's Tragedies: Violation and Identity* (2005) and Pascale Aebischer's *Shakespeare's Violated Bodies: Stage and Screen Performances* (2004) are just two examples. While these two books narrowly focus on Shakespearean texts and performances, one of the many strengths of Deborah G. Burks's book is to approach violation imagery with a wide scope in order to examine the "portability" of the rhetoric of violation not only in the drama but in a broad range of nonliterary texts as well. Fortunately Burks's project does not simply seek to create a catalogue of such instances; instead, her work persuasively demonstrates the "durability and adaptability of violation as a figure for disruptions of the normative relations among superior and subordinate members of society" (12). Another strength of this analysis is that Burks joins other recent scholars who reject the traditional periodization that links Restoration drama with a long eighteenth century. Seeing the seventeenth century as a whole, Burks attends to violation imagery as a "key piece of the history of political discourse" in order to "recapture a sense of the seventeenth century as a continuous series of moments and movements; a sense of continuity that has been lost to students of literature because of the way we tend to break the period into isolated pieces" (24).

For Burks, the drama played a vital role in political debates both before and after the restoration of the monarchy: "Plays initiated, continued, echoed and replied to the debates—about domination and subjection, rule and rights, prerogative and property holding, sovereignty and citizenship—that were central to the events of the period" (29). Burks carefully reads not only the drama, but also the religious and political texts with the eye of a literary critic in order to see the cultural conversation among genres and authors at specific moments within this turbulent century.

The book is divided into three sections, each with three chapters. The first section is entitled "Acts and Monuments of Violation" which has chapters anchored on readings of John Foxe's *Actes and Monuments,* Shakespeare's *Measure for Measure,* and George Chapman's *Bussy D'Ambois.* At the foundation of Burks's project is her careful reading of *Actes and Monuments* which will be recalled throughout the book. One such reoccurring image of violation is when Roman Catholic persecutors enact violence against a victim's body and will. A playwright himself, Foxe's Protestant polemic shares many characteristics of the drama, the tyrant play in particular, and Burks argues that many of the moments are consciously theatrical and interested in representing the spectacle of the horror visited on innocent victims. As every drama needs conflict, Burks identifies the battle here as one where the persecutors abuse the bodies of their victim, but they fail to violate their will. Anne Askew, for example, is tortured but refuses to give in to the demands of her persecutors to name names. The battle of wills is won by the victim, even as her body is violated to the point of death. Polemists like Foxe and John Bale often depict the papist persecutors as imposing their wills on their victims in a way that brings sexual pleasure to the perpetrator. It becomes more about the pleasure of exhorting power over a woman than it is about extracting information. In a fascinating examination of the woodcuts included in *Actes and Monuments,* Burks argues that together they "depict the Marian persecutions as the fruit of an unholy alliance between church and state authorities. The result is a picture of individual tyranny and collective abuse of power on the part of England's highest officials" (43). The woodcuts and Anne Askew's story become keys to her reading of the deceitful rulers of *Measure for Measure* and the scenes of rape and torture in *Bussy D'Ambois.* While Burks acknowledges the multiple ways in which to interpret a character in a play, she suggests that Shakespeare "depends on his audience to hear and apply these polemical echoes [of violation images] as they interpret Angelo's handling of women" (92). By drawing these connections between scenes of violation in these various texts, Burks convincingly shows how Foxe's and Bale's texts would likely shape readers' interpretations of the plays.

The first section of the book examined the way that political and dramatic texts were "encoded" with violation imagery. At the center of the book is a section entitled "Ravishing the Subject's Masculinity." In the first chapter of this section Burks examines property rights, status, and sexual will in literary representations of rape in early seventeenth-century drama (from a previously published and often cited essay). Much scholarly work has been published regarding depictions of sexual violation as a trope for abusive power in rulers, as evidenced by the foundational story of Lucrece. Burks's contribution to the study of representations of rape in literature is her unpacking of the culture's anxiety about a woman's agency or will regarding her own body and her relationship to the subject whom the culture considered the true victim of rape: her father, husband, or guardian. The chapter opens with an example of a notorious power struggle between Sir Edward Coke and his wife, Lady Elizabeth Hatton, over their daughter's marriage to John Villiers. Burks uses the Coke-Villiers case to show how law and custom gave fathers of the propertied class exclusive right regarding marriage negotiations, yet it became increasingly clear "that women as well as men possessed wills, which prompted them to desire and act on their own." Where such agency in men "was seen as the rightful expression of intention, ownership, and familial authority, in women, it was associated with petulance and indulgence, especially sexual indulgence" (152). Here Middleton's *The Changeling* helps Burks to demonstrate the link between representations of ravishment and rights; the play articulates a growing concern about women's will and its impact on the subject's (that is, on men's) rights. Burks identifies the culture's contradictory stance about women's agency: "women, though responsible for their (sexual) actions, are strongly suspected of being incapable of acting responsibly" (158). Burks continues to note throughout the book how women characters are depicted as both vulnerable gatekeepers, but also dangerous and willful. Burks closes the chapter by considering James I and the growing controversy over the subject's rights where the "king's impositions amounted to a seizure or *ravishment* of the subjects property against their will—a violation" (181, original emphasis). In addition to early statute law on rape, Burks explores the connection between debate about subject's rights and ravishment law by examining several proposed bills under consideration in the House of Commons at the beginning of the century (182–83).

The issues of subject's rights, gender, and violation imagery is also examined in a chapter focused on the letters of Arbella Stuart Seymour, a cousin of James I and a potential rival for the throne. For Burks, Stuart Seymour's letters provide further evidence of how a woman might use the images of violation found in Protestant martyrology to argue for the return of her title and property, language that Burks finds Jacobean MPs using as well. More compelling is the final chapter in this section which turns to James Shirley's *The Cardinal* and the political crisis of 1640–41. Burks argues that Shirley "redeploys" the rhetoric of abuse of subject's rights when it depicts "the abuse of the ecclesiastical hierarchy as rape and emasculation, as a violation of the wills, bodies, and rights of English subjects" (21). While this same rhetoric was used by militant Protestants to dismantle the monarchy and the state church, Burks argues that Shirley's play "urges the Crown to reform its own abuses before reform is imposed on it from without" (21).

The final section of the book, "Renegotiating the Rhetoric of Abusive Sexuality" explores the ways in which the rhetoric of abuse was used in texts to support either the Stuart monarchy or the Interregnum by examining notable texts written by Margaret Cavendish, John Dryden, and Aphra Behn. This section opens with a reading of the propaganda mills hard at work at the time; on the one hand persuading English readers to re-embrace the mythology of the monarchy, and on the other hand, discrediting popular pro-monarchy texts such as *Eikon Basilike* with rebuttals such as Milton's *Eikonoklastes*. Burks demonstrates how these regicidal historians revived the earlier language and imagery which linked political impositions with the sexual transgressions of the monarch: "These antimonarchist writers set out to prove that Charles was a tyrant by pointing to the arbitrariness of his will, which they insinuated was not only a will to power, but also a will to pleasure irrational and boundless in its desire" (269). Repeatedly, Charles is depicted as a type of Tarquin, whose exercise of power is continuously given a sexual connotation, denigrating finally to rape. Interestingly, Burks suggests these writers not only deployed the rhetoric to engage their readers emotionally, but also to create a titillating display for readers to witness as if presented from the stage: "these texts draw 'the traverse Curtain' to reveal both a tyrant Charles and a puppet Charles manipulated by his wife, while also exposing a womanish sodomite in the role of James" (277). While Burks's close reading of the deployment of the rhetoric is intelligent and persuasive, it is not clear if there is something inherently different about this engagement of rhetoric from the prewar texts.

Burks is clear that she reads the debauched cavalier rakes in Margaret Cavendish's fictions and plays differently than what will become the all too familiar rakes of Restoration drama. Since the royalist Cavendish is writing at a time when the royalist cause is at its weakest, it is surprising for some readers that her villains are aristocratic, often royal, men. In this way, Cavendish seems to be unintentionally using the "antimonarchist rhetoric to critique masculine behavior" (291). For Burks, Cavendish seeks to uphold the class privilege of which she was a member, and yet her subject position of a woman made her distrust the symbol of that cause: the aristocratic man. Thus, Cavendish offers an "early and uniquely awkward version of royalist mythology" (23).

Heroic drama is also interested in depicting royalist men in need of reform which Burks sees as evidence of the drama "directly confronting the negative portrait of the monarch as presented in the Interregnum press" (302). Again, we see sexual abuse as a metaphor for political misbehavior, but here, the love plots of the plays revise the struggle as the need of Honor to overcome Passion's assault on Reason. Dryden's *Conquest of Granada* is examined in the context of politics surrounding the reign of Charles II.

Burks's contribution to the growing critical conversation about Aphra Behn's Tory politics and the depiction of rape is clear in her final chapter on *The City Heiress*. Burks demonstrates Behn's ambivalence in the depiction of women characters who do not want to be raped alongside of "willing" rape victims who see rape as a "useful social convention that enables her to overcome the restrictive concern for reputation what would otherwise force her to refuse sex" (351). Ultimately, Burks argues that while Behn supports the Tory cause, she repeatedly reveals that "Tory ideology—and Restoration sexual license—benefited men far more than women, and in fact, benefited men at women's expense" (24). While Behn, like Dryden, wrote to please those in power because of the benefits it would bring, Behn also dramatizes the minority position that a woman holds within that ideology.

For some, one weakness of the book might be that violation and abuse are defined too broadly. Rape is a violation, but rights are violated as well. Ironically, this becomes a strength. The book's project is to explore how the language and images of violation and abuse are recycled in ways that try to connect very different experiences. In other words, Burks's point is not to note that writers use the same words to describe how rights and bodies can both be violated, but to notice how often, in the discourse of the seventeenth century, the two violations become conflated. Moreover, Burks usefully tracks the durability of the rhetoric by tracing its use by various political stances, often with very different political agendas.

Shakespeare's Tragedies: Violation and Identity, by Alexander Leggatt. Cambridge: Cambridge University Press, 2005. Pp. ix + 228. Cloth $75.00; Paper $28.99.

Reviewer: RAPHAEL FALCO

It has been a secret creed of my Shakespearean life to avoid *Titus Andronicus*. The play upsets me. It disturbs my equilibrium beyond what I consider (in my innocence) to be the right measure of tragedy. Lavinia's rape and mutilation, which are seminal to the play and its architecture of violent episodes, disgusts me, blurring my experience of all the other dramatic interactions. So, for the most part, I've given the play a miss in my writing and on my syllabi. It was, therefore, with anxious misgiving that I began Alexander Leggatt's *Shakespeare's Tragedies: Violation and Identity,* the first chapter of which is devoted to *Titus*. But if my anxiety was well-founded—Leggatt does nothing to dispel the horror of Lavinia's plight; indeed, if anything, he enhances it—my reluctance to return to the play over the years soon seemed unfortunate. For Leggatt's learned and perceptive analysis of *Titus* revealed a world of nuance I now feel privileged to have encountered.

Shakespeare's Tragedies is in fact replete with analytical subtlety, a lifetime's pondering of the plays and the criticism, of dramatic representation, and of characterologic ambiguity. Leggatt demonstrates familiarity with Shakespeare criticism and with the reigning theories of early modern culture without allowing a clutter of jargon to fuddle his writing. His most obvious debt, which he readily acknowledges in the notes, is to feminist critics. Strong female characters fill *Shakespeare's Tragedies,* in play after play tracing a familiar path from violation to tragic authority. But, *prima inter pares,* Lavinia haunts the book. In chapter 4, Leggatt says of Cressida that "the breakup of Cressida's identity reverberates through the rest of the play" (86), but in fact Lavinia's troubled identity is even more important to him. Her mutilation, her ruined and eventually revived identity reverberate from chapter 1 onward. These reverberations are remarkable, and indeed ironic, in that they give a powerful voice to a female character who, in her own play, is mute.

Leggatt's method of cumulative or aggregate reverberations is not without drawbacks, however. At times the comparisons he draws between Lavinia and other characters seem forced, as when Leggatt suggests, again in *Troilus,* that "the kissing scene . . . is the play's equivalent of the rape of Lavinia" (103). Perhaps *equivalent* is just too strong a word: Cressida may lose her reputation and her chastity, but Lavinia, by any reasonable measure, loses much more. *Shakespeare's Tragedies* suffers, I think, from too many assertions of equivalence between characters and situations in different plays. In the *Hamlet* chapter, for instance, Leggatt suggests that Gertrude has "the same capacity to baffle and disturb" as Lavinia and the Ghost (71). Even less persuasive is Leggatt's linking of Hector and Lavinia: "In his death, set upon by a gang, he is outnumbered as Lavinia is in both rape sequences, and as Cressida is in the kissing scene" (94–95). Not only strained, this comparison misleads us by substituting the critic's metaphorical architecture for the play's.

These instances (and there are others) are disappointing since Leggatt's local analyses—that is, his acute sense of interaction and dénouement within each tragedy—would stand well on their own. Particularly valuable is Leggatt's attention to theatricality itself. He casts an expert eye on the relationship of players and audience in the experience of tragedy. In *Titus* he suggests that "in a sense theatre itself has been threatened in the play: the questions hurled against silence . . . have been a denial of dialogue itself, the medium of drama. Lavinia deprived of language and Lavinia and Titus deprived of hand-gestures have been deprived of two instruments of the actor's art" (24). This superb interpretation of the parallel between the play's action and the actor's presence is the critical maneuver we've come to expect in readings of *Hamlet*. To find it here, in *Titus,* is exciting, and, as I indicated above, forced me to reassess my avoidance of the play.

Among the most interesting readings are those in which Leggatt shows how violation, far from being an end in itself, more often serves to highlight the fluctuations of identity. The best example of this is Leggatt's treatment of *Troilus and Cressida.* He argues against the recent trend to see *Troilus* as a problem play, seeing "a more positive link with the tragedies, based on the connected ideas of violation and identity" (84). He proceeds to demonstrate how the violations of Cressida's reputation confound her identity, inducing the crisis that leads Troilus to utter the notoriously equivocal line, "This is and is not Cressid" (V.ii.53). The heart of the tragedy is found here, as Leggatt shows through close reading of Troilus's self-reflections, but the theme of identity revealed and undone pervades the play. In an excellent passage on the meeting of the Greeks and Romans, for instance, Leggatt notes quite practically that "general introductions are necessary . . . [g]iven that they are used to seeing each other armed and helmeted" (86). He adds, however, that these general introductions "[plant] the thought that these warriors are fighting enemies they know as reputations, as armored shapes, but not as faces or people" (86). As elsewhere, Leggatt here brings to our attention Shakespeare's skill in balancing identity on a knife-edge of concealment and disclosure: the revealed faces of the Greeks and Trojans double as a kind of violation of the relative anonymity of their caparisoned forms (in the absence of heraldic markers). In *Othello,* violation is manifestly the subject on everyone's mind. Yet Leggatt shows how ambiguous this notion of violation can be in this play. "The view of the marriage as an act of violation," he points out," begins to look like a misreading, a false start" (116). His discussion of this paradox—that the marriage is and is not violation—rescues the chapter from somewhat predictable readings of Iago and Desdemona (despite interesting passages on the expectations of gender and, following Karen Newman, on the symbolism of the strawberry decoration in the handkerchief).

Comparably valuable moments of critical acuity occur in other chapters. In his discussion of *Romeo and Juliet,* for example, Leggatt's linking of identity and orgasm struck me as a unique way to explain Juliet's tragic force. He observes that "Juliet's 'Give me my Romeo; and when I shall die / Take him and cut him out in little stars' (III.ii.21–22), making no distinction between her climax and his, not only suggests the blending of identities in perfect love-making but goes straight from sex to death" (47). At other times Leggatt complicates the notion of identity by returning to the audience-actor relationship, and upping the ante. Discussing *Hamlet,* he asserts that "it all goes back to the Ghost," noting that "the identification of performer with role is arguably what makes theatre" (61). Spectators, he explains, know that actors are "figures who are *like* the characters they play, but are not those characters" (61). In *Hamlet,* according to Leggatt, the spectator-actor relationship is moved onto the stage, not so much in the Mousetrap but in the Ghost's role: "the figure who triggers the action is 'like' the late king Hamlet, and this produces *within the play* that slight but crucial detachment from absolute belief that is normally the condition of the audience" (61). *Shakespeare's Tragedies* contains many other equally fascinating meditations on how identity shifts and dissipates as performance melts into tragic experience and the lifelines of reality are lost. Indeed, one of Leggatt's *leitmotifs* is the notion of getting "a fix on reality." He suggests that in *Hamlet* writing is a means of fixing reality. Looking is another—he reminds us of Titus's injunction to "look upon" Lavinia and Romeo's intense staring at Juliet. (Oddly, given the context, Leggatt doesn't cite any of the voluminous criticism on the gaze, even if only to distance himself from it.)

Another *leitmotif* of Leggatt's book is misreading. Othello misreads Desdemona—"he has so thoroughly rewritten her that if she is chaste, as she knows she is, then she cannot be herself" (135)—although Desdemona resists the misreading, and, according to Leggatt, retains as firmly grounded a sense of herself as Juliet. King Lear, perhaps the most stupendous misreader in the tragedies, augments misreading with linguistic violation: "He violates his relationship with [Cordelia] by violating the language of relationship" (149). A distorted variation of misreading is unreadability. In his chapter on *Macbeth,* Leggatt focuses on the unnameable. He observes that vagueness, riddling, and "language [that] dwells obsessively on unnameable deeds" (179) pervade the play. Leggatt thrives in this challenging linguistic atmosphere. His style of close reading is ideal for finding interesting new routes through the maze of "unnameable deeds" to the final unraveling.

The value of *Shakespeare's Tragedies* lies in close readings of this kind. Leggatt says in his introduction that he plans to resist seeing plays as merely cultural documents. His approach, he explains, "is going to involve a close reading of individual texts, rather against the current practice of reading plays as embedded in their culture and determined by it" (1). Leggatt's resistance, as well as his frankness, are to be admired. The absolute quality of his methodology, however, worried me throughout the book. In his conclusion, as a matter of course, Leggatt observes that "*Othello* keeps the focus on a woman, but reacts against *Troilus*" (206). But this statement should not be a matter of course regardless of whether one sees the plays as culturally embedded or not. Nothing is *not* culturally embedded. It's just a question of how much cultural bedrock one wishes to bring to literary interpretation, a matter of measure. The problem with Leggatt's statement—which, to be fair, he elaborates on in the context of the conclusion—is his conceptual model. That is, is it conceptually valid to think of these tragedies as *reacting against* one another? The underlying assumption of such a model strikes me as anachronistic, disclosing Leggatt's critical aims more revealingly than it characterizes Shakespeare's practice. Critical tact might require that we resist the view that Shakespeare wrote his plays one against the other. The weakness, in conceptual terms, of Leggatt's neglect of cultural determination and other influential factors in the composition of the tragedies is nowhere as evident as in this kind of comparison. *Shakespeare's Tragedies* often satisfies—and satisfies deeply—at the level of close reading, but at other times can waken hunger for the *orbis terrarum*.

Magic on the Early English Stage, by Philip Butterworth. Cambridge: Cambridge UP, 2005. Pp. ix + 295. Hardcover $85.00.

Reviewer: MARINA FAVILA

Magic is a marvelous subject, literally. It's not surprising that the wonder of it, magic's promise and allure, held sway over much of medieval and early modern thought. Any scholar interested in the field must choose from a variety of crossroads before gaining access to magic's lair. The intersections are many: alchemy and Neoplatonism; witchcraft and sorcery (black magic and white); the miracles of the saints, their stories and statues; the magician's as well as the mountebank's agile sleight of hand; and, of course, theatrical illusion, cannily staged on a pageant wagon, in a playhouse, for a palace wedding or a royal parade. Though magic's territory is far-reaching, the point of contact between practitioner and audience (and perhaps even the scholar who studies them) is one and the same—not faith, as one might expect, but recognition of what magic has to offer. That is to say, all parties query and answer the same question: Is the "trick," no matter how it is achieved, worth the asking price?

For Butterworth's book *Magic on the Early English Stage,* the asking price is $85.00. It's a fair price, for Butterworth is an accomplished and careful scholar, and his crossroad is clearly marked for the reader. He is not interested in magic as an access to the supernatural, a child of science, or a metaphor for power. He is interested in illusion—the trick of magic, and how that trick is accomplished. What he offers his audience is a thorough analysis of the many illusions performed by the juggler (arguably the most common name for magicians in medieval/Renaissance Europe) as well as some interesting insights into how the juggler's art is appropriated, literally and/or linguistically, by the playwright, the con man, the church and its critics, as well as the culture at large.

Overall, *Magic on the Early English Stage* reads much like a magician's how-to manual. A quick glance at Butterworth's chapter headings (for example, "Conveyance and Confederacy," "Appearances and Disappearances," "Magic through Sound: Illusion, Deception and Agreed Pretence," "Mechanical Images, Automata, Puppets and Motions," "Substitution," and "Stage Tricks") gives you some idea of the vast array of magic tricks and illusions to be spotlighted for the reader. Eyewitness accounts and secondhand anecdotes are particularly tantalizing. Be amazed at the story of Brandon, the King's Juggler, who drew a picture of a bird on the public square, and when he stabbed his drawing with a knife, a pigeon miraculously fell from the sky. (This performance proved so horrifying that Brandon was sworn never to repeat the trick again.) Wonder at the power of Feats, who could test the honor of a maid by commanding his knife to fly from a bucket of water into the rafters above: no flight, no virgin. Marvel at the multiple retellings of the famed Indian rope trick, where a boy, a man, a woman, a hare, a dog, a hog, a panther, a lion, and a tiger were all said (at one time or another) to ascend a rope leading nowhere to disappear before your very eyes.

Of course, we are not allowed to marvel at these feats for long, as Butterworth's goal is to explain the "how" hidden by the magician. His primary sources prove surprisingly specific and illuminate the importance of well-crafted illusion in early modern England. In *Discoverie of Witchcraft* (the first book to betray the juggler's secrets), Reginald Scot offers a detailed explanation of the art of decollation, including an illustration of the contraption needed to decapitate a man and serve his head on a platter. William Vincent, whose early seventeenth-century book on magic boasts his own stage name, *Hocus Pocus Iunior*, not only reveals the appropriate moves to make four balls disappear, but also the needed patter to misdirect the audience. Drawing on countless stage directions and a variety of theatrical sources, including the intriguing *Volume of Secrets of a Provençal Stage Director's Book,* Butterworth explicates numerous references to the illusions required of medieval and early modern drama as well as the equipment needed to create them: slow-moving dumbwaiters to resurrect Christ; trick gibbets to hang his betrayer (though beware, one Judas hung so long he needed reviving); revolving tables that snap into place to make a banquet disappear; exceedingly long leaden pipes used to carry the voices of ghosts and severed heads across the stage; retractable bodkins, false bellies, and hidden bladders of blood to effect the needed carnage for religious drama and revenge tragedies; and my personal favorite, polished bowls carefully placed to catch the light of the sun to create an aura for Jesus and his disciples! Of course, not every explanation is necessarily plausible, but Butterworth is quick to admit that it's "sometimes the case that explanations offered by jugglers or modern-day conjurors of their tricks are in themselves further obfuscations designed to misdirect" (97).

Though the numerous examples provide an impressive behind-the-scenes look at the performance of magic, Butterworth's analysis does offer more than a list of tricks. Emerging from the book is an understanding of the early modern juggler, himself: his fee to perform (or not perform); his place among other popular feats of activity (vaulting, tumbling, rope dancing); his wizard-like cap and wand, and brightly colored costume: billowing sleeves, baggy pants, and magician's purse, all hiding multiple illusions in the making. Here again, Butterworth's primary sources are more than varied, ranging from the obvious to the obscure: dictionaries, diaries, memoirs, letters, travel literature, essays, pamphlets, license records, costume orders, books on magic (then and now), plus a multitude of references where the juggler's magic has been appropriated for the stage: passion plays, moralities, mystery cycles, early modern tragedies and comedies, and all the paperwork that goes with them: account books, performance records, stage directions, and property lists. Of course, the author draws heavily on *Records of Early English Drama* and the *Malone Society Collections* series, but he also provides some hitherto unpublished material in his appendices.

Perhaps equally important, Butterworth takes a look at how the juggler's art was viewed by society, especially in regards to the art of deception. This connection can be quite literal, as some jugglers merged the art of magic with the art of the con; but there are also many theatrical references to the juggler and his art, as one might expect to find, say, in Ben Jonson's comedies. Butterworth's close analysis of language also suggests that the vocabulary of the juggler often emerges in the period like a lawyer joke; that is to say, the magician's image and art can be used to insult not only a pickpocket, a card-sharp, a dice player, a fortuneteller, a charlatan, a mountebank, a quacksalver, and a witch, but also a would-be lover, a Catholic priest, and yes, even a lawyer. The book, however, also offers one fabulous example when the magician is both condemned and saved by his art. While performing abroad in France, Richard Banks and his magical horse Morocco are accused of sorcery, and indeed how else could you explain a horse who could "count coins, identify a specific card picked out by a member of the audience, pretend to be dead by lying on his back with his legs in the air, curtsy, dance, fight, piss and operate whilst blindfolded" (66)? But the wily juggler promptly proves his horse is no agent of the devil. He instructs him to seek out a man with a cross on his hat, kneel in respect, then kiss the rood to prove his master's innocence and that of his own. According to two anecdotes, Morocco bows before the man, then jumps up and slurps the patron's head. Presto! All is forgiven, for what demon would dare do that, even for applause?

I obviously love the subject of this book and commend the author's research; his notes and bibliography are both extensive and impressive. I did, however, sometimes find the prosaic quality of Butterworth's analysis a shade dry. His linguistic analysis of the juggler's vocabulary, while scholarly, can also be a bit repetitive (though his synthesis in the last chapter is quite helpful). To be fair, the subject may demand a no-nonsense approach, especially as this scholar's job is to explain away a magic that enchants by deception.

My own longing for something more suggestive might, in fact, be born from the wealth of the book's references, which indirectly invite the reader to make her own connections. For example, at several points in the book, Butterworth offers examples where magic and death intersect: most notably, jugglers' epitaphs as well as Lydgate's haunting translation of Boccaccio's "The Daunce of Machabree," where "Death speaketh to master John Rikil Tregetour [magician]":

> Master Joun Rikil whilom Tregetour
> Of Noble Henry King of England
> & of Fraunce ye mightie conquerour,
> For al the sleights and turning of thine hond
> Thou must come nere my daunce to vnderstond
> Nought may auayle al thy conclusions,
> For death shortly nother on sea ne lond,
> Is not deceiued by none illusions.
>
> (qtd in Butterworth 49–50)

The "key" point for Butterworth is the phrase "turning of thine hond," which offers more proof that jugglers utilized sleight of hand in their tricks (50). But such a fabulous example (paired with the jugglers' epitaphs and perhaps even theatrical illusions of resurrection) might also lead to some interesting parallels between our attraction to magic and our fear of death: that is to say, our happy willingness to embrace the illusions of the juggler, who seems able to transcend the boundaries of reality with his art, and our denial of death, whose boundary must be crossed and who "is not deceived by none illusions." But again, the book's journey is not to explore our desire to feel wonder, what it gives to us, or the price we're willing to pay to experience it. Instead, *Magic on the Early English Stage* focuses on how the magician manipulates that desire, how he utilizes misdirection, magic words, theatrical patter, and mechanical devices to create the type of special effects demanded by an early modern audience.

If the magician's task is to do the impossible, say, to make the laws of nature seemingly disappear, then the critic's job is to make the trick disappear. Butterworth has done a credible job of illuminating the craft behind the illusion, and thus "stretch[ing] out imaginations even unto" understanding, if not wonder.[1] *Magic on the Early English Stage* offers a much needed synthesis and analysis of not only the importance of illusion, but also the business of magic, in the medieval and Renaissance period. I have no doubt this book will appear in many a future footnote.

Note

1. This phrase comes from Butterworth's epigraph, where he quotes Heinrich Cornelius Agrippa: "For the ende of this skil is not to doo simplely, but to stretche out imaginations euen vnto apperaunce, of whiche there shall afterwarde no sign appeare." I have modernized the spelling in my text.

Textual Performances: The Modern Reproduction of Shakespeare's Drama, Lukas Erne and Margaret Jane Kidnie, eds. Cambridge: Cambridge University Press, 2004. Pp. xv + 229. Cloth $70.00.

Reviewer: BRIAN WALSH

The history of the book has been a hot subject in literary studies for several years now, and its popularity among early modern scholars shows no sign of diminishing. The 2006 MLA convention, for instance, featured no less than three sessions devoted to the topic courtesy of the Renaissance literature division. The new collection *Textual Performances,* edited by Lukas Erne and Margaret Jane Kidnie, deals mainly with one of the perhaps less happening corners of textual criticism: editorial practice. Nonetheless, it is as timely as any of the more cutting edge work being done on book history. This volume should be of interest to anyone who teaches Shakespeare or Renaissance drama on a regular basis, or who cares about how this drama circulates in the world today. Its most pressing questions concern the material traces of these plays as they have come down to us in printed, and more rarely manuscript sources, and how we convert those traces to editions for students, scholars, performers, and general readers. The collection admirably serves as both a primer on the development of what might be called "meta-editorial" scholarship in Renaissance drama, as well as an example of some of the most current thinking on editorial decisions.

The thirteen essays in *Textual Performances* cover a range of topics, from the production of electronic editions of early modern plays to the loaded issue of inferring and inserting stage directions in play texts. With the exception of Leah S. Marcus's essay on editing *Othello,* there are few if any truly controversial arguments to be found in *Textual Performances.* Most of the essays seek merely to highlight and de-familiarize some particular aspect of editorial practice, and perhaps offer alternatives to choices that have hardened into critical orthodoxy. The collection is willing to pose questions and offer solutions without being programmatic. The essays tend to call for a more open-ended approach to editing texts, an approach that cedes authority from editors to readers, or, as some of the essays prefer to term the consumers of play texts, "users."

Essays by H. R. Woudhuysen, Paul Werstine, and Ernst Honigmann nicely survey some of the major figures whose editing practices and philosophies continue to shape the production of texts today, such as W. W. Greg, A. E. Houseman, R. B. McKerrow, and A. W. Pollard. Such mapping of the history of editing the Renaissance allows great insight into many features of edited texts we might assume to be "natural." For instance, Werstine critiques instances where early editors assumed that repetition in a text meant corruption, and therefore found it necessary to determine which lines should be eliminated and which preserved. Michael Warren also usefully takes issue with a tradition of perceived textual corruption and subsequent editorial intervention in the specific case of *Coriolanus* and its unnamed citizens. The sum idea of this group of essays points to the need for continual reevaluation of the criteria by which editors determine which available texts are "good" and which are "bad," decisions that provide the foundations for the editions they produce.

Sonia Massai brings us into the electronic age with her excellent essay on an Internet Shakespeare Edition of *Edward III* she recently prepared. Massai is optimistic about the possibilities for editing that electronic media allow, such as the use of animated types to show textual variants with greater flexibility than would be possible in a print edition. A fascinating counter point to Massai's piece comes toward the end of the volume in John Lavagnino's more skeptical take on editing in the digital age. Lavagnino airs fundamental but easily overlooked concerns about, for instance, the display on computer screens, and concludes that "the highly developed technology of the book is not easy to improve upon" (203). While by no means in direct opposition, taken together these papers form a stimulating starting point for a real discussion about the future of electronic editing.

Kidnie and John D. Cox in separate essays take on the challenging question of stage directions and their place in modern editions, especially those designed with student readers in mind. Kidnie puts forth a novel mode of layout in presenting stage directions—both those provided by the original documents and those inserted by subsequent editors—that moves them to the margins of the page and thus, she argues, allows a reader-user more leeway to determine how physical action, entrances, and exits will take place in their own imagined or actual performances. Cox echoes the call for less intrusive stage directions and thus a more "open" text. Alongside these somewhat radical calls for "un-editing" is David Bevington's more moderate take on modern spelling. Bevington surveys a host of examples where modernizing spelling can obscure original connotations and instances of polyvalence, but ultimately concludes with the "bold, but not too bold" assertion that the "benefits [of modernizing the spelling] outweigh the costs by making early modern texts more available to readers in terms of today's idioms" (157). The volume includes also a collaborative piece by Ann Thompson and Neil Taylor on generating a cast list that assumes doubling in original stagings of *Hamlet*. This may well be the most eccentric essay in the book. Like all casting charts for Shakespeare plays it is necessarily speculative, as the authors freely admit. But as they point out, such questions are more than quaint exercises, for questions of casting have been a central part of efforts to make sense of the Quarto/Folio divisions in textual studies of *Hamlet*. *Textual Performances* concludes with a witty essay by Barbara Hodgdon on producing editions with an eye toward stage performance. It is a meditative piece on the new possibilities enabled by a "paradigm shift" (219) in editorial practices that Hodgdon sees happening now. It is a fitting end to the collection for it is consciously an exercise in problem posing rather than an attempt to preserve or enact rules.

It is only Marcus's essay, as I alluded to earlier, that presents a more forceful critique of editing on political grounds. Marcus claims that the Folio version of *Othello* is more laced with racial "virulence" (30) than the quarto, and that this difference deserves to be better studied, perhaps even in the parallel text tradition of *King Lear* and *Hamlet*. The argument as sketched out here is not yet convincing—part of it depends on the assumption that Roderigo, one of the stupidest and easily the most pathetic dupe in the Shakespeare canon, might speak for Shakespeare's own views on the essential meaning of skin color—but it is a worthwhile line of inquiry that reminds us how high the stakes can be when it comes to editorial decisions.

As any teacher of Shakespeare can attest from the catalogs and examination copies that clog up departmental mailboxes, there is no shortage of new and constantly repackaged Shakespeare editions in assorted series from sundry presses. And yet one cannot help but be struck by the sameness amid the seemingly various editions. A fascinating but underdeveloped critique of the status quo that emerges in *Textual Performances* implicates the rigidities of the publishing industry and the very concept of the "house style" for limiting the ways texts can be presented. A house style assumes that all early modern plays followed the same rules and can thus be converted to the modern print idiom en masse through a uniform, prescribed textual scheme. But we know this is not the case: some plays have come down to us in only one text; others exist in many texts from their era. Some feature heavy stage directions; most are light on the specifics of how physical action can be juxtaposed with spoken language. Given such discrepancy, it seems logical that each play a publisher brings out should be treated according to the specificities of its own condition. This would obviously pose many difficulties for publishers in terms of the logistics of coordinating editorial work and in terms of the physical production of editions. Yet, *Textual Performances* implies, it is time to consider whether the benefits of giving editors freedom to imagine how their plays might be presented outside the restrictions of a house style sheet could outweigh the hassle.

Along with the recent volume *In Arden: Editing Shakespeare: Essays in Honour of Richard Proudfoot* (2003), with which it shares some contributors and some conceptual elements, *Textual Performances* alerts us to issues that we should never lose sight of when working with drama from Shakespeare's era. The title of *Textual Performances* itself helps to frame some larger concerns about the texts that scholars, teachers, students, and general readers employ: if editions are considered "performances" by an editor, they lose some claim to definitive, authoritative status. Like all performances, they become interpretations—in many cases one of many—based on conscious choices that necessarily suppress alternatives. *Textual Performances* is successful in, to extend the terminology, going "backstage" in the editing process to bring out into the open some of the assumptions, debates, traditions, and innovations that have been bustling behind the curtain of textual scholarship for the last century or so. Most importantly, this volume opens the door for more discussion and debate about what to do at the editing table or keyboard once we've seen what goes on backstage.

The English Renaissance Stage: Geometry, Poetics, and the Practical Spatial Arts, 1580–1630, by Henry S. Turner. Oxford and New York: Oxford University Press, 2006. $99.00 (cloth).

Reviewer: DAVID GLIMP

This past summer I had occasion to observe the construction of the sets in advance of the 2007 season of the Colorado Shakespeare Festival, which takes place in an outdoor theater adjacent to the building housing the University of Colorado's English Department. In late May and early June I frequently paused to watch the carpenters, welders, and other workers configure the space of performance, undertake the otherwise invisible labor that makes possible the dramatic entertainment for which people would soon pay. Henry Turner's fascinating new book argues that in early modern England there are deep connections between poetics, dramatic performance, and what some might consider as the auxiliary labor of craftsmen. To invoke a widely employed distinction which Turner's study compels us to treat as a historical result, an assumed opposition between intellectual and manual work elides the many relations between early modern mechanical arts, poetics, and dramatic practice, especially at the epistemological level. The set of assumptions about the world and how one knows and acts upon it constitutes a shared epistemology that defines what Turner names the "practical spatial arts," a domain that links playwrights, surveyors, carpenters, engineers, military artificers, and others who actively apply geometrical modes of thought.

Turner's introductory chapter spells out the polemical dimensions of his work—a general sense that reading plays for the ideology of their themes or intellectual content underdescribes what's going on in any given literary text or performance, obscures the formal dimensions of drama, the concrete way plays make meaning, and the practical epistemological resources upon which they draw to organize action in space. Turner's concern is to show how practical geometry and stage plays share a mode of signification, a "diagrammatic" or (after Pierce) "iconic" way of representing the world that both indicates that world and renders available for thought otherwise imperceptible aspects of reality. This semiotic distinction allows Turner to comprehend and to take seriously the frequent troping of literary production as a form of artisanal craftsmanship, and to explore for example the interrelationships between the two definitions of "plot" in the period, both a technical term within the practical spatial art of surveying and an activity central to the work of playwrights configuring dramatic action on the space of the stage.

Part 1 of *The English Renaissance Stage* establishes the lines of continuity linking poetics and applied geometry. Chapter 2, "Practical Knowledge and the Poetics of Geometry," demonstrates the surprisingly deep connections between mechanical and liberal arts, at the level of university curriculum, of shared epistemological assumptions, and of social networks of intellectual exchange and collaboration between humanists and workmen in trades that put geometry into practice. The most compelling connection—one Turner revisits throughout the book—is the epistemological orientation toward practical deliberation and the analysis of particular circumstances as a prelude to action, an orientation present both in humanist moral philosophy and manuals of practical geometry. Chapter 3 locates these concerns specifically in the realm of poetics through a reading of how Sidney's interest in geometry, and the considerable network of artificers, engineers, and others with whom he associated, inflects Sidney's *"architectonike"* account of poetic activity. Sidney's *Defence of Poesie* comprehends the poet in terms of his ability to mediate between abstract and particular, to generate knowledge about the world, and to train readers in the Aristotelian ethical discipline of "practical, prudential deliberation" (97) as a precursor to virtuous action. "Noun, Foot, and Measured Line," Turner's fourth chapter, develops the argument by tracing how George Puttenham and George Gascoigne's poetry manuals, with their emphasis on quantity, their explicit understanding of poetry as a practical spatial art, and their use of graphic illustrations to describe and detail how to produce poetry, employ and elaborate the quantitative epistemology informing Sidney's poetics.

Part 2 of *The English Renaissance Stage* focuses specifically on theatrical production as a practical spatial art, a shift initiated in chapter 4's concluding discussion of records of masque performances in the Revels Office (notably their detailed "plattes" of past performances maintained for those charged with reproducing or adapting these events in the future) and the use of space in the entertainments conducted in London celebrating King James's accession (as documented in *The Magnificent Entertainment*). Chapter 5, "Theater as a Spatial Art," explores some of the general ways early modern popular drama constituted a spatial art. The chapter adapts Glynne Wickham's thesis of an epochal rupture in modes of stage representation—a shift from an earlier emblematic to a modern realist mode—offering a more dialectically charged version of the spatial and semiotic aspects inherent in this transformation. Revisiting some of the well-known spatial cruxes in *King Lear* (Gloucester at Dover, Lear on "the heath," though this latter is an interpolation that seeks to manage the tensions Turner sees as most crucial to the play), Turner emphasizes how Shakespeare's play self-consciously explores the limits of the stage's capacity to represent space, how the quarto and folio versions of the play differently translate these volatile spatial dynamics to the page, and how critics and editors have sought to manage the play's unruly spaces. This latter dynamic signals Turner's interest in the ideological dimensions of space, how it is organized and depicted onstage, an emphasis developed in chapter 6, "The Topographic Stage." Just as contemporary surveyors sought to map and thereby render London intelligible in a moment of intensified urbanization, playwrights' representation of civic space generates analytical knowledge that helps make sense of an otherwise disorienting and profoundly destabilizing series of transformations. Detailed readings of Dekker and Webster's *Westward Hoe* and *Northward Hoe,* alongside Chapman, Jonson, and Marston's *Eastward Hoe* demonstrate how the playwrights' projection and management of space on stage shapes the action of these plays and informs the critical or moral pedagogy they undertake.

The book's final two chapters focus primarily on Ben Jonson as both a participant in the spatial dynamics the book describes and as a key figure in the disarticulation of poetics from the practical spatial context so central to earlier poetic theory and stage practice. Chapter 7, "Dramatic Form and the Projective Intelligence," locates competing modes of spatial representation in *Every Man Out of His Humor*. If, on one hand, Jonson's play is deeply "emblematic," which implies a kind of static space of quasi-allegorical reference, it is also deeply "topographical," a mode of spatial representation in which the dramatic projection or use of space is centrally implicated in the organization of action on the stage. "Projective intelligence" constitutes something like an ethos adapted to this topographical mode of representation, a way of thinking and acting that embodies the emphasis within the practical spatial arts on comprehending circumstances in their particularity and rearranging circumstances prudentially. The chapter concludes with a somewhat breathless survey of several examples of such projective intelligence—especially its role in structuring a given play's organization of space and action—in Marlowe's *Jew of Malta,* Middleton's *A Mad World, My Masters,* Shakespeare's tetralogies, and the anonymous *Arden of Faversham.* The book's eighth and final chapter, "Ben Jonson's Scenography," shows how much Jonson's critical pronouncements on literature, especially those embedded in his dramatic works, derive from the practical challenges of organizing space and action faced by a working playwright, even as he works to disarticulate drama from its originating practical context. Jonson's critical neoclassicism then becomes an important means for redefining literature as superior to its practical associations by constituting it as a specialized knowledge unavailable to "mechanic" practitioners.

This hasty summary elides much of the nuance of Turner's extensively researched and scrupulously documented study, which works with considerable facility across several different disciplines. In its synthesizing approach, *The Renaissance English Stage* establishes an exciting dialogue between theater history, performance theory, poetics, semiotics, historical epistemology, and materialist social analysis and critique, among other fields. If I have a complaint, though it is unfair to call it such, it deals with Turner's own sense of the payoff of his extensive theoretical and historical efforts. The readings Turner offers tend to be constrained to an established focus of materialist inquiry; Turner's elaborate and sophisticated methodological armature demonstrates how plays participate in an "epistemological project of social analysis" (29). Drama represents a "way of coming to knowledge" (24) about the forces structuring social reality. What other things might drama do? What other kinds of insights might Turner's findings generate? For example, the predominantly cognitive focus on literary production leads Turner to elide the affective dimensions of poetry and drama, dimensions crucial to how Sidney understands poetry to produce its effects (which Turner treats as a matter of intellectual engagement), as well as to theatrical entrepreneurs' ability to commodify drama. The study also adheres pretty closely to a standard historical narrative of epistemological transformation, which is not to deny that decisive developments impacting the formation of modern disciplines of scientific inquiry aren't taking place, but to wonder how Turner's research might help locate alternative temporalities or ways of narrating literary history that emphasize its dislocation from these developments. But rather than characterize these as shortcomings of the study, or note other points where the inquiry might have been qualified or developed in interesting directions, I would prefer to emphasize the considerable accomplishments of this book and its deep suggestiveness for future research. Turner's important book offers extraordinary resources for energizing the discussion of Renaissance literature, and reimagines what a materialist account of form might be and what it can contribute to our understanding of Renaissance poetics and the drama of the period.

Performance Approaches to Teaching Shakespeare, by Edward L. Rocklin. Urbana: NCTE, 2005. Pp. xxvii + 431. Softcover $39.95 ($29.95 NCTE member).

Reviewer: SHARON A. BEEHLER

In the epilogue to his useful book, *Understanding Shakespeare's Plays in Performance,* Jay L. Halio observes, "To enjoy Shakespeare today we require an open mind and a receptive sensibility. Fixed ideas about how a play should be performed can be and usually are self-defeating."[1] This basic tenet of modern thinking about Shakespeare's works provides the underpinning for Edward L. Rocklin's guide to teaching Shakespeare through performance. What makes Rocklin's work especially valuable is the thoroughness with which the approach has been theorized, detailed, and practiced, or as Rocklin might say, conceptualized, rehearsed, and performed. For as Rocklin shows us, the act of teaching Shakespeare through performance is itself a dramatic enterprise.

Rocklin believes that his performance approach to Shakespeare encourages the open-minded attitude advocated by Halio and by other Shakespeare scholars invested in pedagogical issues. He begins his book with a prologue designed to set out the principal ideas he will develop in the rest of the text. There he remarks, "one of the simplest but most fundamental skills we must master in learning to read drama is the skill to discover how the same speech can be used to perform different or even radically divergent speech acts, and thus to create surprisingly divergent situations both within the world of the play and in the play-audience relation" (xviii). His objective, as he explains in the first section of the book, is to help students, at both the secondary and college levels, to encounter Shakespeare's plays as the performance vehicles they were designed to be. What is striking about his approach is his ability to introduce and teach strategies of the stage while avoiding the slip into theater arts instruction. His instruction remains firmly grounded in the domain of English.

His success in this regard stems from two factors: (1) his attention to language as an "act" of "doing," and (2) his emphasis upon imaginative possibilities. To accomplish the first of these factors, Rocklin adopts a speech act approach by asking students to consider "What does X do?" not only about such aspects as plot and stage directions, but also about particular words and scenes. To ask this question encourages students to consider the play's relationship with the audience and how that relationship might be altered by different answers to the question. The second factor follows logically from the first in that by raising "doing" to consciousness, he manages to lead students to imagine widely diverse possibilities for enactment.

Following the first section, entitled "Learning How to Read in a Different Language: Framing and Initiating the Study of Drama," Rocklin proceeds to offer three specific accounts of his approach in action. He calls this second section "Imaginary Rehearsals and Actual Engagements," a subtitle that highlights the sort of activities he will describe. The three subsections relate very specifically to single plays—*The Taming of the Shrew, Richard III,* and *Hamlet.* Because these three works reflect different periods in Shakespeare's career, as well as different genres, they provide examples that will be valuable to teachers shaping their courses around such topics. Moreover, the strategies Rocklin describes for each play could easily be adapted to other plays of similar date or type. In response to the complaint that performance strategies cannot be incorporated into a literature class because of time constraints, Rocklin demonstrates that by focusing student attention on select separate yet sequential scenes the necessarily time-consuming process of investigating performance choices can indeed occur while maintaining the integrity of the entire work through discussion.

Rocklin teaches students how to ask questions that will direct their thinking toward performance possibilities. For example, when teaching *Shrew,* he asks, "What does the Induction do?" and "What does a title do?" In both cases, he forces the students to consider the impact of these features on an audience: what expectations do they create? To emphasize this audience perspective, Rocklin introduces the Expectation Log, an assignment that requires students to record their presumptions about what will come next. As students engage in this assignment, they become accustomed to thinking in this anticipatory fashion, so that another level of critical thinking has been achieved. Rocklin maintains this activity throughout his course, layering new habits of thought and questioning upon established ones in order to heighten students' abilities to read with an active set of performance questions in mind.

In addition to guiding students to new ways of private reading, Rocklin also immerses them in physical activities designed to make them aware of the difference between silently reading a text and actively performing a script. As students undertake to perform scenes and speeches for their peers, Rocklin involves the class in discussion about the specific choices made by the actors and how those choices create particular responses in the audience. Through this endeavor students come to realize, for instance, that *Richard III* relies upon a series of doubled actions and that *Hamlet* offers far more performance options than they ever dreamed. When confronted with the stage direction "She dies" at the moment when Gertrude expires, students suddenly realize that a great deal of thought must accompany that action—What knowledge does she possess in dying? Does she realize Claudius's duplicity? Does she know her son is doomed? Does she try to warn Hamlet? To answer such questions requires students to engage closely with the text and with prior performance choices.

Throughout the book Rocklin presents strategies that include the examination of how to transform a "role" into a "character," how to identify and perform soliloquies, how to become alert to the discrepant awareness of characters and audience, how to recognize and exploit repetitions in plot and language, how to contend with conflicting frames of reference, how to think about endings, how to use and ignore act and scene divisions, how to imagine alternative stagings, how to understand coded props and imagery, how to make blocking choices, how to critique editorial choices, how to make performance history expand possibilities, and how to avoid the strictures of genre.

Each of these strategies is coupled with at least one writing assignment, usually short paragraphs intended to focus on a single question or issue. For instance, while studying *Richard III,* students received this assignment: "as you reread *Richard III,* please note all the repetitions, of any sort and on any level, and any type, literary and theatrical, verbal and visual, that you hear or see . . . Come to class with a written list of some of the repetitions you have noted and begin to develop your answer as to how you would interpret those repetitions" (226–27).

In short, this book (to which I cannot do justice here) provides teachers of Shakespeare with a wealth of techniques and good thinking about using a performance approach in their classes. Because Rocklin has spent many years developing and practicing his instruction, the assurance with which he writes and shares his ideas gives us confidence in his methodology. As he says in the epilogue, "learning something about the poetics of Shakespeare's drama, we can also learn about the poetics of our own pedagogy . . . [because the performance approach] will enable teachers themselves to learn more about both the plays and how students learn" (351, 352). And he concludes, "The performance-oriented teacher is often much less interested in telling his or her students what to learn from a particular playtext than in suggesting how they might best go about exploring its potentials and learning from their own performance" (364). In the end, Rocklin calls for reflection upon performance choices and makes his book the reflection of his own pedagogic practice.

Note

1. Jay L. Halio, *Understanding Shakespeare's Plays in Performance* (Manchester, UK, 1988, and Houston, 2000), 83.

Shakespeare, from Stage to Screen, by Sarah Hatchuel. Cambridge: Cambridge University Press, 2004. Pp. 190. Cloth $75.00.

Reviewer: DOUGLAS M. LANIER

An unfortunate by-product of current Shakespearean ideological criticism has been the tendency for critics to minimize the differences between stage and screen Shakespeare by collapsing the two under the banner of "performance," treating interpretive choices as if they were conditioned only by a director's high concept or reigning sociopolitical contexts. Sarah Hatchuel's *Shakespeare, from Stage to Screen* provides a timely reminder of the specific formal demands of the medium for Shakespearean performance. Concern with the problem of transposing Shakespeare from theatrical to cinematic form is, of course, not new—indeed, Shakespearean film criticism has its genesis with that issue. Hatchuel's study is thus the latest in a genealogy that stretches from Jack J. Jorgens's *Shakespeare on Film* (1977) and Roger Manvell's *Shakespeare and the Film* (1979) to Lorne M. Buchman's *Still in Movement: Shakespeare on Screen* (1991). What distinguishes Hatchuel's book is its interest less in offering full-scale readings of individual Shakespeare films than in schematizing and methodly analyzing the formal resources and choices available to Shakespearean filmmakers. The focus falls on the capabilities, conventions, and meanings of specifically cinematic techniques compared against those of the stage, all illustrated with examples drawn from a range of canonical Shakespearean films. Hatchuel's approach owes much to the school of film analysis championed by David Bordwell, a school that emphasizes precisely articulating the grammar of the cinema—the nature of its formal elements and the conventions of their use, particularly within the mode of the classic Hollywood realist narrative—rather than generating close readings or ideological critiques of films or treating films as catalysts for excursions into theory.

The six chapters of *Shakespeare, from Stage to Screen* provide a brisk but reliable survey of the technical resources of Shakespearean film. The opening chapter surveys the history of Shakespearean performance from a formal perspective. A valuable historical overview, it nonetheless implies perhaps too smooth and natural a progression of Shakespeare from stage to screen, suggesting that Shakespearean film was a necessary outgrowth of nineteenth-century naturalistic staging conventions. In the second chapter, Hatchuel examines the differences between theatrical "telling" and cinematic "showing" through a discussion of how cinematic techniques of editing, flashback and flashforward, film speed, and camera movement allow film directors to reshape Shakespearean stage narratives for the screen. She makes the interesting observation, for example, that Kenneth Branagh's *Henry V* showed Shakespearean filmmakers how they might take fuller advantage of the narrative resources of cinema, exploiting its capacity to reshape time through slow-motion, quick-cutting, ellipses, and flashbacks. Her third chapter addresses most directly how Shakespearean narratives are reshaped to accommodate the cinema's dominant narrative mode, classic Hollywood realism, discussing, for example, how Shakespearean soliloquies are recast so as not to reveal the invisible presence of the camera and how film music works to provide continuity across cuts and thus to mask the director's moment-to-moment manipulation of the viewer's perceptions. Hatchuel's emphasis upon the drive of cinematic realism to present the fictional world of the film as natural rather than constructed leads to the fourth chapter, which considers cinematic counterparts for such metatheatrical, anti-illusionistic devices as the play-within-the-play, the chorus, and direct address to the audience. She argues provocatively that "whatever film directors may do, the very nature of the cinematic experience forbids any radical exposure of illusion: enunciation generally dissolves into narration" (95). It is in the screenplay, she argues in chapter 5, where the "subtext" of a Shakespearean film—both the director's interpretive concepts that unify the Shakespearean narrative and the technical choices that create the illusion of reality—is most clearly revealed, though, she acknowledges, few viewers of Shakespearean films ever get access to one. This chapter, which offers close readings of passages from several *Hamlet* screenplays, provides a particularly novel and valuable approach to the study of screenplays. As a way of demonstrating the power of formal analysis for Shakespearean film criticism, the final chapter offers case studies of key scenes from five Shakespeare plays, discussing how different directors have handled the same material in different ways.

Hatchuel's study has several virtues. First among them is the sheer clarity of her definitions and categories. Though her discussion necessarily entails a certain amount of jargon and technical elements of narrative theory, the terms and concepts are carefully, precisely defined, in the manner of an extremely adept lecture on the topic. In fact, occasionally the categories and definitions feel somewhat too sharply delineated, with not enough attention paid to problem cases. Secondly, Hatchuel is fully conversant with the state of the art in the analysis of film form. The book is especially strong in cinematic narrative theory and thereby marks a considerable advance over its predecessors in Shakespearean film studies. Lastly, whereas earlier formal analyses of Shakespearean film have tended implicitly or explicitly to privilege arthouse Shakespeare—what Jorgens calls the "cinematic" mode of adaptation—Hatchuel stresses the sophistication and value of the classic realist mode, the dominant style of most Shakespearean film adaptation. In this, her study reveals the influence of the Shakespeare films of the nineties, which definitively brought Shakespearean film adaptation in line with mainstream narrative cinema. Understandably, the work of Kenneth Branagh—which Hatchuel addressed at length in an earlier study—looms large in her analysis. She pushes against the predominantly negative reaction to Branagh among Shakespearean film scholars by stressing the distinctiveness and sophistication of Branagh's formal choices, in effect sidestepping the issue of the ideological conservativeness of his interpretations. Despite the occasional factual lapse—the Shakespearean briefly glimpsed onscreen in Almereyda's *Hamlet* is John Gielgud (in Humphrey Jennings's *A Diary for Timothy*), not Johnston Forbes-Robertson (112)—the book is generally very well-researched and documented.

Even so, Hatchuel's study demonstrates not only the power but the limitations of a formalist approach to Shakespeare on film. When in the final chapter Hatchuel does make analysis of Shakespeare films her central concern, her exclusive focus on film technique precludes consideration of the wider implications of directorial choices in the films at hand. The study thus seems rather disconnected from the dominant modes of analysis in Shakespearean film studies. In line with Bordwell's approach, the study stops short of exploring the ideological implications of formal choices or situating them within some specific historical context. Some very intriguing observations—that, for example, Olivier's *Henry V* "borrows from the Hollywood western" (114)—thus remain unelaborated. Hatchuel rightly stresses that classic Hollywood realism is a formal system that tends to naturalize ideology, but the implications of that tendency for Shakespearean film adaptation demands much more discussion. When, for example, at the end of chapter 3 Hatchuel engages the argument that film music in Shakespearean film manipulates the viewer and thus poses an ideological trap, she argues that "criticizing the creation of emotion often betrays a denial of the nature of the cinematic experience" (92) rather than addressing the relationship between the orchestration of emotion and the not-always-unified operations of ideology. Whether "the very act of going to the cinema already implies a certain kind of surrender to a particular vision of the world" (92) is true—what kind of surrender? full or partial, particularly in an era of media savvy?—or, more to the point, desirable seems an issue very worth discussing, and nowhere more so than in Shakespearean film, where the powerful cultural authority of Shakespeare is often placed in service of ideology. When Hatchuel turns to considering whether the Brechtian alienation effects Shakespearean theater is capable of can be produced in screen Shakespeare, her conclusion is that film is so powerfully recuperative that it defeats all attempts to bare its devices (indeed, she argues that metacinematic devices only strengthen the illusion of realism). This conclusion has large implications for Shakespearean film adaptation that deserve further discussion and investigation, raising, at the very least, the question of whether Shakespeare on film betrays some of the ideological qualities we most value Shakespeare for. It is surely a conclusion that might be challenged by, say, Jean-Luc Godard's *King Lear* or Peter Greenaway's *Prospero's Books,* films she does briefly discuss.

A second issue has to do with the specificity of the adaptational challenges posed by Shakespeare's plays for filmmakers. As the title suggests, *Shakespeare, from Stage to Screen* is concerned with the adaptation of drama to film, and its great strength is its emphasis on the *dis*continuity between these two media. Paradoxically the place of Shakespeare in that analysis seems somewhat insecure. The unwillingness to offer a full reading of any one Shakespeare film has the unintended consequence of making the many (and generally well-chosen) examples from Shakespeare films seem oddly superfluous to the book's main concern: offering a taxonomy of cinematic techniques. Though Hatchuel's extensive examples are drawn from Shakespeare films, it is not clear how the adaptational issues she discusses are specific to Shakespeare rather than endemic to most transpositions of stage plays to films. To be fair, Hatchuel does take up elements of dramatic form common in Shakespeare—soliloquies, for example, or gaps in the action between scenes—though, of course, these elements are not exclusive to Shakespeare. To put the matter another way: if one would focus the analysis on the challenges of transposing Shakespeare in particular (not merely drama in general) to film, how might that analysis illuminate peculiarities of form particular to Shakespeare's plays—specific modes of narrative construction, relations of word to stage image, uses of theatrical devices? Might examining specific patterns of resistance or amenability of Shakespeare's drama to film adaptation reveal something precise and otherwise imperceptible about Shakespeare's own formal techniques in constructing his plays?

There is much of value in this well-organized and well-written study. Hatchuel updates and refines earlier formalist analyses of Shakespeare on film, and her emphasis on realist modes of cinematic adaptation is apropos in light of Shakespearean cinema of the nineties. The book's primary contribution to Shakespearean film scholarship is that it brings to bear a sophisticated Bordwellian style of analysis on Shakespearean film adaptation. The great clarity of its taxonomies of cinematic techniques and well-informed discussions of their implications are especially welcome. Those in need of a reliable primer on the formal challenges of adapting plays to the screen will find this a most useful addition to their bookshelf. This is a book which will be particularly useful for advanced students or those Shakespearean scholars new to formalist film criticism, and it is a very timely corrective to the collective inattention of performance critics to the demands, limits and potentialities of specific media. Those who are willing to combine the formalist analytic techniques Hatchuel demonstrates with the insights of recent ideological analyses of Shakespeare on film will find themselves in possession of very powerful critical tools indeed.

Female Mourning and Tragedy in Medieval and Renaissance Drama: From the Raising of Lazarus to King Lear, by Katharine Goodland. Aldershot and Burlington: Ashgate Publishing Company, 2005. Pp. 254. Cloth $94.95.

Reviewer: KATIE NORMINGTON

Katharine Goodland's *Female Mourning and Tragedy in Medieval and Renaissance Drama* is a welcome addition to the growing field of study that crosses the previous critical boundaries of medieval and Renaissance drama and instead analyzes the influences and echoes that can be found within these two eras. It is much to Goodland's credit that she spends equal time discussing each period rather than compressing the discussion on medieval theater to favor the Renaissance, as is often the case.

Goodland sets out to show how grieving women on the early modern stage are not influenced only by classical drama but developed from the Catholic past (2), and the importance of the cultural trauma of the Reformation in shaping mourning (7). She does this by identifying a series of laments that can be found within the medieval Lazarus plays, the Nativity and Passion plays, and the Resurrection plays before examining mourning women in early modern English tragedies: *King John, The Spanish Tragedy, The White Devil, Hamlet, Lucrece,* and *Titus Andronicus,* as well as looking at how lamentation frames *Richard III* and the figure of King Lear as symbolic of a female mourner.

During the introduction Goodland interweaves examples from classical, medieval, and Renaissance drama. The examples demonstrate a large and impressive arena of scholarship, but often there is a tendency to dash between the examples without making clear the substantial differences between the contexts of the chosen plays. For example, Goodland begins by stating that, "In the world that extends from Homer to Hamlet grief is a performance incumbent upon the female relatives of the deceased, simultaneously a responsibility, a right, and a source of pride" (9). She illustrates her point by reference to *The Trojan Women,* the N-Town *Raising of Lazarus,* the Digby *Mary Magdalene, Electra,* and *Antigone.* So while the breadth of Goodland's examples is to be commended, she often fails to distinguish how these dramas are also part of differing cultural worlds. In fact this is symptomatic of a larger problem: Goodland gives little time to establishing the cultural, social, or political milieus of the worlds that she examines. She often makes useful references to other literary writings, but this in fact increases the sense of drama existing in a vacuum with little attachment to real life. This problem decreases during the course of the book, however, so that by the final couple of chapters the textual analysis and argument is more grounded.

Part 1 of the book examines the figures of women mourners across a range of medieval "cycles" and the Digby *Mary Magdalene* play. In the first of these sections she concludes that the Lazarus plays "attempt to resolve the inherent opposition between the residual practice of lament and the dominant Christian eschatology" (52). This section, and the two that cover the Nativity, Passion, and Resurrection plays, undertake detailed textual reading of the plays. The thoroughness of these readings is to be commended, but is reminiscent of that of Rosemary Woolf whose 1970s study Goodland frequently draws upon. It is an approach which seems rather old-fashioned these days and leads Goodland to frequently treat drama as though it amounts to words on a page. When Goodland strays into considering the performative production and reception of drama her analysis is immediately lightened. For example, reference to actresses playing Constance (120) and Alexandra Johnston's writing on the experience of playing the N-Town virgin (122) produces a more dynamic reading. Goodland's dense textual commentary is not aided by an editorial decision to run textual quotations into the prose rather than indent them on new lines.

The second part of the book shifts to Renaissance drama, and it is here that the structure seems less secure. While the chronology of medieval pageants serves Goodland well in the first part, the second part is less clearly defined. Her link between the traumatized society of post-Reformation England and the world of *King John* is convincing, and the reading of *Richard III* as explorations of the "consequences for England's communal memory of the suppression of mourning practices" (155) is interesting. However, the "monstrous mourning women" identified in a chapter that embraces Kyd's *The Spanish Tragedy,* Shakespeare's *Titus Andronicus* and *Rape of Lucrece,* and Webster's *The White Devil* makes a less convincing case that "the ritual destruction of English icons of the Virgin Mary seem to haunt these moments" (170) given the vast historical shifts that occurred during these various works.

Goodland approaches the chapter on *Hamlet* with greater control, drawing on textual readings, references to pamphleteers, and critical readings, to argue that Ophelia's laments shape the reception of the play (198). However, there is no consideration given as to how her laments might be read differently given that they were performed by a boy actor. The final chapter examines Lear as an inverted Pietà, pointing out that in his direction of "look there" he calls the audience's attention to the corpse of Cordelia in a manner that was now forbidden within the funeral service.

Goodland's book will be of value to those searching for specific texts in this area, but there is a sense that there is an embryonic book of much greater appeal and importance lurking here. Had Goodland been more selective and directional about her use of critical perspectives (for example, on page 7 she dashes through six alone), she could have carved out a very influential book.

Women Players in England, 1500–1660: Beyond the All-Male Stage, Pamela Allen Brown and Peter Parolin, eds. *Studies in Performance and Early Modern Drama,* edited by Helen Ostavich. Aldershot, Hampshire and Burlington, VT: Ashgate, 2005. Pp. xvii + 329. Cloth $99.95.

Reviewer: SHEILA T. CAVANAUGH

Women Players in England, 1500–1660: Beyond the All-Male Stage offers a number of valuable essays concerned with the role of women in performance during the years noted. Unfortunately, the title of the collection is misleading. Only a few of the essays in question actually address what the title suggests is the central issue: female performers in early modern England. The other pieces in the collection discuss related topics, including drama produced on the Continent during this period. While many of these essays serve as eloquent and erudite contributions to the project, their discontinuity with the purported topic of the collection is disconcerting. Readers are advised, therefore, that this series of essays is well worth perusal despite the unfortunate title that promises something different than the volume actually provides.

The previous caveat notwithstanding, Pamela Allen Brown and Peter Parolin have gathered essays from an impressive range of scholars, who help illuminate the role of women in performative events during this period. As they judiciously note, they are focused on female "players" rather than actresses since this term acknowledges that for both male and female performers, "their art encompassed many mimetic forms, such as singing songs and ballads, dancing jigs, cross-dressing, miming, jesting, and masking" (4). They also offer an appropriately capacious understanding of "performance," calling it "any act of embodied display or representation intended for an audience" (5). Although their justification for including continental players is less convincing namely, "to assess the ways that [Italian and French] performances intersected with, and affected, the English scene" (5) they rightly seek to open up our conceptualization of the numerous early modern performative activities thriving outside the professional stage. They also highlight the many avenues of research that will be supported by the Records of Early English Drama (REED) project. This collection, moreover, helps identify fruitful areas for future research by these scholars and others.

The first section, "Beyond London" contains the essays that best exemplify the ways that REED and other archival sources can invigorate our understanding of the activities of early modern female performers. James Stokes, for instance, in "Women and Performance: Evidences of Universal

Cultural Suffrage in Medieval and Early Modern Lincolnshire," details how REED documents make women visible in ways that much twentieth-century theater history did not. As Stokes acknowledges, this essay marks only the beginning of the work that can be done on socioreligious guilds in this period, but he convincingly demonstrates that "women participated as players, sponsors, producers, and audiences in revels; in customary mimetic games, processions, and enactments blending worship and play; in mimetically conceived ceremonies publicly enacting the rituals of power, authority, and life's passages" (41). Similarly, Gweno Williams, Alison Findlay, and Stephanie Hodgson-Wright offer a jointly authored essay entitled "Payments, Permits and Punishments: Women Performers and the Politics of Place" that considers the evidence about female performers offered by REED for York, Lancashire, and Gloucestershire. This essay also highlights the importance of religious ceremonies in the history of female performance, but concurrently urges scholars to look more closely at "the importance of women's role as producers rather than performers" (64). Like Stokes's contribution, this essay underscores the important archival work in this area that remains to be done.

The subsequent essays in the collection, which offer glimpses into the larger research projects most of them are drawn from, are divided according to their common themes: "Beyond Elites," "Beyond the Channel," "Beyond the Stage," and "Beyond the 'All-Male.'" Most of these pieces explore different realms where scholars can locate women's theatrical performance. Bella Mirabella, for instance, considers female mountebanks; Melinda J. Gough focuses on the plays undertaken by Henrietta Maria; Julie Crawford explores Margaret Cavendish and the "Dramatic Petition"; Bruce R. Smith examines early modern ballads; and Pamela Allen Brown expands upon her previous work on jest books. Other contributions, such as those by Jean E. Howard, Julie D. Campbell, and Rachel Poulsen, approach the topic of female performance through dramatic analysis.

These individual essays frequently offer significant insight into areas that are relatively unknown to many scholars, and they will whet the reader's appetite for longer works on these topics. Melinda Gough's essay, Peter Parolin's analysis of "The Venetian Theater of Aletheia Talbot, Countess of Arundel, and Bruce R. Smith's discussion of "Female Impersonation in Early Modern Ballads," for instance, offer well-documented accounts of material that falls outside the expertise of many early modernists. Natasha Korda and M. A. Katritzky, on the other hand, provide new information about more established topics, i.e., Moll Frith and female commedia performers respectively. By focusing on performers rather than actors, the editors have supported work on a fascinating range of theatrical representations both in England and on the Continent.

Taken as a whole, this volume offers a range of evidence to strengthen our knowledge about the ways that early modern women participated in performance. As Phyllis Rackin notes in her afterword, "The essays in this collection provide us with evidence that was previously unknown or neglected of the widespread participation of women in the production of every possible kind of show" (317). At the same time, the volume illustrates both the strengths and weaknesses of this kind of project, which has become increasingly popular in the current academic publishing world. Beginning life as a 2000 Shakespeare Association of America seminar on "Women Players In and Around Shakespeare," the collection gathers a group of talented scholars whose work sometimes, but not always, fits well within the chosen rubric. As a result, the audience receives a rich gathering of scholarly material whose interrelationship is not always clear. In the case of this volume, readers wanting a glimpse at some of the exciting new work in this area will be well-served; those expecting a cohesive presentation are less likely to find it. Still, Brown and Parolin deserve our gratitude for providing a tantalizing preview of the scholarship approaching on the horizon as an important area of theatrical history comes more sharply into focus.

Global Economics: A History of the Theater Business, the Chamberlain's/King's Men, and Their Plays, 1599–1642, by Melissa D. Aaron. Newark: University of Delaware Press, 2005. Pp. 250. Cloth $47.50.

Reviewer: NORA JOHNSON

Every scholar who wishes to read early modern plays as reflections of their economic, material, and professional contexts faces the difficulty of explaining precisely how the drama can be said to perform such an act of reflection. Are plays somehow allegories of the economic conditions under which they are produced? Do they supply discursive constructions of authorship, collaboration, or patronage that shape and are shaped by the theatrical milieu? Are the plays simply to be mined for discrete bits of information about commercial practices, or do they make more complex statements about the business of playing through larger thematic structures? Each of these possibilities—and there are doubtless many others—suggests a different way of thinking about metatheater, about base and superstructure, about the possibility of theatrical self-consciousness.

Melissa Aaron's study of The Chamberlain's/King's Men proposes a program of "economic readings," seeing the plays as, whatever else they may be, "snapshots" of the company's material and financial circumstances at various moments in its collective life. At best, this strategy leads Aaron into some very interesting ways of combining material and thematic concerns (it does not, by the way, lead her to consider economics in any way that could be considered "global"; the pun in the title is somewhat misleading). Her pursuit of the evidence about costumes that may have been given to theatrical companies by aristocrats, for instance, causes her to speculate that the same bear costume might have circulated from *Mucedorus* through the *Masque of Oberon* to *The Winter's Tale,* "from the public theater to the court and back again" (90). This hypothesis in turn allows her to argue that when The King's Men use the bear costume they are implicitly critiquing the claims of the royalty-friendly productions in which the costume had shown up previously. Mucedorus had been able to protect Amadine from a bear, Aaron notes, as the presence of Henry and James had been able to tame the bears who pull Henry's chariot in *Oberon,* but neither the infant princess Perdita nor her tragically absent parents have the power to keep Antigonus from dying an awful death. While highly speculative, the argument is intriguing. It suggests that attending to specific props and particular performance contexts may make a real difference in critical debates about individual plays and in larger arguments about the relation of the players to their royal sponsors. It also helps to fill in the endlessly fascinating gap in our knowledge of the material world of early modern theater.

Aaron reads *Henry V* in the context of the construction of the Globe theater in 1599. She argues that the Prologue's famous references to the "wooden O" and the "unworthy scaffold" are in fact apologies not for the general inadequacy of the stage to represent Henry's reign so much as for the specific problems of the outworn Curtain theater. Contending that *Henry V* had been written for the new Globe, which was not completed in time for its first performance, Aaron uses the play and its surrounding business environment as a way of talking about the Chamberlain's company at that stage in its economic development, about "the precarious financial position of the Chamberlain's Men in 1598/99 and the marketing and investment strategies they used to combat it" (47). The audacious building of the Globe theater does reward intensive scholarly focus. Here, however, the notion of "economic reading," while it poses interesting questions in theater history, tends unfortunately toward a flattening of the text. This objection may well go double for a reading of *Hamlet* that brings to light a string of references that may or may not be about rivalry with the Admiral's Men. Given that the fact of the rivalry is already well established and the professional reflections on playing in *Hamlet* are very clear, one hopes for a more significant engagement with textual evidence.

In a very detailed and illuminating study of *The Roman Actor,* Aaron claims that the play is "prophetic" in its depiction of a form of patronage that draws players away from popular audiences and leaves them dangerously dependent upon royal approval. She establishes a clear set of similarities between the business of playing as represented in the play and the conditions that would weaken The King's Men disastrously under the sponsorship of Charles I and Henrietta Maria. The royal couple, Aaron argues, "loved theater to death," appropriating the King's Men for their own purposes in a way that ultimately crippled the company, making them especially vulnerable as the monarchy approached its point of crisis. The picture given of court sponsorship in this period is both helpful and convincing, but in the end it is hard to understand why even the most prescient member of the King's Men should want to stage a prophecy about the company's own downfall, especially one that insults royal patrons while proclaiming alienation from larger audiences. If, as Aaron wants to argue, the company consistently made its choices for reasons that were heavily determined by economics and not politics or ideology, more explanation is required for this strangely negative form of self-publicity. Again, while the connections between the text and the economic and professional life of the King's Men are clearly worth exploring, the use of the text as evidence for the economic history of the company needs some further consideration in methodological terms.

That said, this useful and ambitious history of the Chamberlain's/King's Men offers many strong arguments about a broad range of economic and professional questions. On the way to talking about *Henry V,* Aaron makes important interventions in the debates about when the Globe might have been completed, and what the costs and financial gains of this complex transaction might have been. Her reading of the King's Men's relationship to Jacobean patronage is a wonderful corrective to the New Historicist emphasis on court control. Stressing in particular the power of the playing company to represent the court before courtiers from other nations and before more popular audiences, Aaron helps convincingly to salvage the repertory from lockstep obedience to a putatively absolutist monarchy. She provides some finely detailed studies of the masques in *Henry VIII* and *The Tempest,* as well as *The Winter's Tale,* and she makes an excellent case for reading the First Folio as a document with as much to say about theater history as it says about the history of print or textual studies. The book moves deftly from analyses of court politics to the larger economic background of the period to specific performances, props, and actors. Its picture of "the bold strategies of 1624," in which the King's Men risked punishment by producing both *A Game at Chesse* and *The Spanish Viceroy,* does much to solidify our understanding of the relative independence and stability of the company during that period (145). Though Aaron perhaps too self-consciously avoids writing what she calls a "master narrative" of the company's history, the series of institutional moments she stitches together do nevertheless describe an enterprise that begins in chaotic struggle, achieves the stability to take economic and political risks, and finally loses its audience because of an excessive dependence upon royal favor. *Global Economics* may be something less than sure-footed in its use of the plays themselves; the work of Heather Hirschfeld or of Scott McMillin and Sally-Beth MacLean provides a better model of integrated institutional and textual analysis. As a self-professed set of snapshots, though, this is an illuminating and much-needed chronicle of the leading theater company of its time.

Representing the Professions: Administration, Law, and Theater in Early Modern England, by Edward Gieskes. Newark: University of Delaware Press, 2006, Pp. 365, $60.00 (cloth).

Reviewer: REBECCA LEMON

In *Representing the Professions,* Edward Gieskes uses the sociological theory of Pierre Bourdieu to chart the formation of the professions of administration, law, and theater in early modern England. In doing so, he offers an ambitious study, ranging through the drama of Shakespeare, Jonson, Dekker, Beaumont, Massinger, Middleton, and others, in order to demonstrate the parallels between these three professional fields as each moves from the status of trade or guild into a profession. Complementing extant studies on the topic of the professions, including Wilfred Prest's edited collection on *The Professions in Early Modern England* (1987), Gieskes brings a particular insight to the discussion with his research on the labor of theatrical staging. By connecting the craftspeople and workers of the theater to playwrights, *Representing the Professions* challenges strictly literary approaches to drama and instead argues convincingly for the interplay of dramatic writing and theatrical practice.

Rather than viewing the professions through the economic frame that he finds typical of Marxian studies on the topic, Gieskes offers a "Bourdieuian literary history." This sociological approach has real advantages: Gieskes ambitiously considers a number of fields implicated in the rise of the professions—literary, historical, economic, legal, theatrical, and political—without privileging any one field. Yet this reliance on Bourdieu also presents difficulties for readers coming to the book with a primary interest in the early modern period: each chapter's extended engagement with Bourdieu comes at the expense of direct, detailed engagement with literary and historical texts. In the chapter on the law, for example, Gieskes offers a rich analysis of the rise of the legal profession, tracking the vast number of handbooks on the law that proliferated in the sixteenth century to support law students in their studies. Yet this discussion begins and ends with Bourdieu's terminology, locating the payoff of the legal history in the terms "habitus" and "field." In returning consistently to Bourdieu throughout its chapters, the book, as a result, allots proportionately much less space for the analysis of plays. This latter aspect of the book is disappointing given that Gieskes has skillfully assembled a fresh selection of understudied texts, which readers may be eager to see analyzed at greater length.

The book's first case study, on public administrators, traces the new men, such as the Bacons and the Cecils, who made up a professional administrative cadre. This chapter argues, following G. R. Elton, that the Tudor revolution in government affected an administrative shift from a tradition of service based on noble rank to one based in talent. Gieskes's case for administration as a profession with its own set of talent-based standards is less convincing than subsequent arguments for law and theater, considering that bureaucrats in the Tudor period used their "professional" positions to achieve noble status, demonstrating a persistent concern for rank within the context of state service. Here, soldiers or clergy members might have conformed more convincingly to the book's definition of professionals. The chapter nevertheless offers insightful readings of Shakespeare's *King John* and the anonymous *The Troublesome Raigne of John, King of England* to help support its argument about the tension between nobility and talent in the period. For example, Gieskes compares the linguistic range of Philip in *Troublesome Raigne* with the Bastard in Shakespeare in order to juxtapose innate nobility and hard work: while Philip's language-use is remarkably consistent, suggesting his noble birth despite his illegitimate status, Shakespeare's Bastard acquires royal language over the course of the play, suggesting instead his talent.

Chapter 3 argues for the emergence of the profession of law in the period. With increasing numbers of law students and lawyers, professional training became more institutionalized. The chapter offers a particularly rich discussion of the resulting educational requirements for lawyers, the differentiation of barristers and lawyers in the period, and the proliferation of printed books and manuals on the law to help support these emerging professionals. Literary depictions of lawyers, Gieskes argues, register the law's newfound professional status. Specifically, Massinger's *A New Way to Pay Old Debts,* Middleton's *Michaelmas Term,* and S.S.'s *The Honest Lawyer* represent the pervasive fear that a group of socially ambitious upstarts might take over a role formerly reserved for the upper classes. Thus, while these plays preserve a sense of respect for the law itself as a source of social order, they condemn the scheming practitioners who give the law a bad name.

The book's most compelling argument concerns theater as a profession, since it is here that Gieskes demonstrates his deepest literary and archival engagement. Chapter 4 examines the field of theater through the lens of the artisans who constructed the stage, the props, and the costumes. This chapter demonstrates how playwriting was affected by other theater-based trades and crafts, emerging as professions. As the author writes, "I contend that professional dramatic writing owes as much to a body of stage techniques and design principles that derive from a usually underconsidered group of theatrical craftsmen as it does to a 'literary' tradition" (212). The chapter traces the many hired workers who were routinely employed in the staging of seasonal entertainments, and later to stage productions in London's permanent theaters. The impact of these professional craftspeople on playwriting is most apparent in metatheatrical plays, including Beaumont and Fletcher's *Knight of the Burning Pestle* and Greene's *James IV*. These plays, as Gieskes skillfully demonstrates, reveal a preoccupation with issues of craft, exploring the tensions between and among both different staging conventions and theories of acting. Continuing the exploration of theater, chapter 5 focuses on the War of the Theatres, or Poetomachia. The stakes of this conflict, Gieskes argues, "were the right to define the nature and structure of the emerging professional field of writing" (218). Specifically, in his contributions to this Poetomachia, Ben Jonson struggles to define the role of writer as one worthy of respect, and thus turns, Gieskes argues, an initially minor conflict into a field-defining one.

After tracing the rise of these historical professions in its main chapters, the book's concluding chapter reveals how the term "profession" operates in the book in another, more methodological, respect: the term invokes current debates about the crisis in the humanities and the state of "the profession" itself. While this methodological discussion helps to illuminate the book's critical stakes, it also raises some questions about the relationship between the fields of history, theory, and literature in *Representing the Professions*. As suggested above, in using Bourdieu to avoid the potential pitfalls of new historicism, the book celebrates the insights of social science while, at times, ignoring evidentiary methods, such as sustained analysis of historical and literary materials, typical of much distinguished work in the humanities. Yet when, in chapters 4 and 5, Gieskes turns from Bourdieu to bring forward his own readings of literary and historical texts, the book's argument proves original and compelling. The result is fresh insight into the complex relationship between dramatic literature and theatrical staging, between professionalism and craft.

Public Theatre in Golden Age Madrid and Tudor-Stuart London: Class, Gender, and Festive Community, by Ivan Cañadas. Burlington, VT: Ashgate, 2005. Pp. xiii + 233. Cloth $94.95.

Reviewer: OLGA VALBUENA

Hispanists and Anglicists working in both areas of early modern studies look forward to new offerings in the relatively under-explored field of comparative Anglo-Hispanic literature. A careful perusal of Ivan Cañadas's useful bibliography (twenty-four pages in length) draws attention to the need for further inquiry in this field and goes partway to explain why Cañadas's contribution falls short of its stated goal (more on this below). In his own words, Cañadas proposes to extend "recent critical revisions of the *comedia*, and to demonstrate the hybrid relationship between different discourses, such as gender, race, and rank, in dramatic appeals to the audience, in addressing the theatrical cultures of both Madrid and London in the period" (18). He argues that certain plays in England such as Thomas Dekker's city comedy *The Shoemaker's Holiday* and a selection of Lope de Vega's Spanish peasant dramas challenge or even supersede traditional aristocratic (or gender or racial) privilege through collective action and appeals to the audience's own hybrid interests in a festive and communal celebration of class identity.

Cañadas's book evinces the fatigue of the dissertation writer. There is a template-like quality to the argument as carried from the brief introduction to the fifth chapter: in his hands, most texts under inspection are "hybrid" in their ideological tendencies, and, indeed, "subversive." Those not openly subversive prove "ambiguous." By the time Cañadas finishes his discussion of any given drama, as in chapter 4 with Lope de Vega's *El villano en su rincón* (*The Peasant in His Corner*), the reader is likely to recognize that for Cañadas the terms *ambiguity, hybridity,* and *polyphony* are synonymous with *subversion.* Similarly, in his discussion of *Peribañez y el Comendador de Ocaña,* the eponymous peasant who slays the *comendador* or overlord is eventually "honored as a *noble*" (110, my emphasis). This conclusion seems incongruous with the celebration of the lower class that the author claims for this play, for in both instances, the monarch not the peasant gives closure to events surrounding the *comendador*'s actions and the peasant retribution. Doing so, he consolidates his power in his own royal person. Similarly, Cañadas argues in chapter 5 that the peasant uprising culminating in the murder of Fernán Gómez, due to that *comendador*'s and other knights' and nobles' widespread rapine in Lope's *Fuente Ovejuna,* effects "a revision of traditional aristocratic notions of heroism" based on the collective retributive action of the united peasantry. Arguably, however, when King Fernando's inquest fails to produce a guilty creature because members of the entire collectivity endure the state's coercive measures (principally torture), the peasants have paid a high price for "the claims of the community as a whole to an ideal of common dignity" (139).

This heady "no end of subversion," then, is purchased at considerable cost, not only to the actual complexity of Lope's plays but also to the work of Dian Fox and various other Hispanists whom Cañadas labels "neo-conservative" (108). He expends so much energy refuting other critics that the reader becomes distracted by that and the author's recourse to the fixed set of talking points regarding hybridity and subversion found in each successive chapter. Cañadas's discussion of "theatrical transvestism," for example, contains all the reflexes of what he associates with queer, cultural, and gender-inflected historicism but makes no new observation, breaks no new ground in either English or Hispanic studies. He asserts, to no one's surprise, that a complex of subject positions could well have resided in the individual (and in the plurality) of character types and audience members that the theater might bring together in the flux of the performative moment:

The subversion of patriarchal notions of gender suggests the specific influence of both female actors and female spectators in the theatrical culture. It points to the coexistence, from the perspective of the heterogeneous audience, of a range of positions regarding gender, as well as analogies evident in the dramatic conflict between aristocratic and humanist notions of human identity and conduct. By these means, the polyphonic approach to rank and gender in the early modern theaters of both Madrid and London argues social contexts of uncertainty, anxiety, and flux, rather than the conditions of conservative, monolithic cultures. . . . Lastly, the dramatic motif and theatrical practice of crossdressing in both theaters provided another means to question identity, a complex web of practices in view of institutional differences between the all-male English theater and the Spanish stage, in which female actors played a leading role. (61)

Cañadas is to be commended for his effort to bring together Spanish and English theatrical texts and social contexts, but the *dialogic* potential between the theater of Spain and England just does not resound in the pages of his book. And the juxtaposition of two texts from different cultures should pass the "merely adventitious" test for which neo-historicism is faulted, though this qualification applies not only to Cañadas's book but to any practitioner tempted to throw in, somewhat randomly, Lope's *X* with Shakespeare's *Y*. The book's weaknesses are not altogether Cañadas's own but reflect the absence of a quantum cross-disciplinary knowledge base among most literary critics. For this area deserves more attention and certainly more theorization than it has received since Walter Cohen's 1985 groundbreaking *Drama of a Nation: Public Theater in Renaissance England and Spain.* Nor does the dearth of authentically dual-language studies available today help Cañadas situate his own work in something like a "field."

A project of this nature might incorporate the rich possibilities of a play such as Thomas Middleton's satirical and wildly popular 1624 *A Game at Chess.* Written in the wake of Prince Charles's abortive efforts to woo the Infanta Maria, the play rejects cultural hybridity, most notably in the equation of the marriage match with a plot to revconvert England to Catholicism. This text would seem but one apt choice for establishing a dialogic examination of "class, gender, and festive community" that truly mobilized the audience across class and gender lines while satirically aspersing the whole enterprise of the Spanish Match and James I's diplomacy. As popular art "made tongue-tied by authority" this play was summarily forbidden by order of the king after its unprecedented nine-days' run.

While isolated work has emerged since the 1980s and Cohen's book, the groundbreaking *Drama of a Nation: Public Theater in Renaissance England and Spain*—of course John Loftis's *Renaissance Drama in England and Spain: Topical Allusion and History Play* (1981); the Fothergill-Paynes's essay collection, *Parallel Lives: Spanish and English National Drama 1580–1680* (1991), as well as a smattering of dissertations and articles along the way—more work is needed to properly situate, historicize, and recognize the dialogic potential of *both* literatures *together.*

Index

Aaron, Melissa D., 296–99
Actresses, 294–96
Africans, 19–55
Arden of Faversham, 170–73, 175–76, 178, 180–83, 185
Armin, Robert, 218, 220
Audiences, 157–69
Augustine of Hippo, 164–65

Bacon, Anthony, 35, 38
Bacon, Francis, 162
Basadonna, Giovanni, 35–36
Battle of Alcazar, 39
Beehler, Sharon A., 285–88
Berek, Peter, 170–88
Blackfriars playhouse (first and second), 163–64
Blayney, Peter W. M., 91–93
Bosch, Hieronymus, 41
Brown, Pamela Allen, 294–96
Brown, Thomas, 40–41
Burks, Deborah G., 266–70
Butterworth, Philip, 274–78

Cañadas, Ivan, 301–3
Catholicism, 207, 242–45,
Cavanaugh, Sheila, 294–96
Chambers, E. K., 58, 90, 112, 214
Chettle, Henry, 184, 186
Clifford, Anne, 21, 22
Clopton, Hugh, 217
Cockpit (Drury Lane), 128, 158, 164
Cox, John D., 242–45
Crawford, Julie, 236–42
Curtain playhouse, 209

Danter, John, 88–93, 112
Dawson, Anthony B., 255–58
DeWitt, Johannes, 191
Dekker, Thomas, 157, 160, 165, 184–86
Detmer-Goebel, Emily, 266–70

Devereux, Robert (Earl of Essex), 207
Domestic tragedy, 170–88
Dürer, Albrecht, 41

Elizabeth I, 26, 67, 210
Erne, Lukas, 278–81

Falco, Raphael, 271–74
Favila, Marina, 274–78
Field, Richard, 35–36
Film, 288–92
Fleay, F. G., 60–61
Foakes, R. A., 258–66
Forker, Charles R., 225–32
Forman, Simon, 24, 112

Gieskes, Edward, 299–301
Glimp, David, 281–85
Globe Playhouse (first and second), 163, 209, 210, 213, 219
Goodland, Katherine, 292–94
Greg, W. W., 62, 90, 128, 130, 132, 145, 147, 149
Griselda plays, 183–84
Gurr, Andrew, 150, 157–69

Hadfield, Andrew, 232–35
Hakluyt, Richard, 43
Hamilton, Donna B., 242–45
Hammill, Graham, 232–35
Harington, John, 20, 38–39, 41
Hartmann, Franz, 191–200
Harvey, Gabriel, 37
Hatchuel, Sarah, 288–92
Haughton, William, 184, 185
Hawkins, John, 25
Helgerson, Richard, 175
Henslowe, Philip, 209, 213–14, 217
Heywood, John, 57
Heywood, Thomas, 128–56, 160, 163, 170, 179–81, 183, 186
History play, 87–127, 245–48

INDEX

Holinshed, Raphael, 173, 175
Holland, Peter, 258–67
Hollar, Wenceslaus, 62
Honselaars, Ton, 245–48
Horace, 40

Jack Straw (play), 87–127
James VI and I, 159, 191
Johnson, Nora, 296–99
Jones, Inigo, 191
Jonson, Ben, 191, 207

Kemp, Will, 218, 219
Kidnie, Margaret Jane, 278–81
King's Men, 158, 220
Kyd, Thomas, 171, 174

Lady Elizabeth's Men, 128, 149, 150
Lanier, Douglas M., 288–92
Law, 299–301
Lemon, Rebecca, 299–301
Lesser, Zachary, 248–55
Logan, Robert A., 225–232
Long, William B., 129, 137, 149, 203–21
Lord Admiral's Men, 213
Lord Chamberlain's Men, 19, 38, 213, 216, 218, 220

McCarthy, Jeanne H., 56–86
Madrid, 301–3
Magic, 274–78
Marlowe, Christopher, 171, 225–232
Marston, John, 74, 219
Memory, 255–66
Middleton, Thomas, 160, 165
Miseries of Enforced Marriage, 171, 179–80, 186
Montaigne, Michel de, 204
More, Sir Thomas (play), 56, 63
Mourning, 292–94
Munday, Anthony, 56, 59–60, 63, 129, 157, 242–47

Neale, J. E., 205
Normington, Katie, 292
Nunes, Hector, 32–34

Ovid, 40

Parolin, Peter, 294–96
Patterson, Annabel, 205

Pavier, Thomas, 89–93
Pérez, Antonio, 34–38
Performance, 285–88
Petrarch, Francesco, 183
Pollard, A. W., 205
Porter, Millicent, 23
Preiss, Richard, 248–55
Professions, 299–301
Protestant/-ism, 59, 162, 236–42
Public Theater, 301–3
Purkis, James, 128–56

Rebellion, 87–127
Red Lion playhouse, 209
Republicanism, 232–35
Revels, Master of, 128, 131, 148–51, 205, 210, 219
Robinson, Grace, 21–22
Rocklin, Edward L., 285–88
Rose playhouse, 209, 217
Rowse, A. L., 36–7

Sackville, Margaret, 22
Schillinger, Stephen, 87–127
Schlueter, June, 191–200
Shakespeare, William: 112, 129, 203–21, 225–35, 245–48, 258–66, 271–74, 285–88, 288–92
—Plays: *Antony and Cleopatra,* 44, 218; *As You Like It,* 180, 210, 214, 218, 219; *The Comedy of Errors,* 37; *Coriolanus,* 208; *Hamlet,* 215, 216, 218–20; *Henry IV, Pt. 1,* 215, 218; *Henry IV, Pt. 2,* 215, 218; *Henry V,* 214, 218, 220; *Julius Caesar,* 210, 214; *Love's Labors Lost,* 37, 77; *The Merchant of Venice,* 44; *The Merry Wives of Windsor,* 215; *Much Ado About Nothing,* 214; *Othello,* 44, 218; *Richard III,* 171, 218; *Romeo and Juliet,* 219; *The Taming of the Shrew,* 163, 185; *The Tempest,* 44; *Titus Andronicus,* 19, 34, 38–40, 42; *Troilus and Cressida,* 216, 219; *Twelfth Night,* 215
Shapiro, James, 203–21
Shirley, James, 164
Spectacle, 266–70
Stage, 281–85, 288–92
Staging, 56–86, 133–37
Street, Peter, 212
Sullivan, Garrett A., 255–58

Swan playhouse, 209
Szatak, Karoline, 157–69

Textual studies, 88–93, 128–56, 248–55, 278–81
Theater/Theatre (playhouse), 209
Tiffany, Grace, 236–42
Tragedy, 170–88, 271–74
Turner, Henry S., 281–85

Valbuena, Olga, 301–3
Van Heemskerck, Maarten, 193

Van Meer, Michael, 191
Violation, 266–74

Walsh, Brian, 245–48, 278–81
Webster, John, 131
Warning for Fair Women, 171, 173–78, 181, 185–86
Women, 21–25, 157–69, 292–96
Wyndham, Thomas, 25

Yorkshire Tragedy, 170, 179–80, 186